Islamic Financial Products

Mohd Ma'Sum Billah

Islamic Financial Products

Principles, Instruments and Structures

palgrave
macmillan

Mohd Ma'Sum Billah
Islamic Economics Institute
King Abdulaziz University
Jeddah, Saudi Arabia

ISBN 978-3-030-17623-5 ISBN 978-3-030-17624-2 (eBook)
https://doi.org/10.1007/978-3-030-17624-2

This Palgrave Macmillan imprint is published by the registered company Springer Nature Switzerland AG
The registered company address is: Gewerbestrasse 11, 6330 Cham, Switzerland

This book is dedicated to the memories of my most beloved parents, Allamah Mufti Nur Mohammad (r) *and* Ustazah Akhtarun Nisa' (r), *who have nourished me with their love and wisdom. May* Allah (swt) *shower them with His Love and Mercy and grant them* Jannat al-Ferdaus Nuzulah. *I also like to dedicate this book to my lovely wife, Dr. Khamsiah Nawawi, and our children, who bring joy to our hearts, Dr. Ahmad Mu'izz Billah, Ahmad Mu'azz Billah, Ahmad Muniff Billah and Akhtarun Naba' Billah, for their continuous support and sacrifices. May they all be blessed with* Muwaddau Wa Rahmah, Qurratu A'yun *and* Mardhaati Allah (swt) *in this life and the next.*

This book is also dedicated to the Ummah, *the whole of humanity and other creatures.*
Mohd Ma'Sum Billah

Foreword

Dr. Abdullah Omar Nasseef

Contemporary Islamic financial activities began in 1963, since which time Islamic finance has been blessed by having secured a significant global platform. It is not merely confined within Muslim countries, but has been warmly welcomed in the non-Muslim world. Islamic financial assets stand at almost US$2.5 trillion and the annual growth rate is about 18%, a significant achievement when compared to in the achievements of conventional counterparts.

Islamic financial products and services are not a new dimension in the modern economic era; they have been growing rapidly in different classes of the global market despite the numerous shortcomings of the situations in which they operate.

Worldwide, and particularly in Muslim communities, people are expecting niche *Shari'ah* compliant financial products to meet the demand in multi-dimensional markets. It has been observed that no adequate customer friendly Islamic financial products are yet available. It is worth noting here that there are numerous product developers claiming to have designed sufficient *Shari'ah* financial products; this may apply in certain areas but is not the case globally.

Although there are books, articles and other research on Islamic finance, there is still a lack of comprehensive Islamic financial product solutions and structures with which to meet the global demand of academia, industries, professionals and policy makers.

The initiative of Prof. Dr. Mohd Ma'Sum Billah of Islamic Economics Institute, King Abdulaziz University, in producing this book *Islamic Financial Products - Principles, Instruments and Structures* is timely with regard to meeting the demand of the modern world to benefit from *Shari'ah* compliant financial products and structures. This book addresses the subject with comprehensive analyses, intellectual discussions and empirical solutions, and stands as a pioneering work alongside the guides and references for academia, researchers, professionals, industrialists, customers, entrepreneurs, decision-makers, promoters, programmers, students and people in general who are involved with, or have interest in, *Shari'ah compliant financial products and structures.*

It is my honour and privilege to write the Foreword for this prestigious title. May we all be blessed with true knowledge and its rightful practices.

Jeddah, Saudi Arabia

H.E. Dr. Abdullah Omar Nasseef
President of the Muslim World Congress
Former Vice-President of the Saudi Arabia
Shura Council
Former Secretary-General
of the Muslim World League

Preface

There is a great deal of literature available concerning Islamic finance but, sadly, no comprehensive literature exists that exclusively addresses Islamic financial products and their structures. This causes significant confusion not only within the industry, but also for customers, promoters, professionals and even academia. This book is therefore a timely contribution to the literature, discussing as it does a series of Islamic financial products and their structures that are applicable in the reality of modern socio-economics. This title, comprising 30 chapters and presented in three parts, is specifically focused on *Shari'ah* compliant financial product solutions as practised in and applicable to modern socio-economic reality. It contributes to the literature applied Islamic financial product solutions, their policies, structures, mechanisms and empirical analyses.

Part I provides an overview of the Islamic financial system, and consists of three chapters addressing different core issues. Chapter 1 presents the Islamic financial system in a nutshell, clearly demonstrating that Islamic finance is not merely a product with a commercial objective. Rather, it is an integrated system with spiritual, moral, economic and humanitarian values that benefit all mankind and encourage a worthy universal ethos. Chapter 2 provides a case study of the role of the Organisation of Islamic Cooperation (OIC) in the effective development of Islamic financial products and services in a way that shows care for humanity, both globally and among OIC member nations in particular.

Chapter 3 focuses on the dynamic and sustainable evolution of Islamic financial products and services that may be an essential element with which to attract the market.

Part II focuses on the governing principles and strategies of Islamic financial products and services. Chapter 4 focuses on various aspects of Islamic financial policies and enforcement. Chapter 5 analyses the role and functions of the Islamic Financial Services Board (IFSB) with regard to the regulation of Islamic financial industries. Chapter 6 analyses the controversial doctrine of *Bay' al-Ina* and its impact on financial products and services. Chapter 7 goes on to analyse various classes of *Shari'ah* instrument that facilitate Islamic financial products and services. Chapter 8 analyses the pricing techniques of Islamic financial products and services within *Maqasid al-Shari'ah*. Chapter 9 provides a comprehensive analysis of remedies available for the breach of any financial contract under *Shari'ah*.

Part III deals with the various classes of Islamic financial product, along with structures, mechanisms and empirical solutions. Chapter 10 analyses Islamic equity financing mechanisms applicable in today's financial world. Chapter 11 discusses the *Shari'ah* compliant interest free debt financing model. Chapter 12 analyses the Islamic trade financing model, its facilitating instruments and operational mechanisms. Chapter 13 contributes a *Shari'ah* framework for a trade financing model. Chapter 14 analyses an international trade financing model and structure under *Shari'ah* principles. Chapter 15 discusses the practicality of Islamic international trade and shipping. Chapter 16 analyses how an Islamic accepted bill functions in modern international trade. Chapter 17 focuses on an Islamic model of lease financing (*al-Ijarah*) and its structure. Chapter 18 discusses the model of Islamic leasing leading to ownership (*al-Ijarah tantahi bi al-tamleek*). Chapter 19 addresses the Islamic hire-purchase model (*al-Ijarah thumma al-Bay'*). Chapter 20 discusses the Islamic manufacturing model (*al-Istisna'*). Chapter 21 analyses the Islamic manufacturing contract (*'Aqd al-Istisna'*). Chapter 22 discusses the Islamic venture capital model and structure. Chapter 23 contributes a *sukuk* model and structure. Chapter 24 discusses the *Shari'ah* model for a loan (*al-Qardh*). Chapter 25 analyses the *Halal* model of financial wealth management. Chapter 26 goes on to analyse Islamic financial planning. Chapter 27 addresses the Islamic model of unit trust applicable in today's world. Chapter 28 analyses Islamic financing for sustainable development goals (SDG). Chapter 29 contributes the model structure of Islamic fin-tech and digital financial product. Chapter 30 presents an Islamic model of cryptocurrency to benefiting everyone.

Finally, exclusive research on Islamic financial products focusing on *Shari'ah* compliant financial products to meet the demands of academia, researchers, industrialists and professionals for specific solutions is not yet widely available. Thus, this book may be among the pioneers on the subject to offer possible academic, empirical and hypothetical solutions that may be a guide for academia, researchers, practitioners, decision-makers, programmers, professionals, promoters and students in their future research, and support the development of specific financial products under *Shari'ah*. Should this book contain any shortcomings, we would be grateful to any reader that shares their observations with us so that we may further improve this work.

Jeddah, Saudi Arabia — Mohd Ma'Sum Billah

Acknowledgements

بسم الله الرحمن الرحيم

There is no strength and power except in *Allah (swt)*, To Him comes the praise, the Savant, the Wise, the Omniscient, the most beautiful names belong to Him. May the blessing of Allah (swt) and peace be upon *Muhammad (saw)* and all the Prophets (*aws*) from the first to the last.

First, I would humbly like to acknowledge King Abdulaziz University, Kingdom of Saudi Arabia and its prestigious wing, the Islamic Economics Institute, for supporting this work with every facility available to enable our research into academic, human capital and professional development activities, and thereby reach out to the global *Ummah*. It is also a great honour for me to extend humble acknowledge to His Excellency Professor Dr. Abdulrahman Obaid AI-Youbi (President of KAU), Professor Dr. Yousef Abdul Aziz Al Turki (Vice President of KAU) and Dr. Abdullah Qurban Turkistani (Dean of the IEI, KAU), Dr. Mohammad A. Naseef (Vice Dean, IEI-KAU), Dr. Marwan G. A. Andejani (Vice Dean, IEI-KAU), Dr. Hasan Mohammad Makhethi (Vice Dean, IEI-KAU), Dr. Maha Alandejani (Vice Dean, IEI, KAU), Dr. Faisal Mahmoud Atbani (Head, Department of Insurance, IEI-KAU),

Dr. Adnan M. A. Al-Khiary (Head, Department of Finance, IEI-KAU) and Dr. Albara Abdullah Abulaban (Head, Department of Economics), for their continuous support and encouragement towards dynamic professional development, excellent academic contributions and specialized advance scientific research activities. Humble acknowledgement is also extended to my respected colleagues from the IEI, KAU, including Dr. Yousef Abdullah Basodan (Associate Professor of Accounting, FEA-KAU), Dr. Ibrahim M. S. Abolola, Dr. Omar Hafiz, Professor Dr. Abdulrahim Al-Saati, Sheikh Dr. Ali Ahmed Al-Nadwi, Professor Abdul Azim Islahi, Dr. Ahmed Mahdi Belouafi, Dr. Fadul AbdulKarim Al-Bashir, Dr. Abdul Razzaq Belabes, Dr. Hichem Salem Hamza and my talented colleague, Mr. Mohammed Alabdulraheem, Lecturer (Islamic banking and finance), IEI-KAU. Further acknowledgement is extended to Bank Negara Malaysia, Bank Islam, Bank Mu'amalat, RHB, CIMB, HSBC, Standard Chartered, other universities, industries and professional firms including my research assistant, Hafiz Akram bin Mohd Ghani, whose support, direct and indirect, with knowledge, experiences and resources, was of inestimable value.

Mohd Ma'Sum Billah

Introduction

Even though Islamic finance began its journey more than half a century ago, in 1963, it has been observed that Islamic financial products are still influenced by conventional product structures. This is due, perhaps, to a lack of research in designing and structuring niche products created in the spirit of *Maqasid al-Shari'ah* to meet modern market demand. Decision-makers are concerned with prioritizing commercial goals over *Shari'ah* normative compliance. Marketers do not truly focus on *Shari'ah* compliance but, rather, promote what is assigned to them to pursue commercial objectives as the prime goal. Furthermore, management goes on to offer the products created without investigating the degree to which they are *Shari'ah* compliant, and the extent to which they encompass ethical concerns or humanitarian care. Instead, marketability and profitability are among the prime concerns of today's Islamic financial industry. In the face of such calamitous challenges, financial products and services that reflect the true spirit of Islam may have a hard time to making significant growth. Islamic financial products should not merely aim at a commercial goal; rather, they should be an integrated platform that reflects *Shari'ah* concern, ethical cohesion, commercial goals, humanitarian concern and a just ethos. An Islamic financial product should be unique and provide benefits for all, sustaining a success rate that is compatible with holistic universal values. Before designing an Islamic financial product, a target must be established; this should encompass *Shari'ah* compliance, Divine ethical standards, smart marketability, *Halal* profitability, socio-humanitarian concerns, minimum risk and a lower level of competition with mainstream financial products. The design of the product should be competitive and unique so as to attract the market strategically, intelligently and easily.

Today, Islamic finance continues to grow at a rate of between 12% and 15% per annum, and its total assets are estimated to have reached US$2.5 trillion. The Islamic financial industry has not been confined to Muslim countries, but has also spread to important finance centres in Europe, Africa, the United States of America, Russia, the Asia Pacific, India and the Far East. The value orientated ethos of Islamic finance has enabled the industry to attract monies from Muslims and non-Muslims alike. In recent years, conventional institutions have also shown growing interest and increasing participation in the sector. This has assisted the Islamic financial industry worldwide, helping it to keep pace with sophisticated financing techniques and to develop *Shari'ah* investment instruments that are not only profitable, but are also Divinely ethically motivated and cultured. Despite these significant achievements, there is still a lack of realization, understanding and utilization of the Islamic model of financing and its various structures. This modest book aims to provide industrialists, professionals, practitioners and academia with an understanding of financial products and their structures that accord with *Shari'ah* principles so as to enable them to explore the salient features of Islamic financial product solutions. The intention of this is to help to ensure the continued growth of the application of Islamic financial products and services, and their attendant benefits.

This book provides a series of applied Islamic financial products and their structures together with *Shari'ah* rulings and mechanisms. It is a pioneering volume in that it focuses exclusively on Islamic financial products and services that aim to meet market demand with the best possible results for all concerned. This volume may be an effective guide for academia, researchers, industrialists, professionals, product designers, decision-makers, promoters and students in the specialized field of Islamic finance, its products and services, and perhaps offers empirical solutions for the finance industry.

Contents

About the Author

Mohd Ma'Sum Billah, D.B.A., Ph.D., M.C.L., M.M.B., L.L.B. (hons) is a Professor of finance, insurance, fintech and investment, Islamic Economics Institute, King Abdulaziz University, Kingdom of Saudi Arabia. Billah has been serving and contributing to both academic as well as corporate industries for more than 20 years with management, teaching, research, solution proving and sharing of strategic and technical thoughts towards the advancement of Islamic finance and insurance (*Takaful*) besides *Halal* standard. Billah has published 32 books and chapters in books besides more than 200 articles in journals and social media. He has presented in more than 300 conferences, seminars, executive workshops and industrial training in different parts of the world. In addition, he has also been affiliated with corporate, academic and financial industries including central banks, international corporate organizations, governments and NGOs in his capacity as a member in boards, advisor, strategic decision maker, transformer and reformer with strategic solutions. Among the areas of his interest and contributions are: Islamic finance, insurance (*Takaful*), crowd-funding, investment, capital market (*Sukuk*), social finance, petroleum finance, trade, fintech and cryptocurrency models and standards.

List of Figures

Chapter 26

Chapter 28

List of Tables

Chapter 28

Chapter 30

PART I

An Overview of Islamic Financial System

CHAPTER 1

The Islamic Financial System

1 Introduction

From the perspective of the Western legal system, modern principles are extremely basic. It is precisely because secularism is such an intrinsic part of our thinking that we mention its principles. Indeed, secularism is so fundamental to Western regulatory framework awareness that the laws generated from Islamic and other God-given or 'received' legal frameworks can appear irrational and inflexible. Furthermore, in the absence of an understanding of the foundations underlying a non-secular legal system, Western ability to understand and appreciate revisions to the laws of such a system may be severely limited. In contrast, the scope and origin of Islamic law are fundamentally different from those of common and civil laws. The scope of Islam is not limited to religious matters. Rather, Islam is an entire way of life: it is a religion, an ethic, a lifestyle, and a legal system rolled into one, and includes economics and financial systems.

Western jurists are, consequently, empowered to alter their systems as social and economic demands emerge. Conversely, the two primary sources of Islamic law are the Qur'an—the word of God, and the Sunnah—the pronouncements and practices of the Prophet. Having sources that are, by nature, sacred and unchanging has influenced the legal system in a way that has restricted Islamic jurists' power to interpret and amend laws according to contemporary values and needs.

M. M. Billah, *Islamic Financial Products*,
https://doi.org/10.1007/978-3-030-17624-2_1

1.1 Sources of the Islamic Legal System

Since the objective of Islamic law is to define and regulate an individual's duties according to God's will, historically there has been no distinction between legal rules and rules of religion. *Shari'ah*, or 'the Way', is the term used to describe Islamic law. There are two primary, independent sources of *Shari'ah* law: the Qur'an—the Holy book of Islam, and the Sunnah—the pronouncements and practices of the Prophet Muhammad (*SAW*). There are also three secondary sources: *ijma'* (consensus), *qiyas* and *ijtihad* (reasoning by analogy), which are not sources in the strict sense of term, but are means of revealing the law.

1.2 Al-Qur'an

The Qur'an is considered to be 'the bedrock of Islamic jurisprudence'. It represents, to Muslims, the word of God as revealed to and spoken through his prophet, Muhammad (*SAW*). Although more than 80 verses deal with topics Westerners would consider being legal matters, the 6000 verses that comprise the Qur'an constitute an entire code for a moral, spiritual and social life. The guidelines and commandments of the Qur'an, including those that can be termed as legal matters, must be read as an integrated whole, and not as individual parts. However, the scarcity of actual law within the Qur'an creates the need to look to other sources.

1.3 Al-Sunnah

The Sunnah, which literally means 'customary procedure or action' or 'norm', is a set of rules deduced from the pronouncements and conduct of the Prophet. When Qur'anic verses did not expressly address an issue at hand, Muslims resorted to the Sunnah, which became Muslim customary law. Over time, the notion of the Sunnah became more restricted. Currently, the Sunnah is regarded as being limited to the collective traditions, pronouncements and conduct of the Prophet, as opposed to tradition in general. The Sunnah includes stories or traditions of the Prophet, called *hadith*, as well as the prophet's deeds and tacit approval of the actions or practices of others. The Sunnah is regarded as a source of law, second only in authority to the Qur'an.

The word 'Sunnah' means a manner of acting, a rule of conduct, a mode of life. The term *hadith* refers to the report of a particular occurrence. Although, in the context of Islamic law, the words are often used interchangeably, *hadith* refers in particular to a tradition or story of the Prophet, while Sunnah signifies the rule of law deduced from the *hadith*.

1.4 Al-Ijma'

As Islam spread rapidly in Asia and North Africa, questions of personal and societal rights, obligations and relationships arose to which neither the Qur'an or the Sunnah could provide direct answers. *Ijma'*, a secondary source, provided a way to meet the needs of changing times. *Ijma'*, which literally means 'unanimity', is a way of discovering the law by resorting to the general consensus of opinion among Islamic legal scholars of a particular era.

Rules unanimously agreed, provided they do not conflict with the Qur'an or the Sunnah, become fixed and definite elements of Islamic jurisprudence. At first glance, *ijma'* may appear to be a built-in mechanism for integrating Islamic teachings with evolving social practices and technology. However, the Hanbali school of Islamic law, to which Saudi Arabia subscribes, has historically limited *ijma'*, recognizing only the *ijma'* of the companions of the Prophet.

1.5 Al-Qiyas

If the Qur'an, the Sunnah, and *ijma'* fail to provide a rule that adequately addresses a problem, jurists may, as a last resort, use *qiyas*—logical reasoning by analogy to precepts of the Qur'an or Sunnah. Essentially, by using *qiyas*, the underlying principles of the Qur'an and Sunnah may be extended by analogy to deal with matters similar, but not identical, to those covered by the Qur'an and Sunnah.

Imam Shafi'i (AD 767–820) was the founder of the Shafi'i school. His leading work, *Risala*, sets forth a fixed framework of rules within which *qiyas* can be used. To Shafi'i jurists, *qiyas*, through the proper application of these rules, effectively became a fourth source of law. Adherents to this school are mostly in southern India, southeast Asia, east Africa, and the Arabian coastline.

1.6 *Al-Ijtihad*

Early in the evolution of Islamic law, any qualified Islamic jurist had the authority to reason and interpret original sources of the law independently through a process known as *ijtihad*. *Ijtihad* literally means 'effort', 'endeavour' and, in the Islamic legal context, means 'independent judgement of a legal or theological question'. *Ijtihad* allowed Islamic jurists to interpret the law when circumstances demanded, presumably through logical reasoning.

By the ninth and tenth centuries, the notion of using human reasoning to interpret the Divine word fell out of favour; increasingly, it was argued that nothing more could be gained through interpretation and reason. By the tenth century, *ijtihad* was repudiated in an event called 'the closing of the gate of independent reasoning'. Jurists were regarded as *muqallids*, 'those whose duty it was to accept the opinions of their great predecessors without the exercise of private judgement'.

Although *ijtihad* and *qiyas* may appear to be identical, they are distinct concepts. *Ijtihad* connotes the entire field or process of ascertaining the terms of *Shari'ah* law, whereas both *qiyas* and *ijma'* can be viewed as products of *ijtihad*. Without the general endeavour to determine *Shari'ah* principles by using independent reasoning, consensus and reasoning by analogy would have never evolved. *Qiyas* and *ijma'* can also be regarded as particular ways in which *ijtihad* is expressed; for example, by reasoning through analogy or through consensus.

2 The Islamic Financial System

Some of us may wonder what the financial world would be like were Islam to become the basis of the present day financial system. Could it have prevented the stock market and currency crises from occurring? Some will say that this depends on the version of the Islamic financial system (IFS) that we have now. In Malaysia, the IFS has been moulded along conventional philosophy but blended to claim *Shari'ah* legitimacy by virtue of contracts employed in financial transactions. In essence, a financial system is a set of rules and regulations or principles that governs the flow of funds from the surplus spending unit (SSU), to the deficit spending unit (DSU). The household, business and government sectors make up the SSU and DSU.

Simply, in the IFS, the guiding rules and regulations are taken from the Qur'an. The *Shari'ah* spells out the Qur'anic teachings in three dimensions: the *aqidah* (ethics and morality) and *muamalat* (transactions). The role of reason and experience, too, has been given a higher order by the Qur'an, in that they help convey the truth that God wants mankind to acknowledge. When the IFS is guided by rules and regulations determined by God, some would ask what they are. Again, the answer is quite simple. There are two types of guidelines to observe: the legal and the ethical.

On the former, the Qur'an prohibits *riba* in financial transactions (2:275). It also does not condone the creation of wealth by means of investment in *al-bathil* transactions such as financial gambling and liquor-based production (2:219). On the ethical side, the Qur'an enjoins trustworthiness (2:282), and prohibits deceit and greed in profit-taking. All these enjoinments and prohibitions are meant to generate harmony in economic and business activities such that justice prevails and, thus, mankind obtains peace of mind. Once the rules and regulations are clearly spelt out, it is easier to appreciate how surplus funds are channelled to the DSU.

The financial market is where investors buy stocks, bonds and short-term securities. Investments in higher risk securities, such as stock and long-term bonds, are made in the capital market, while lower risk securities, such as treasury bills, negotiable certificates of deposits and overnight funds, can be bought in the money market. Overall, Islamic capital and money markets, as well as Islamic financial intermediaries to some extent, operate well in Malaysia. In the Islamic capital market, there is the issuance of Islamic private debt securities, while, in essence, investments in stocks are a *Musharakah* phenomenon. In the money market, we also observe the *murabahah* interbank money market. In the financial intermediaries, we have the Islamic Banking System in the banking sector, while some insurance companies practice *takaful*. These activities show that an ISF really works in modern Malaysia, although in the most humble form. What is important now is not its mere existence or application but, rather, what it does to the economy.

3 Governing Laws and Policies

To enable a bank to meet the objectives of a central bank, it is vested with comprehensive legal powers under the following legislation that regulates and supervises the financial system. Among those regulations are the:

- Islamic Financial Services Act (Malaysia) (2013) (IFSA 2013).
- Central Bank of Malaysia Act (1958) (Revised 1994).
- Banking and Financial Institution Act (1989) (BAFIA) (repealed by IFSA 2013).
- Exchange Control Act (1953).
- Islamic Banking Act (1983) (repealed by IFSA 2013).
- Insurance Act (1996).
- Takaful Act (1984) (repealed by IFSA 2013).
- Emergency (Essential) Powers Act (1979) and Essential (Protection of Depositors) Regulations (1986).
- Loan (Local) Ordinance (1959).
- Treasury Bills (Local) Act (1946) (Revised 1977).
- Government Investment Act (1983).

4 The Central Bank of Malaysia Act (1958) (Revised 1994) (Direct Art Company, 1999)

The Act provides for the administration and objectives of the Central Bank. It also enumerates the powers and the duties of the Central Bank in relation to the issuance of currency, maintenance of external reserves, the authorized business of the bank, and specific powers to deal with ailing institutions. The Act also contains general provisions on a bank's accounts, powers to compound, and so on.

4.1 The Banking and Financial Institutions Act (1989) (BAFIA) (Repealed by the Islamic Financial Services Act, 2013)

The BAFIA, which came into force on 1 October 1989, provides for the licensing and regulation of institutions carrying on banking, finance company, merchant banking, discount house and money-broking businesses. The Act also provides for the regulation of institutions carrying on scheduled business comprising non-bank sources of credit and finance, such as credit and charge card companies, building societies, factoring, leasing companies and development finance institutions. Non-scheduled institutions that are engaged in the provision of finance may be subject to Parts X and XI of the BAFIA should the Minister of Finance so decide.

4.2 *The Exchange Control Act (1953) (Kuala Lumpur: Direct Art Company, 1999)*

The Act restricts dealings in gold and foreign currencies, payments to and from residents, the issuance of securities outside Malaysia, imports and exports, and settlements. The Act also empowers the Controller for the Foreign Exchange to grant permissions and consent regarding the foregoing matters and to enforce the provisions of the Act.

4.3 *The Islamic Banking Act (1983) (Repealed by the Islamic Financial Services Act, 2013)*

This Act provides for the licensing and regulation of Islamic banking business. The Act, *inter alia*, has provisions covering the financial requirements and duties of an Islamic bank, ownership, control and management of Islamic banks, restrictions on the business of Islamic banks, powers of supervision and control over Islamic banks, and other general provisions, such as penalties and so on.

The Islamic Banking Act was introduced into Malaysia by the Islamic Banking Act, 1982. The scope of Islamic banking business is defined in the Act, as 'banking business whose aims and operations do not involve any element which is not approved by the religion of Islam'. This enables Islamic banks to provide certain facilities (for instance, leasing) that are strictly non-banking business under the Banking and Financial Institutions Act (1989). The granting of financing facilities by an Islamic bank, though based on principles of the *Shari'ah*, are nevertheless commercial and banking transactions, which therefore come within the jurisdiction of the civil courts.

The Islamic Banking Act (1988) defines an Islamic bank as any company that carries on Islamic banking business and holds a valid licence. 'Islamic banking business' is defined as meaning banking business the aims and operations of which do not involve any element that is not approved by the religion of Islam. The Act also provides that the central bank shall not recommend the grant of a licence and the Minister of Finance shall not grant a licence unless the central bank or the Minister of Finance, whichever the case may be, is satisfied.

The aims and operations of any banking business that it is desired to conduct must not involve any element that is not approved by the religion of Islam.

The articles of association of the bank concerned must contain provision for the establishment of a *Shari'ah* advisory board to advise the bank on the operations of its banking business in order to ensure that they do not involve any element that is not approved by the religion of Islam.

4.4 The Insurance Act (1996) (Direct Art Company, 1999)

The provisions of the Act deal with the licensing of insurers, insurance brokers adjusters and reinsurers. It also deals with the setting up of subsidiary companies and offices, establishment of an insurance fund, direction and control of defaulting insurers, the control of the management of licensees, licensees' accounts, examination and investigation powers of the central bank, winding-up, and the transfer of business of licensees. The Act also provides for matters relating to policies, an insurance guarantee scheme fund, the enforcement powers of the central bank, offences and other general provisions.

This Act should be read along together with the Financial Services Act (2013).

4.5 The Takaful Act (1984) (Repealed by the Islamic Financial Services Act, 2013)

This Act provides for the registration and regulation of *takaful* business in Malaysia and for other purposes relating to or connected with *takaful*. *Takaful* in this context means a scheme based on brotherhood, solidarity and mutual assistance that provides for mutual financial aid and assistance to the participants in the event of need whereby the participants mutually agree to contribute for that purpose.

4.6 Essential (Protection of Depositors) Regulations (1986) (Direct Art Company, 1999)

This Act gives the central bank the powers to investigate the affairs of any person it suspects or has reason to believe is a deposit-taker. It empowers a bank to freeze the properties of the deposit-taker and other persons associated with the deposit taker, assume control over the deposit-taker, and to appoint receivers and managers. The Act also enumerates the powers of managers, and provisions on priority of payment and cost.

4.7 The Loan (Local) Ordinance (1959)

This Ordinance authorizes the raising of loans, and matters connected thereto, within the Federation by the government for the purposes of the Development Fund. The Act, amongst other things, appoints the central bank as the agent of the government and enables the raising of the loans by way of book-entry; that is, scrip less.

4.8 The Treasury Bills (Local) Act (1946) (Revised 1977)

This Act provides for the issuance of Treasury Bills in Malaysia. The Act, amongst other things, appoints the central bank as the agent of the government and permits issuance by way of book-entry; that is, scrip less.

4.9 The Government Investment Act (1983)

This Act confers on the Minister of Finance power to receive investments of moneys for a fixed period and to pay dividend thereon. The Act, amongst other things, appoints the central bank as the agent of the government and allows the issuance of the investment by way of book-entry; that is, by scrip.

5 Conclusion

While deregulation has been increasing in a number of countries, the traditional set-up of registered joint stock companies remains. As an extension and attachment, the departments of the Ministries of Industry of several developing countries were replaced by quasi autonomous bodies known as corporate law authorities and are now functioning under autonomous securities and exchange authorities. Therefore, regulatory frameworks are being strengthened to maintain a vigilant watch on financial markets. Financial managers should to comply with the regulatory frameworks.

Reference

Rosly, S. A. (2002). *Islamic Banking and Finance.* Kuala Lumpur: IIUM, p. 469.

CHAPTER 2

Role of the OIC and Other International Organizations in the Sustainable Development of Islamic Finance

1 Introduction

Islamic rules apply to every moment of our daily life. As Muslims, we may not prevent or reject what has been revealed in the Qur'an. The need for insurance is very important in the modern business world of the new millennium. Insurance is one of the ways to reduce the risk of loss due to misfortune, or to provide funds with which to overcome misfortune. The concept of insurance is where resources are pooled to help the needy that do not contradict *Shari'ah*.

Islamic insurance (*takaful*) is insurance where resources are pooled to help the needy according to *Shari'ah* principles. The concept is in line with the principles of compensation and responsibilities shared among the community. It is not a new concept; in fact, it was practised in the ancient customs of Arab tribes. It was also practised during the time of the Prophet (*PBUH*). It is generally accepted by Muslim jurists that the operation of conventional insurance does not conform to either the rules or the requirements of *Shari'ah*. Conventional insurance involves elements of uncertainty (*Al-Gharar*) in the insurance contract, gambling (*Al-Maisir*) as the consequences of the presence of uncertainty and interest (*Al-Riba*) in the investment activities of conventional insurance companies, which is in contradiction to *Shari'ah* rules. *Takaful* is an alternative form of cover of which a Muslim may avail himself against the risk of loss due to misfortune.

M. M. Billah, *Islamic Financial Products*,
https://doi.org/10.1007/978-3-030-17624-2_2

Due to the rapid development of *takaful* throughout the nation, this chapter will present the OIC as one of the Islamic bodies involved in the development of *takaful*. This chapter also presents the structure, functions and contribution of the OIC to the *takaful* industry globally.

2 Background

The OIC is an international organization grouping 57 states that have decided to pool their resources, combine their efforts and speak with one voice to safeguard the interests and to secure the progress and well-being of their peoples and of all Muslims worldwide.

The OIC was established in Rabat, Morocco, on 12 Rajab 1389H (25 September 1969) when the first meeting of the leaders of the Islamic world was held in the wake of the criminal Zionist attempt to burn down the Blessed Al-Aqsa Mosque on 21 August 1969 in the occupied city of Al-Quds. Six months after that historic event, in Muharram 1390H (March 1970), the first Islamic Conference of Foreign Ministers (ICFM) was held in Jeddah, Saudi Arabia, during which the OIC General Secretariat was established to ensure the coordination of member states. The ICFM appointed a Secretary General for the Organization and chose Jeddah as the city to house its temporary headquarters pending the liberation of Al-Quds Al-Sharif, to which the General Secretariat would then be transferred as the permanent seat of the Organization.

3 Objectives

The main aims of the OIC are to strengthen, coordinate action for and work for the Islamic community.

3.1 Strengthen the Islamic Community

- Instil Islamic solidarity among member states.
- Extend cooperation in the political, economic, social, cultural and scientific fields.
- Support the struggle of all Muslim people to safeguard their dignity, independence and national rights.

3.2 Coordinate Action for the Islamic Community

- Safeguard the Holy places.
- Support the struggle of the Palestinian people and assist them in recovering their rights and liberating their occupied territories.

3.3 Work for the Islamic Community

- Eliminate racial discrimination and all forms of colonialism.
- Create a favourable atmosphere for the promotion of cooperation and understanding between member states and other countries.

4 Principles

- The OIC management has a duty to pursue the following principles in order that any decision may be made; there should be:
- Full equality among member states.
- Observation of the right to self-determination and non-interference in the internal affairs of member states.
- Observation of the sovereignty, independence and territorial integrity of each state.
- The settlement of any dispute that may arise among member states by peaceful means, such as negotiations, mediation, conciliation and arbitration.
- A pledge to refrain, in relations among member states, from resorting to force or threatening to resort to the use of force against the unity and territorial integrity, or the political independence of any one of them.

5 The Organization of the OIC

5.1 The General Secretary

The General Secretariat is headed by a Secretary General appointed by the ICFM for a period of four years, renewable once only. The Secretary General is assisted by four elected Assistant Secretaries General. As the highest authority of the General Secretariat and its subsidiary bodies, the Secretary General is responsible to the ICFM for their work and submits reports to the ICFM on the execution of his duties. In the exercise of his duties, the Secretary General is assisted by the Assistant Secretaries General, officials and experts.

The Assistant Secretary General for Political Affairs is in charge of the following departments:

- Department of Political Affairs.
- Department for Arab Affairs.
- Department for African Affairs.
- Department for Asian Affairs.

The Assistant Secretary General in charge of Information and Cultural and Social Affairs coordinates the work of the following two departments:

- Department of Information
- Department of Cultural and Social Affairs.

The Assistant Secretary General in charge of Economic Affairs coordinates the work of the Department of Economic Affairs. The Assistant Secretary General in charge of Science and Technology coordinates the work of the Department of Science and Technology. The Director of Coordination with Palestine (who holds the rank of Assistant Secretary General) coordinates the work of Palestine and Al-Quds. The High Commissioner for the Boycott of Israel (who holds the rank of Assistant Secretary General) coordinates the work of the Boycott of Israel Bureau. He also supervises the *Da'wah* section.

5.2 *Responsibilities of the Department of* **Al-Quds Al-Sharif** *and Palestine*

The Department is responsible for the drawing up of plans, and the undertaking of such political, economic, social, military and information studies and programmes as are designed:

- To support the struggle of the Palestinian people for their legitimate rights.
- To protect the Holy places against desecration by the Zionist enemy.
- To prevent and check Jewish immigration to Palestine and to counter all forms of Zionist action.

- To lead information campaigns in conjunction with information bodies of Islamic countries.
- To help the OIC play an effective role during meetings dealing with the cause of Al-Quds Al-Sharif and Palestine.
- To follow up the implementation of decisions relating thereto.

5.3 *Bureau for the Islamic Boycott of Israel*

The Bureau coordinates the efforts of member states of the OIC in boycotting Israel.

5.4 *Islamic Bureau for Military Coordination with Palestine*

The Bureau's tasks consist in coordinating aid of a military nature granted to Palestine by member states of the OIC.

5.5 *Department of Political Affairs*

The Department is responsible for:

- The harmonizing and coordination of political action among member states at the international and inter-regional levels in order to adopt unified Islamic political positions.
- Following up on the implementation of decisions taken in this respect.

5.6 *Department of Muslim Communities and Minorities*

The purpose of this Department is:

- To collect information, data and statistics on Muslim communities in non-Islamic countries.
- To promote contact with them.
- To look after their interests while observing the sovereignty of the states in which they live.

5.7 Department of Legal Affairs

This Department is responsible for:

- Dealing with legal matters and providing legal counsel relating to the work of the General Secretariat, its bodies and institutions.
- Examining international draft treaties to which member states adhere or with which such member states are concerned. It prepares legal texts of conventions and treaties to be concluded within the Organization and takes legal steps for their signing, ratification, adherence, deposit, registration and publicizing.

5.8 Department of Economic Affairs

This Department deals with the:

- Drawing up plans and undertakes the development studies and programmes created.
- Fostering economic, technical and trade cooperation in priority fields as defined by the OIC.
- Accelerating the economic progress of OIC member states through the development of their economic and human potential and protecting their natural resources in cooperation with banks and other relevant bodies and institutions.

5.9 Department of Science and Technology

The purpose of this Department is:

- To promote the development of science and technology in the Islamic world.
- To ensure the implementation of the decisions adopted by the OIC on inter-Islamic cooperation in the field of science and technology.
- To follow up on the activities of the Standing Committee for Scientific and Technological Cooperation (COMSTECH) and of subsidiary bodies.

5.10 *Information Department*

The aims of this Department are:

- To keep the public informed about the activities of the General Secretariat and its bodies and institutions.
- To coordinate the activities of the news media of member states with those of the General Secretariat and the inter-Islamic information bodies.
- To disseminate information on the Islamic *Ummah*, its cultural heritage, its achievements and position.
- To work to bring OIC states and peoples closer to each other.

5.11 *Cultural and Social Affairs Department*

- The purpose of this Department is to promote cooperation among member states in the fields of culture and sports through.
- The organization of meetings, training courses, competitions and seminars for their nationals.
- The support of and coordination among centres and other institutions clearly involved in cultural and sports activities.
- The creation of an appropriate cultural framework.
- The encouragement of studies and publications on Islam, Palestine and Al-Quds Al-Sharif.

5.12 *Administration and Finance Department*

This Department draws up the administrative and financial draft regulations of the General Secretariat and its subsidiary bodies, deals with the personnel matters, prepares and executes the budgets, manages the accounts and holds the ledgers of the General Secretariat.

5.13 *Conference Department*

This Department plans, coordinates and makes all arrangements relating to the holding of OIC conferences and meetings, and provides secretarial support to the Departments of the General Secretariat.

5.14 *Protocol and Public Relations Department*

This Department deals with matters of protocol, and handles contacts concerning the privileges and immunities of the OIC. It is also in charge of public relations.

5.15 *Department of Coordination for Subsidiary Bodies, Specialized and Affiliated Institutions*

This Department follows up on coordination activities between the General Secretariat, subsidiary bodies, and specialized and affiliated institutions.

5.16 *Department of* Da'wah

This Department aims to rationalize and coordinate the various activities of official and public organizations working in the domain of the *Da'wah* in member states and elsewhere, to avoid duplication or overlapping in their action.

Further, the OIC also establishes other bodies in order to cater to any new *Ummah* problems that may arise. These other bodies are:

5.16.1 The Islamic Summit Conference

The Islamic Summit Conference is the supreme body of the OIC entrusted with defining strategies for OIC policies and actions. It convenes once every three years.

5.16.2 The Islamic Conference of Foreign Ministers (ICFM)

The ICFM considers the means of implementing the general policy of the Organization and adopts resolutions accordingly. It meets regularly once each year. The ICFM also holds special sessions as required by circumstances.

5.16.3 The General Secretariat

The General Secretariat carries out duties entrusted to it by the conferences mentioned above as the OIC's executive organ. The headquarters are in Jeddah, Saudi Arabia. The General Secretariat is headed by a Secretary General elected by the ICFM for a period of four years, renewable once only.

5.16.4 The International Islamic Court of Justice

The establishment of the Court was decided by the Third Islamic Summit. It is envisaged that it will have seven members elected by the ICFM and to have headquarters in Kuwait City, Kuwait.

5.16.5 Subsidiary Bodies

The subsidiary bodies of the OIC are:

- The Statistical, Economic and Social Research and Training Centre for Islamic Countries (SESRTCIC), Ankara, Turkey.
- The Research Centre for Islamic History, Art and Culture (IRCICA), Istanbul, Turkey.
- The Islamic Institute of Technology (IIT), Dhaka, Bangladesh.
- The Islamic Centre for the Development of Trade (ICDT), Casablanca, Morocco.
- The Islamic Fiqh Academy, Jeddah, Saudi Arabia.
- The Islamic Solidarity Fund, Jeddah, Saudi Arabia.
- The International Commission for the Preservation of the Islamic Heritage, Istanbul, Turkey.
- Islamic University of Niger.
- Islamic University of Uganda.

5.16.6 Specialized Institutions

The specialized institutions of the OIC are:

- The Islamic Development Bank (IDB), Jeddah, Saudi Arabia.
- The Islamic Educational, Scientific and Cultural Organization (ISESCO), Rabat, Morocco.
- The International Islamic News Agency (IINA), Jeddah, Saudi Arabia.
- The Islamic States Broadcasting Organization (ISBO), Jeddah, Saudi Arabia.

5.16.7 Affiliated Institutions

The affiliated institutions of the OIC are:

- The Islamic Chamber of Commerce and Industry (ICCI), Karachi, Pakistan.
- The Islamic Committee of the International Crescent (ICIC), Benghazi, Libya.

- The Organization of the Islamic Ship Owners Association (OISA), Jeddah, Saudi Arabia.
- The International Association of Islamic Banks, Cairo, Egypt.
- The Organization of Islamic Capitals and Cities (OICC), Makkah Al-Mukarramah, Saudi Arabia.
- The Sports Federation of Islamic Solidarity Games, Riyadh, Saudi Arabia.
- The World Federation of International Arab-Islamic Schools, Jeddah, Saudi Arabia.

6 International Organizations Contributing to the Development of Islamic Finance

6.1 Islamic Development Bank (IDB)

The Islamic Development Bank (IDB) was established by the first ICFM of member countries of the OIC, convened on 24 Dhul Qa'da 1393H (18 December 1973). Its purpose is to foster economic development and social progress in member countries and Muslim communities worldwide based on the principles of *Shari'ah* (i.e. Islamic jurisprudence). The Bank commenced its activities officially on 15 Shawwal 1395H (20 October 1975).

The main operational activities of the IDB are geared towards projects, technical assistance for studies, trade financing aimed at the promotion of cooperation between the member countries through the exchange of expertise and trade for their economic and social development. The Bank also extends support to Muslim communities in non-member countries under the Special Assistance Programme and offers two scholarships to meritorious students, especially in science and technology. In line with its overall objectives of fostering economic development and social progress, the Bank finances productive projects and programmes in both the public and private sectors in member countries. It invests in economic and social infrastructure projects; provides technical assistance to member countries; and assists in the promotion of foreign trade, especially capital goods. The Bank also assists Muslim communities in non-member countries and undertakes *Shari'ah* based research studies in Islamic economics and banking through special funds established for this purpose. The IDB finances development projects in member countries through a number of *Shari'ah* compatible modes such as loans, leasing, instalment sales, *Istisna'a*, equity participation, lines of financing, and so on. In addition to its trade financing schemes, such as import trade financing operations (ITFO), export financing schemes (EFS), an Islamic banks portfolio (IBP), unit investment fund (UIF), and so on, the IDB promotes trade among member countries.

During the period 1396–1418H (1976–1998), the IDB approved a total of ID14,017.03 million (US$ 19,624 million) for 2452 operations. In 1418H (1997–1998), the Bank approved ID1147.12 million (US$ 1606 million) for 189 operations covering project financing, technical assistance, trade financing operations, and special assistance projects for member countries and non-member countries.

The IDB is one of the specialized OIC bodies. Specialized bodies usually have their own governing boards independent of the OIC governing machinery. The Bank is a permanent observer in all OIC meetings and committees. It cooperates closely with other subsidiary, specialized and affiliated bodies. However, being an economic organization, the Bank has a special relationship with the Standing Committee on Economic and Commercial Cooperation (COMCEC).

6.1.1 Purpose

The purpose of the IDB is to foster the economic development and social progress of member states and Muslim communities, individually as well as collectively, in accordance with the principles of *Shari'ah*.

6.1.2 Functions

The functions of the IDB are to provide equity participation and to grant loans for productive projects and enterprises. It also gives financial assistance to member states in other forms for their economic and social development, and to foster foreign trade among member countries.

6.1.3 Membership

The basic condition for membership is that the prospective member country be a member of the OIC.

6.1.4 Organization and Administration

Board of Governors

Each member state is represented on the Board and nominates a governor and a deputy governor. The Board meets once each year in an ordinary session.

Board of Executive Directors

The Board consists of 10 members who are not members of the Board of Governors. They are elected for a mandate of three years by the Board of Governors. They can be re-elected.

The President

The President is the legal representative of the Bank and its Chief Executive Officer (CEO). He is elected by the Board of Governors for a period of five years and can be re-elected.

Capital

The authorized capital of the Bank is ID6 billion divided into 600,000 shares among subscribers. The value of the Islamic dinar, which is the unit of account of the Bank, is equivalent to one Special Drawing Right (SDR) of the International Monetary Fund. The subscribed capital of the Bank is ID4 billion. One Islamic Dinar is equivalent to US$1.3.

Development

The Islamic Development Bank and MIMOS Berhad of Malaysia have signed a joint venture agreement to implement the OIC information systems network project. It will interlink the OIC member countries and enable improved flow, exchange and dissemination of information amongst them. The company, with a paid up capital of $14.47 million, will be based in Kuala Lumpur. The IDB will hold a 51% share in the company, and MIMOS will hold the remaining 49%. The company will develop an interest based network infrastructure and content for OIC member countries and Muslim communities. This will include providing information services. The company will also launch an Internet portal incorporating advanced search engines and e-commerce, as well as providing consultancy services.

In view of the need to be a content aggregate, the joint venture partners have engaged in discussions with potential strategic alliance partners to ascertain their willingness to participate in the different aspects of implementing this project, according to a press statement issued by the IDB. The company aims to be a major catalyst in accelerating the deployment of Internet technology and e-commerce in OIC member countries with a view to enhancing trade between them and increasing their economic development.

Besides IDB involvement in information technology, the IDB has also had certain impacts on Islamic economics and the Islamic state:

- Expresses its deep satisfaction in the devotion and efficiency with which the IDB President and his assistants ensure the effective functioning of this institution, which continues to make an invaluable contribution to the development and progress of Muslim people.
- Calls on the IDB to continue its beneficial action and increase the necessary resources for augmenting its services to the member states, and to the Islamic *Ummah* at large.
- Congratulates the IDB on having set up the Islamic Corporation for Insurance of Investment and Export Credit.
- Calls on the member states to participate in various schemes recently launched by the IDB and to benefit from the Longer Term Trade Financing Scheme, Islamic Banks Portfolio, IDB Unit Investment Fund, the Islamic Corporation for Insurance of Investment and Export Credit, together with the IDB's other existing schemes, programmes and operations.
- Appeals to the member states who have not yet done so to sign and ratify the Articles of Agreement of the Islamic Corporation for Insurance of Investment and Export Credit and to pay their respective shares to its capital so that its benefits would be extended to as wide an OIC area as possible.
- Requests the General Secretariat, the IDB, the Islamic Chamber of Commerce and Industry and the Islamic Centre for Development of Trade to organize joint seminars on a regional basis on the various schemes approved by the COMCEC; namely, the Longer Term Trade Financing System, the Islamic Export Credit and Investment Guarantee Corporation, the Framework Agreement on the Trade Preferential System among OIC member states and the Islamic Clearing Union, with a view of ensuring efficient and speedy implementation of these schemes for the benefit of the business community of the Islamic *Ummah.*
- Invites the member states that have not yet done so to subscribe to the second capital increase of the IDB and to settle their outstanding contributions and other financial commitments.
- Calls upon the member states to lend their support to the IDB so as to enable it to fulfil its obligations and commitments towards fostering economic development and the social progress of the member states.

- Appreciates the efforts of IDB in assisting Member States in their relationship with the World Trade Organization (WTO) and urges all OIC Member States to participate in the consultation/coordination meeting which was organized by the bank during the period 29–30 April 1998 in preparation for the second WTO Ministerial Meeting to be held in May 1998.

6.2 *Islamic Corporation for the Insurance of Investment and Export Credit (ICIEC)*

The Islamic Corporation for the Insurance of Investment and Export Credit (ICIEC) is a subsidiary corporation of the IDB established on 1 August 1994 as an international institution with full juridical status. The ICIEC commenced operations in July 1995 from its principal office in Jeddah, Saudi Arabia. The idea for the establishment of an entity to provide investment and export credit insurance for Islamic countries originated from the Agreement for the Promotion, Protection and Guarantee of Investment among Member Countries of the Organization of the Islamic Conference. This Agreement provided that the OIC shall, through the IDB, establish an Islamic institution for investment guarantee to undertake, in conformity with *Shari'ah*, the provision of insurance for investments in the territories of signatory parties of the Agreement (Article 15). The impetus came from the First Session of the OIC Standing Committee for Economic and Commercial Cooperation (COMCEC), held in Istanbul Safar 1405H (November 1984), which requested the IDB to take the necessary steps to establish an export credit guarantee scheme for OIC member countries. At its sixteenth Annual Meeting held in Tripoli, Libya, in Sha'ban 1412H (February 1992), the IDB Board of Governors approved the Articles of Agreement of the Islamic Corporation for the Insurance of Investment and Export Credit.

On 4 Muharram 1413H (4 July 1992), 28 member countries signed the Articles of Agreement. Two member countries later signed the Articles, making a total of 30 signatory countries.

6.2.1 *Objective*

The objective of the ICIEC is to enlarge the scope of trade transactions and the flow of investments among member states of the OIC by:

- Providing export credit insurance to cover the non-payment of export receivables resulting from commercial (buyer) or non-commercial (country) risks.

- Providing investment insurance against country risks, mainly the risks of exchange transfer restrictions, expropriation, war and civil disturbance, and breach of contract by the host government.

6.2.2 Capital

The authorized share capital of the Corporation is ID100 million, made up of 100,000 shares at ID1000 each. The IDB has subscribed to half of the authorized capital, while the remaining half was left for the subscription of the member countries of the OIC. Each member country may subscribe to a minimum of 250 shares. As of 30 Dhul Hijja 1421H (March 2001), the IDB and 29 member countries had subscribed to a total of 94,990 shares for a nominal value of ID1,000 per share, the equivalent of ID94.99 million. The called-up instalments amounted to ID72.50 million, of which ID70.94 million has so far been paid up. The balance of ID1.56 million is receivable from the subscribing member countries.

6.2.3 Organization and Management

In accordance with the Articles of the Agreement, the ultimate responsibility for the management of the ICIEC rests with the Board of Governors, which is composed of governors and deputy governors of the IDB. All powers of the Corporation are vested in the Board of Governors; however, it may delegate any or all of its powers to the Board of Directors of the Corporation. The Board of Directors is responsible for the direction of the general operations of the ICIEC and is also composed of the Board of Executive Directors of the IDB. The Chief Executive of the Corporation, responsible for conducting its affairs under the direction of the Board of Directors, is the President of the Corporation. The President is the legal representative of the ICIEC and has the power to approve its operations and the conclusion of contracts pertaining thereto. This position is held, ex officio, by the President of the IDB. The President may delegate any of his powers to the Manager of the Corporation, who is responsible for conducting the day-to-day business of the Corporation.

In order to advise the President on the overall management of the Corporation, a Consultative Committee was established on 16 Ramadan 1417H (25 January 1997). The members of the Consultative Committee are prominent personalities from member countries who are well-versed in matters relating to export credit and investment insurance, international trade and banking. The Committee meets periodically to discuss and advise the President on relevant issues. The Corporation is organized into three main departments reporting to the Manager of the Corporation; underwriting, marketing, and finance and accounting. Three ancillary units dealing with administrative affairs, information technology, and country risk analysis provide technical and administrative support to the main departments. Legal, internal audit, investment services and certain administrative services are currently provided by the IDB for a fee in accordance with a Memorandum of Understanding signed between the IDB and ICIEC.

Board of Governors

The Board of Governors shall be composed of the governors and deputy governors of the IDB. The Chairman of the Board of Governors of the Bank shall be the ex officio Chairman of the Board of Governors of the Corporation. All powers of the Corporation shall be vested in the Board of Governors. The Board of Governors, and the Board of Directors to the extent authorized, may adopt such rules and regulations as may be necessary or appropriate to the conducting of the business of the Corporation, including rules and regulations pertaining to staff, retirement and other benefits.

Board of Directors

The Board of Executive Directors of the IDB shall be the Board of Directors of the Corporation. All regulations, by-laws and procedures of the Board of Executive Directors of the Bank shall apply to the Board of Directors of the Corporation as if the latter were the Board of Executive Directors of the Bank.

The Board of Directors shall be responsible for the direction of the general operations of the Corporation and, for this purpose, shall, in addition to the powers assigned to it expressly by the Agreement for the Promotion, Protection and Guarantee of Investment among Member Countries of the Organization of the Islamic Conference, exercise all the powers delegated to it by the Board of Governors. The Board of Directors also:

- Prepares the work of the Board of Governors.
- Lays down guidelines for the carrying out of the business of the Corporation and its operations in conformity with the general directions of the Board of Governors.
- Approves the budget of the Corporation.

The President

The President of the IDB shall be the ex officio President of the Corporation. The President shall be the Chief Executive of the Corporation and shall conduct the affairs of the Corporation under the direction of the Board of Directors. The President shall be responsible for the organization, appointment and dismissal of the officers and staff in accordance with the rules and regulations adopted by the Board of Directors.

The President shall be the legal representative of the Corporation and shall have power to approve the operations of the Corporation and the conclusion of the contracts pertaining thereto within the general guidelines issued by the Board of Directors.

6.3 *Islamic Financial Services Board (IFSB)*

The establishment of the Islamic Financial Services Board (IFSB) is in response to the growing significance of the Islamic financial services industry. The setting up of the IFSB is the culmination of an extensive two-year consultative process initiated by a group of governors and senior officials of the central banks and monetary authorities of several Islamic countries, together with the IDB and the Accounting and Auditing Organization for Islamic Financial Institutions (AAOIFI), and with the support of the International Monetary Fund (IMF).

6.3.1 Purpose

The objectives of the IFSB include promoting, disseminating and harmonizing best practices in the regulation and supervision of the Islamic financial services industry.

6.3.2 Functions

The IFSB will serve as an association of central banks, monetary authorities and other institutions that will be responsible for the regulation and supervision of the Islamic financial services industry. In brief, the IFSB will:

- Set and disseminate standards and core principles, as well as adapt existing international standards, for supervision and regulation consistent with the *Shari'ah* principles governing the industry, and for voluntary adoption by member countries.

- Liaise and cooperate with other setters of standards in the areas of monetary and financial stability.
- Promote good practices in risk management in the industry through research, training and technical assistance.

Besides the above departments that undertake a variety of tasks, the OIC also establishes affiliated institutions in order to cater for Islamic economics that have an indirect relationship with *takaful*.

6.4 *Affiliated Institutions*

6.4.1 Idea Groups

These groups bring together entities or moral persons. Membership to these institutions is optional, and is open to institutions and bodies of OIC member states. Their budgets are independent of the budget of the Secretariat General and those of subsidiary and specialized bodies. These groups were established under the auspices of the Islamic Conferences of Heads of State and Government or the ICFM.

Affiliated institutions may be granted observer status by virtue of a resolution of the ICFM. They may obtain voluntary assistance from the subsidiary and specialized bodies, as well as from member states.

Seven affiliated institutions have been established that are located in different capitals and cities in the Islamic world. They are the:

- Islamic Chamber of Commerce and Industry (Karachi).
- Organization of Islamic Capitals and Cities (Makkah Al-Mukarramah/Jeddah).
- Sports Federation of Islamic Solidarity Games (Riyadh).
- Islamic Committee of the International Crescent (Benghazi).
- Islamic Shipowners Association (ISA) (Jeddah).
- World Federation of International Arab-Islamic Schools (Jeddah).
- International Association of Islamic Banks (Jeddah).

6.4.2 Islamic Chamber of Commerce and Industry (ICCI)

Establishment

A recommendation to establish the Islamic Chamber of Commerce, Industry and Commodity Exchange was made in accordance with a resolution adopted by the Tenth Islamic Conference, held in Fez in May 1979. It is affiliated to the OIC.

Objectives

- To promote and encourage trade, industry and handicrafts among the member states.
- To make recommendations to safeguard economic interests and commercial activities of the Islamic world.
- To promote cooperation between the Islamic Chambers and other international commercial, industrial and agricultural organizations.
- To promote the exchange of commercial delegations and to organize trade fairs, exhibitions, seminars, lectures and publicity campaigns.
- To promote investment opportunities and joint ventures among the member states.
- To provide for arbitration in the settlement of commercial and industrial disputes.
- To promote the exchange of commercial, technical, industrial, management and scientific information and expertise among the member states.

6.4.3 Organization of Islamic Capital Activities

Establishment

The establishment of the Organization of Islamic Capital Activities was approved by resolution No. (9/9-E) adopted by the ICFM held in Dakar, Republic of Senegal. The Statute of the Organization was approved by the ICFM held in Fez, Morocco.

Objectives

- To strengthen the bonds of friendship, brotherhood and solidarity among Islamic capitals and cities.
- To promote, develop and expand the scope of cooperation among the Islamic capitals and cities.
- To preserving the identity and heritage of Islamic capitals and cities.
- To seek to implement comprehensive urban architectural plans that may guide the growth of Islamic capitals and cities in accordance with their actual economic, social, cultural and environmental characteristics.
- To upgrade the standards of public services and utilities in the Islamic capitals and cities.

CHAPTER 3

Evolution of Islamic Financial Products and Services

1 Introduction

Today, the market segment of Islamic financial products and regulations is no longer confined within a limited territory but, rather, is in the borderless space of the Internet, having exposure to almost all groups of people worldwide. The market mechanisms adopted by potential marketers include dynamic strategies and mechanisms of governance to match the Internet, where both Muslim and non-Muslim participate on an equal footing to market Islamic financial products. The results are promising.

The arena of Islamic corporate application and governance has captured the attention of both Muslims and non-Muslims, both participating equally in establishing and offering competitive and sound Islamic financial products. As a result of this, besides having almost 300 fully fledged Islamic financial providers in the modern market, almost all conventional players also offer Islamic financial products. They achieve this by establishing segregated windows and divisions, and by adopting suitable *Shari'ah* compliant mechanisms.

Numerous options of *Shari'ah* justified instruments are being applied by product specialists and technical experts in Islamic financial industries, who are developing competitive Islamic financial products with innovative cultural and dynamic corporate outcomes. As a result, these products for investors, customers and bankers are paving the way for Islamic financial industries. The products are designed to satisfy not only retail

M. M. Billah, *Islamic Financial Products*,
https://doi.org/10.1007/978-3-030-17624-2_3

groups, but also corporate levels. If such dynamic product innovation continues, the growth rate of Islamic financial business, based on the historical rate, may achieve 40–50% by the year 2020.

However, such an achievement definitely requires the reworking of the mechanisms for product innovation, the culture of product reviews, reviews of professional standards, and improvement of the relevant policies, regulations and governing standards in line with ethical guidelines, as these will not be ignored in any sector of the Islamic industrial movement.

Strategic planning for every move of Islamic financial industry is of utmost importance to ensure the smooth and successful growth of the industry. Strategic planning should be consolidated with dynamic actions. Therefore, it is essential to ensure the presence of experts in *Shari'ah*; decision-making; and technical, operational and marketing fields, together with proper professional standards and legitimate behaviours in accordance with *Shari'ah* requirements.

2 Resurgence of Islamic Financial Products and Services

The modern growth of the Islamic financial industry began in Egypt and the Arab world, while Malaysia caught the wave in the early 1980s; subsequently, we have seen a rapid and steady development throughout both the Muslim and non-Muslim worlds. Due to the present phenomena of development and dynamic offerings of applied Islamic financial products, Malaysia, Bahrain and the United Arab Emirates hold the top-ranking roles in the global Islamic financial market.

Applied Islamic financial sectors have developed a global dimension that is highly dynamic and growing rapidly, which is greatly appreciated not only by among 1.8 billion Muslims, but also by non-Muslims worldwide. This leads *Halal* industries and the Islamic financial market to perform as a stable alternative to conventional industries and markets, affording a sustainable existence for all.

The global *Halal* industries; Islamic financial market; and *Shari'ah* compliant industries, activities and markets achieve business in trillions of dollars, there being almost 400 Islamic financial institutions worldwide. According to the Global Islamic Finance Report 2013, the global Islamic finance market value is purported to be worth US$1.631 trillion, with a growth rate estimated to be around 20.4% per annum.

Among the master players of Islamic finance in the contemporary world are the Middle East, Malaysia, Iran, Indonesia, Brunei, Singapore, North America, Pakistan, Bangladesh, South-West Africa and the UK. The clientele of Islamic financial institutions are not confined to Muslim countries but are spread throughout Europe, the USA, south Asia, southeast Asia, the Asia Pacific and the Far East. Providers are not confined to local institutions; global players increasingly play major roles in the industry today by aiming satisfy everyone regardless of their religion, colour, culture or status.

Apart from the existing world players, the next wave of industrial growth from the non-Muslim world can be predicted with reasonable accuracy. Among those countries we could anticipate seeing Singapore, the UK, Hong Kong, Germany, Canada, Russia, Australia, China, Japan and South Africa. It may be anticipated that, within the next seven to ten years, Islamic financial products with the required *Shari'ah* regulatory frameworks may attract almost 60–65% of total financial business globally, offering Islamic financial products to both Muslims and non-Muslims with beneficial results.

It is widely accepted that the adaptation of the *Shari'ah* compliant financial paradigm is one of the fastest growing areas of international banking and finance. The forecasts predict that there will be significant growth in this sector over the next five to ten years. However, this growth is dependent on successful risk management, professionalism, product innovation, regulatory frameworks, marketing strategies, research and development, and customer satisfaction—matters to which all professionals, regulators, practitioners, and customers and participants in the banking and financial industry must attend. Such a practice can be only achieved with the appropriate knowledge, information and behaviours.

3 Rational Outlook of the Sustainable Growth of Islamic Financial Products

The Islamic approach is not simply based on religious grounds. Its ethos comprises a wide range of principles—socio-eco-cultural, logistic, authentic and hypothetical—that undeniably support and justify the sustainable growth of Islamic finance. Thus, there are positive opinions regarding the growth of Islamic finance in the modern world, as evinced by the *Borneo Post Online* (www.theborneopost.com), as the following sections will show.

3.1 *Mutual Cooperation with a Risk-sharing Culture*

Islamic finance is not a mere product; rather, it is a holistic integrated system for all mankind based on the Divine principle of mutual cooperation with a risk-sharing culture for the legitimate benefit of all, irrespective of their religious background, race, colour, gender, status or nationality (see the *Qur'an* 5:2).

3.2 *Green Financing Platform*

Islamic finance offers the ideal platform on which to boost 'green financing' and promote socially responsible investment (SRI). As *Shari'ah* rules prohibit participation in businesses involving alcohol, pork, and gambling, Islamic banks only support businesses that adhere to ethical and moral natural values where investments are involved.

3.3 Shari'ah *Compliant Products*

Demand for *Shari'ah* compliant products continues to rise together with a growing Muslim population. Muslims were predicted to account for more than 25% of the world population in 2013, growing twice as fast as the world's non-Muslim population. Islamic banks address this group's needs and natural inclination to prefer *Shari'ah* compliant financial products.

3.4 *Fast and Steady Growth*

The Islamic financing industry is growing 50% faster than conventional banking. As of 2011, the global asset value of the Islamic finance industry was estimated to be at US$1 trillion. The figure was expected to reach US$5 trillion over the subsequent five years. Indeed, there would appear to be no stopping the rapid growth of Islamic banking, with Islamic banks setting up shop in countries under the Gulf Cooperation Council (GCC), Malaysia, the UK, and even in Africa, among many other regions.

3.5 *Attracts Non-Muslim Investors*

Even non-Muslim investors see the potential for profit in Islamic banking. Islamic financial products, as a rule, carry lower risk investments while enabling investors to earn a profit and, at the same time, diversify their portfolio to further reduce risk.

3.6 Global Indexing

Western investors can track the Islamic financing industry through international rating systems. When purchasing *sukuk* (Islamic bonds), they can easily assess the strengths, weaknesses, and risk of the bonds by simply referring to the benchmarks that track the financial industry.

3.7 Oil-rich Countries Adopt Islamic Finance

Countries belonging to the GCC want *Shari'ah* compliant products for investment. Those belonging to this group are some of the wealthiest countries in the world. As the economies of Europe and the USA struggle to stabilize their budgets, GCC nations are well-funded and their needs are well-met by Islamic banks.

3.8 Effective Decision-making

Islamic investors avoid choices that cause harm to people and the environment. Through a thoughtful decision-making process, investors are able to make socially responsible choices that encourage investments that are good for the long-term.

3.9 Streamlined and Simpler

Islamic financial products, though they may come with their own set of complex rules, are far simpler to understand than their conventional counterparts. For instance, the contracts are stricter and their content focused. Islamic financial institutions also have scholars that offer consumers guidance on every venture and proceeding. They follow strict principles that ensure every single transaction is carried out according to *Shari'ah* law.

3.10 'No Crisis' Zone

Islamic financing saw a 25% increase in the value of its assets from 2007 to 2008, while most of the world's economies battled with a dire financial crisis. It is therefore safe to say that investing in Islamic financing is a possible way forward to avert potential crises in the world economy.

3.11 *Humanitarian Concerns*

It is not against Islamic laws to accumulate wealth; however, all investors need to exercise awareness and shared responsibility for the poverty in the world. Through the concept of *zakat* (giving a portion of wealth to charity), Islamic finance aims to reduce economic disparity around the globe.

3.12 *Industrial Catching Up*

Malaysia's Islamic assets reached US$65 billion in the financial year 2012/13, according to a report by the Ministry of Finance. National Islamic banking assets registered an average annual growth rate of between 18 and 20% to reach US$65.6 billion. The government has recently invested in the development of human resources for the Islamic financing industry so as to ensure it catches up to the industry's phenomenal growth.

4 Literature Initiative to Support the Growth of the Industry

4.1 *Islamic Trade Finance*

Despite this development, quality refereed materials on the Islamic law of trade and finance do not yet satisfy the demand for this information. *Applied Islamic Law of Trade and Finance* (Sweet and Maxwell) provides a possible practical exposition of the current Islamic law of trade and finance. Comparison between Islamic law and civil law highlights the differences between the systems and greatly assists in the understanding of both. Regular quotations of Qur'anic verses and prophetic traditions, accompanied by English translations, set out the religious foundation underlying the practicality of each Islamic law of trade and finance.

Applied Islamic Law of Trade and Finance covers topics such as commercial contracts, the sale of goods, partnership, the capital market, Islamic currency, *takaful* and the institution of *zakat*. Islamic finance practitioners, bankers, lawyers, business owners and their financial and legal advisers may gain valuable information, including practical solutions, on the Islamic law of trade and finance.

Islamic finance has grown exponentially in since 1963 and has reached over 70 countries around the world. The Islamic financial system today comprises a sizeable asset base, and there is evidence of sustained demand for Islamic financial products and services in the global market, with demand outstripping supply.

The forthcoming title *Applied Islamic Finance: Law and Practice from a Global Perspective* provides a new source of reference to aid in the understanding of the laws and practices of Islamic finance from a global perspective. Besides providing an overview of the regulatory structure overseeing the Islamic financial system, the book discusses the sources of law and the applied principles of *Shari'ah* governing Islamic financial instruments, products and policies. An entire chapter is devoted to surveying the laws of several countries in the Muslim world that govern Islamic financial institutions.

As Islamic finance involves a wide array of global players—including borrowers, lenders and their bankers, policy-makers, and legal and financial advisers—harmonization and rationalization are important in order to foster an efficient and dynamic system. To that end, the book discusses the *Shari'ah* standard of contemporary financial business, the roles and functions of a *Shari'ah* advisory body, and the impact of *fatwa* in Islamic financial practices.

This book may be regularly consulted by banking and finance practitioners, in-house legal counsel, business owners, policy-makers, participants, players, researchers and persons responsible for the further development of the Islamic financial system globally.

4.2 Takaful *and* Re-takaful *Products*

The understanding of *takaful* (Islamic insurance) and modern insurance will be greatly enhanced by reading *Applied Takaful and Modern Insurance* (Sweet & Maxwell), which deals with regulatory and practical matters. This book presents a comparison in clear and succinct language between the principles and practices of *takaful* and those of modern insurance. The comparison of these two systems reveals the differences between the two systems and their similarities so as to facilitate a better appreciation of the systems, which run in parallel to cover the various risks faced in the reality of daily life today.

The topics covered in the book include the subject matter at risk, insurable interest, good faith, insurance contracts, risk management, insurance intermediaries, nomination, beneficiaries, claims, distribution and legal formalities. The modern experience of *takaful* operation is also discussed and recommendations are given for the future development of the industry in the contemporary world of advanced economies.

The book has been useful for *takaful*, *re-takaful* and insurance practitioners, business owners, in-house *Shari'ah* and legal counsel, *takaful* or insurance advisors, and persons responsible for risk management.

4.3 E-Commerce Products

The increasing volume of *Shari'ah* compliant business transactions backed by Islamic financial arrangements together with the widespread use of the Internet and information technology (IT) afford a good understanding of Islamic e-commerce law and practices. Being a developing area, there is a lack of good literature and it is the aim of *Applied Islamic e-Commerce: Laws and Practice* (Sweet and Maxwell) to fill the need.

The book gives a practical and enlightening account of Islamic law, comparing modern principles as they apply to the field of e-commerce. Part I of the book sets out the general principles of e-commerce law, which includes ethics in e-commerce and the sources of e-commerce law. Part II discusses the *Shari'ah* perspective, comparing modern practical matters such as Internet marketing and advertising, virtual stores and payment systems, as well as personal rights and the protection of privacy.

The practices of e-commerce law under *Shari'ah* compared with the practices of modern principles are explored in Part III. These include the components of an e-contract, the principles governing data protection, and the concept and practical application of digital signatures. Part IV surveys offences and liabilities in e-commerce, particularly those associated with hackers and torts in e-commerce dealings under *Shari'ah* compared with those associated with modern principles.

Applied Islamic e-Commerce: Laws and Practice is an illuminating text and provides valuable guidance from the Islamic law standpoint compared with modern principles on practical issues which arise in the conduct of e-commerce. This is the first publication to consider *Shari'ah* standards in comparison with modern principles and should not be overlooked by corporate lawyers, finance and business advisors, business owners, in-house legal counsel, marketers, IT professionals and those involved in e-commerce activities in worldwide business.

4.4 *Strategies Ahead*

In the past, the Islamic financial industry had grown through hardship strategies; its present success is being achieved through dynamic strategic and smart applications, giving Islamic financial products the potential to be an alternative option for global conventional players. If this phenomenon continues, the Islamic banking and financial platform could undoubtedly secure a sustainable place in the world's growing financial picture.

For this to occur, professionalism, public awareness, appropriate reviews and product innovations must strictly be observed. Furthermore, dynamic mechanisms should be continuously researched to provide tools for risk management at all levels of the Islamic financial industry. In addition, IT hardware and software should be upgraded regularly to facilitate the smooth running of hi-tech Islamic financial activities. This will help meet the objective of providing the best and most competitive offerings for the present and the future.

PART II

Governing Principles and Strategies of Islamic Products and Services

CHAPTER 4

Islamic Financial Policies

1 Introduction

Bank Islam Malaysia has been one of the providers of Islamic financing in Malaysia. Islamic financing is an alternative to the conventional financing offered by other banks. The principles that the bank follows are those contained in *Shari'ah* laws, which principles meet the demand from Muslim societies for business capital from the Islamic banks.

The financing techniques offered by the Bank fall into two categories: debt and equity financing. Bank Islam Malaysia does not separate their financing into these two categories; the nature of the debt raised is distinguished by the various products that are offered to meet public need. Based on this, we can see that Bank Islam Malaysia has introduced many products for the benefit of society, especially Muslim society, either to finance a new venture or to refinance a home loan.

By analysing Bank Islam Malaysia's debt and equity financing figures, we are able to see how the Bank manages its financing techniques and tries to differentiate the various types of financing available. We will further discuss financing such as *mudharabah*, *ijarah* and *al-rahn*, and others in due course.

This chapter will also discuss *takaful* in connection with the financing options offered by the Bank because when acquiring finance customers need to know the coverage that the bank can offer. For this reason, *takaful* was introduced by the Bank on 29 November 1984 to cater for customers' insurance requirements.

M. M. Billah, *Islamic Financial Products*,
https://doi.org/10.1007/978-3-030-17624-2_4

The primary goal of Islamic banking and finance is the development of economic resources, and regulation of the monetary and financial policies of the Muslim *Ummah* in accordance with the *Shari'ah*. Islam has a unitary approach to life. It considers mankind to be an integral whole; in other words, the sum total of the numerous functions that he performs—economic, political, social, in line with his moral values, in accordance with his cultural heritage and, above all, with his religious belief.

2 Central Concept

Financing is crucial for an entrepreneur wishing to start new venture; an example here would be a person who wishes to start a new business, or to buy a new house or a new car, or perhaps to obtain personal financing. Since it is an important decision, each person must make the right decision in determining the appropriate kind of financing that will not only afford the best method of financing their project, but also provide them with the appropriate cover if matters do not transpire as anticipated.

Therefore, Bank Islam Malaysia has introduced their own version of financing to cater for society's needs, especially those of Muslims. Muslims are very sceptical regarding the nature of conventional financing. The idea of Islamic financing is not only to provide finance, but also to provide cover for the participants. An additional benefit is the encouragement of Muslim entrepreneurs to expand their business and compete in the market with other non-Muslim entrepreneurs.

In addition, *takaful* is also provided to protect the participants should they face business problems or be unable to repay their loan instalments due to unforeseen circumstances. The coverage provided is directly related to the type of financing offered by the Bank. With regard to debt financing, the Bank will provide a loan for an entire project or for the purchase of equipment. At the end of the term of the loan, the debtor will pay back the loan principal plus any interest due, such sum of interest depending on the period of the loan. With regard to equity financing, the Bank will be a joint partner in an enterprise and will provide half, or more, of the required capital to enable the debtor to do business. In this situation, the Bank has the option to bear the cost together with the debtor, or give the capital to the debtor and, should a loss be incurred, the debtor will not be responsible therein. Equity financing is used by a person who wishes to start new business. At the end of the financing period, the Bank will receive profit according to the profit ratio agreed between the Bank and the debtor.

3 Application of Islamic Financing in Islamic Banking

3.1 *Debt Financing*

3.1.1 Al-Rahn (Rahnu)
Al-rahn means to hold a *maal* as a mortgage to a loan in such a way that the loan can be settled from the value of the mortgaged *maal* in the event of default or the inability to pay. Islamic banks are similar to conventional banks in that they prefer to secure a loan through either personal surety (a guarantor) or a pledge.

4 *Shari'ah* Ruling

The holy Qur'an also supports the idea of furnishing a pledge against a debt. It is laid down in *Surahal-Baqarah* (2:283):

> And if you are on a journey and cannot find a scribe, pledges [may be taken] in hand, but if you trust one another, then let them who is trusted fulfil his trust, and let him be conscious of God, his sustainer.

In the *Mejelle*, Article 701 defines *al-rahn* as 'to make a property a security in respect of a right of claim, the payment of which in full from that property is permitted'

Hadith

Narrated by Bukhari and Muslim from *Aishah* (*RA*): 'Verily the Messenger of Allah (*SWT*) bought some food from Yahudi and he mortgaged an iron armour' (Agreed).

5 Application of *Al-Rahnu*

Al-rahnu is used for a shorter period of loan. This scheme will enable a person to obtain an immediate amount of money for finance purposes. Bank Islam Malaysia Berhad (BIMB) collaborated with the Yayasan

Pembangunan Ekonomi Malaysia (YPEIM) in introducing this scheme. Customers are required to offer collateral, such as gold bullion.

BIMB plays a role in the field of *al-rahn* (mortgage/loans), guaranteeing the safety of customers' property while dealing with their financial needs, such as managing debts. Such property may be sold, with payment being deferred, in order to meet the liability of the second party to the guarantee. So, BIMB could use *al-rahn* to service customers' obligations.

A person can secure a loan amount to the maximum value of $5000, or up to 60% of the market value of the collateral or the gold, whichever is the lower.

For example, the gold cost price = $10,000 * 60% = $6000

Whatever the value of the collateral held by the Bank, the loan is limited to $25,000.

The duration of the financing period is up to a maximum of six months.

The process that secures the loan takes the following steps:

- The Bank grants a benevolent loan (*qard al-hasan*) to the applicant.
- The applicant provides collateral (gold) as security for the loan.
- The Bank safeguards the collateral based on the *wadiah yad dhamanah* contract.
- The Bank charges a fee for the custody of the collateral.

This scheme can be related to the general *takaful*; that is, the *takaful* mortgage plan. The *takaful* will guarantee the payment of financing in the event of death or other unavoidable circumstances.

5.1 Al-Ijarah

Al-ijarah means to give something on the basis of it being rented. Technically, *ijarah* means employing the services of a person on wages given to him as a consideration for his hired services, or transferring the usufruct of a particular property to another person on the basis of a rent claimed from him. There are two types of *ijarah*: *ijarah al-ain* and *ijarah al'amal*.

5.1.1 Shari'ah *Ruling*

The Qur'an mentions *ijarah*:

(*Surah Al-Saff*, verse 2):

> O you who believe, why do you profess what you not practice? (61:2)

Surah Al-Saff, verse 3:

> Saying what you do not practice is odious to God. (6:3)

Surah Al-Qasas, verse 26:

> Truly the best man for you to employ is the man who is strong and trusty. (28:26)

5.1.2 Hadith

Prophet Muhammad (SAW) said:

Give the employee his due wage before his sweat dries.

Al-ijma':

> All scholars from *sahabah* time agree that *ijarah* is permissible since people need benefits.

5.1.3 Application of Ijarah

In the case of direct leasing financing, the lessee is required to pay the amount equivalent to the market purchase price of the object as the lease rent. This contract is called hire purchase finance (*ijarah thumma al-iktina/bay*).

The process is as follows:

- The Bank will acquire the asset from the house developer, as agreed by the customer.
- The customer will pay the Bank the amount of purchase under the contract, as monthly rental for a specified number of months.
- The rental could be agreed as a fixed amount, or as a percentage of the amount related to the cash flow of the projects.

- When the amount of rental equals the value of the asset cost, the asset ownership will be transferred to the customer.

  The asset cost = $100,000
  Duration of rental = 20 years
  $100,000.00/20/12 = $416.67
  Payment per month = $416.67

This relates to the general *takaful* of *takaful* for house owners, where they have coverage if they find themselves unable to pay. In this situation, the cost will be borne by the other participants first.

5.2 Al-Qard *(Loan Contract)*

Qard literally means 'to cut'. This refers to a proportion of the lender's property being the security for a loan. Technically, it is a contract of payment to be repaid with the same.

5.2.1 Shari'ah *Ruling*

Shari'ah does not permit a bank to set a profit margin at the time a contract is made. *Hadith* provides that, 'Every loan which is draws benefit is *riba*'. Therefore, a contract for a loan in Islamic finance is called a benevolent loan (*qard al-hasan*). However, it is recommended that the borrower gives something in return for the benevolent act of the bank. The two *hadiths* of the prophet are self-explanatory:

Hadith reported by Abu Rafi that the prophet was lent a young female camel. He could not find a similar type of camel and returned a pregnant camel instead.

> Indeed a good person among you is he who settles the loan with something better.

Hadith narrated by Jabir (*RA*):

> I had the right (of loan) on the prophet-settled it made additional payment.

In another narration by Anas that Prophet Muhammad (*SAW*) said:

> I saw on the night I travelled, written on the door of '*al-Jannah*': *sadaqah* is rewarded tenfold the value of its amount; whereas a loan is preferred to charity. He answered; a beggar asks for (something) he already has (which means he is not in real need). A debtor will not ask for a loan unless he is in real need.

In a narration by Ibn Mas'ud, the Prophet said:

> Not so a Muslim whenever he gives a loan (*al-qardh*) twice, except it is like one *sadaqah*.

A narration from Abu Hurairah recounts that the Prophet said:

> Whoever relieved/banished from a Muslim a burden/sorrow of this world, Allah will relieve from him a burden/sorrow in the next world, and whoever make someone in an impoverished circumstances happy, Allah will make him happy in this world and in the next world; and Allah is ever ready to help his servant (man) if the servant is ever ready to help his fellow man.

Another *hadith* related to *qard* is the Prophet saying that whoever performs a good deed for you, you should reciprocate. If you cannot afford to do so, pray to Allah for his pleasure to express your gratitude.

5.2.2 Application of Qard *in Modern Islamic Banking*

Currently, the practice of *qard al-hasanah* is limited to discharging a bank's social or charitable obligation and buying government investment certificates.

5.3 Al-Murabahah *(Mark-Up Lump Payment Sale)*

The term *murabahah* is derived from the word *ribah*, which means profit or gain. *Murabahah* is generally defined as a sales plus profit margin, which is the profit margin or mark-up created purely by time.

Many Islamic banks and financial institutions are using *murabahah* as an Islamic mode of financing. This term is commonly used in current economic circles as a method of banking operation, even though the original concept of *murabahah* is different from this.

In *murabahah*, if a seller agrees with his buyer to provide a specific commodity with a certain amount of profit added to his cost, it is called *murabahah* transaction. This profit may be in the form of a fixed lump sum, or based on a percentage. Payment in *murabahah* can be done either on spot, or at a future date agreed by the parties. *Murabahah* is different from other kinds of sale because the seller in a *murabahah* transaction expressly tells the buyer how much cost he has incurred and how much profit he is going to charge in addition to that cost.

The term *murabahah* means a sale. Islamic banks and financial institutions use this type of sale by adding certain other elements to it so as to create a mode of financing. The validity of such transactions, however, depends on certain conditions that must be observed to make them acceptable under *Shari'ah* law.

Bank Islam Malaysia normally buys the asset at the market price, and then sells it back to the consumers at the cost or selling price; here, there is no risk-taking, which is the element of *gharar* and the additional value of *riba*. Banks can add the value of risk-taking (*ghurmi*)—for example, in risk-taking, the bank must have legal ownership of goods before it can sell the goods to a customer. With legal ownership, it bears the risk of not making a sale should a customer change their mind, which they have the right to do. Without legal ownership, the bank is functioning a financier and this is not what the Qur'an intended it to be. In addition to the ownership factor, the bank must also honour the customer's option to reject the goods if they were found to be defective, or if they were not delivered as specified.

5.3.1 Application of Al-Murabahah

Vehicle Financing

This type of financing will enable a customer to own the car they desire. With a deferred payment, a customer will be able to afford the full amount. The financing is applicable to any car, whether national or made abroad.

- The amount for financing is up to 100% for any national car.
- For non-national cars, the amount is 90%.
- The duration of instalment payments is 84 months.
- Customers will receive a discount (*ibra*) should they settle the loan early.

As in general *takaful*, there is insurance coverage for commercial vehicles. Customers who do not make any claims can have two benefits;

- The no-claims benefit
- The profits from *murabahah*.

The bank provides the source of finance by means of a *murabahah* trust receipt; in conventional banking, a trust receipt is set up as a trade financing loan. In the case of an Islamic trust receipt, the bank buys the goods from supplier and sells them on to a customer at a credit price. The customer will pay in a lump sum. The mark-up or profit is equal to the credit price minus cash price (see Table 1).

A *Bai' bithaman ajil* (BBA) arrangement is very similar to *murabahah*. BBA is a long-term credit sale/deferred sale where payments are made in instalments. The profit created from BBA is *halal* (permissible exchange) and is based on a sale contract. The rules of BBA are:

An object must exist, otherwise the contract is void.

- The seller (bank) must have title to the object.
- The sale is immediate and absolute; it is not dependent on a future date or event.
- The price is fixed; otherwise it would be tantamount to two sales in one transaction, which is prohibited by the holy Prophet Muhammad (*SAW*).
- In a BBA transaction, the customer may buy an asset from an owner or seller even though he may not have sufficient money to pay in cash.

Table 1 Vehicle financing

Murabahah *trust receipt*	
Facility	\$100,000
Tenure	3 month (1/6/00–1/6/00) or 91 days
Annual profit	10%
Profit	(FV × annual rate of profit × no. of days) divided by 365
Profit	\$100,000 × 0.1 × 91/365 = \$2493.15
Selling price	Cost price + profit \$100 000 + \$2493.15 = \$102493.15

Source Author's own

Table 2 Past experience with *Al-Bai' Bithaman Ajil* (BBA) (deferred/credit sale)

Calculation of selling price based on BBA	
Cost of financing	$40,000
Profit rate (flat)	7%
Period of financing	5 years
Selling price (SP)	CF + (CF × i × n)
CF	Cost of financing
I	Rate of return perannum
N	Period of financing in years
SP	$40,000 + $14,000 = $54,000
Monthly repayment	SP / (n × 12) $54,000 / 60 $900.00

Source Author's own

For example, the bank purchases the asset from the owner at $40,000. The bank then sells the asset to Mr. Muhammad at $40,000 plus a profit margin; this is the selling price. The customer repays the selling price in instalments over the course of five years. The profit margin is $14,000. The selling price is therefore $54,000. From this, we can see that Mr. Muhammad has to pay $900 per month (see Table 2).

The difference between *murabahah* and BBA:

- In the case of a *murabahah* contract, the buyer must be informed the cost price of the goods; in a BBA contract, no need to inform the cost price of an asset.
- *Murabahah* financing is for small items, while BBA financing is for assets such as building, machinery, and so on.
- In a *murabahah* contract, the customer will pay for the goods over a shorter period (not longer than between 6 and 12 months). Under the terms of a BBA contract, the customer will pay for the assets over a longer period; for example, between 10 and 30 years.
- A BBA contract deals with the deferred payment of capital in instalments. *Murabahah* is also a deferred payment but is due to be paid as a lump sum.

The *al-baiti* home financing offered by a bank will enable a customer to own their ideal house. Under BBA, payments can be deferred and the debt settled by equal monthly payments.

5.3.2 Application of Al-Bai-Bithaman Ajil
House Financing (*al-baiti*)

- The total amount of finance available is up to 100%.
- The period of repayment is up to 32 years, including a discount for the first 24 months.

This relates to *takaful* in two ways:

- Long-term house owner's *takaful*: to protect the house from any disasters throughout the financing period.
- *Takaful* mortgage plan: this guarantees settlement of any outstanding portion of the loan if the customer dies, or is permanently disabled.

5.4 *Equity Financing*

5.4.1 Al-Mudharabah
Mudharabah, also known as *qirad* or *muqaradah*, is a special kind of contract of partnership based on risk and profit sharing in which one party provides funds (*rabbul mal*) and the other provides work and management (*mudharib*).

***Shari'ah* Rulings**
The scholars of all schools of *fiqh* are in agreement that *al-mudharabah* contracts are allowable based on the indications in the Qur'an, the Sunnah, *al-ijma'*, and *al-qiyas*.

Allah (*SWT*) said in *surah al-Muzammil* (73:20)

> and others travelling through the land, seeking Allah's bounty.

Surah al-Jum'ah (62:10)

> and when the prayer is finished, then you may disperse through the land and seek the bounty of Allah.

Surah al-Baqarah (2:195)

> and spend of your substance in the cause of God, and make not your own hands contribute to (your) destruction; but do good; for God loveth those who do good.

The above three verses indicate that the contract of *mudharabah* is allowed on wealth.

In the *hadith* narrated by Ibn Abbas, he says: 'Sayidna Abbas bin Abdul Mutalib, when he handed over his wealth for *mudharabah*, made it conditional that his friend [the worker/*mudharib*] should not trade his wealth overseas but in the valley, and should not to use his wealth to buy animals. If the condition were to be broken, then the worker would be responsible for any loss. The *mudharabah* and its conditions came to the knowledge of the Prophet (*SAW*) and received his approved.

In another *hadith* narrated by Ibn Majah, from *Suhaib* (*RA*) that the Prophet (*SAW*) said: 'Three things in which there are blessings (from Allah); the sale of barley for home (consumption) and not for trade.'

There is another trade arrangement in the form of *mudharabah* approved by Umar (which therefore became the Sunnah and, in another form, became a consensus of the companion).

Application of *Al-Mudharabah* in Islamic Banking

In *mudharabah* banking, there are actually two separate contracts between three parties; the suppliers of the capital (depositor, or *rab-bul mal*), the intermediary links (the banks) and the users of the capital (*mudharibs*, or manager).

The first contract is the arrangements that the bank will receive deposits of various kinds from the public on the basis of *mudharabah* and will have a share of the profit (or loss) from them on certain mutually agreed terms. The second contract is when bank then uses these funds by advancing loans to individual businessmen or firms on the same principle of profit sharing with them. To have greater understanding of the principles of *mudharabah* in the Islamic banking system, see Fig. 1.

In a *mudharabah* as described above, the depositor (*rabbul mal*) puts the money into the bank as capital; say, $10,000. The bank then gives the money as an investment in a second tier. Profit generated by the second tier investment will be shared between bank and the entrepreneur at a ratio of, say, 45:55 (45% for bank and 55% for the entrepreneur). If the contract makes a gain, the bank receives $45 for every $100 profit

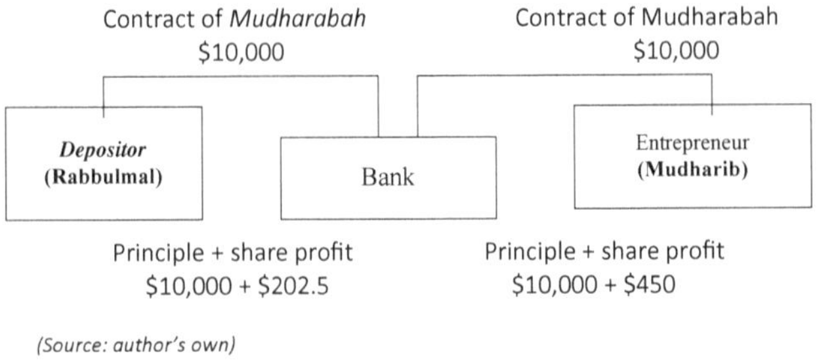

Fig. 1 Application of *al-mudharabah* in Islamic banking (*Source* Author's own)

and the entrepreneur receives $55 for every $100 profit. In the first tier, profit will be shared between bank and depositor at a ratio of, say, 55:45 the bank receives $55 and the depositor receives $45 for every $100 of business profit.

According to the example given above, the total investment of the *mudharabah* bank is $10,000 and the net profit from the business enterprise is $1000. In the second tier, the entrepreneur will obtain a net profit of $550 (55% * 1000) and the *mudharabah* bank obtains a net profit of $450 (45% * 1000).

The bank then has to share the profit with the depositor at the same ratio. So, the *mudharabah* bank receives $247.5 (55% of $450) and the depositor receives $202.5 (45% of $450). The depositor will eventually obtain $10,202.5 (10,000 + 202.5) from the business (Gain).

In the event of a loss—for example, the *mudharabah* bank invests $10,000 in the entrepreneur and received $8000, the loss will be borne by depositor (*rabbul mal*), not the entrepreneur (*mudharib*).

Mudharabah contracts can also be used in situations when it is prohibited to make any interest, thereby enabling the channelling of more funds. Engaging in *mudharabah* would satisfy the ethical and Islamic requirements of using funds productively, and not involve *riba'*. *Mudharabah* permits the drawing of funds currently held by devout Muslims who are dissatisfied with conventional banking.

There are differences between interest rates from a *mudharabah* bank and a conventional bank. If a gain is made in a *mudharabah* bank, payment will be calculating based on profit. For example, when the *rabbul mal* gives \$10,000 to a *mudharib* with a profit ratio of 40:60, the *mudharib* will give \$400 for each \$1000 profit to the *rabbul mal*. This means that the *rabbul mal* will receive \$10,400 in return. If a business has incurred loss, it will be borne by the *rabbul mal*.

In conventional banks, when they make a loan to an entrepreneur—for example, \$10,000 with fixed interest, such as 4% per annum—the entrepreneur has to pay principle as well as the fixed interest regardless of whether they make a profit or incur a loss. In this situation, the entrepreneur must pay \$104 to the bank. In both the examples above, it can be clearly seen that the concept of *mudharabah* is suitable for modern financing practice because the profit not based on interest. In a conventional bank, because the interest is fixed it places a burden on the entrepreneur if the business incurs losses.

Another objection is that, when the interest rate is reduced to a very low rate under an interest free economy, there will be a great rush on the banks to contract loans, causing the demand for money to exceed the supply. This will require additional funding to be made available on the money market, which will lead to inflation with all its consequences.

5.4.2 Musharakah

Musharakah originated from the discussion of *shirkah* (a joint venture or partnership). *Shari'ah* defines *musharakah* as a participative arrangement in which two or more persons enter into a business contract and participate in the management of a project, and there are rights in favour of a specific partner.

It has two forms:

- Equity participation
- Joint venture projects.

According to the equity participation form, the bank will be one of the shareholders of the company. This is similar to venture capital investment. This typically happens where there is a newly established company and an existing company whose bank has a representative who sits on the bank board of directors. The bank will receive returns either in the form of of dividends or any disposal of shareholdings.

In the case of joint venture projects, the bank will finance selected projects of the company, and will share the profit and loss of those particular projects based on the agreed ratios.

Causes of the Failure of Islamic Banks to Adopt *Musharakah*

There are various reasons why Islamic banks prefer not to adopt *musharakah*.

- Profit and loss financing techniques are extremely vulnerable to the problems of moral hazard. Information uncertainty may lead the bank to choose weak or dishonest enterprises. It may be difficult to review the actual working results of the firm due to widespread malpractice of defaulting profits, and loss.
- Over-valuation of the opening inventory and under-valuation of the closing inventory.
- Over-valuation of assets to inflate depreciation, in order to reduce the element of profit.
- Excessive remuneration charged by the directors of an enterprise—who are, in most cases, relatives of the enterprise owners. An audit is of little help in deciphering the true profit and loss position, as the auditors are typically more concerned with legality, rather than propriety.
- A lack of institutional frameworks that would facilitate appropriate contract mechanisms as means of enforcement. Without clear-cut legal support, the monitoring costs involved in ensuring the elimination of morally hazardous issues would be extremely high.
- Competition with interest-based banks has sometimes compelled Islamic banks to deploy their financial resources in short-term trade financing, as they have to pay sizeable profits to the depositors and shareholders to maintain confidence in the Islamic banking system.
- Lack of short-term financial instruments and inter-bank Islamic money markets create problems for Islamic banks in terms of liquidity at a time of need. For this reason, they prefer to invest in short-term trade financing operations. This mode of financing on the basis of mark-up for short periods also leads to a concentration of the asset portfolio on trade related investments, and has no improving effect on the investment environment and the economic development of the country.
- Lack of strong, reliable and efficient project appraisal mechanisms may lead Islamic banks into an adverse selection situation if they decide to extend finance on the basis of profit and loss sharing. This is the main reason why Islamic banks rely more on financing techniques based on mark-up, rather than profit and loss sharing financing techniques.

5.4.3 Al-Wadiah

Al-wadiah can be defined as a contract of trust or safe keeping. There are two types of *al-wadiah* contract.

- *Al-wadiah yad dhamanah* (guarantee custody)
- *Al-wadiah yad amanah* (trusted custody).

The former is more practical in the modern bank.

There are two *wadiah* accounts available at the Bank Islam Malaysia: current accounts and saving accounts. For saving accounts, the Bank can use a customer's money to invest in a short-term project. Bank Islam Malaysia is responsible for the safety of that money by means of a guarantee (*yad dhamanah*).

The same situation applies to current accounts; however, Bank Islam Malaysia has fewer opportunities to use or invest the money because its owner may take back his *wadiah* at any time by issuing a cheque. Further, Bank Islam Malaysia can charge a payment fee on current accounts.

Application of *Al-Wadiah*

For customers looking to have their funds held safely and to have easy access, the Bank accepts deposits in the form of current accounts or savings accounts. The Bank requests customers' permission (written into the contract) to make use of their funds so long as such funds remain with the Bank. The customers may withdraw a part or the whole of their balance at any time, and the Bank guarantees the deposits at all times and in all circumstances. In return, all profits generated from the depositors' money belong to the Bank.

6 Recommendations

The objective of the financing that is offered by Bank Islam Malaysia is to cater for the growing demand among Muslim society. This is because there are not many financing institutions that offer types of financing that are based on *Shari'ah* laws. As Muslim entrepreneurs, we should take this opportunity to expand our business to compete with other entrepreneurs, or to finance our asset buying so that we may afford to own the assets that we desire.

With the various kinds of financing on offer, a borrower will be able engage with a business that operates purely under *Shari'ah*, and have no need to worry about the source of money that provides their financing. This is a great opportunity that Muslim society should not miss out on.

The bank itself should play an important role in communicating to the people about the financing facilities it offers. This is because not many people are aware of these opportunities. Sometimes, people are very sceptical about the benefits that they could obtain if they used the Islamic type of financing. Bank Islam Malaysia should therefore be very aggressive in advertising and communicating their products and the benefits that society could reap. Some promotions that they should consider are:

- Organizing some educational programmes regarding the significant of financing under *Shari'ah* laws. This can be achieved by arranging seminars, conventions, talks and awareness campaigns at schools, higher learning institutions, hospitals, government agencies, and so on.
- Wide promotion through the mass media. Bank Islam Malaysia has to broaden their promotion through the mass media, such as television, radio and news articles, for example. This form of promotion would assist the Bank in gaining ample exposure, which should be widespread, precise and have a high public profile.
- Online registration. This will enable customers to register through the Internet.

7 Conclusion

Regarding the survey report, the financing offered by the Bank Islam Malaysia is important, especially for those of us in Muslim society. It is part of the continuous effort to encourage other banking firms to provide financing that follows the rules of *Shari'ah*. Based on the benefits that are offered, it is likely that the demand for this type of financing will increase in the future. Thus, it will benefit not only the Bank, but also Muslim society as a whole. It will give society confidence in our Muslim products and demonstrate the significance of products do not harm the *Ummah*. The products also have the benefit of being superior to other banking products, that they provide no *gharar*, interest taking or value addition. So we, as Muslims, should encourage those around us to use this type of financing in their daily dealings, by indicating the real benefits they could realize.

Islamic banking started with the advent of Islam. The nature of Islamic banking and Islamic finance cannot be understood in isolation from Islam as the centre and as a way of life. Islam is a complete way of life and Islamic finance is a very important aspect of that way of life. In fact, Islamic society needs Islamic finance. Muslim community leaders are calling for Islamic retail bank products in Malaysia. The financial needs of Malaysia's Muslim community are estimated at approximately $80 billion, with an expected growth rate of 15%. Malaysian banking is targeting 5% of its banking system to provide Islamic banking products by the year 2000. Most financial institutions—commercial banks, finance companies and merchant banks—are now required to operate Islamic banking windows side-by-side with the interest-free banking system.

It is clear that Islamic banking is wider in its scope and more suited to people's needs than a system based on the secular system of economics. Islamic banking is in the course of evolving. We have to strive continuously to develop and redefine its boundaries by providing better services and better products. It also has to help the cause of the Islamization of society. It is hoped that, with the interest of the government and with the support of the people, the challenges will be met and goals will be achieved.

CHAPTER 5

Islamic Financial Services Board and Its Regulatory Functions in the Islamic Financial Industry

1 Introduction

The first *takaful* company, the Islamic Insurance Company of Sudan, was established in 1979. Today, there are more than 28 registered *takaful* companies worldwide writing *takaful* directly, and 10 Islamic windows or marketing agencies placing insurance risk with conventional and with *takaful* companies. In fact, the number of *takaful* companies in Sudan is even higher, as all insurance companies in Sudan are deemed to operate based on the principles of Islamic *Shari'ah.*

The development of *takaful* as an alternative to conventional insurance can also be seen through the establishment of new *takaful* companies in Sri Lanka and Tunisia, and at least four more *takaful* companies are in course of being established in the Middle East.

However, the *takaful* industry in the Middle East is still under-developed compared to other *takaful* markets, such as that in Malaysia. The most successful *takaful* company in the Middle East only stated growth of 10% per annum whereas, in Malaysia, it has achieved a rate of growth of 60% per annum.

The growth and development of *takaful* in Malaysia performed well in the period 1998–2000. For the year 1998–1999, it stated an increase in total *takaful* for both general and family *takaful* whereas, in 1999–2000, there was a 27% increase in these types of *takaful* product.

The demand for Islamic products is increasing due to the success of the Islamic financing and banking system in Malaysia. In order to create

M. M. Billah, *Islamic Financial Products*,
https://doi.org/10.1007/978-3-030-17624-2_5

consumer confidence in the *takaful* industry as a provider of Islamic product, efforts to develop and manage *takaful* business must be genuine and effective. The establishment of *takaful* companies in non-Muslim countries—such as the Australia Takaful Insurance Company, Takaful UK Ltd., and Takaful USA Management Services—shows that the implementation of Islamic insurance is acceptable to all regardless of race, culture and religion.

Malaysia has shown its commitment to the development of this industry by establishing many institutions; for example, the ASEAN Takaful Group (ATG) (founded in 1995) and the ASEAN Re-Takaful International (Labuan) Ltd. (founded in 1997) or ARIL (founded in 1997). At present, the establishment of the Islamic Financing Services Board (IFSB), which is a response to the growing significance of the Islamic financial services industry globally, is also expected to contribute to the development of *takaful* industry globally, as this industry is mostly related to Islamic financial products.

2 Background of the IFSB

The development and growing significance of Islamic financial services globally lead to the establishment of the IFSB on 3 November 2002. The formation of the IFSB is the culmination of a two-year effort initiated by a group of governors and senior officials of the Central Bank and monetary authorities of several Islamic countries, together with the Islamic Development Bank (IDB) and Accounting and Auditing Organization for Islamic Financial Institution (AAOIFI), together with the support of the International Monetary Fund (IMF).

On 3 November 2002, the IDB and 10 Muslim countries signed an agreement to launch the IFSB in order to create awareness of the Islamic way of dealing with investment, banking, the capital market and other financial instruments.

The establishment of the IFSB in Kuala Lumpur will make Malaysia the regional centre for Islamic Financial Services. The IFSB's secretariat, which is based in Kuala Lumpur, and the selection of the Malaysia Bank Negara (Central Bank) Governor, Dr. Akhtar Aziz, as chairman of the IFSB's steering committee will contribute to the development of the Islamic financial industry not only in Malaysia, but also globally.

As information on the development of the IFSB is only available for the few months since November 2002, it will place greater focus on the growing of the Islamic financial industry. However, the IFSB also intends to pay attention to the development of the *takaful* industry globally, even though it is still in the process of forming its committee and planning department.

2.1 Objectives and Functions of the IFSB

Other than managing Islamic financial services, the main objectives of the IFSB are: to disseminate information regarding the availability of Islamic financial services, and to harmonize and to promote best practice in the regulation and supervision of the industry among participant countries.

The establishment of the IFSB is also response for the growing significance of the Islamic financial services industry. Its scope is directed more towards the setting up of international standards for Islamic financial instruments. In addition, the IFSB will serve as an association of central banks, monetary authorities and other institutions that will be responsible for the regulation and supervision of the Islamic financial industry.

The IFSB is expected to devise and disseminate standard and core principles in compliance with the *Shari'ah* (Islamic legislation) for adoption by member countries. Hence, the IFSB will cooperate with other standards setting organizations in the areas of monetary and financial stability, and promote good practice in risk management through research, training and technical advisory services.

The IFSB also will serve as an association of central banks, monetary authorities and other institutions entrusted to develop and promulgate internationally accepted prudential regulatory standards and practices. Here, the board will examine which of the existing international best practices need to be adopted that are consistent with *Shari'ah* principles. With a view to achieving these aims, the IFSB will collaborate with other international standards setting bodies in achieving the stability of international financial services.

Based on the Articles of Agreement of the IFSB, the following points are among the objectives of the established IFSB that is located in Kuala Lumpur, Malaysia:

- To promote the development of a prudent and transparent Islamic financial services industry by either introducing new international standards consistent with *Shari'ah* principles, or adapting existing practices. These practices will then be recommended for adoption.
- To provide guidance on the effective supervision and regulation of institutions offering Islamic financial products, and to develop for the Islamic financial services industry the criteria for identifying, measuring, managing and disclosing risks, taking into account international standards for valuation, income and expense calculation, and disclosure.
- To liaise and cooperate with relevant organizations currently setting standards for the stability and the soundness of international monetary and financial systems and such systems of the member countries.
- To enhance and coordinate initiatives to develop instruments and procedures for efficient operations and risk management.
- To encourage cooperation amongst member countries in developing the Islamic financial services industry.
- To facilitate training and personnel development in skills in areas relevant to the effective regulation of the Islamic financial services industry and related markets.
- To undertake research into the Islamic financial services industry and to publish studies and surveys thereon.
- To establish a database of Islamic banks, financial institutions and industry experts.

2.2 *The Structure of the IFSB*

Every organization has its own structure for the purpose of the smooth running of its operations. The IFSB is likewise restricted to having a permanent structure; this comprises several constituent organs, including the General Assembly, the Council, the Technical Committee and the Secretariat. These constituent organs shall have the powers and duties that are set out in its Articles of Agreement.

2.3 *The General Assembly*

According to Articles 13–19 in the Articles of Agreement of the IFSB, the General Assembly shall be the representative body of all the members of the IFSB. The IFSB membership consists of three categories: full membership, associate membership and observer membership. Here, the General Assembly shall have, inter alia, to implement certain duties and responsibilities: for example, to review and approve the final audited accounts of the IFSB; to approve the appointment of the external auditor of the IFSB; to determine membership fees for the various membership categories, including any exemptions or reductions for individual members, exemptions or reductions to be determined on a case-by-case basis; and to discuss issues that are related to the objectives of the IFSB itself.

In addition, this body should meet annually at such time and place as the Secretariat shall determine on the giving of not less than three months' notice of the meeting, with the exception that no such notice shall be required in respect of the first meeting. At any meeting conducted by this assembly, it is necessary that valid and binding decisions shall be based on the votes of two thirds of all full members, each full member having one vote. Resolutions of this assembly shall be effective with a simple majority of the full members present. No member is allowed to act as a proxy or representative of another member. Hence, the chairman of this assembly will determine any challenge to or right of a person to represent any other members.

A chairman must preside over each meeting. Such chairman is elected by the full members at the previous meeting of the General Assembly.

2.4 *The Council*

The second constituent body in the IFSB is the Council, which is the senior executive and policy making body of the IFSB. The Council consists of one representative from each full member organization who shall be the senior executive officer of that full member. Council duties consist, inter alia, of formulating and approving the policies and strategies of the IFSB; approving and making the by-laws of the IFSB; adopting and approving for issuance prudential and supervisory standards and guidance on Islamic financial services on such terms as it deems fit, following the advice and recommendations of the Technical Committee; establishing one or more Technical Committees and establishing guidelines and procedures to be followed by any Technical Committee when preparing standards and guidance for approval by the Council.

The Council's duties are also: to refer technical Islamic financial services issues to the Technical Committee for its review, advice and recommendations; to constitute the Technical Committee, appoint its Chairman and Deputy Chairman, and determine its term of reference; to appoint the Secretary-General of the IFSB and determine his term of reference; to approve the budget of the IFSB; to set guidelines for the maintenance, management and monitoring of funds as may be established in pursuance of the objectives of the IFSB; and, lastly, to be responsible for the assessment and approval of applications for membership.

As the General Assembly shall meet annually, the Council shall meet at least twice a year at such time and place as determined by Secretariat on the giving of not less than two months' notice. At this meeting, three quarters of the members of the Council may require the Secretariat to convene an extraordinary meeting of the Council on such terms and conditions as it may require. In order that decisions made are valid and binding, a quorum of two thirds of all members of the Council is required to be present. As in the General Assembly, no member of the council may be the representative or proxy of another member. This meeting should be presided over by the Chairman and the Deputy Chairman is also required to be present.

2.5 *The Technical Committee*

This body is responsible for advising the Council on technical issues within terms of reference as determined by the Council. The Council should select 10 members of this Committee for a term of three years. The members of this body should be qualified with regard to the relevant technical expertise and skills; should ensure the equitable distribution between the specific technical skills required by the Technical Committee and the geographical and industrial composition of the sector; and should ensure the continuity of the Committee's work. As with as all other bodies in the structure of the IFSB, this body is also in course of the implementation of certain duties.

First and foremost, the Technical Committee is responsible for presenting draft prudential and supervisory standards and guidance for Islamic financial services for the consideration of and formal adoption by the Council. Its function also includes advising and making recommendations to the Council on various specific technical issues referred to it by the Council. Its duties also include advising the Council on technical issues and making any recommendations, the appointment and approval of the work plans of specific working groups who are not among the members of the Committee, and assisting with any matters regarding technical issues that the Council may request from time to time.

The Chairman of the Technical Committee shall determine the place and time for each meeting, and determine the procedural rules of meetings in accordance with the law. During meetings, each member may only one vote on any matter.

2.6 *The Secretariat*

The Secretariat is the permanent administrative body of the IFSB. A full time Secretary General appointed by the Council will lead this body. Any actions must be within the objectives of the IFSB and the Secretary General shall be assisted by such other administrative and support staff as are required for the effective functioning of the Secretariat. There is a Senior Secretariat, selected by the Secretary General or seconded by full members. It is important to note that the Secretary General is entitled to attend any meeting of the General Assembly, the Council, the Technical Committee or any working group appointed by the Technical Committee.

2.7 Shari'ah *Rulings*

Simply put, the guiding rules and regulations of the IFSB are from the Holy Qur'an. The *Shari'ah* spells out the Qur'anic teachings in three dimensions: *aqidah* (faith and belief), *akhlaq* (ethics and morality) and *muamalat* (transaction). The role of reason and experience, too, has been given a higher order by the Qur'an in that these attributes help convey the truth that God wants mankind to acknowledge.

Insurance business is invalid if it involves any element that contradicts *Shari'ah* principles. The Takaful Act (Malaysia) 1994 rules that *Shari'ah* based insurance is enforceable if its 'aims and operations do not involve any elements which are not approved by the *Shari'ah*' (Billah 2001). When the IFSB is guided by rules and regulations determined by God, some may ask what they are. Again, the answer is quite basic and simple. There are two types of guidelines to be observed by the IFSB: legal and ethical. Legal guidelines are related to the concept of *riba*: the Qur'an prohibits *riba* in any financial transaction. Islam regards *riba* as an economic evil that is harmful to society, not only economically and socially, but also morally (Shafie 1992). Therefore, the Holy Qur'an forbids Muslims to give or take *riba*:

> Those who devour usury shall not be able to stand except as stands he whom Satan has demanded with his touch. This because they say: trade is but as usury; whereas Allah has allowed trade and has forbidden usury. So he who receives an admonition from his Lord, and has desisted, may keep what is past, and his affair is with Allah but he who reverts, such shall be the inmates of the Fire, therein they shall abide. (al-Qur'an, 2:275)

It is also does not condone the creation of wealth by means of investment in *al-bathil* transactions, such as financial gambling and liquor-based production. All forms of gambling and betting are prohibited and considered acts of impiety and abomination (Shafie 1992):

> They ask thee of wine and gambling. Say thou: 'in both is a great sin and some benefit for men, but the sin of them is greater than their benefit'. And they ask thee as to what they shall spend. Say thou: 'the redundant portion'. Thus does Allah expound to you His commandments so that you may ponder. (al-Qur'an, 2:219)

Regarding ethics, the Holy Qur'an enjoins trustworthiness, and prohibits deceit and greed in profit taking of any economic or financial activities. As one verse of the Holy Qur'an states:

> O you who believe! When you borrow one from another for a time stated, write it down, and let a scribe write it down justly between you, and let not the scribe refuse to write according as Allah has taught him... And call witnesses when you are transacting business with one another, and let not the scribe come to harm nor the witness. (al-Qur'an, 2:282)

It is worthy of note that the process of product design or the development of Islamic banking products require us observe the two principles of the *Shari'ah*: the removal of hardship, and the prevention of harm. The Qur'an, for example, says:

> God never intends to make religion a means of inflicting hardship. (al-Qur'an, 22:78)

In *Surah al-Maidah*, verse 6, the Qur'an again says 'God intends to make things easy for you'. So, when the Qur'an says that 'Allah allows trade but prohibits *riba*' (*Al-baqarah*: 278), trade is supposed to control the elements that can prevent harm and hardship in spending activities involving delayed or instalment payments.

Allah commands us to tolerate each other for the development of *Ummah* in this world and hereafter. Therefore, the concept of brotherhood and cooperation among Muslims has been mentioned clearly in the Holy Qur'an:

> Cooperate with each other in virtue and piety, and do not cooperate in sin and transgression. (al-Qur'an, 5:2)
>
> The faithful are but brethen; so affect reconciliation between your brethen and fear Allah that haply mercy may be shown to you. (al-Qur'an, 49:10)

The structure of the IFSB is related to both of these concepts because it consists of several organizations from different Muslim and non-Muslim countries. In Islam, there is no difference between people in this world in terms of ethnicity, race, or religion. If they are committed to one main objective on one particular path, it is not possible for them to be united in the current situation.

All these enjoinments and prohibitions by God are meant to generate harmony in economic and business activities such that justice prevails and, thus, mankind obtains peace of mind.

2.8 *Expected Contribution to the Development of* Takaful *Globally*

As the IFSB consists of several central banks of Muslim countries, members and established financial institutions such as the IDB, with support from the AAOIFI and the IMF, the development of the Islamic banking and finance industry is not limited due to its important role in the growth of the financial sectors; the development of the *takaful* industry can also be achieved.

For instance, Bahrain, one of the member countries, is currently well-developed in the area of *takaful* and *re-takaful*. Several *takaful* companies operate in Bahrain, including the al-Salam Islamic Takaful Company, Bahrain Islamic Insurance Company, Islamic Insurance and Re-Takaful Company, Sarikat Takaful al-Islamiyah, and Takaful International and Global Islamic Insurance. As the central bank of Bahrain is involved in the IFSB, it can cooperate with those *takaful* companies to develop the *takaful* industry. There should be a mutual guarantee or shared responsibilities among institutions in order to reduce certain risks involved in that area.

The support from the AAOIFI to the IFSB is one way to create a high level of consumer confidence in becoming involved with the *takaful* industry, rather than in conventional insurance. The AAOIFI is most commonly known in in regard to calculating the amounts of *takaful* payments. As the founding committee of the IFSB consists of several governors of the central banks of the 10 member countries, more *takaful* companies will be set up and we can be assured that matters will be conducted in a professional manner, provided the IFSB plays its role in accordance with the objectives of its foundation.

Risk management in *takaful* operations should be undertaken with precision. In the event of inaccuracies, operations will contain *gharar* elements, which are totally prohibited in Islam. With the establishment of the IFSB, at least *takaful* companies can run their business based on the rules and regulations of *Shari'ah* principles, as one of the objectives of the IFSB is to enhance and coordinate initiatives to develop instruments and procedures for efficient operations and risk management, enabling total profit and loss to be distributed fairly to the participant and *takaful* operator.

As the Washington based IMF assisted in the establishment of the IFSB during the two years of its establishment, the key members of this organization can create major markets for the *takaful* industry globally. As we know, the IMF already has a strong base in terms of the funds of its country members. As the IMF was selected as a facilitator of the IFSB, one of the objectives is that the IFSB should cooperate with standards setting bodies in the area of monetary and financial stability. Making investments through a *takaful* fund should therefore be straightforward.

The IFSB can also contribute by protecting the global coverage of *takaful* through the international cooperation network, as the use of modern technology is currently expanding widely. At the same time, as the IFSB has become a centre for the management of *takaful* operations based on the *Shari'ah* principles, it can establish a database of *takaful* companies and industry experts. Furthermore, the implementation of new computerized systems that link all *takaful* desks and branch offices in most of the *takaful* institutions to the IFSB headquarters will make it easy for the IFSB to supervise them well.

3 Recommendation

The IFSB took two years to establish and within three months of its formation on 3 November 2002 the organization was officiated by the then Prime Minister of Malaysia, Dato' Seri Dr. Mahathir Mohammad, in Kuala Lumpur. Some consider that the existence of this body is redundant, bearing in mind the founding of the Islamic Bank of International Settlement (BIS) with an 'Islamic Basle Concordat' whose task is effectively to set prudential and supervision standards for the global Islamic banking industry.

The central bank and governors of the G-10 control operations for the BIS. Hence, there will be no conflict regarding the settlement of Islamic rules and regulations on Islamic financing matters because countries other than those that comprise the G-10 will refer to the IFSB, whereas the G-10 countries will refer to the BIS. However, it would be better if both bodies could form only a united body and cooperate with each other in solving any issues related to Islamic banking and the coming development of *takaful* planning by the IFSB in order to stabilize the Islamic financial market.

An annual conference or seminar should be held correspondingly amongst each country's members. Each country should be given the opportunity to host the conference on *takaful*. It would then be easy for them to introduce new *takaful* products, or to adapt existing products that accord with *Shari'ah* principles to the *takaful* companies as well as to the target consumers in that country.

The availability of a trained and skilled workforce is essential for the rapid development of the *takaful* industry (Bank Negara Malaysia 1999). Therefore, the IFSB should organize appropriate programmes to facilitate training and personal development in the *takaful* industry globally.

4 Conclusion

The establishment of *takaful* companies to provide for Muslims cover that conforms to the rules and practices of the *Shari'ah* is a new development in the Muslim world, having begun in the 1970s (Mohammad 1995). However, currently, *takaful* companies have become well-established not only in Muslim countries, but also in non-Muslim countries.

Globalization means that there are no barriers to anyone using the services afforded by Islamic products. As the basic concept of *takaful* is the provision of insurance as a form of business in conformity with

Shari'ah and is based on the Islamic principles of *al-tabarru* and *al-mudarabah*, it is necessary for a body or organization such as the IFSB to guide and supervise the *takaful* industry in terms of its rules and regulations. In addition, the establishment of the IFSB will help any institutions in this industry to face any challenges to the smooth running of *takaful* operations, as well as the development of the *takaful* industry globally.

References

Bank Negara Malaysia. (1999). *The Central Bank and the Financial System in Malaysia*, Bank Negara Malaysia, Kuala Lumpur, p. 259.

Billah, M. M. (2001). *Islamic Law of Trade & Finance: Some Contemporary Issues*, IIUM Press, Kuala Lumpur, p. 64.

Mohammad, R. (1995). *Insurance Contract and Its Provision in the Islamic (Law) Shari'ah*, International Islamic University Malaysia, Petaling Jaya, p. 88.

Shafie, M. R. M. (1992), *Insurance Law and the Islamic System of Mutual Insurance (Takaful) in Malaysia*, IIUM, Petaling Jaya, pp. 80, 84.

CHAPTER 6

Bay' Al-Inah (Buy Back Sale) and Its Position in Modern Islamic Finance

It is well-known that every society has its norms, values and traditions in life. These traditions and norms undergo tremendous challenges, making them controversial and subjecting them to adjustments to the new situation. Islamic transactions today should be taken into consideration with the huge challenges facing the Muslim nation in the contemporary world. Since financial challenges are of leading significance, Muslim scholars have to diminish the widening spaces between Islamic principles and the dominant styles of banking and financing criteria and procedures.

There should be collective criteria for financing and banking derived from the highest objectives of Islamic law that present themselves as appropriate to a contemporary perspective on life. Nevertheless, Islamic law managed to deal with a certain stage in financial concepts in the ancient times; it possessed the flexibility to adapt to the new systems and additional concepts that people subsequently created, to which Muslim society has adjusted. The flexibility of Islamic laws in terms of transactions was applied well by the previous scholars. They extended the style of traditional Islamic contracts to determinants that could include variable contracts and joint transactions with the purpose of creating a viable means of producing and consuming.

To obtain responses to the questions raised by the new challenges diffused throughout the arena of world economy, we should generate new translations for the values and rules that Islamic jurisprudence has advocated and applied to the arena in which people live and surrender to the

M. M. Billah, *Islamic Financial Products*,
https://doi.org/10.1007/978-3-030-17624-2_6

influence of its pressures. This does not imply that we have to replicate the same picture, or deal with contemporary issues following the guidelines the rest of the world has suggested, followed and adopted.

In this chapter, I would like to focus on a certain type of transaction discussed by the Muslim jurists of old and the different opinions, with variable justifications and reasoning, that have arisen therefrom: *bay' al-inah*. Therefore, I will offer a comparative view and assessment, then analyse the applications possible when implementing this kind of transaction in a live banking system.

1 Definition

Bay' al-inah is generally recognized as a sale based on a transaction of *nasi'ah* (deferment). Person A (the prospective debtor) sells some object to Person B (the prospective creditor) for cash which is payable immediately. Person B immediately buys the object back from Person A for a greater amount to be paid on a future date. Thus, the transaction amounts to a loan. The difference between the two prices represents the interest.

Due to the length of time between the initial transactions and the agreed deferred date by which payment of the greater price is due to be made, a good has two different prices simultaneously. Moreover, the good is back in the hands of Person A. Person B does not receive the due payment immediately and pays Person A (his customer) an amount of money as a due of the good itself, purposely to achieve a potential profit at the future date. In consequence, Person A (the customer) satisfies his present needs by obtaining the desired amount of money and loses an amount of money as the cost of the loan.

2 Legal Evaluation

Scholars have differing legal opinions when evaluating this type of contract due to its dual nature. It appears to be two contracts rolled into one, or could be seen as a loan that brings about a profit. In such an arrangement, provided the contracts are performed without the intention of making a profit as the result of a loan, there should be no quibbles as each contract fulfils its legal preconditions. However, an overall view of the entire arrangement reflects a kind of legal device (*hilat*) to circumvent usury (*riba*), which is prohibited.

Abu Hanifa, Malik and Ahmed hold that in such a situation the contract is not valid and should not be allowed. It is an indirect way to create a usurious contract. The Shafi'i school considers it valid since the legal preconditions are apparently fulfilled.

The main evidence of Shafi'i was analogy (*qiyas*). He said: 'Since the customer is allowed to sell the good to everyone else, there are no considerable reasons to invalidate a contract being held with the ex-vendor' (the previous good's owner).

The mainstream of *Jamhur* jurists took an overview of the situation and considered it a form of usury disguised as a formally legitimate contract. They justified their view with several pieces of evidence:

Malikiyyah proclaimed:

> It is a loan that brings about a profit and jurists agreed on considering it a prohibited contract upon the legal maxim of: 'That every loan entailing benefit is usury'. (*Kullu Qardin jarra nafa'an fahwa riban*)

Hanafiyyah proclaimed:

> The price of the good does not get secured '*Daman*' by the vendor, so if he reincorporates the good and pays the buyer (customer) a price, it means that he receives a monetary advantage without giving a counter value. Therefore, this type of transaction should be invalidated upon the legal maxim of '*al-Ghunmu bil ghurmi*', meaning that no person is allowed to invest in a way that generates profit without exposing himself to the risk of loss.

The *Hanabilah* opinion is derived from different evidence:

> To prevent the causes of bad consequences *Sadduz'zari'ah*, because if we permit such a contract, it may cause the diffusing of interest among society and this leads, gradually, to the bad consequences for which usury was forbidden.

Prophetic traditions such as that:

> Narrated by Abi Ishaq Al-Subaie's wife, she said: 'Zaid bin Arqam's son's mother and I visited A'ishah. My companion said: "I sold Zaid my slave for eight hundred dirham till the time of capability, and then I bought

> the same slave from him by six hundred dirham on the spot." A'ishah said: "How badly you have sold? How badly you have bought?" Zaid announced that his *jihad* with the prophet was null and void except when he has regrets.' They hold that A'ishah could not blame Zaid without depending on a prophetic tradition.

The *hadith* in which Allah's messenger says:

> A time is certainty coming to mankind when they validate (*Yastahillun*) the *riba* under the name of *Bay'* (trade concerning intended usury circumvented by the words of a sales contract).

Ibn Umar said:

> I heard the Prophet of Allah (*SAW*) say, 'when you enter into an *'inah* transaction, hold the tails of the oxen, be pleased with agriculture, and give up conducting *jihad*, Allah will make disgrace prevail upon you, and will not withdraw it until you return to your original religion'.

The Shafi'i school defended their opinion by rejecting the validity of what was narrated regarding the prophet's wife and considering Zaid's practice as a different opinion, proclaiming that if the companions of the prophet believed in different opinions, the authority is whosoever's opinion is according to *qiyas*. Moreover, *'inah* is just like '*'Bi' al-jam'a bi ad-darahimi wa ibta' bi ad-darahimi janiban*'.

3 Application

Although *al-inah* is immensely controversial and totally rejected by the majority of scholars and Middle-Eastern investors, it is implemented in Malaysia, where acceptable due to the fact that they follow the Shafi'i school of jurisprudence. They may have wide scope to apply *'inah* as private deals, corporation models and bond trading in the secondary market. *Bay' al-inah* is involved in certain underlying assets owned by the Malaysian government, such as land, buildings, shares, bonds and reserves in hard currencies. For liquidity purposes, bond trading in the secondary market is crucial. However, Islamic banks may apply this type of transaction in order to create a dynamic secondary market by securitizing debt certificates so that they become property. As such, they can then be discounted in order to encourage investors to buy them and collect the benefit at a pre-arranged time, perhaps after one year or six months. It means that the banks are able to gain a capital sum, which is very important for projecting their position and evolving the economy.

CHAPTER 7

Instruments that Facilitate Islamic Financing

1 Introduction

Theoretical work on Islamic banking sought a complete change from interest to profit sharing and equity participation. *Mudarabah* and *musharakah* were supposedly the main activities of the Islamic banking service. This means that Islamic banks are no longer sharing profit and loss; instead, they assume the capacity of a classic financial intermediary.

There are certain realities in modern life that need to be considered from a *Shari'ah* perspective. The population in every country looks to its government as a source of many valuable goods and services, such as health, education and welfare, as well as economic development. Islam aims to establish a social order where all individuals are united by bonds of brotherhood and affection, as though members of one family. Islam is not bound by any geographical boundaries and encompasses the whole of mankind, rather than a single family group, tribe or race.

A non-Islamic government will experience no difficulties as it may always resort to interest-bearing credit. However, this is not the case for a government of people who are keen to remain within the realms of *Shari'ah* needs and alternate solutions. It is a part of our faith that Islam is suitable for every time and every place, because it is the final message for all humanity. It is only because of a lack of effort on our part that appropriate Islamic solutions are not found. The purpose of this chapter is to make thorough examination of the framework for *musharakah* and other financial instruments of Islamic banks.

M. M. Billah, *Islamic Financial Products*,
https://doi.org/10.1007/978-3-030-17624-2_7

2 *Al-Murabaha* (Cost Plus Mark-up)

A *murabaha* transaction is defined by *fuqaha* (jurists) as the sale of goods at cost plus an agreed profit mark-up. The word 'cost' is meant to include the purchase price and any other expenses incurred by the possessor of the goods. The characteristics of such a transaction are that'the seller should inform the purchaser of the price at which he purchased the product and stipulate an amount of profit in addition to this'.

2.1 *Conditions of* Al-Murabaha

a. The Islamic bank should make the cost or capital outlay known to the client.
b. The first contract should be valid.
c. The contract should be free of usury.
d. The Islamic bank should disclose any fault that occurs after the purchase and should disclose all details related to the fault.
e. The Islamic bank should disclose the terms applicable to the purchase price; for example, if the purchase was on credit.
f. If any of the conditions in (a), (d) or (e) is not met, the purchaser shall have the option to:

- Proceed with the sale as it is;
- Have recourse to the seller for the discrepancy;
- Cancel the contract.

2.2 *Types of* Al-Murabaha

2.2.1 Ordinary Al-Murabaha *Sale*

Ordinary *murabaha* sales involve two parties: the seller and the buyer. The seller is an ordinary trader who buys a commodity without depending on a prior promise of purchase; he then displays it for *murabaha* sale for a price and a profit to be agreed upon.

2.2.2 Murabaha Sale Linked to a Promise

There are three parties involved in this sale: the seller, the buyer and the bank as an intermediary trader between the buyer and the seller. In this situation, the bank does not purchase the assets unless the buyer specifies his desire to purchase and indicates there is a prior promise to purchase.

The mode of a *murabaha* sale linked to a promise is used by Islamic banks to undertake the purchase of commodities according to the specifications requested by the customer and to resell them on *murabaha* terms to the person who promised to buy the asset for its cost price plus a pre-agreed profit.

2.2.3 The Practical Steps of the Murabaha Sale

- The purchaser determines his needs:
  - *The purchaser*: Determines the specifications of the commodity he wants and requests the seller to determine the price.
  - *The seller*: Sends a quotation valid for a certain period.
- Signing a promise to purchase agreement:
  - *The purchaser*: Promises to buy the commodity from the bank on the terms of a *murabaha* sale for the cost of the commodity plus the agreed profit.
  - *The bank*: Studies the request and determines the conditions and security approval.
- The first sale contract:
  - *The bank*: Notifies the purchaser of its approval to purchase the commodity and that bank may pay the price either immediately or in accordance with the agreement.
  - *The seller*: Expresses his approval of the sale and sends the invoice.
- Delivery and receipt of the commodity:
  - *The bank*: Authorizes the beneficiary to receive the commodity.
  - *The seller*: Sends the commodity to the agreed place of delivery.
  - *The purchaser*: Undertakes the receipt of the commodity in his capacity as a representative and notifies the bank of the promise to purchase.
- The *murabaha* sale contract:
  - The two parties (the bank and the purchaser) sign the contract for the *murabaha* sale according to the agreement of the promise to purchase.

3 *Al-Mudhraba* (Partnership in Profit-Sharing)

This is an agreement (contract) to form a partnership between two parties; one provides the capital and the other participates in terms of his management and efforts. The party who provides the capital is called the *rabb al-mal* (financier); the second party, who manages the partnership, is called the *mudharib*.

3.1 *The* Mudharib

The *mudharib* is a trustee (*amin*) for the capital entrusted to him in accordance with the terms of *Mudharaba*. He takes possession of the capital with the permission of the owner (by entering into a contract after an offer and acceptance has taken place). If the capital is destroyed in his possession without any negligence on his part, then there is no liability on him.

The *mudharib* is also an agent of the *rabb al-mal* in whatever transactions he undertakes entailing the wealth of the *mudharaba*. He is the person responsible for buying and taking delivery of stock, he is the person entitled to return faulty goods and to whom any legal action will be directed.

If he is grossly negligent, or if he violates the conditions of the contract—such as if the *muwakkil* has placed any restrictions on him in the way he can dispose of his property—then the *mudharaba* may be invalid and the *mudharib* becomes liable.

3.2 *The* Muwakkil*: The Owner of the Property*

The owner of the property has no right to dispose of the property that belongs to the company, either for or on behalf of the company. Thus, it is invalid for the owner of the property to work with the *mudharib*, even if the owner stipulates that he do so. Rather, it is the *mudharib* who disposes of items and undertake the work, and he has full control over the property.

Furthermore *mudharaba* is not valid until the property is given to the worker by the *muwakkil* and the *mudharib* is given free control over it, because the *mudharaba* system requires that the property is handed over to the *mudharib*.

In *mudharaba*, the worker's share must be defined and the property used in the *mudharaba* contract must be of a stated value. If the amount is undefined or unknown, the *mudharabah* is not valid, as this will lead to uncertainty with regard to the profit.

3.3 *Rules of* Al-Mudharaba

- *Limiting a mudharaba contract to a certain period*
  Some *fuqaha* permit the limiting of a *mudharaba* to a certain period; others do not permit this on the grounds that a *mudharaba* contract is permanently binding.
- *Making the contract conditional on a future matter or event*
  The implementation of the contract should not take place unless the conditional matter occurs or the future event takes place.
- *Guarantee in mudharaba contracts*
  This refers to the responsibility of the *mudharib* to return the capital to the owner of the funds in all cases. This is not permissible due to the fact that the *mudharib*'s possession of the fund is made as a trust, and the trustworthy person does not guarantee the fund except in the event of his omission.
- *Ruling pertaining to profit*
  Realization of profit: According to the Islamic Fiqh Academy, 'profits are due when realized, and owned by declaration or revaluation and become payable only upon distribution' (Islamic Fiqh Academy resolution).
  Entitlement to profit: *Hanafis* and some *Shafis* say that profit should be recognized on a realization basis, whereas the *Malikis* and *Hambalis* believe that profit should be reorganized only when distributed between two parties (cash basis).

4 Al-Ijarah

4.1 *Definition*

Al-ijarah literally means sale of benefit. Imam Hanafi defined *ijarah* as a contract of benefit with return or exchange. While Shafie opined that *ijarah* is a contract of determined permissible benefits that are known to be available for use, where return or exchange is allowed. Rashid Ahmad Osman stated that, according to this method, the bank purchases capital assets (equipment, buildings or other facilities) as requested by the customer and leases such assets to the beneficiary (lessee) in return for an agreement (Osman, n.d.). The contract is dependent on an annual or monthly rent. *Ijarah* also can be defined as a hire contract. The basic security under the *ijarah* arrangement is the ownership of the equipment. The title of ownership to the equipment remains with the leasing company and, in the event of serious default, the equipment is repossessed.

4.2 Modern Concept of Al-Ijarah

The Islamic technique of *ijarah* is comparable to leasing. Leasing is based on the same fundamental concept as that of *ijarah*, according to which one does not have to own an asset in order to enjoy the benefits of it. *Ijarah* is now widely being applied to business activity.

A comparison between leasing and other similar forms of transaction, such as rental, will give a clearer picture. Ghifari and Muzaffar (n.d.) said that 'rent'—such as is shown by the car rental business—forms part of a contract according to which the objects are leased to individuals or a number of users for a much shorter period than their actual useful life.

In contract law, the 'rental contract' specifies the lease and usage for an indefinite period. While the users of the equipment leased on a rental system are major enterprises and their usage is continuous, the rented equipment is usually used in a transient manner. Whether the situation is 'rental' or'rent', the lessor is charged with the responsibility for maintenance. This is especially so in the case of 'rental', where the lessor is also charged with the responsibility a product's obsolescence. This may therefore be termed a service-oriented business.

4.3 Application of Al-Ijarah

In applying the concept of *ijarah*, *ijarah walqtina* has been practised in order to manage financing. It is a lease purchase financing arrangement based on profit sharing in which the bank buys the capital assets (equipment, buildings or other facilities) and leases them to the client for a limited period of time.

The amount of rent collected from the lease, which constitutes the bank's return, is calculated on the profitability of the asset once the beneficiary puts it to use, with careful reference to the cash flow.

The client (lessee) makes payment into a savings account that eventually permits the bank's capital to be repaid; ownership is then transferred to the borrower. Leasing, then, according to Islam, does not involve interest since its outcome is either a sale–purchase type of transaction or a rent transaction.

5 Al-Musharakah

5.1 Definition

Sharikah literally means the mixing of two properties so that they cannot be distinguished from each other. It also means sharing, participation. Technically, it is a contract between parties who are partners in the capital and the profit. The *Majellah* defines partnership as an agreement for association, on the condition that the capital and its benefits are common between two or more persons. Imam Maliki's opinion states that *musharakah* is an agreement between all the owners of the assets of a sharing group that each of them may have the use and enjoyment of such assets. Hambali said *musharakah* is a joining in the acquiring of rights or utilization. Shafie defined *musharakah* as conferred rights for something shared to two or more persons. Hanafiah defined *musharakah* as a contract between sharing partners in the capital and profit. According to Rashid Ahmad Osman, *musharakah* is a profit–loss sharing venture designed for a particular operation and ending within an agreed period of time (Osman, n.d.).

5.2 Classification of Sharikah

Sharikah can be classified into three categories which are *sharikah al-amlak*, *sharikah al-uqud* and *sharikah al-mudarabah*.

Sharikah al-amlak is when two or more persons share an asset due to particular reasons for obtaining ownership in which no differentiation can be made between their respective wealth but not due to the terms of the contract.

Sharikah al-uqud is a partnership of two or more persons, for involvement in commercial activity, where the wealth and profit are shared according to their agreed terms.

Sharikah al-mudarabah is the giving of wealth to a worker for commercial activity from which the profits are shared according to the terms agreed between them.

5.3 *Distribution of Profit and Loss*

The proportion of profit to be distributed between the partners must be agreed at the time of the contract. It is based on a proportion of the actual profit gained by the business.

Imam Malik and Imam Shafie opined that the ratio should be in relation to the proportion of the capital invested. According to Imam Ahmad, the ratio of the profit may differ from the ratio of the investment according to the agreement of the parties, but any loss must be borne between them in the same ratio as the capital invested. Imam Abu Hanifah has same opinion as Imam Ahmad except for when a partner is a sleeping partner. In this situation, as a sleeping partner does not undertake any work for the partnership, their share of the profit cannot be more than the ratio of their investment.

In the event of a loss, all the Muslim jurists are unanimous that each partner shall suffer the loss exactly according to the ratio of their investment.

5.4 *Application of* Al-Musharakah

The sources of this operation depend on the ability of the bank to do the following:

- Choose appropriate customers;
- Make a realistic feasibility study of the project;
- Follow up the project through audit and periodic control.

Musharakah mutanaqisah has been chosen as a concept that can be used to develop instruments for the Islamic capital market. It is a form of partnership contract whereby the financier allows his partner to buy assets either by means of a single payment or in instalments based on terms agreed by both parties.

An illustration of *Musharakah mutanaqisah* in the capital market is where Company A buys a building worth $80 million and sells it to its customers for $100 million, based on the principle of BBA, within 120 months. As Company A requires liquidity, it can involve project investors by issuing shares through *Musharakah mutanaqisah*. For that purpose, Company A put its share (the smaller part, say 10%) into *Musharakah mutanaqisah* for the purchase of the building. The investors hold the majority share (say, 90%). Company A will then buy back all the shares from the investors every month according to the amount and duration agreed. This arrangement ends at the point when Company A owns all the shares.

6 Al-Istisna'

6.1 *Definition*

Istisna' is a contract whereby a party undertakes to produce a specific item that can be made in accordance with agreed specifications at a pre-determined price and for a fixed date of delivery. The majority of jurists consider *Istisna'* as one of the categories of *salam*.

In *istisna'*, it is not a condition that the work be accomplished by the undertaking party; this work, or part of it, can be done by others under his control and for whom he is responsible. *Istisna'* is an instrument of pre-shipment financing and is a contract where the deal can refer to an item that does not exist at the time the contract is made.

According to the *Usrah* module, *istisna'* is the giving of an order to a workman to make a specific item with an agreement to pay a fixed wage or price for that item once it has been made (*Usrah* module, n.d.). *Istisna'* cannot be cancelled unilaterally after the manufacturer has started the work. *Istisna'* combines two distinguishing traits that are distinctive of *salam*. These elements relate to the permissibility of the contract even though the subject of the contract does not exist at the time the contract is made, and to the fact that the contract relates to an ordinary absolute sale whereby the price is fiduciary, not necessarily be advanced in *salam*, because *istisna'* involves labour in addition to the materials.

6.2 *Rules of Law*

It is a condition of an *Istisna'* contract to state in the clearest of terms the type, dimensions and all the specifications of the item required in order to avoid subsequent dispute.

An *Istisna'* contract is valid for items that can be manufactured. It is invalid for corn, wheat, barley or fruit, and all natural products, the sale of which on liability is a *salam* and not *istisna'*. An item sold under the terms of an *Istisna'* contract is a fixed liability debt; therefore, it is permissible that the item be a valuable asset made according to particular specifications. Regarding this feature, *Istisna'* is different than *salam*, which is only permissible in terms of similar 'assets'.

The materials should be supplied by the maker. If they are supplied by the buyer, the contract is *ijara* and not *Istisna'*. *Istisna'* is not confined to the item the seller makes after he entered into the contract; the maker will be considered to have satisfied his obligation provided he supplies an article conforming to all the buyer's specifications, whether the item was made by him or by someone else. The specifications demanded by the buyer are the most significant element, as the item the subject of the contract is a liability debt.

An *Istisna'* contract is binding on both parties, and neither party has the right to retract. Only if the item does not conform to the required specifications demanded can the buyer have the option to retract. Once the contract is drawn up, the ownership of the asset is affirmed to the buyer and the ownership of the price is affirmed to the maker. It is not a condition in an *Istisna'* contract to pay the price in advance; it is, however, permissible to pay the price in advance, to defer payment, or to make payment in instalments.

Typically, part of the price is paid in advance and the balance will be withheld until the time of delivery and receipt of the item. It is a condition that the period of delivery is specified, whether this is short-term or long-term, so as to avoid any conflict between the two parties. It is also a condition that the place of delivery is specified and whether any loading or transportation expenses are to be met. In an *Istisna'* contract, a buyer may stipulate that an item shall be manufactured or produced by a specific manufacturer, or manufactured from specific materials. This is not permitted in the event of a *salam* sale.

6.3 Application of Al-Istisna'

Istisna' contracts afford wide fields of application for Islamic banks to finance the public's needs and the vital interests of society so as to develop the Islamic economy. *Istisna'* contracts are applied in high technology industries, such as the aircraft industry, and the locomotive and ship building industries, in addition to the different types of machines produced in large factories or workshops. *Istisna'* contracts are also applied in the construction industry, such as for apartment buildings, hospitals, schools, universities, and to whatever that creates the network of modern life. *Istisna'* contracts are also applicable to a variety of industries as long as they can be monitored by measurement and specifications, such as the food processing industry. As a mode of Islamic bank finance, *Istisna'* can be used to finance the construction of a house. It is suitable for this in terms of payment and the rules of sale. The bank can enter into a parallel contract of *Istisna'* with a third party, or may hire the services of a manufacturer. The payment of instalments may start during or after the construction of the house.

7 Advantages of the Islamic Financial System

There are several advantages in applying Islamic project financing. The advantages of such instruments are that:

- They create a framework for the public's participation in financing government projects, including those of infrastructure, such as roads, bridges, ports, airports and others, on the basis of *murabahah* and *istisna'*.
- Sami Hassan Hamond (n.d.) stated that they can help Islamic banks to create a suitable outlet for investing surplus liquidity and to establish an Islamic capital market.
- The existence of these instruments and the generalization of their use is expected to be helpful in reducing the budget deficit by enabling the private sector to contribute to the financing of infrastructure projects.
- They help to raise investment funds, especially for industries where rapid technological innovation is either under way or desired, and for top class firms that are in course of the rapid expansion of their business, or for small and medium-sized enterprises and firms that would typically have insufficient assets and capital.
- Using the instruments available will allow the financing of tangible assets such as gas and electricity services. They also could finance infrastructure projects such as roads and buildings.

8 Issues and Challenges Faced by the Islamic Financial System

Islamic financial markets are operating far below their potential because of some reasons. In the practice, the Islamic banking by itself cannot take root in the absence of the other necessary components of an Islamic financial system. Certain limitations should be addressed before any long-term strategy can be formulated; these include the absence of a regulatory and legal framework; the lack of an organized financial centre operated in accordance with Islamic principles; the slow pace of innovation; and the of uniformity in accounting standards and procedures.

8.1 No Regulatory and Legal Framework

There is no a uniform regulatory and legal framework supporting the Islamic financial system. The existing banking regulations in Islamic countries are based on the Western banking model. Therefore, a regulatory and legal framework that supports the Islamic financial system will enhance the integration of Islamic markets and international financial markets.

8.2 No Single, Sizable, and Organized Financial Centre Operated in Accordance with Islamic Principles

Although stock markets are active in emerging Islamic countries such as Egypt, Jordan and Pakistan, they are not fully compatible with Islamic principles. The stock markets in Iran and Sudan may come closest to operating in compliance with Islamic principles. Furthermore, the secondary market for Islamic products is extremely light and illiquid, and money markets are almost non-existent, since viable instruments are not currently available.

8.3 The Pace of Innovation Is Slow

For quite some time, the market has offered the same traditional instruments—instruments that are unable to handle maturities at the extremes. In addition, the market lacks the necessary instruments to provide viable alternatives for public debt financing.

8.4 Lack of Uniformity in Accounting Standards and Procedures

An Islamic financial system needs appropriate accounting standards and procedures in the operation of its business. Western accounting procedures are not adequate for this purpose due to the different nature and treatment of financial instruments in the Western system. Therefore, well-defined procedures and standards are crucial for the disclosure of information and the building of investors' confidence, as well as to help the integration of Islamic financial markets with international markets.

8.4.1 Lack of Uniformity in Application of Religious Principles

In the absence of a universally accepted central religious authority, Islamic banks have formed their own religious board for guidance. Islamic banks have to consult their respective boards, or *Shari'ah* advisors, to seek approval for each new instrument. Variations in the interpretation of Islamic principles by different schools of thought may mean that identical financial instruments are rejected by one board but accepted by another. Hence, this problem should be resolved by forming a unified council representing the different schools of thought to define cohesive rules and to expedite the process of introducing new products.

9 Conclusion

The further growth and development of the Islamic financial system will depend largely on the nature of innovations introduced in the market. The immediate need is to organize human and financial resources to develop instruments to enhance liquidity, to undertake the management of assets or liability and risk, and to introduce public finance instruments. The Islamic financial system can also offer alternatives at the microfinance level.

At the microfinance level, the application of Islamic finance will promote entrepreneurship and risk-sharing, and its expansion to the poor could be an effective development tool. By practising this method, the poor can be protected from paying usurious rates at the hands of the lenders.

In conclusion, an Islamic financial system can play an important role in the economic development of Islamic countries by mobilizing dormant savings that are intentionally being kept out of interest-based financial channels, and by facilitating the development of capital markets. Furthermore, the development of an Islamic financial system would enable savers and borrowers to choose financial instruments compatible with their business needs, social values and religious beliefs.

References

Ghifari, N. M., and Muzaffar, M. (n.d.). Ijarah and Islamic Modern Application. Paper Presented at the Seminar on Islamic Financing Technique, Islamabad, pp. 11–12.

Homond, S. H. (n.d.). Islamic Financial Instrument Based on Intermediary Contracts, p. 229.

Islamic Fiqh Academy Resolution No. 5, para 7, issued in respect of Muqaradah bonds and investment certificates in the fourth session of the Academy held in Jeddah during the period 18–23 Jumada II, 1408H (corresponding to 6–11 February 1988).

Osman, R. A. (n.d.). Islamic Financial System, p. 18.

Osman, R. A. (n.d.). Islamic Financial System, p. 20.

Usrah Module. (n.d.). Muamalat, IIUM, p. 30.

CHAPTER 8

The Pricing Techniques of Islamic Financial Products

The rules and norms of Islam derive from the Quran and Sunnah of the Holy Prophet, and other dependent sources are consensus (*ijma'*) and reasoning by analogy (*qiyas*). Islam is comprehensive and covers all aspects of life. Thus, these sources are guidelines for mankind throughout his life in this world.

Thus, in business matters, Islam permits the implementation of a wide range of business activities and financing methods provided they are within the principles of *Shari'ah*. Some of these methods of financing were developed during the early stages of Islam. Others have emerged recently to meet ever-changing requirements and technology.

Hence, Islamic banking is practised as an alternative to conventional banking and to meet contemporary financing requirement in the light of the teaching of Islam. An Islamic bank cannot provide its products or services with interest. Islamic banks have had to create a number of special products and services that are suitable and attractive to their existing and potential customers. These new products and services conform to *Shari'ah* principles such as *murabahah*, *mudarabah*, *ijarah* (leasing) and certain other methods of financing.

Pricing is very important in marketing; however, a bank's products are more complex than other products and the prices have to be fixed. The blessing of the Islamic transaction is that both the customer and the bank operator gain economic and spiritual revenue, as their aim is to gain reward from Allah.

M. M. Billah, *Islamic Financial Products*,
https://doi.org/10.1007/978-3-030-17624-2_8

Recently, almost all conventional banks have begun to offer Islamic financing. One could question how true such financing is to *Shari'ah* principles. Thus, the Islamic banking system should ensure that it becomes a truly viable alternative banking system and is able to meet the demands of the modern banking industry.

1 Regulatory Framework for Pricing of Islamic Products

The modern system of banking and investment was fundamentally based on the economy and legal norms of Islamic Law. For example, consider the model for an economy system not based on interest that seized on the principles of partnership, particularly *mudarabah*. In *mudarabah* concepts, it offers the opportunity of pure finance, enabling the owner of capital to invest his capital without himself becoming involved in managing such capital and exposing himself to liabilities in excess of the capital.

The important point for the practice of *mudarabah* is that it is not permitted to claiming of either a fixed profit or the assured return to be received by the capital provider, no matter how much the return on the investment will be. The capital provider profits only in the proportion to a venture's profits and it is his capital that is hostage to a venture's losses, although the capital provider will not be liable beyond the amount of such capital.

Muslim economists justify an Islamic financial system competing with the western system on the basis of two partnership principles: the return on capital cannot be fixed in advance but must be a proportion of profits, and the capital (not the labour) is liable for the financial risks of the venture.

Nagle is a prominent western economist, in his writing regarding the strategy and tactics of pricing, states, 'it is the firm's attempt to capture some of that value in the profits it earns. In effective product development, promotion and distribution sow the seeds of business success, effective pricing is the harvest.'

The different between successful and unsuccessful pricing lies in how the process is approached. Nagle has pointed out certain questions that aid in achieving superiority and sustainable profitability. A strategic pricing approach will consider:

- What costs can our business afford to incur, given the price achievable in the market, and still earn a profit?
- What is our product worth to this customer and how can we better communicate that value, thus justifying the price?
- What level of sales or market share can our business most profitably achieve?

Basically, Nagle suggests that strategic pricing requires more than just a change in attitude; it also requires changes to when, how and who makes pricing decisions. For example, strategic pricing requires that management take responsibility for establishing a coherent set of pricing policies and procedures, consistent with the company's strategic goals. According to Nagle, strategic pricing requires, most importantly, a new relationship between marketing and finance.

2 *Al-Murabahah* (Mark-Up Pricing)

Murabahah is a kind of absolute pure sale, which based on the sale of an asset for a price or a mark-up price. Mark-up transactions account for 80–90% of investments by Islamic financial institutions (Warde, n.d.). It is one of the most widely used methods of finance by Islamic banks and is suitable for the partial financing of the investment activities of customers in industry, trade and other such engagements.

Murabahah is a selling something for its cost price plus a specified profit, provided that both the seller and the buyer know the cost price. The seller says, my capital, or the cost price, is a 100, and I will sell it to you for a profit of 10. This is permitted as there is no doubt about its legitimacy. No scholar is reported to have regarded it with legal 'dislike' (Kahf and Khan, n.d.).

In a *murabahah* contract, an Islamic bank buys commodities or assets from a supplier, who can provide a better discount, and then sells them to customers at a calculated profit. It involves three parties: the purchaser, the supplier and the bank. The purchaser approaches the bank for assistance; the bank offers to purchase the commodities from the supplier and sell them to the purchaser for a profit, with repayment by the purchaser on a pre-agreed date. The act of buying from the supplier and selling to the customer removes any elements of interest, which is prohibited in Islam, as the transaction is not a loan but, rather, is a pure trading transaction. The bank assumes the risk by purchasing the commodity before it sells it at a mark-up price. A *Murabahah* transaction does not apply if the purchaser wants to obtain funds for a purpose other than that of purchasing a commodity; for example, for the payment of salaries, or to settle bills or other liabilities.

2.1 Al-Murabahah *Legal Framework of Pricing*

A *murabahah* price is payable at a later date. The bank or financier naturally wants to make sure that the price will be paid on the due date and may ask for security in the form of a mortgage, or some other kind of charge.

2.2 Calculation of Cost in murabahah

The transaction of *murabahah* is based on the concept of cost plus sale. Therefore, this type of transaction can only come into effect when the seller can ascertain the exact cost of acquiring assets or commodities. In the event this is not possible, the sale must be made on the basis of *musawamah* (a sale without reference to the cost). Another principle affecting the legitimacy of a *murabahah* transaction is that it should be based on the same currency in which the banker has purchased the commodity from the supplier. Any elements that lead to any uncertainty regarding the price at the time of sale lead to the invalidity of a *murabahah* transaction according to classical Muslim jurists.

2.3 Rescheduling of Payment

Even though it may have been stated in the agreement that the purchaser should pay a certain amount to the banker at specified periods (i.e. monthly), there may be time when the purchaser is unable to pay accordingly. The purchaser then requests the banker to reschedule the instalments. In conventional banking, any rescheduling of payments leads to the incurring of additional interest. This is not the case in non-interest banks. If the instalments are rescheduled, no additional amount should be charged. The amount of the *murabahah* price should remain the same in the same currency.

This is mentioned in the Holy Quran, which states that:

> If the debtor is in difficulty, grant him time till it is easy for him to repay. But if ye remit it by way of charity, that is best for you if ye only knew (2:280). ('Ali, n.d.)

2.4 *Discount on Early Payment*

Sometimes a purchaser is able to pay earlier than the specified date. In the event that he wishes to earn a discount on the agreed deferred price, some jurists have held that this agreement is permissible; however, most Muslim jurists hold that, if the discount is held to be a condition for earlier payment, it is not allowed.

The permission regarding discount is held based on the following *hadith*:

> Abdullah Ibn (*RA*) is reported to have said that when the Jews belonging to the tribe of Banu Nadir were banished from Madinah, some people came to the Prophet (*SAW*) and said, 'You have ordered them to be expelled, but some people owe them some debts which have not yet matured.' Thereupon, the Prophet (*SAW*) said to them [the Jews who were the creditors] 'Give discount and receive (your debts) soon.'

However, the majority of jurists held that early payment with the reward of a discount is not permissible based on the following *hadith*.

> Al-Waqidi has narrated that Sallam b. Abi Huqaiq, a Jew of Banu Nadir, had advanced 80 dinars to Usaid Ibn Hudayr (*RA*) payable after one year with an addition of 40 dinars. Thus, Usaid (*RA*) owed him 120 dinars after one year. After this arrangement, he paid the principle amount of 80 dinars and Sallam relinquished the remainder of the debt.

Nevertheless, if the banker gives a rebate of his own volition, this is permissible, especially when the purchaser is a person in need. Thus, this means that an Islamic bank or financial institution may effect *murabahah* transactions.

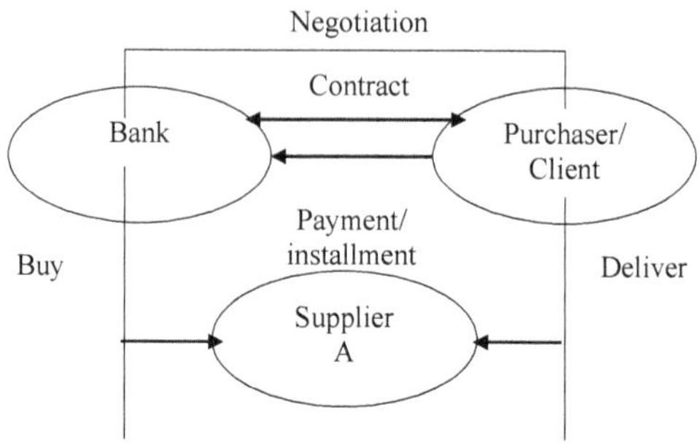

Fig. 1 *Murabahah* pricing techniques (*Source* Author's own)

2.5 *Other Features That Form Part of a* murabahah *Contract*

- Flexible repayment terms.
- Competitive pricing.
- Fixed and reducing balance basis.
- The minimum amount considered for *murabahah* finance is US$50,000 (http://www.barakaonline.com) (Fig. 1).

Ahmad (the client) requests Bank Islam to purchase a house and sell it to him at cost plus a certain amount of profit. Bank Islam purchases a house from Supplier A at $100,000 and sells it to Ahmad at $100,000 (cost) plus $8000 (profit/mark-up). Ahmad will pay the amount of $108,000 by instalments at specified periods. Bank Islam will assume the risk and the ownership of the house as long as the payment by Ahmad remains outstanding.

3 *Al-Mudarabah* (Profit Sharing)

Mudarabah is another financing method used by Islamic banks in their relationship with depositors (*rab al-mal*) who tender their money to banks. The capital provider (*rab al-mal*) may specify a particular business for the banker (*mudarib*), which is known as restricted *mudarabah* (*al-mudarabah al-muqayyah*), or may otherwise enter into unrestricted *mudarabah* (*al-mudarabah al-mutlaqah*). After the operation is concluded, the capital provider receives the principal and the pre-agreed share of the profit.

3.1 *The Legality of* mudarabah *from an Islamic Perspective*

> And when the prayer is finished, then may ye disperse through the land, and seek of the Bounty of God: and celebrate the Praises of God often (and without stint): that ye may prosper (62:10). ('Ali, n.d.)

Haziat Ibn Majah has recorded a narrative by Shuib (*RA*) that the Prophet (*SAW*) said:

> Three things are blessed: ratified sales, *mudarabah*, and mixing wheat with barley as a substance for home food (not for sale). (Shingeri, n.d.)

3.2 *Distribution of Profit and Loss*

No particular proportion has been prescribed by the *Shari'ah* but, rather, has been left to the mutual consent of the capital provider and the managing trustee. They can share the profit in equal proportions, or allocate different proportions, such as a ratio of 50:50, 60:40, or 70:30. However, the division of the profits between the two parties must be on a proportional basis; they cannot be a lump sum, neither can they determine the share of any party at a specific rate tied up with the capital. Apart from that, the managing trustee cannot claim any periodical salary or any fee for the work done. All the schools of the Islamic *fiqh* are unanimous on this point.

3.3 *Distribution of Profit and Loss in* mudarabah takaful

The general accepted ratio in *mudarabah takaful* is 70:30, between the capital provider and the managing trustee, and for a family business, and 50:50 for a general business (i.e. non-life insurance).

In the case of a loss, this is to be borne completely by the capital provider. He is not liable for losses beyond the capital he has contributed. The managing trustee does not share in the losses except for the loss of his time and efforts. Different *fiqh* traditions have resulted in differences between the various schools. *Hanafi* and *Hanbali* argue, for example, that the profit can be shared only when the activity is completed and the financier has been reimbursed his principal, whereas *Maliki* and *Shafie* permit the distribution of the profit even before the operation has come to an end and the principal has been reimbursed.

3.4 *Investment Amount of* mudarabah

A contract between an investor and an Islamic bank is specified by the investor. An Islamic bank will invest money deposited in accordance with *Shari'ah* principles at a pre-agreed profit sharing ratio.

3.5 *Features of Investment*

- The minimum investment is $500.
- The investment period is from 1 month to 60 months.
- The minimum investment for 1 month is $5000, and is $500 for an investment of 3 months and above.
- The profit sharing ratio is in favour of the investor; for example, investor 70% and Islamic bank 30% (http://www.mud3.mpbb.com.my).

3.6 *Application of* mudarabah *Contract*

Consider the following example:
Ahmad wants to invest $100,000 with Bank Islam for three months. The agreed rate of profit sharing between Ahmad and Bank Islam is 75:25, respectively.

3.6.1 Profit Distribution

Assume that the venture earned a profit of $3750 in three months' time; that is, a return of 15% on the investment.

Ahmad's proportion (75% × $3750) $2812.50
Principal investment $100,000.00
Total invested fund $102,812.50
Bank Islam proportion of profit (25% × $3750) $937.00

3.6.2 Loss Venture

Assume that the venture incurs a loss of $1750; that is, 7% of the invested amount.

Invested amount $100,000.00
(Less) loss incurred $1750.00
Net investment $98,250.00

In the *mudarabah* system, the capital provider is entitled to share in the profit based on the agreed profit; however, the capital provider is not bound to share in any loss that the partnership may have incurred.

4 *Qardh Al-Hasan* (Benevolent Loan)

Al-qardh (benevolent loan) also known as *ad-dayn* or *as-salf*, which means debts, owings or borrowings. A debt is a kind of contract that transfers the right of the owner to the lender or borrower to a certain amount of money or certain goods that it then becomes the responsibility of the borrower to pay back in the same amount and on the due date as agreed in the contract. *Al-qardh al-hasan* is a kind of debt where there is no condition or promise to pay more than the amount borrowed but a voluntary award is made.

4.1 Qardh Al-Hasan *Legal Framework of Pricing*

A bank will apply a *qardhu hasan* contract when lending where it has a legal claim solely on the principle loan. This is because a *qardhu hasan* loan pays no contractual interest. The borrowed funds raised from a *qardhu hasan* loan must be made from the bank's own special *mudarabah* investment deposits. As a managing trustee, the bank invests funds in the open market. If *musharakah* is applied, the bank places part of its own capital in the fund. Dividends and capital gains will be distributed based on a contractual profit and sharing ratio. Since a *qardhu hasan* loan is interest-free, the profit sharing ratio must reflect the opportunity cost of the *qardhu hasan*, which is non-contractual in nature. For example, the profit sharing ratio for investment derived from a customer's own capital should be designed to give relatively less return to the bank compared to the customer who is using the *qardhu hasan* share financing scheme.

4.1.1 Al-Qardh *Share Financing with Profit Sharing Fund Management*

Consider the following example:

(a) With own funds $50,000
Profit sharing ratio: 70%:30% between investor and bank, respectively.
If the rate of return is 20% or $10,000 per annum:
The return on investment is $7000 or $7000/$50,000 = 14%

(b) Using the *al-qard* facility $50,000
Profit sharing ratio: 40%:60% between investor and bank, respectively.
If the rate of return on investment is 20% or $10,000 per annum:
The return on investment is $4000 or $4000/$50,000 = 8%

5 *Al-Bai' bithaman ajil* (Deferred Payment): A Past Experience

Bai' bithaman ajil (BBA) financing is one of the better-known financial instruments in Malaysian Islamic banking. It is a contract involving a deferred sale where payments are made in instalments. BBA financing allows an Islamic bank to involve itself in deferred purchase/sales activities.

5.1 BBA Legal Framework of Pricing

In BBA, the offer price will include some time element, since payment will be made at some point in the future. It was argued that Islamic jurists have no objection to the setting of credit price higher than the cash or spot price. The profit generated from the BBA sale is legitimate under *Shari'ah* principles, since it is derived from trade rather than debt.

The fixing of profits is allowed in trading because it involves risk such as losses and uncertainty. Such as, if the profits are prefixed in a particular trade, the amount of the expected profits remains uncertain. As mentioned earlier, a BBA transaction takes place with the purchase of a property and its resale involving the repayment of that resale price on deferred payment terms. With regard to a property sale agreement, an agreement is made between the bank, the supplier and the customer to secure the purchase of the property by the customer.

BBA is not a loan but, rather, a direct purchase from the vendor/supplier by an Islamic bank at market price and the subsequent sale of that good to the customer at a mark-up price. The determination of the mark-up or selling price depends on the stipulated annual rate of profit the bank desires from the transaction. After the determination of profit and the specification of the period of the loan, the selling price can be computed using the annuity factor table.

The difference between the market price (cost price) and the mark-up price (selling price) is the profit created over the instalment period, which is allowed, since the transaction is based on a deferred sale contract rather than debt.

To practice the spirit of the *al-bay'* fully, the bank must take the risks of the possession of the property before the sale is completed. This will make the profit generated from the BBA sale legitimate, as it involves the element of risk-taking; that is, the risk of having the possession of property.

5.2 *Determination of Selling Price*

A BBA facility requires the selling price to remain fixed, since only one selling price is allowed. This implies that the rate of the profit in each contract remains unchanged. To avoid violation of the contract, the selling price cannot be changed even though Islamic banks are widely exposed to economic volatility.

In order to calculate the selling price of a BBA contract, the cost of financing (the market price of the asset), is multiplied by the annuity factor. As some Islamic jurists approve credit sales with a preference for a specific time, a conventional annuity table is applied when determining the sales prices of BBA assets.

5.3 *Calculation of Selling Price*

The cost of financing is $50,000 and the payment period is 12 years or 240 months. An annual profit rate of 10.5% will give an annuity factor equal to 0.0093145. Multiplying the annuity factor by the cost of financing derives monthly payments of $499 per month.

To find the selling price, the monthly payment of $499 is multiplied by 240 months, which give the selling price of $119,105. The profit of the transaction is the difference between the selling price $119,105 and the cost of financing of $50,000, which is equal to $69,105.

6 Conclusion

The beauty of Islamic methods of financing and the legality of its pricing system in *Shari'ah* law not only attracts customers, but has also lead other conventional financial institutions to implement and offer these Islamic methods of financing in their operations.

However, a truly viable and transparent method should be implemented to ensure that the concept of these methods of financing is not misinterpreted. One could draw a comparison between Islamic products and conventional products of financing in terms of their practicality, availability, ease of use and terms of pricing. How well these Islamic financing methods perform in the banking industry is subjective; however, the important point that should not be overlooked is that, in Islamic transactions, both the customer and the bank operator gain economic and spiritual revenue because their aim is to gain reward from Allah.

Thus, it is very important that everyone should cooperate to ensure that these Islamic financing products may present themselves as truly viable methods of financing. As mentioned in the Quran:

> Help ye one another in righteous piety, but help ye not one another in sin and rancour: fear God, for God is strict in punishment. (5:2) ('Ali, n.d.)

References

'Ali, A. Y. (n.d.). *The Holy Quran: Text and Translation*, Islamic Book Trust, Kuala Lumpur.

Kahf, M., and Khan, T. (n.d.). *A Survey (Research Paper No. 16): Principles of Islamic Financing*, p. 28.

Shingeri, M. S. (n.d.), *A Model of Pure Interest Free Banking*, Islamic fiqh, p. 27.

Warde, I. (n.d.). *Islamic Finance in the Global Economy*, p. 133.

http://www.barakaonline.com.

http://www.mud3.mpbb.com.my.

CHAPTER 9

Remedies for Breach of Financial Contract Under *Shari'ah*

1 Introduction

To contract (*al-'Aqd*) means to tie or to bind. In Islam, Muslims are free to enter into any kind of contract, provided that it does not contradict *Shari'ah* principles. Thus, a contract to sell wine or to steal money from a bank, for instance, is not accepted or acknowledged under *Shari'ah*.

In Islam, once a contract is concluded the parties are obliged to perform and fulfil their obligations in accordance with the terms of the contract. This is supported by two verses in two different *surahs* in the Qur'an:

> O you who believe, fulfil your obligations. (Al-Quran, Al-Maidah: 1)
>
> Again fulfil every engagement for every engagement will be enquired into (on the day of Reckoning). (Al-Quran, Al-Israa: 34)

Financial contracts in general are bilateral contracts whereby at least two parties are involved. In each contract, one party shall make a proposal (*ijab*), while the other accepts (*qabul*). In bilateral contracts, both parties to the contract must concur; that is, their agreement must be related to the same subject matter, and the contract must be able to produce legal and beneficial results to both parties (Billah 2003). For instance, Ahmad decided to sell his shares to Abu for a certain amount of money; thus, he approached Abu and offered him his shares. Abu then agreed to buy Ahmad's shares for the exact amount of money Ahmad demanded.

M. M. Billah, *Islamic Financial Products*,
https://doi.org/10.1007/978-3-030-17624-2_9

Thus, here, offer and acceptance are present, and the subject matter is the shares. Once the payment is made and the shares are transferred, both parties will gain: Ahmad will receive the money while Abu will own the shares.

Despite the fact that contracts are binding on both contracting parties, there are instances where one of the parties to the contract fails to fulfil their obligations, either intentionally or unintentionally. As a result, the other party will be in a position of loss. In order to protect or to compensate this party to the contract, remedies for breach of contract are available and enforceable, either by going to the court, or sometimes by resorting to the remedies stipulated in the agreement (thus, there is no need for the court to grant remedies to the aggrieved party).

In this chapter, we will first briefly discuss some of the elements of a contract, and then present the remedies for breach of financial contract that are available under Malaysian *Shari'ah* law. Then, we will look at the current practices in Malaysia, followed by a case study on breach of financial contract and the remedies granted, in Malaysia and under *Shari'ah* principles. Finally, we will make recommendations in relation to financial contracts and their governing *Shari'ah* law in Malaysia.

2 Elements of a Contract

Under *Shari'ah*, a contract is valid when its essence and attributes are in line with *Shari'ah*, and it is binding when there is no defect in the substance (this refers to offer, acceptance and subject matter) or description of the contract (this refers to the characteristics of a contract, such as the price or the quantity of shares to be traded) (Billah 2003). However, a contract is considered invalid under *Shari'ah* either when the substance is lawful, but the description is not; or when both its substance and description are unlawful in the eyes of *Shari'ah* (Billah 2003).

An element of a contract that we need to look at is the parties to a contract. There is a need to establish the fitness of a person for the application of the law on his actions (legal capacity), in order to force that person legally to fulfil his obligations under a contract. There are instances when a person will be labelled as unfit for the law to be applied on his actions; thus, if he enters into an agreement, the law cannot be used against him if he refuses or fails to fulfil his part of the agreement. Examples are: insane and idiotic people, a person who is in the state of forgetfulness, a dying person, a drunk person who was forced to consume or who unknowingly consumed liquor, or a person who is forced to enter into a contract (Billah 2003).

Aside from the parties to a contract, the subject matter of a contract is also an important element. For a subject matter to be valid under *Shari'ah*, the following conditions must be satisfied (Billah 2003):

- The subject matter should exist at the time of the contract in order to avoid the element of *gharar*. However, for *salam* (deferred), *istisna'* (manufacturing), *ju'alah* (reward) and *ijarah* (service, hiring or employment) contracts, the subject matter need not necessarily exist at the time of contract, subject to several conditions (Billah 2003).
- The subject matter must be legally owned by the seller, meaning that the seller has legal title to the subject matter and not mere possession thereof. Therefore, for example, if a person entrusts the safe-keeping of some shares to his friend in that friend's home, the friend cannot sell those shares to a third party, even though the shares are in his possession.
- The subject matter is beneficial to both the contracting parties. If only one of the contracting parties sees the subject matter as valuable, then it defeats the purpose of entering into the contract because the parties to the contract may not be able to expect the contract to turn out to be the way they want it to be.
- The subject matter must be of commercial value under *Shari'ah* principles, meaning that, besides having commercial value, the subject matter must also be *halal*.

The elements of offer and acceptance must exist in order to conclude a contract and to bind the parties to that contract. Offers can be made by word (orally), in writing, by gesture, conduct, or by post, telegram, telex, fax, phone or e-mail. Acceptance may be communicated orally, in writing, by gesture, delivery (of the subject matter), payment (in consideration of the subject matter), performance or conduct, letter, telex, fax, phone or e-mail (Billah 2003). Offers will be terminated and the contract will not be concluded if any of the following situations take place (Billah 2003):

- *Revocation*: when the offeror changes his mind and revokes his offer; this may take place at any time after the offer is made and before the offer is accepted. For instance, if a person made an offer on 30 September 2003 to sell his shares to a friend and the friend was given one week to consider the offer, and the next day the offeror changed his mind and wanted to keep the shares before his friend accepted the offer. When the offeror conveyed his intention to keep the shares, this implies that the offeror is revoking the offer; thus, the offer will be terminated.
- *Rejection by the offeree*: if the offer is not accepted. In relation to the above example, if the offeree (the friend) chose not to purchase the shares and conveys his rejection of the offer to the offeror, then the offer is terminated.
- *Counter-offer*: when the offeree wants to accept the offer, but with his own additional conditions, which is seen as a counter-offer to the original offer. Hence, in this case, the original offer will be terminated. For example, A wants to sell his bonds of Company XYZ to B for $1 million. However, on receiving the offer, B made a counter-offer to A, saying that he is willing to purchase the bonds for the same price, provided that A also sells his shares of Company ABC at a price that is 5% less than the market share price. As a consequence of the counter-offer, the original offer from A to B is terminated.
- *Absence of acceptance*: when an offer is made but no acceptance has been received. For example, A offered B a lot of shares of Company GYM in 1999. But even two years later, in 2001, B had not yet accepted the offer. Two years is a long time during which to consider whether or not to buy shares from A; thus, the absence of acceptance during the two-year period results in the termination of the offer.
- *Death*: if either the offeror or the offeree dies before the offer is accepted, the offer is automatically terminated.
- *Lapse of time*: an offer is made and it is to be accepted within a specific time period. If the offeree fails to accept within the time limit, the offer will be terminated. For instance, an offeror made an offer on 1 October 2003 and said to the offeree that he expected a reply in one week's time. However, after the week had passed the offeree did not contact the offeror. Hence, the offer would be terminated.

3 Remedies for Breach of Financial Contract Under *Shari'ah*

Figure 1 shows the types of remedy available for breach of financial contract under *Shari'ah*.

Remedies for breach of contract (*'ilaj naqd al-'aqd*), as noted earlier, arises when a party to a contract refuses or fails to perform their obligations under a contract. Under *Shari'ah*, the party who experiences a loss due to a breach of contract by another party can seek remedy from the defaulting party by either going to a court of law, or through self-help remedies (which will be discussed later in this section), which does not require a court order (Billah 2003).

Shari'ah law in Malaysia comes from different sources. The primary sources are: al-Quran, which contains the words of Allah, and the Sunnah, which comprises the sayings and practices of the Prophet Muhammad (*SAW*). In additions to these primary sources, the writings of Islamic jurists are also a source for *Shari'ah* law, subject to acceptance by other jurists. Islamic jurists sometimes wrote opinions of legal rulings; these may contain revealed sources (from al-Quran and the Sunnah), opinions of the writers themselves or a collection of opinions of other jurists (*Halsbury's Laws of Malaysia* 2002). Under *Shari'ah* law in

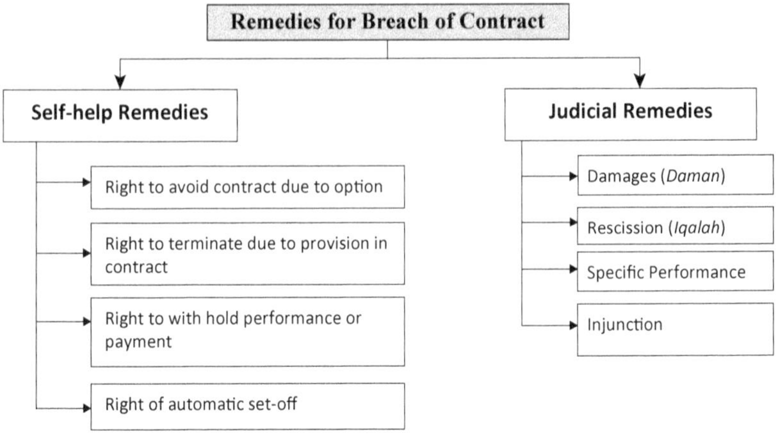

Fig. 1 Remedies for breach of financial contract under *Shari'ah* (*Source* Author's own)

Malaysia, case law or judgements made on disputes brought before the *Shari'ah* courts cannot be used as an authority on *Shari'ah* law. That is, the legal principles arising from the judgement of each piece of case law cannot be considered as a source of *Shari'ah* law; each piece of case law is only enforceable in that particular dispute (Billah 2003). Nevertheless, the judgements of other *Shari'ah* courts can be referred to as a supporting basis for a judgement in other cases (Billah 2003).

Despite the fact that there is *Shari'ah* law and there are *Shari'ah* courts for disputes on Islamic financial contracts, the cases are brought before the civil court of Malaysia. The sources of law relating to remedies in Malaysia are found in various sources: the adaptation of common law (the common law of England), the Contracts Act 1950 and the Specific Relief Act 1950 (Billah 2003).

3.1 *Self-Help Remedies*

Now, referring back to the self-help remedies, they can be classified as follows (Billah 2003):

- A party to a contract has the right to void a contract due to the existence of an 'option'. Under *Shari'ah*, once a contract is concluded, parties to the contract are not allowed to modify or disturb the agreement; hence, through options, the parties are granted a period of 'reassessment' or 'cooling-off' in order to allow them to rationalize their decisions, or to reverse their decisions (Billah 2003).
- A party to a contract has the right to terminate the contract due to specific provisions that are provided in the contract. For instance, in a contract related to the buying and selling of goods, if it is stipulated that, in the event that the seller is late in delivering the goods, the buyer has the right to terminate the contract, the buyer can exercise his right to terminate the contract if the seller makes late delivery.
- The right of one party to withhold (*haqq al-habs*) performance or payment when the other is in breach of contract. For example, a housing developer and a financier enter into a contract to build a housing area by means of an *istisna'* contract, on behalf of the financier. As stipulated in the contract, the financier should provide 10% of the finance in mid-May 2003 so that building of the houses

may begin in June 2003. However, if the financier fails to provide the finance in mid-May, he is in breach of contract; consequently, the developer can withhold the performance of building the houses until such time as the financier provides the finance.

- If a party to a contract is in breach, the other party can seek redress or compensation (the right of automatic set-off), as stipulated in the contract. For example, if it is stipulated in a contract that, if any party fails to perform their part of the contract, the other party will be compensated by way of entitlement to a certain sum of money. Thus, if one of the contracting parties does breach the contract, then the aggrieved party can automatically offset his loss through monetary compensation given to him by the party in breach.

3.2 Judicial Remedies

Unlike the self-help remedies, which can be settled out of court, judicial remedies, as the term suggests, require the aggrieved party to go to court in order to seek remedy for the loss he suffered due to the breach of contract by the other party to the contract.

There are basically four types of judicial remedy available under Malaysian law for breach of financial contract:

(i) Damages;
(ii) Rescission;
(iii) Specific performance, and
(iv) Injunction.

Each of these remedies will be discussed in Sects. 4, 5, 6 and 7, respectively. Where necessary, certain relevant and real cases will be included, although such cases may not relate to financial contacts.

4 Damages (*Daman*)

The Court grants damages to a party as a form of compensation for the damage, loss or injury such party has suffered as the result of a breach of contract (by the other contracting party) (Sinnadurai 1987). Section 74 of the Contracts Act sets out the consequences of a breach of contract (Sinnadurai 1987):

- When a contract has been broken, the party who suffers by such breach is entitled to receive, from the party who has broken the contract, compensation for any loss or damage caused to him thereby, which naturally arose in the usual course of things from such breach, or which the parties knew, when they made the contract, to be likely to result from the breach of it.
- Such compensation is not to be given for any remote and indirect loss or damage sustained by reason of the breach.
- When an obligation resembling those created by a contract has been incurred and has not been discharged, any person injured by the failure to discharge it is entitled to receive the same compensation from the party in default as if such person had contracted to discharge it and had broken his contract.

Below are the items under the heading of damages that are available in Malaysia (Fig. 2).

We shall now examine a few cases being given under the heading of recovery of damages. One of the cases is the case of Teoh Kee Keong *v.* Tambun Mining Co. Ltd. (1968) (Sinnadurai 1987). In this case, Long Kee Nyean was a director of certain private companies, one of which held a mining certificate. The appellant eventually came to have a contract transferred from Ipoh Mining to the respondents. The work was to mine land on a cliff, which required heavy work and costly initial outlay. After the mining operations had progressed and began to yield ore, deliveries were able to flow for some months (the work of the appellant). The respondent then gave notice of the cessation of the operations, thus terminating the contract. The appellant then claimed $290,000.45 as

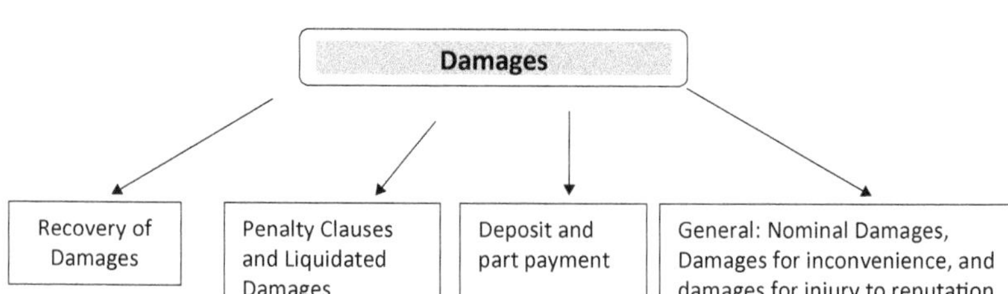

Fig. 2 Damages (*daman*) (*Source* Author's own)

the value of the work done, outlay for materials used and for labour and expenses. The trial judge held that there was a breach of contract and the respondent was required to pay $99,272 to the appellant. Dissatisfied with this result, the appellant went to the Federal Court, which later ruled in favour of the appellant for $121,220 with interest thereon at 5% per year from 7 February 1963.

Under penalty clauses and liquidated damages, reference is made to Section 75 of the Contracts Act. The case of Wearne Brothers (M) Ltd. *v.* Jackson (1966) is given to describe this type of damages (Sinnadurai 1987). This case was in relation to a breach of contract with respect to a hire purchase agreement for a car. The appeal was that the learned president of the Sessions Court failed to consider whether the relevant clause in the agreement was a penalty clause or a genuine pre-estimate of the damage as on the date of the agreement. In view of Section 75 of the Contracts Act 1950, it was irrelevant whether the clause in the agreement was a penalty clause. Section 75 also says that, in every case, the court must determine reasonable compensation. In the application of Section 75 to the case, it was held that the plaintiff was disentitled to recover simpliciter the sum fixed in the contract, whether as a penalty or liquidated damages, and must prove the damages suffered by him unless the sum quoted was a genuine pre-estimate. If a clause in the agreement stated a genuine pre-estimate of the damages for depreciation beginning from the time when they entered into the contract, and if the damages fixed by the parties did not appear to be unreasonable or disproportionate to the nature and extent of depreciation, then, the court may award such damages.

The case of Linggi Plantations Ltd. *v.* Jagatheesan (1972) (Sinnadurai 1987) is an example of the difference between a deposit and part payment. In this case, the issue was the determination of whether a vendor was entitled to forfeit a deposit paid on a contract for the sale of real property following its non-completion by the purchaser, although the vendor was not in a position to prove actual damage due to the purchaser's breach of contract. It was held that the contract meant that, in the event of failure by the purchaser to complete and notice to terminate being given, the vendor was entitled to forfeit the deposit and claim for any damage that he had suffered over and above the amount of deposit, after giving credit for the amount of the deposit.

Other types of damages available are:

- *Nominal damages*: As in the case of Hilborne *v*. Tan Tiang Quee, Chung *v*. Tan Tiang Quee (1972) (Sinnadurai 1987), it was held that, even though the plaintiff has suffered no pecuniary loss due to defendant's breach of contract, he was in general entitled to nominal damages (determined by the court).
- *Damages for inconvenience*: It was held in the case of Hong Leong Co. Ltd. *v*. Pearlson Enterprises Ltd. (No. 2) (1968) (Sinnadurai 1987) that, due to the plaintiffs' breach of contract, which caused the defendants considerable inconvenience and unreasonably delayed the construction of a block of flats, the plaintiffs should pay the defendant the costs of the retrial and original trial of the counterclaim.
- *Damages for injury to reputation*: Under this, damages are given to a party who suffers an injury to his reputation as a consequence of the other party's breach of contract. For instance, Company A, a reputable company, announces to the public that it is going to receive a huge sum of finance from a bank, after the contract had been signed between the company and the bank. Suddenly, the bank decides not to give the agreed financing to Company A, which resulted in the value of the company's shares dropping and unfavourable comments being made by financial analysts. As a consequence, Company A is entitled to claim damages from the bank under this heading as it suffered an injury to its reputation as a result of the breach of contract by the bank.

According to *Shari'ah* principles, the award of damages granted by a court of law is aligned with that of the *Shari'ah*; that is, that the aggrieved party should be put in the same position as he would have been had the contract not been breached (Billah 2003). The right to receive damages as a result of breach of contract is based on the legal principle that:

> There shall be no unjust loss nor causing of such loss. (Billah 2003)

5 Rescission (*Iqalah*)

Rescission is another type of remedy for breach of contract, whereby an innocent party has the right to rescind a contract in all 'reciprocal' obligations in cases where the breach is material and the contract cannot be specifically performed due to the seriousness of breach (Billah 2003).

The Specific Relief Act 1950 generally provides for rescission in cases where the contracts are written. However, in relation to compensation payable when rescission is granted, there is no need for the agreement to be written (*Malayan Law Journal*, Sdn. Bhd., Kuala Lumpur, 2002).

Rescissions may adjudged by the court in lieu of any of the following cases:

- where the contract is voidable by the plaintiff;
- where the contract is unlawful but is not clear about its unlawfulness, and the defendant is more to blame compared to the plaintiff; and
- where a decree for specific performance of a contract of sale, or a contract to take a lease, has been made and the purchaser or lessee defaulted in the payment of the purchase money or other sums that the court had ordered him to pay (Billah 2003).

In general, rescission can take place without the involvement of a court, so that the parties to a contract can restore any benefits received under the defective contract; that is, if both parties agree to recognize that there was never a contract in the first place. If only one party accepts this interpretation, then the matter of rescission will have to go to the court to be settled (Billah 2003). In cases where a contract is defective due to a breach of contract (rather than the contract being defective due to faults in the formation of the contract), rescission under the headings of damages, rescission, or specific performance would be the only way to terminate the contract (Billah 2003).

However, rescission of a contract cannot be adjudged for mere mistake, unless the party against whom it is adjudged can be restored to almost the same position as though the contract had not been made (Billah 2003). Furthermore, a plaintiff who is establishing a suit of specific performance of a contract may wish to rescind, or even cancel, the contract if he sees that the contract cannot be enforced; or the court may refuse to enforce the contract specifically, and thus may opt for the contract to be rescinded (Billah 2003).

Additionally, the court may also require the party to whom the relief was granted (when the court adjudged the rescission of a contract) to make any compensation to the other party, if it sees that justice will be restored by doing so; this normally takes place when the plaintiff may have received a benefit under the contract that he is not in the position to return to the defendant (Billah 2003).

Thus, rescission can take place in cases where there is a defect in the formation of the contract, or when the performance of the contract is impossible. Thus, the court will only grant rescission to the innocent party if it finds that there is no possibility of the party performing the contract, had the court ruled him to do so. Therefore, in this case, breach of contract is so important that it justifies rescission in favour of the innocent party (Billah 2003).

6 Specific Performance

Under Islamic law, specific performance is another important remedy for breach of contract. This happens when a party to the contract fails to fulfil his part of a contract (breach of contract) and the other party applies to the court for an order that will force the party in breach to perform the contract according to its terms and conditions (Billah 2003). This is in line with the teachings of Islam; that is, for Muslims to honour and fulfil their obligations. Nevertheless, the court will first assess the possibility of the performance being carried out before granting remedy under specific performance. Hence, if the order of specific performance will result in 'hardship amounting to injustice', the court will not grant specific performance, even though there is material breach (Billah 2003). This is in line with the following Qura'nic verse:

> And when you judge between man and man, that you judge with justice. (Al-Quran, An-Nisa': 58)

Let us now discuss the issues and types of specific performance that are available under the Specific Relief Act 1950 (revised in 1974) (Sinnadurai 1987) (Fig. 3).

For specific performance, as a remedy for breach of contract, contracts may be specifically enforced. To illustrate, we refer to the case of Zaibun SA Binti Syed Ahmad *v.* Loh Koon Moy & Anor (1982) (Sinnadurai 1987), where the respondent had claimed specific performance of a contract for the sale of land against the appellant. The judge favoured the respondent but found that there was an oral agreement enabling the respondent to pay damages for breach; thus, the judge gave damages in favour of the respondents. The respondents appealed to the Federal Court seeking specific performance of the contract. The Federal Court held that the respondents were entitled to it because there was

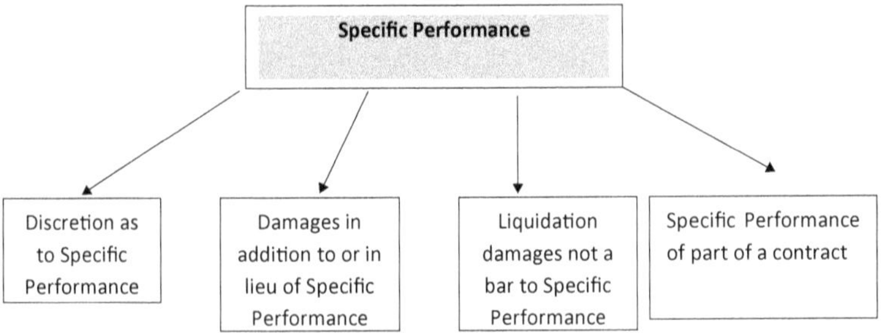

Fig. 3 Specific performance (*Source* Author's own)

insufficient evidence to show that the vendor had agreed to pay money to the purchaser in consideration of defaulting if the purchaser agreed not to claim specific performance and to claim only damages.

Regarding discretion as to specific performance, an issue in relation to specific performance can be illustrated with the case of Venkatachalam Chettiar & ORS *v.* Arunasalam Chettiar (1953) (Sinnadurai 1987). In this case, an agent negotiated with the plaintiff regarding the sale of land; an oral agreement was entered into and the agreed purchase money was paid in full. However, there was a delay in the delivery of the document of title due to the government's delay in assessing tax, which, under the law, had to be paid before registration could take effect. After tax was assessed, the purchasers immediately paid it to enable the transfer of land to be registered. However, registration could not be made due to the death of the registered proprietor. The administrator of the deceased proprietor refused to complete the contract and the plaintiffs sought for specific performance in court. The defendant resisted on two grounds: that the plaintiffs' claim was barred by limitation, and there would be hardship if the court were to exercise its discretion as requested. The judge ordered for specific performance on the basis that under Section 21(2) of the Debtor and Creditor (Occupation Period) Ordinance the court may exercise its discretion not to order specific performance where the performance would involve some hardship to the defendant that he had not foreseen, whereas its non-performance would involve no such hardship to the plaintiff. In this case, however, if the court had not ordered specific performance, the plaintiff would be in hardship as he would have been deprived of being the owner of the land.

The case of Lee Hoy & Anor *v.* Chen Chi (1971) (Sinnadurai 1987) refers to damages in addition to, or in lieu of, specific performance. In this case, parties agreed for the purchase and sale of land. The area of land was not stated in the agreement but the option for sale signed by the appellants was for nine acres (the sale price stated was $16,300). However, when the title document was issued, the area of the land was only 5.281 acres. The respondent thus applied for rescission and reimbursement. The judge refused to grant rescission because there had been no misrepresentation by the appellants. However, since the respondent had paid for nine acres, instead of the actual area, the judge ordered that the respondent be reimbursed accordingly.

In relation to liquidation of damages not being a bar to specific performance, Jones and Goodhart (Sinnadurai 1987) said that although a contract contains a liquidated damages clause, or a clause of a similar nature, it is not generally an admission that the parties have agreed that damages are an adequate remedy, or that one party has the option to pay or perform. Specific performance will still be granted if it is the appropriate remedy.

Finally, under the heading specific performance of part of a contract, this happens when parties have entered into an agreement and only part of the contract has been performed. Hence, the court may grant specific performance of a part of a contract whereby the party in breach will have to perform the balance of the contract. For instance, A and B entered into an agreement whereby A agreed to sell 100 lots of shares to B, but he sold only 50 shares, in anticipation that the prices would rise. Hence, B may claim for remedy under specific performance of part of a contract for A to sell to him the balance of the shares, at the agreed price.

7 Injunction

An injunction is 'an order of the court against a party to the effect that he shall do or refrain from doing a particular act' (Billah 2003). There are two principles governing the granting of an injunction (Sinnadurai 1987) (Fig. 4).

The first principle, the 'balance of convenience/prima facie' test, states that to be granted an injunction, the applicant must establish a probability or a strong prima facie case that he is entitled to the right due to breach of contract and, subject to this being established, the consideration granted will be the 'maintenance of status quo pending the trial'

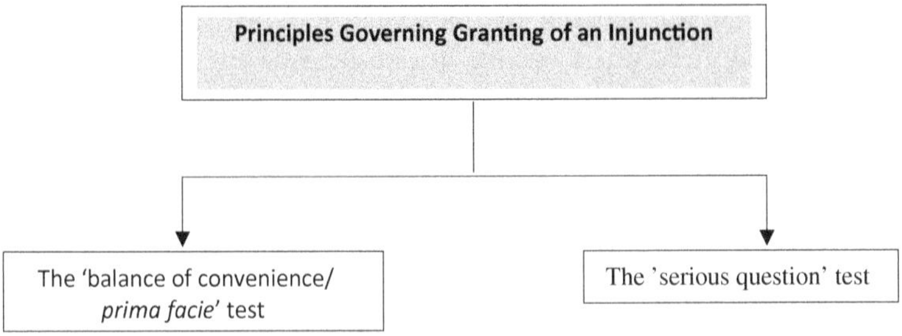

Fig. 4 Injunction (*Source* Author's own)

(Sinnadurai 1987). A case example in relation to this is Holiday Inns Inc. & Anor *v.* Hotel Enterprises Ltd. (1976). In this case, both parties entered into an agreement whereby the first plaintiff was to manage a hotel. The benefit of the management agreement was then passed to the second plaintiff, a wholly owned subsidiary of the first plaintiff. The defendant was dissatisfied with the management of the hotel and sought to terminate the contract. After some discussion, the first plaintiff was given (by the defendant) a 'grace period' of one month to wind up the operation. On expiration of the 'grace period', the defendant removed the first plaintiff's signs and took over management. In a previous action brought by the plaintiff, the court ordered an interim injunction that restrained the defendant from interfering with the second plaintiff's performance of the management agreement. The plaintiff then applied for an order from the court to allow the continuance of the injunction against the defendant. It was held that, since the management agreement was neither a contract of service, nor a contract of personal services, damages would be an inadequate remedy and the balance of convenience was in favour of the plaintiff—that is, the plaintiff was able to establish a strong *prima facie* case that it was entitled to an injunction.

As to the second principle governing the granting of injunction, the 'Serious Question' test needs to be fulfilled. For instance, in the case of Mohamed Zainuddin Bin Puteh *v.* Yap Chee Seng (1978) (Sinnadurai 1987), there was a Notice of Motion to set aside an injunction that was granted two years earlier (in 1976). From the Notice and affidavits supporting the application, the basis for the application of setting aside the injunction was because the plaintiff had not stated the facts fully and accurately to the court, and that he had not disclosed all material facts.

It was held that the motion to dissolve the injunction should be dismissed because there was a serious question to be tried and, thus, measures must be taken to preserve the status quo; that is, to maintain the injunction. It is said that, at that stage, the court was not justified in confronting anything that resembled a trial of the action on conflicting affidavits. Furthermore, in another case, Sivaperuman *v.* Heah Seok Yeong Realty Sdn. Bhd. (1979) (Sinnadurai 1987), it was held that for any plaintiff seeking interlocutory relief, it is necessary to show that there was at least a serious question to be tried, and to provide sufficient and accurate evidence to satisfy the court the he had a real prospect of succeeding in his claim.

For remedies for breach of contract, by way of injunction, there are two types of injunction: prohibitory and mandatory (see Fig. 5).

A prohibitory injunction, as its name suggests, is an order by the court that restrains a party from doing certain things that are contradictory to *Shari'ah* principles, or contradictory to the terms of a contract (Billah 2003). For instance, in the case of Broome (Selangor) Rubber Plantations *v.* R. H. Whitley (1919) (Sinnadurai 1987), the defendant entered into an agreement to serve the plaintiff for a period of three years and eight months. However, about one and a half years after the commencement of the contract, the defendant chose to terminate the contract. The plaintiff then sued for an injunction. It was held that, under Section 57 of the Specific Relief Act, the plaintiff were entitled to an injunction restraining the defendant from entering into employment as a manager or assistant on any plantation in the states of Selangor and Negeri Sembilan other than on the estate of the plaintiff until the expiry of their contract.

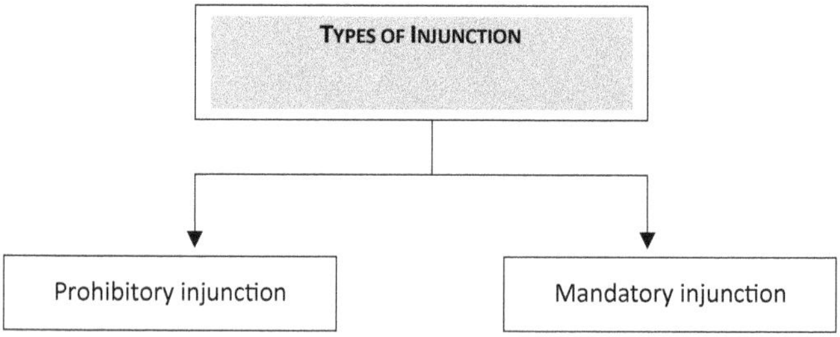

Fig. 5 Injunction (*Source* Author's own)

A mandatory injunction, on the other hand, is an injunction whereby the court may force a party, by way of law, to perform certain positive acts in relation to the stipulated contract. This type of injunction is akin to the court's order for specific performance (Billah 2003). An example is the case of Neoh Siew Eng & Anor *v*. Too Chee Kwong (1963) (Sinnadurai 1987). According to this case, the plaintiffs were the tenants of rent-controlled premises of which the defendant was the landlord. One of the terms of tenancy was that the defendant would pay $2 towards water charges and the plaintiffs would pay the sum in excess of that amount. Thus, the plaintiffs had an uninterrupted flow of water until later, when the water supply ceased due to the corroded state of the pipe. The defendant did nothing to repair the pipe and, thus, the plaintiffs sought an injunction. It was held by the court that the defendant was under an obligation to ensure the flow of water to the plaintiffs' premises and also to ensure that all pipes were in a proper state of repair, in order to comply with all regulations of the Waterworks Department. Thus, the plaintiffs were entitled to damages and a perpetual injunction that required the defendant to keep the water supply open.

For injunctions, there are instances where an injunction can be dissolved, or it can vary from the original cause for its existence. For instance, when there is the suppression of material facts, an injunction can be dissolved (Sinnadurai 1987). For example, in the case of Sari Artists Film Sdn. Bhd. *v*. Malaysia Film Industries Sdn. Bhd. (1974) (Sinnadurai 1987), there was an application to dissolve an *ex parte* injunction that restrained the defendant from distributing, screening or exhibiting an Indonesian film within Malaysia. Initially, the Indonesian court granted the injunction, but it was not disclosed that the order had been stayed, or that the defendant had denied distribution of the film in Malaysia. It was held by the Malaysian court that the plaintiff had suppressed material facts in his application for the *ex parte* injunction; hence, the injunction must be dissolved.

An injunction can also be dissolved if the facts on which the injunction was granted no longer exist (Sinnadurai 1987). For instance, referring to the above case of Broome (Selangor) Rubber Plantations *v*. R. H. Whitley (1919), if, for example, the company sold all its estates and plantations in Selangor and Negeri Sembilan before the employment agreement between the parties had ended, the facts no longer existed. That is, the plantations no longer belonged to the company. Consequently, the injunction imposed on the defendant could be dissolved.

The concept of an injunction is justified under *Shari'ah*, under which it is known that every individual has a common duty to 'enjoin good and forbid wrong' (Billah 2003). Allah said in the Qur'an:

> You are the best of people, evolved for mankind, enjoining what is right, forbidding what is wrong. (Al-Quran, Al-Imran: 110)

8 Current Phenomena

There are two court systems operating in Malaysia: the civil courts and the *Shari'ah* courts. The jurisdiction of the *Shari'ah* court is given in paragraph 1 of the State List in the Ninth Schedule of the Federal Constitution, which states that the *Shari'ah* courts shall have jurisdiction only over persons professing the religion of Islam and in respect of any of the matters set out in the paragraph, which includes:

> Islamic law and personal law and family law of persons professing the religion of Islam, including the Islamic Law relating to succession, testate and intestate, betrothal, marriage, divorce, dower, maintenance, adoption, legitimacy, guardianship, gifts, partitions and non-charitable trusts; *wakafs* and the definition and regulation of charitable and religious trusts, the appointment of trustees and the incorporation of persons in respect of Islamic religious and charitable endowments, institutions, trusts, charities and charitable institutions operating wholly within the state; Malay customs; *Zakat*, *fitrah* and *Bait-ul-mal* or similar religious revenue; mosque or any Islamic public places of worship; creation and punishment of offences by persons professing the religion of Islam against precepts of that religion, except in regard to matters included in Federal list; the constitution, organization and procedure of *Shari'ah* courts, which shall have jurisdiction only over persons professing the Islam and in respect only of any of matters included in this paragraph, but shall not have jurisdiction in respect of offences except in so far as conferred by federal law, the control of propagating doctrines and beliefs among persons professing the religion of Islam; the determination of matters of Islamic law and doctrine and Malay custom. (Wu 1996)

The jurisdiction of the *Shari'ah* court in the above matters is subject to certain federal law. The Federal List in Item 4 Civil and criminal law and procedure and the administrative of justice includes:

- Constitution and organization of all courts other than the *Shari'ah* courts;
- Jurisdiction and power of all such courts;
- Remuneration and other privileges of the judges and officers presiding over such courts;
- Persons entitled to practice before such courts;
- Subject to paragraph (ii) of the following:
  - Contacts, partnership, agency and other special contracts; master and servant; inns and innkeepers; actionable wrongs; property and its transfer and hypothecation, except land; *bona vacantia*; equity and trusts; marriage, divorce and legitimacy; married women's property and status; interpretation of federal law; negotiable instruments; statutory declarations; arbitration; mercantile law; registration of business and business names; age of majority; infants and minors; adoption; succession, testate and intestate; probate and letters of administration; bankruptcy and insolvency; oaths and affirmations; limitation; reciprocal enforcement of judgements and orders; law of evidence.
  - The matters mentioned in paragraph (i) do not include Islamic personal law relating to marriage, divorce, guardianship, maintenance, adoption, legitimacy, family law, gifts or succession testate and instate (Ibrahim 2003).

Item 7 of the Federal List includes 'banking, money lending, pawnbrokers, control of credit; bill of exchange, cheques, promissory notes and other similar instruments'.

From the above legislation, there is a clear-cut situation where all disputes arising in banking transactions are brought before the civil court and not the *Shari'ah* court. Even though Islamic banks and conventional banks operating Islamic counters are governed by the Islamic Banking Act (1983) and the Banking and Financial Institution Act (1989), neither of these acts exclude the application of civil law to Islamic banking transactions. In addition, there is no provision in either Act stipulating that Islamic law shall apply exclusively to Islamic transactions.

So, which law is to prevail in Islamic banking transactions? In this situation, Section 55 of the Islamic Banking (1983) should be considered. It reads as follows:

> An Islamic bank which is incorporated under the Companies Act 1965 shall be subject to the provisions of that Act as well as the provisions of this Act, save that where there is any conflict or inconsistency between provisions of that Act and the provisions of this Act the provisions of this Act shall prevail. (Islamic Banking Act 1983)

The purpose of Section 55 is to resolve any conflicts that may arise between the provisions of the Companies Act and the Islamic Banking Act. But the effect of Section 55 may be far-reaching due to the definition of Islamic banking business in Section 2 of the Islamic Banking Act. Furthermore, there may be a conflict between the Act and Islamic law, which is not specified in the Act. Thus, which Act should an Islamic bank use, especially in matters of disputes?

Due to the lack of such a specification, it has been presumed that both Islamic law and civil law can be applied to Islamic banking transactions, and that it has to be applied within the existing common law system of courts.

However, most of those laws and procedures were designed before the introduction of Islamic banking in Malaysia. Thus, those laws were not drafted or designed with Islamic principles in mind, or to facilitate the application of Islamic law. This raises different problems in enforcing Islamic law-based transactions in civil courts. There have been a number of decisions in the civil courts involving Islamic banking.

In the case of Bank Islam *v.* Adnan b. Omar (Ibrahim, n.d.; Rosly 2003), where Bank Islam had filed a suit in the Kuala Lumpur High Court for the recovery of an amount owing pursuant to a guarantee, the defendant raised a preliminary issue that, as the plaintiff was an Islamic bank, the civil court had no jurisdiction to hear the case since Item 4 of the Federal List states that the High Court has no jurisdiction in respect of any matter within the jurisdiction of a *Shari'ah* court. However, the judge overruled that preliminary objection. The plaintiff relied on the Ninth Schedule, List I and II, wherein it is stated that banking comes within the Federal List.

In Tinta Press Sdn. Bhd. *v.* Bank Islam Malaysia Bhd. (Ibrahim, n.d.; Rosly 2003), the respondent had agreed to provide facilities by issuing a letter of credit for the purchase of printing equipment that would be leased to the appellant, subject to certain conditions as laid down in the letter of offer. The appellant defaulted in the lease amount, leading to the respondent bringing an action to recover possession of the equipment and to recover the rent arrears. In addition, the respondent also made application for a mandatory injunction to enable the appellant to recover possession of the equipment. The court granted the injunction and the appellant applied to the High Court to set aside the injunction. The application was dismissed and the appellant appealed to the Supreme Court.

The appellant had argued that the lease agreement was, in fact, a loan agreement. However, the Supreme Court dismissed the appeal of the appellant. It was held that the relationship between the parties was that of lessor and lessee. As the respondent was the legal owner of the equipment, it had the right to restrict the appellant's possession and use of the equipment due to there being no rental receipt, based on the agreement. In this case, no reference was made to the Islamic Law relating to *ijarah* (leasing).

In Dato' Nik Mahmud bin Daud *v.* Bank Islam Berhad, there was a conflict between *Shari'ah* law and conventional laws. This case involves a *bai bithaman ajil* (BBA) transaction. The customer applied for financial assistance to the bank for a facility and the bank agreed to grant the customer the assistance under the BBA principle. Under this principle, the customer sold a property that he owned to the bank at a price pursuant to a property purchase agreement. Then, according to this principle, the bank would pay the purchase price and then immediately resell the said property to the customer at its purchase price plus profit pursuant to the property sale agreement. The consumer would pay the bank in instalments over a period of time stipulated in the contract. As security, the bank would create a charge on the property.

In this case, the land involved in the transaction was Malay reserve land subject to the Kelantan Malay Reservations Enactment 1930. The legal effect of such classification is that the land cannot be sold or transferred to a person who is not Malay (Kelantan Malay Reservations Enactment, 1930). All dealings or disposals in favour of a non-Malay are null and void (Ibrahim, n.d.; Rosly 2003). A transfer to a non-Malay may only be made with the approval of the State Ruler. However, the enactment allows non-Malays, such as banks, to make charges on Malay reservation land subject to their names being entered in Schedule D of the said enactment.

The customer has filed an application in court asking for the declaration that the property purchase agreement, property sale agreement and the charge created by Bank Islam were null and void on the ground that

Bank Islam is not a Malay. However, the court dismissed the application due to the fact that the name of Bank Islam is in the Schedule D list.

However, in the decision, the judge made a statement that has resulted in conflict between conventional and Islamic law. The judge gave the argument for the bank, mainly on the ground that the transaction is a financing transaction and not a sale and purchase transaction, which required the title to be transferred in a manner contrary to the enactment. However, this is contrary to the BBA principal, which involves a sale and purchase transaction and, supposedly, the title needs to be transferred.

In the cases above, the civil courts appear to have decided in favour of Bank Islam, but the cases were decided based on the principles of civil law and legislation. Although there were references to Islamic concepts such as *ijarah*, *qard al-Hasan* and *bai bithaman ajil*, there was no discussion of such concepts from the perspective of Islamic law. In the next section, we will discuss the case of Bank Islam Berhad *v.* Adnan bin Omar (Rosly 2003) in the light of Islamic law.

9 Case Analysis: Bank Islam Berhad *v.* Adnan bin Omar [1987] CLJ 396/[1987] 2 MLJ 192

9.1 Facts of the Case

In this case, the respondents had leased certain printing equipment to the appellant under the lease agreement of its letter of credit financing facility. The appellant having defaulted in payment of the monthly rentals, the respondent brought an action to recover possession of the equipment and to recover the arrears of rent. The respondent also made an ex parte application for and obtained a mandatory injunction to enable the respondent to recover possession of the equipment. The appellant then applied to dissolve and set aside the mandatory injunction. This was refused and the appellant appealed (https://uaelaws.files.wordpress.com/2012/05/brief-of-islamic-finance-cases-1987-2009.pdf).

The plaintiff had granted a loan of $583,000 to the defendant. The loan was secured on a charge on a certain parcel of land. The plaintiff granted this facility under the Islamic BBA loan scheme which, in effect, involved the execution of three simultaneous transactions between the parties:

- The sale of the subject property by the defendant to the plaintiff for \$265,000, which was duly paid by the plaintiff;
- The plaintiff's resale of the subject property to the defendant for \$583,000, payable in 180 instalments;
- The defendant executed a charge on the land as security for the debt of \$583,000.

It was a term stated in the charge document that, in the event of any default on the loan instalments by the defendant, the plaintiff would be entitled to sell the charged land. Subsequently, the defendant defaulted in his repayment and the plaintiff filed an originating summons under the Order 83 Rules of the High Court (1980) praying for an Order for Sale of the land to recover the said land.

The defendant raised the objection that the application and affidavit file in support did not comply with the Rules of the High Court, which required the amount 'advanced' by the bank, the interest paid and a daily interest amount to be stated in the affidavit in support of the application. According to the defendant, the plaintiff had not complied with the following Order 83 rule:

- *Order 83 rule 3(3)(a)*: The amount stated in the loan agreement, which was \$583,000, was never received by him as a loan. It was simply a facility amount and he received only \$265,000, which derived from the sale of the land.
- *Order 83 rule 3(3)(c)*: The plaintiff's claim did not include a claim for interest in the affidavit in support.
- *Order 83 rule 3(7)*: The plaintiff had omitted the clause 'the amount of a day's interest' in the supporting affidavit.
- *Order 83 rule 3(3)(d)*: The amount of \$543,995.89, which unpaid under the charge, was subject to rebate (*muqassah*).

The High Court gave judgement and granted order for sale in favour of Bank Islam based on the following reasons:

- *Order 83 rule 3(3)(a)*: The court accepted the amount of \$583,000 as the advanced amount in the plaintiff's claim. The transactions were made between both parties with the full knowledge of the defendant. He knew that the entire process had derived to the loan given to him by the bank; the repayment of that loan inclusive of a profit margin by him, and the charge was placed on his land as security for the loan. His knowledge of those transactions was evidenced by his acceptance of the letter offer. The transactions took place within the limits of Islamic law. Moreover, the two sale and purchase agreements in respect of the said land made reference to the BBA scheme. The court found that the parties were treating the amount of $583,000 as the facility amount given to defendant by the plaintiff, since the amount coincided with the cost of the land under the sale and was the amount intended to be secured by the charge.

- *Order 83 rule 3(3)(c)*: The context of this subsection stated that there must be an amount of interest or an amount of instalment payments in arrears on the given date, but not necessarily both. The court stated that the crucial condition was the fact that the defendant had defaulted on the payments. Since the loan was Islamic in nature, there was no question that the element of interest need be there. The plaintiff proved that the defendant has defaulted on his repayments, thus complying with this provision.
- *Order 83 rule 3(7)*: The act of omission of the plaintiff, who had omitted the clause 'the amount of a day's interest' in the supporting affidavit, was accepted by the court. This was because the loan was granted under Islamic principles. Thus, the plaintiff need not state the 'amount of the day's interest' since no interest was charged for the facility.
- *Order 83 rule 3(3)(d)*: The defendant was not entitled to a rebate; thus, the amount claimed by the plaintiff was deemed correct. Even though the loan had matured by this time, any payment he made would not entitle him to any rebate on the sum owed on the loan facility. A rebate (*muqassah*) is given by the plaintiff on a discretionary basis. In this event, the plaintiff was not required to give the defendant a rebate since he had defaulted on his repayments, which constitutes a breach of contract. Under these circumstances, the plaintiff could exercise his right to terminate the facility and demand the immediate full repayment of the loan. Thus, the plaintiff was entitled to $543,995.89.

9.2 Analysis of the Case

Based on the facts of the case, Bank Islam is entitled to remedies since the defendant had breached the contract. From the discussion in the previous section, there are several types of remedy available to Bank Islam. However, what remedies are applicable for Bank Islam in this situation?

From our point of view, the remedy available for Bank Islam is the self-help remedy; that is, the remedy that has been stated in the contract, which would come into effect on the breach of the contract. One of the remedies is that Bank Islam can take possession of the land and sell the land in order to recover the debt amount. In addition, Bank Islam is entitled to claim penalties due to the defendant failing to make repayment of the financing he had received. If the amount of any penalty is stated in the contract, Bank Islam is only entitled to claim penalties up to the stated amount. If the amount of the penalty is not stated in the contract, the aggrieved party (i.e. Bank Islam) can apply to the court for the amount of the penalty as compensation for the breach of contract.

We would now like to examine the decision of the case in the context of *Shari'ah* principles. First, we would like to examine the nature of the transaction. The loan was granted to the defendant under the BBA facility. The concept of BBA refers to the sale of the goods on a deferred payment basis at a price that includes a profit margin agreed by both parties.

So, the transaction between the parties is a sale and purchase transaction and not a loan transaction, as it had been treated by the court. This treatment by the court was against Islamic principles. To regard the transaction between the parties as 'the grant of a loan to the defendant by the Bank, the repayment of that loan inclusive of a profit margin by him and the charge of his land as security for the loan' would make the transaction illegal under Islamic law, as it would involve the payment of interest (Ibrahim, n.d.; Rosly 2003). Hence, in the eyes of Islam, the contract is not valid in the first place.

The court also needs to make distinctions between the 'advanced' amounts; that is, the loan amounts and the sale amount. Because the transaction is a sale and purchase transaction, it should be dealt with accordingly. The requirement by Order 83 (3)(3)(a) to state the advanced amount may not have been applicable in this case as there was no advance amount involved in this case. The amount that was applicable was the sale amount (i.e. $583,000).

With regard to the interest portion that was subjected to Order 83 (3)(3)(c) and Order 83 (3)(7), we as agree with the court's position, as no amount of interest should be stated in the affidavit in support of an Islamic contract. This is due to no element of interest being involved in the transaction, since the transaction is based on the Islamic principles.

In relation to the amount claimed and the rebate that should be given to the defendant, again, we as agree with the court. According to the Guidelines on the Interest-free Scheme 1993, a rebate (*muqassah*) is available to customers who make prepayments. We believe that no rebate should be given to the defendant, since he is in default. Any payments that he made previously should not constitute prepayment since the amount paid was to service the instalment arrangement.

However, looking at the position of the defendant in default, Bank Islam may wish to exercise its right to provide some rebate to the defendant based on the fact that a rebate can be given at the Bank's discretion. The Bank may apply the concept of *istihsan* in this situation.

The general definition of *istihsan* is equity. *Istihsan* literally means to approve or to deem something preferable (Azizan, n.d.). *Istihsan* is a method of exercising personal opinion in order to avoid rigidity and unfairness that may result from the literal enforcement of the existing law. In addition, *istihsan* also involves the process of setting aside the established ruling based on an available alternative, in order to protect and ensure the protection of justice and the public interest (Azizan, n.d.).

Istihsan needs to be used because the law available sometimes is either too general, or is too specific and inflexible. So, *istihsan* can play a role as the means to avoid the causing of hardship due to the course of law and as a solution that coincides with the *Shari'ah* objectives. *Istihsan* can also be used when the cases in question are not regulated by the incontrovertible authority of the Quran, the Sunnah of the Prophet or *ijma'* or when there is a conflict of principles (Azizan, n.d.).

Istihsan is an equitable concept that is based on the determination of the course underlying an existing legal rule. Therefore, it provides a systematic and rational process of reasoning because it is based on equitable consideration that may sometimes override the inequitable result of the legalistic analogy (Azizan, n.d.).

Now, let us analyse the case in the context of *istihsan*. In order to apply the *isthisan* concept to the case, Bank Islam could choose one of the following options:

- Forgive the defendant on the debt amount:

In this context, Bank Islam will make no claim on any of the amounts outstanding from the defendant. This act is the most preferable to Islam, based on the following *ayat*:

> If the debtor is in difficulty, grant him time, till it is easy for him to repay. But if you remit it by way of charity, that is best for you if only you knew. (Al-Quran, Al-Baqarah: 280)

This option might sound illogical for the Bank if it were to forgive the defendant for the whole sum of the loan while the said land remained with the defendant. However, Bank Islam may forgive the defendant for any shortfall of his facility after the land has been sold.

- Bank Islam can ask for part payment from the defendant. The amount that should be given has to be less than the sale price of $583,000. According to Article 256 of the *Majallah*:

> The reduction of the price by the seller, made after the contract, is good and effect is given to it. (Billah 2003)

However, the amount has to be a reasonable amount; this to ensure that no party is in a position of loss.

- If Bank Islam still wants to claim the whole outstanding balance, it should give the defendant an extension of time to enable the defendant to settle the whole sum. The Holy Prophet (*SAW*) spoke to this effect:

> Imran bin Husain (*R*) reported that the Messenger of Allah (*SWT*) said, Who has his dues from a man and gives time to him [for payment], he will be rewarded from the charity every day (Ahmad). (Billah 2003)

The time frame that will be given to the defendant has to be a reasonable period so as to ensure that the bank will not be in a position of loss.

- Bank Islam can also ask for part payment now and for the balance to be settled at a later date. For example, Bank Islam can ask the defendant to pay $100,000 as a part payment and that the balance of the debt owed to the bank (i.e. $453,000) to be settled by the defendant over a period of three years.

The act of the Bank operating under the principle of *istihsan* is aligned with the doctrine of Masalih al-Mursalah. According to this doctrine, any acts that are done in the public interest shall be accepted if they are to the benefit of the *Ummah*. The concept of *istihsan* in bank dealings did arise to the benefit of the *Ummah*. It allows Muslims to own property such as cars and homes, and encourages Muslims to invest. However, this should only be applicable in the case of a necessity—for example, needing houses and cars for personal use, and not for the purpose of the accumulation of wealth.

10 Recommendations

In order to ensure that the correct laws are used when making decisions on a dispute that relates to an Islamic banking transaction, we believe that the ideal solution is to separate cases related to Islamic finance transactions from the civil court. This means that any dispute regarding an Islamic banking transaction should be heard by a judge at a *Shari'ah* court, instead of by a judge at a civil court.

To make our suggestion viable, first, we need to extend the jurisdiction of *Shari'ah* courta to encompass a wider perspective. *Shari'ah* courts should be granted power to hear all cases involving Islamic financial transactions so that the applicable set of laws can be used. For example, the power of a *Shari'ah* court should be extended to cover all financial transactions that use *Shari'ah* principles, such as *musharakah*, *mudarabah*, *BBA*, *ijarah* and *istisna'*.

In addition, Malaysia will also need to establish a set of Islamic laws that will cover all the important aspects of Islamic financial transactions. These laws can act as guidelines and ensure that any dispute can be solved in an appropriate way by means of Islamic law. The new set of laws should include the specific criteria of Islamic banking transactions and the remedies available if a contract is breached.

However, to implement such a suggestion may not be viable for several reasons. First, it is costly and time-consuming to make drastic amendments to the current system. This is due to the range of resources required to conduct the changes. Moreover, political issues could be an obstacle for us to implement such a system. Politicians play an important role in passing and amending new legislation. Some politicians may not agree with the idea and lobby other politicians to reject it.

If the separation of powers cannot be achieved, some changes to the current legislation are needed in order to minimize the problems encountered in resolving matters relating to Islamic banking transactions. This is crucial due to the fact that there is an increase in the numbers of cases relating to Islamic banking matters.

First and foremost, the legislation needs to ascertain clearly which laws are applicable to Islamic banking, the sources of Islamic Banking law, and the basis on which the courts should decide whether one or more principles are in conflict. The legislation must also clearly state that, in the event that there is a conflict between civil laws and Islamic laws, Islamic laws shall prevail. The following amendments need to be made to ensure the current law can be made appropriate for current banking environments (Azizan, n.d.):

(i) Amendments to the Islamic Banking Act and the Banking and Financial Institution Act are needed to clarify the position of Islamic law in Islamic banking transactions. Both the Islamic Banking Act and the Banking and Financial Institution Act should have a general all-embracing provision to deal with situations of conflict among laws.
(ii) There are several existing laws that need to be amended to make them applicable to Islamic banking: the Contract Act (1950), the National Land Code (1965), the Stamp Act (1949), the Companies Act (1965), the Malay Reservations Enactment of the various states of Malaysia, The Rules of the High Court (1980) and the Subordinate Court Rules (1980). A comprehensive study is needed before any amendments can be passed by Parliament.

In accordance with the current law of evidence, expert evidence cannot be called if the issue relates to local law. In Malaysia, Islamic law is considered to be the local law. Thus, this prevents experts from being called to explain or clarify an Islamic legal perspective to a judge. We believe that this rule need to be relaxed in order to allow expert evidence to be given in court on any Islamic issue, or at least to allow for judges to be advised on Islamic law.

We feel that there is a need for Malaysia to establish one *Shari'ah* Advisory body for the whole country. The body should be called the National *Shari'ah* Advisory Council. This would require all the *Shari'ah* bodies currently in existence to be merged. This new Council should have a broad composition that includes Islamic scholars and jurists, bankers, lawyers and academics so that the advice given by the Council could incorporate the requirements of the banking community and the law in everyday practice, and also to take into account current thoughts and trends. This is important to ensure that the advice and rulings of the National *Shari'ah* Advisory Council is relevant and contemporary.

Furthermore, we foresee the need to have Islamic banking codes in Malaysia. This is due to the fact that Islamic banking services are offered not only by Islamic banks, but by almost all conventional banks. It is noted that there are differences in the practices of these banks and in the products that they offer. If the differences are not of a fundamental character, this is welcomed as the design will attract customers by offering them better services. However, if the differences conflict with *Shari'ah* principles this is not good for the development of Islamic banking, and can cause confusion among the public, including Muslims. So, Islamic banking codes should be set to cover all matters necessary for the proper and orderly conduct of Islamic banking.

11 Conclusion

We would stress once more that fulfilling contracts or agreements is a must for Muslims. Failing to do so for no concrete reason but simply choosing not to honour a contract is seen as a very bad act in the eyes of Islam and God Almighty. It is written in the Qur'an:

> For the worst of beasts in the sight of Allah are those who reject Him. They will not believe. They are those with whom you did make a covenant but they breach their covenant every time and they have not the fear of Allah (*SWT*). (Al-Qur'an, Al-Anfal: 55–56)

Based on the above verses, it implies how serious it is if a person were to breach a contract. When a person breaches a contract, the other parties to the contract are affected and may incur huge loss, be it in wealth or property. Nevertheless, Islam is not that rigid. There are instances where contracts can be cancelled; for example, if all parties to the contract unanimously agree to terminate the contract, or where it is impossible for one of the parties to undertake his obligations due to circumstances beyond his control.

As the consequence of a breach by only one party to a contract, as we have seen, there are remedies available to the other party who may suffer as a result of the breach. Hence, in the event that a contract has been breached, the aggrieved party has experienced a loss; by way of granting of remedies, either through courts or self-help remedies, the aggrieved party will be compensated, or his position may be restored as though the contract had not been terminated.

Relating to the issue of conflicting or confusing orders by the Malaysian court in relation to Islamic financial contract disputes, the authority needs to resolve this issue quickly and efficiently before confusion sets in for the whole community. Judges who handle disputes in relation to Islamic financial contracts must be proficient in this area; also, they must not use conventional and Islamic terms interchangeably in court, as this will confuse matters. Using proper Islamic terms is crucial to ensure correct understanding in matters of dispute.

References

Azizan, S. N. (n.d.). An Islamic Law Approach Where the Contract of Sale of Land Provides the Time Is of the Essence: A Particular Analysis to the *Union Eagle Ltd. v. Golden Achievement Ltd.* Available at www.mlj.com.my.

Billah, M. M. (2003). *Modern Financial Transactions Under* Shari'ah, Ilmiah Publishers, Selangor.

Halsbury's Laws of Malaysia (2002). Remedies, *Shari'ah* Law, *Malayan Law Journal*, vol. 14, Sdn. Bhd., Kuala Lumpur, at para. 250.008.

Ibrahim, A. (2003). *Resolution of Legal Dispute in the Financial Sector Accordance with Islamic Principles*, Institute of Islamic Understanding Malaysia (IKIM), Kuala Lumpur.

Rosly, S. A. (2003). Islamic Banking and Finance, Compilation of Articles and Papers for the Islamic Financial System.

Sinnadurai, V., Dr. (1987). *Law of Contract in Malaysia and Singapore: Cases and Commentary*, 2nd edition, Butterworths & Co. (Asia) Pte Ltd., Singapore.

Wu, M. A. (1996). *The Malaysian Legal System*, Longman Malaysia, Petaling Jaya.

PART III

Islamic Financial Products

CHAPTER 10

Islamic Equity Financing: *Al-Musharakah*, *Al-Mudharabah*, and *Al-Qiradh*

1 Introduction

The development of Islamic equity financing in Malaysia is a very interesting phenomenon that began to grow rapidly in the late 1970s and early 1980s with the establishment of the first Islamic banking with Bank Islam. Since that time, conventional banking has also taken on the provision of Islamic banking facilities. This is due to of the increase in demand for an Islamic banking system because of the growing awareness of the Muslim nation in Malaysia who wish to increase their wealth in accordance with Islamic principles and in interest-free arrangements.

The development of Islamic banking in Malaysia has come about for several reasons. First, positive environment with regard to the development of Islamic banking and support from interested monetary policy makers—such as our own government authority, the Ministry of Finance; and Bank Negara Malaysia. Second, the creativity of the financial institution itself in developing new products and services also played a vital role in this development. Bank Muamalat provides a variety of products and services, such as Muamalat BBA home or fixed asset financing, *al-wadiah* current or savings accounts and so on. None of these services was available in the early days of Islamic banking.

Third, current competition for foreign capital also improved the competitiveness of Islamic banking, rather than that of conventional banks.

M. M. Billah, *Islamic Financial Products*,
https://doi.org/10.1007/978-3-030-17624-2_10

The lack of foreign capital investment at the time had been considered an obstacle to sustaining the high growth rate of the Malaysian economy. The introduction of Islamic banking decreased reliance on foreign capital, as well as increased funding to Malaysia. Fourth, the nature of Islamic financing has shown that Islam promotes fairness and justice, which eventually lead to stability in the political and socio-economic environments. These are the reasons that attract the public invest in Islamic banks and their financing methods.

With the increase of Islamic institutions, the concept of *al-mudharabah*, *al-qiradh* and *al-musharakah* will be widely practised. This is because these concepts are the major source of financing in Islamic banks. This chapter analyses the basic concept of these methods that can be implemented in current practice. Here, we provide facts and information that we think are relevant to our topic; we believe that with the increased in Islamic institution there will certainly be growth in the services of *al-mudharabah* and *al-musharakah*.

2 Bank Islam Malaysia Berhad (BIMB)

Established: 1982

Principle: Entire operations and regulations are interest free. Offers all kinds of conventional banking system based on *Shari'ah* principles and deposits based on the *al-mudharabah* principle.

Products: Islamically accepted bills and Islamic export credit refinancing.

2.1 Interest–Free Banking Scheme

Objective: To open interest-free counters and offer Islamic banking services based on *Shari'ah* principles and deposits that use the *al-mudharabah* principle.

Participants: Malayan Banking Berhad (May Bank), Bank Bumiputra Malaysia Berhad (BBMB) and United Malayan Banking Corporation (UMBC). There were only three participants initially.

Achievements: 24 participants planned within one year comprising 13 commercial banks, 2 merchant banks, 8 financial companies and 1 Islamic bank (BIMB).

3 Equity Financing Instruments

3.1 Al-Mudharabah

One of the major sources of financing in Islamic institutions is the application of *al-mudharabah*. The practice of *al-mudharabah* is widely used in Islamic banking as it is an effective tool that coordinates well with the concept of an interest-free banking system.

In conventional banking systems, financing come from sources such as debentures, bonds, preference share and the like. In the case of a debenture, the debenture holder will usually receive payment or benefit in the form of dividend or interest. However, with the concept of *al-mudharabah*, financing through borrowing may be reduced or minimized as the *al-mudharabah* uses the concept of capital and entrepreneur. No borrowing or loan is involved. The capital provider will earn profit (not interest) generated by the entrepreneur. This concept will be further discussed later.

The literal meaning of *al-mudharabah* is 'aiming an arrow'. Here, we could relate that the target for the arrow is the objective of profit. However, the basic technical meaning of *al-mudharabah* can be divided into the views of two well-known schools of thought:

Hanafi school of thought: *Al-mudharabah* is a partnership with a view to profit, where capital is contributed by one party (the capital owner) and the other party (the *mudharib*) contributes the expertise of his labour.

Maliki school of thought: *Al-mudharabah* is the practice of hiring labour in which to invest one's capital and to share the profit jointly.

The Quranic ruling relevant to a *al-mudharabah* transaction is:

> O ye who believe! Eat not up your property among yourselves in vanities: But let there be amongst you traffic and trade by mutual good-will: Nor kill [or destroy] yourselves: for verily God hath been to you Most Merciful! (Ali, n.d.)

> He knoweth that there may be easy [some] among you in ill-health; others travelling through the land, seeking God's bounty; yet others fighting in God's Cause. (Ali, n.d.)

3.2 Traditional Practise of Al-Mudharabah

The practice has been widely applied during the time of the Prophet Muhammad (*SAW*) and also during the rule of the four Caliphs. Here, we are going to highlight two examples of the practice, which has become one of the most important *Shari'ah* rulings:

- *Al-mudharabah* was encouraged by the Prophet Muhammad (*SAW*) himself, and it was a common form of trading in the early days of Islam. Commercial enterprise in the time of the Prophet used to be organized under the charge of a caravan leader commissioned by one or more rich persons in the society (I. Doi, n.d.). One of the most apt examples is the wife of the Prophet himself, Saidatina Khadija, who could be considered to be a rich person that practises this type of transaction.
- Umar al-Khattab, Uthman Ibn Affan, Abdullah Ibn Mas'ud and Saidatina Aisha Ibn Abu Bakr used to invest the wealth of the orphanage. They acted as the regulators (played the role of entrepreneurs) of the wealth at that time. The rationale behind it was to further increase the wealth so as to avoid the wealth being exhausted by *zakah*, and to inject more funds into economic transactions—which we certainly know, at that time, was only at its inception.
- During the time of Caliph Umar al-Khattab, he assigned two of his sons, Abdullah and Ubaidullah, to Iraq. Their mission was to bring back treasury money for the *baitul mal* in Medina. A prominent leader in Iraq suggested that they buy some valuable merchandise from Iraq and sell it in Medina. They did what was suggested and bought the merchandise using the trusted money. When Umar al-Khattab was told about it, who at that time was known as the most trust worthy of men, became very angry. He commanded that both of his sons explain and justify their actions to the Shura Council. Following discussion, most of the scholars approved the transaction as *mudharabah* because the capital had been provided by the *baitul mal* and each of them had made the transactions as a *mudharib* (entrepreneur). Hence, the profit should be shared.

3.3 *Pillars of* Al-Mudharabah

According to Islamic *fuqaha*, there are five main pillars of *mudharabah*:

- *Performers*: These are the capital owner and the entrepreneur. The issue arises whether we could do business if one of the performers were a non-Muslim. According to Imam Shafie, whose view concurs with that of Imam Hanafi, a non-Muslim would be allowed to take part in *mudharabah* transactions. However, according to Imam Malik, non-Muslims should not be allowed to participate in *mudharabah* transactions as the source of funds may tainted by connection with *haram* activities, which would affect the dignity of the Muslim performer. Taking a modern perspective, we are in agreement with Imam Shafie and Imam Hanafi, as it is not easy to separate the two categories. Furthermore, we are living in a society that comprises various ethnicities, religions and cultures. So long as the transaction is in line with *Shari'ah* principles, it is agreeable to us that *mudharabah* transactions should be permitted. In this type of contract, a fixed amount of capital is handed over to the entrepreneur. The capital provider remains the owner of the capital and the entrepreneur is only in possession by virtue of the trust placed in him. He is only held responsible for negligence, or for breaking the rules of the contract.

- *Capital*: The capital should not consist of a debt owned by a debtor to his creditor; neither should it consist of a pledge or a security. The traditional practice specifies that capital should be in the form of money (e.g. gold and silver). Recent practice now allows it in the form of cash, stocks and cheques so long that the parties in a transaction know and recognize the value of the capital.
- *Labour*: The labourer or entrepreneur is the agent of the capital provider in his transactions. As an agent, he should run the business as agreed by the capital provider. The labourer is also obligated to run the business smoothly. If a loss is incurred by the business, he should explain the reasons for the loss, whether within or beyond his control. This is vital to both the capital provider and the labourer so they may analyse the problems and make further decisions regarding the business. As an agent, the labourer should act only within the stipulated terms agreed prior to entering into the transaction. He should not go beyond the authorized limits and should consult the capital provider or owner before making any major decision.
- *Profit*: Profit should be defined before the performers begin the transaction. Profit can be paid on a basis of percentage, ratio, or fraction of the capital and expertise. Profit should be distributed between the capital owner and the entrepreneur in the agreed

proportions. In the event of loss, the capital owner will bear the capital loss and the *mudharib* will have lost his effort and the expertise he provided.

- *Expression*: Both performers should have the intention of performing the transaction willingly without any pressure or coercion. The expression of this intention (*sighah*) in *al-mudharabah* should be clearly understood by both the entrepreneur and the capital provider and should be made either verbally or in writing by both parties because it prevents any harm befalling either partner in the future.

3.4 *Modern Practice of* Al-Mudharabah

Having seen the practice of *al-mudharabah* from the traditional perspective, we can form the general idea that its practice during early times was very simple, since the performers may be involved in only minor transactions. In modern practice, however, transactions will be more complex so as to suit the current economic situation, which involves a significant amount of capital and expertise. *Al-mudharabah* is now widely practised in the Islamic Bank of Malaysia, such as Bank Islam and Bank Muamalat. Further studies on the practice of *al-mudharabah*, which is also known as 'participation financing' in current practice, have revealed that transactions fall into three categories: demand deposits, mutual investment deposits and special investment deposits.

3.4.1 Demand Deposits

Customers deposit money in a bank. These deposits are not restricted in amount and are repayable on demand to the depositor, who share in the profits is given in the form of a dividend (see Fig. 1).

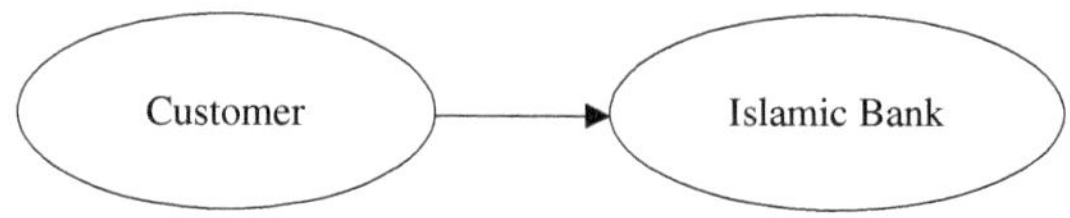

Fig. 1 Demand deposits (*Source* Author's own)

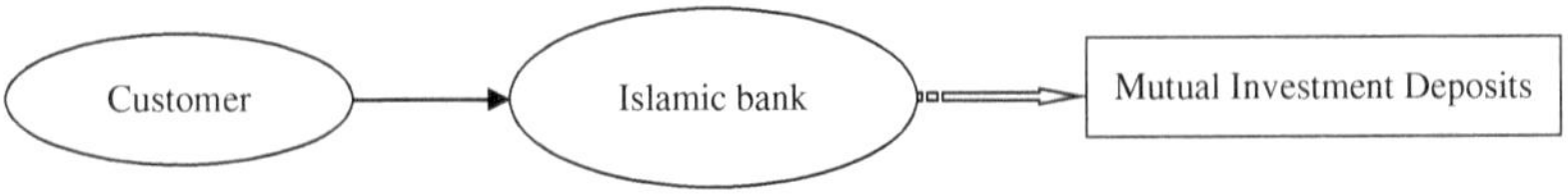

Fig. 2 Mutual investment deposits (*Source* Author's own)

3.4.2 Mutual Investment Deposits

Customers deposit money in a bank and the Islamic Bank will combine these deposits with the Bank's money in order that the customers may participate in mutual investment transactions conducted by the Bank. The percentage of profit generated by these deposits is fixed at the end of the Bank's financial year. Bank Muamalat Malaysia currently offers this investment method as *Al-Mudharabah* General Investment Accounts (see Fig. 2).

3.4.3 Special Investment Deposits

Customers deposit money and the Islamic Bank will invest these deposits in a specific project or investment at the request or on the approval of the depositors. The depositor in this case will be entitled to receive profit and is liable for any losses, provided that the Bank is not negligent or in default. At the end of the deposit period, the Bank receives its share of profit for its contribution of experience and management, while the depositor receives his share of profit as a capital share contributor. This method is currently practised in Bank Muamalat Malaysia as *Al-Mudharabah* Special Investment Accounts (see Fig. 3).

In all categories, we could see the depositor as the capital owner and the Bank as the entrepreneur who provides experience and management. There is, however, a reversal of this situation where the Islamic Bank contributes funds and the client (not the depositor) contributes expertise

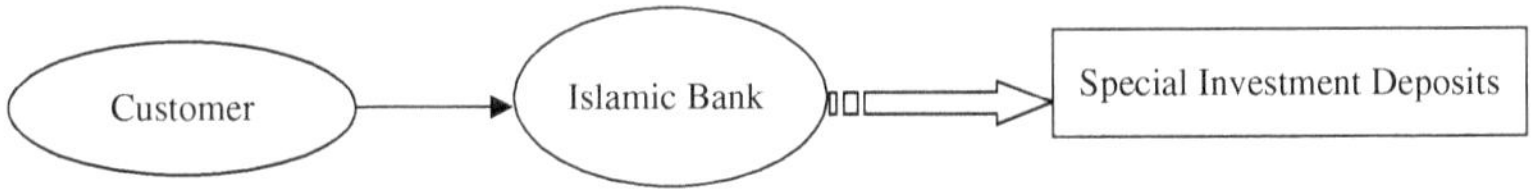

Fig. 3 Special investment deposits (*Source* Author's own)

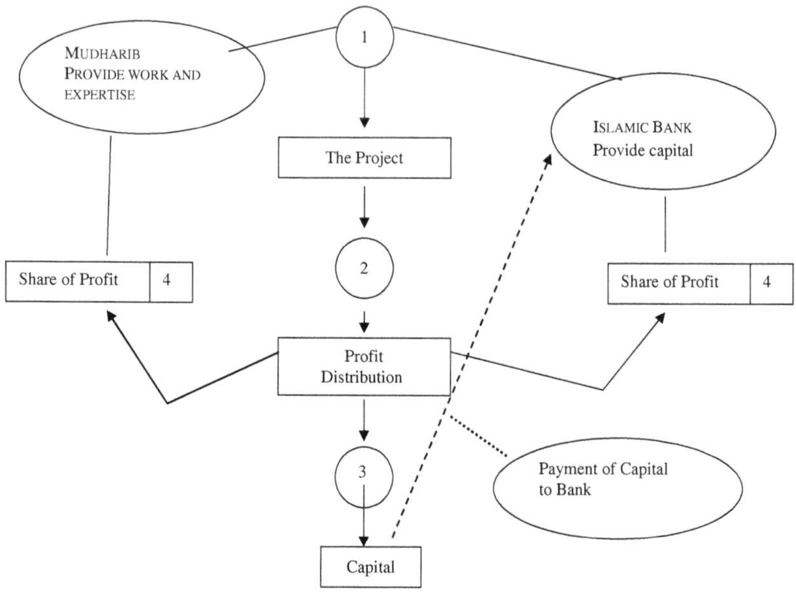

Fig. 4 Special investment deposits (*Source* Author's own)

and works to execute a potentially successful project. Profits are distributed in percentages agreed beforehand (see Fig. 4).

3.5 *Establishing an* Al-Mudharabah *Project*

- The Bank provides the capital as a capital owner.
- The *mudharib* provides his effort and expertise for the investment of capital in exchange for an agreed share of the profit.

3.6 *The Results of* Al-Mudharabah

- The two parties calculate the earnings and divide the profits at the end of the project. This can also be done periodically in accordance with the agreement provided there is observance of any legal rules.

3.7 *Payment of* Al-Mudharabah *Capital*

- The Bank recovers the *mudharabah* capital it contributed.

3.8 *Distribution of Wealth Resulting from* Al-Mudharabah

- In the case of loss, the capital owner (the Bank) bears the monetary loss (Al-Omar and Abdel-Haq, n.d.).

4 *Al-Qiradh*

Al-qiradh is very similar to the concept of *al-mudharabah*. The term *al-qiradh* also refers to the term *al-muqarada*, which connotes the same meaning as *al-mudahrabah*. Some scholars even classify it as the same transaction as *al-mudharabah* because the pillars of *al-qiradh* are more or less the same as those of *al-mudharabah* (Rukaini and Yaakob, n.d.), However, there are differences, which we will discuss below.

Al-mudharabah is based on the concept of a profit and loss sharing ratio. In the case of profit, the profit will be distributed as agreed; in the event of loss, only the capital owner will bear the capital loss while the entrepreneur will bear the loss of work, effort and expertise provided, as it is he who had undertaken the daily management activities. However, in *al-qiradh*, even though the distribution of profit is the same as with *al-mudharabah*, a significant difference exists regarding the distribution of loss. In *al-qiradh*, the entrepreneur bears the loss of capital as he must pay the amount of capital lost back to the capital provider, plus he has lost all the effort he provided. The capital provider is actually secured before the contract has even begun. This is known as securitization (see Fig. 5).

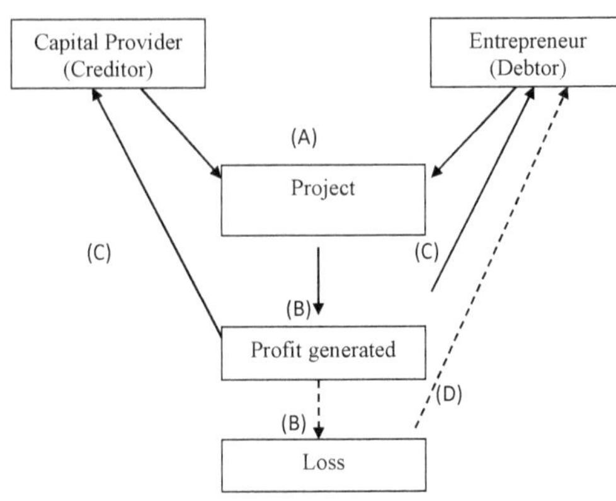

Fig. 5 *Al-qiradh* (*Source* Author's own)

- Both parties will enter into the contract; the capital provider will provide capital and the entrepreneur will provide experience and effort.
- Profit or loss will be generated from the project.
- In the event of a profit, the amount will be distributed based on the agreed proportions.
- If a loss is incurred, only the entrepreneur will bear the amount of loss and will need to pay such sum back to the capital provider. Hence, the entrepreneur will become a debtor to the capital provider.

In the *al-mudharabah*, we can see that the risk is distributed equally between the capital provider and the entrepreneur. This is confirmed by looking at the loss distribution. However, in *al-qiradh* the risk is not distributed; it is the responsibility of only one of the parties (the entrepreneur).

Al-mudharabah is a method of financing that can be used for either long-term or short-term finance. However, *al-qiradh* it is typically used for short-term finance. According to this, we would classify *al-mudharabah* as belonging to macro financing, while *al-qiradh* belongs to micro financing.

The practice of *Al-mudharabah* is in line with the requirements of *Shari'ah* compliance. This form of contract is accepted by all Muslim scholars. The concept of *al-qiradh*, however, is not in total compliance with *Shari'ah* ruling. Most Muslim scholars do find this type of contract acceptable.

Looking at current practice, *al-mudharabah* can be applied in the case of a limited company, as whatever the parties contribute will be the amount of loss borne by either party. *Al-qiradh*, in contrast, can be applied to an unlimited company; this is because we can clearly see that the entrepreneur will still bear liability for an amount that he did not contribute. The entrepreneur has to pay the amount of the loss to the capital provider even if he has to find the amount from his own property.

4.1 Positive Impact on the Concept Al-Mudharabah *and* Al-Qiradh

These contracts:

- bring together the potential of human and capital resources for the benefit of not only economic development, beneficial social aspects;

- increase wealth in efficient and permissible ways as prescribed in the *Shari'ah*;
- permit those who have ample capital to be involved in any business so that their money will generate profit and wealth in a permissible manner;
- permit those with expertise and experience to play an active and productive role in business transactions; hence, this will upgrade their status in life;
- caters transactions for financiers and entrepreneurs alike, encouraging or promoting Muslim participation in business and eventually promoting the welfare of the nation in terms of the standard living, also promoting society's employment rate and its daily benefits;
- give direct awareness to the nation of Islam that wealth and quality expertise is an important asset to a country.

5 *Al-Musharakah*

Al-musharakah can be classified as a group of shareholders financing a project. It also can be defined as a combination of wealth from various groups being used for business purposes. In return, the persons or bodies providing the finance will receive a proportion of the profit. Therefore from its very definition, *al-musharakah* can be classified as a type of equity financing. Generally, *al-musharakah* can be further classified as:

5.1 Al-Inan

Al-inan is a partnership formed by the combination of wealth by the partners for business purposes and, in return, the profit or loss achieved is distributed based on the proportions of the contributions of capital.

5.2 Al-Abdan

Al-abdan is a partnership performed by two parties that contribute labour, expertise or effort as capital to the business. Examples of this are the service industries, such as doctors, legal firm, or auditing firms. The partners will share in the profit based on the labour, expertise or effort contributed.

5.3 Al-Mutawadhah

Al-mutawadhah is when partners agree to work together on an operation or project with the condition that any investment, management or responsibility of the company will be under the control of all the partners equally.

5.4 Al-Wujuh

Al-wujuh is a partnership formed when partners agree to work together to buy something on credit where they are wholly dependent on such credit, and any profit gained is distributed among them.

Based on agreement between the famous Islamic schools (*Maliki*, *Hambali*, *Shafie*, *Hanaafi*) *al-inan* is allowable and is recommended to a greater degree in comparison with other forms of *al-musharakah*. This is due to the fact that each school holds a differing opinion regarding the types of *al-musharakah*.

5.5 *Traditional Practices of* Al-Musharakah

Al-musharakah has been practised since the time of the Prophet Muhammad (*SAW*) and he, in fact, took part in certain kinds of partnership and approved of them. Examples from a *hadith* and the Qur'an discuss the permissibility of *al-musharakah*:

> The Prophet Daud (*AW*) said: 'He has undoubtedly wronged thee in demanding thy (single) ewe to be added to his [flock of] ewes; truly many are the Partners [in business] who wrong each other: Not so do those who believe and work deeds of righteousness, and how few are they?'… And David gathered that we had tried him: he asked forgiveness of his Lord, fell down, bowing [in prostration], and turned [to God in repentance]. (Ali, n.d.)

> Rasulullah (*SAW*) said, 'Allah (*SWT*) had commanded that, I will be the third from two people who commenced business, as long as one of them did not disobey each other.' (Sahih al-Bukhari)

5.6 *Pillars of* Al-Musharakah

- Based on the *Hanafi* school of thought, only two pillars are required: *ijab* and *qabul*.
- The percentage of profit distributed to the partners needs to be clarified.

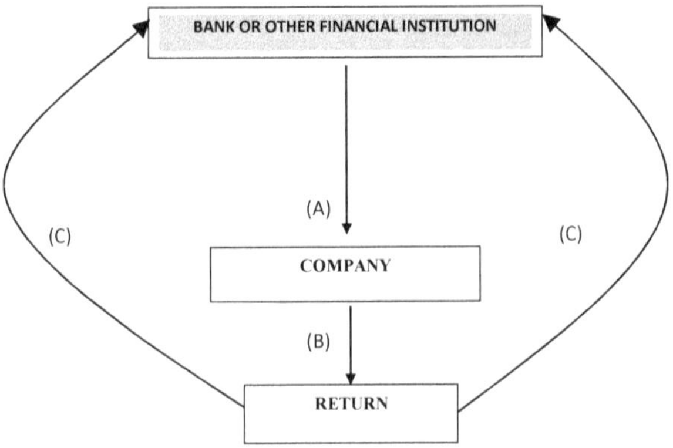

Fig. 6 Equity participations (*Source* Author's own)

- Profit must be distributed to all partners.
- Capital is in form of movable property and is easily measured (e.g. cash) and in existence during *ijab* and *aabul* (not being in the form of debt) (Fig. 6).

5.7 *Modern Practices of* Al-Musharakah

Modern practices of *al-musharakah* are similar to venture capital investment, whereby the bank or some other financial institution becomes one of the shareholders in a company. The company can be either newly established or an existing company. In both of these cases, the investing body will be represented on the board of that company. In return, the capital provider will receive return in the form of a declared dividend or the disposal of shareholdings at the appropriate time (Fig. 7).

5.8 *Joint Venture Projects*

In joint venture projects, the parties to the agreement:

- finance a project by providing cash or other valuable assets;
- are responsible for any profit or loss generated by a project;
- share any profit or loss generated according to the percentage of their shareholdings in the company.

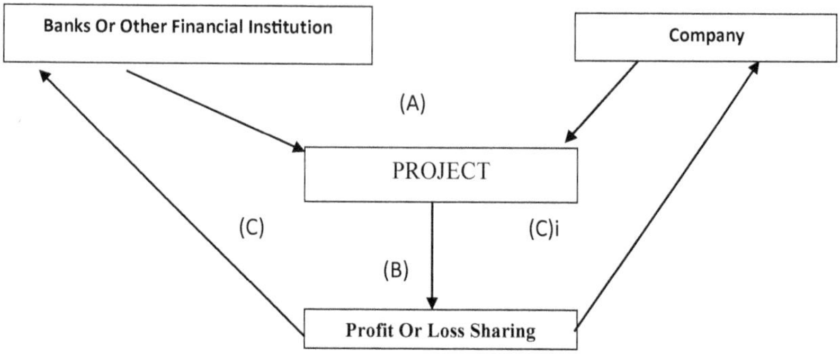

Fig. 7 Joint venture projects (*Source* Author's own)

Alternatively, a financial institution may finance a selected project of a company (rather than the company itself) and will share the profit or loss of that particular project based on pre-agreed ratios. In this case, both parties will provide capital in terms of cash and both parties jointly own other valuable assets and the pool of assets. Losses are shared according to the percentage of shareholding in the company.

References

Al-Omar, F., and Abdel-Haq, M. (n.d.). *Islamic Banking: Theory, Practise & Challenges*, Kuala Lumpur.

Al-Omar, F., and Abdel-Haq, M. (1996). *Islamic Banking: Theory, Practice & Challenges*, Bangalore Town.

I. Doi, A. R. (n.d.). *Tijarah: Trade and Commerce: Shari'ah the Islamic Law*, Kuala Lumpur.

Rukaini, A. R., and Yaakob, M. A. (n.d.). *Siri Teras Ulum Islamiah Muamalat: Teras Pembangunan Sosio-ekonomi*, Kuala Lumpur.

CHAPTER 11

Islamic Debt Financing

1 Introduction

Islamic banking activities in Malaysia began in the early 1980s with the enactment of the Islamic Banking Act 1983, which defines the nature and function of an Islamic bank. In the Qur'an, the explicit prohibition of *riba* has made *al-bay'*—trade and commerce—the alternative to debt contracts in the banking business. The Malaysian Banking and Financial institution Act 1992 (BAFIA) stipulates that commercial banks can only perform lending and borrowing activities. By virtue of the nature of *al-bay'*, the Islamic Banking Act 1983 therefore gave Islamic banks the opportunity to provide non-traditional banking facilities, such as venture capital, stockbrokerage, fund management, insurance and the like to be offered under one roof.

Since March 1993, banks and finance companies have been competing against each other to come up with an interest-free or *Shari'ah* based products. Despite the fact that conventional banking and finance have been in practice for centuries, the Islamic concept is here to stay. Nowadays, Muslims are returning to religion for spiritual strength and the dictates of Islam, which forbid any element of interest such as that found in conventional banking.

There are three major components to finance in an Islamic banking scheme; these are offered by our local banks: overdrafts, term financing and bill financing. These three schemes can provide capital for many

M. M. Billah, *Islamic Financial Products*,
https://doi.org/10.1007/978-3-030-17624-2_11

industries in our nation; for example, agriculture, manufacturing, construction, residential property, real estate, transport and so on.

2 Central Idea

Two of the most common debt financing instruments in the Islamic banking system are BBA and *murabahah*. These two instruments are mostly used in the banking sector in Malaysia as products provided to the public to finance their needs. We will be focusing on Malaysian Banks for this chapter to research these instruments and also to compare their offerings with those of other commercial banks. We will see how these two instruments are used as part of the ongoing objective to provide the public with Islamic banking products.

The chapter will discuss *Shari'ah* rulings and the framework that governs Islamic debt financing. Such *Shari'ah* rulings or laws will ensure that practitioners stay on the right track when developing Islamic debt financing. This will attract not only Muslim customers, but also non-Muslim customers to use Islamic debt financing, which will propagate Malaysia's economy, rather than choosing to use the conventional banking and finance systems that are widely available in the current market.

The application or practical scenario of Islamic debt financing will also be discussed, as it will clarify the picture of practice so far, and the achievements by those practitioners and the benefits gained by the consumer. The chapter goes on to touch on the issues related to the topic and offers various recommendations so as to show the level of our understanding of the topic. This chapter may be of benefit to the industry.

3 *Shari'ah* Rulings

3.1 Islamic and Interest-Free Financing

One of the common features of Islamic debt financing today is the fact that it is free from any kind of *riba*, which seems to be the only visible attribute of Islamic financing in Malaysia (Rosly, n.d.). The application of interest-free transactions is the best approach through to fulfil our responsibilities to society as a whole. The application of debt financing without any addition to the interest is important, since *riba* has been expressly prohibited in Islam, as set forth in the following Qur'anic passage:

> O you who believe, do not consume riba with continued redoubling and protect yourself from God, perchance you may be blissful. (Al-Imran: 130)

> Those who devour usury will not stand except as stand one whom the Evil one by his touch had driven to madness. That is because they say: Trade is like usury, but God had permitted trade and forbidden usury. Those who after receiving direction from their Lord, desist, shall be pardoned for the past; their case is for God [to judge]; but those who repeat [the offence] are companions of the fire: they will abide therein [forever]. God will deprive usury of all blessing, but will give increase for deeds of charity; for he loved not creatures ungrateful and wicked. (Al-Baqarah: 274–276)

The Qur'anic verses quoted above are very clear in the prohibition of *riba*. That is not all. The highly heinous nature of *riba* is evidenced by the fact that the Qur'an and *hadith* articulate its prohibition, in the strongest terms that are not used for any other sin, and its prohibition is mentioned several times. One *hadith* repeats several times that it is a sin worse than incest.

In Islamic banking, we see the application of BBA and *murabahah* contracts as alternatives to interest-based loans. The creation of profit in *murabahah* and BBA financing is consider legitimate because trading and commerce (*al-bay'*) is capital with labour. *Riba* profits are not a legitimate form of income because they are created from 'capital divorced from labour'. That is, the bank does not take an active and meaningful role in converting the capital input into final output.

However, as an intermediary a bank may find it too demanding to be directly involved in production, such as manufacturing or farming. The risks in production are too overwhelming. Banks have refused to combine their loan capital with labour out of fear that the business entity in which both capital and labour are combined will close down due to market risks. As a consequence, Muslim economists further argue that *riba* is prohibited because there is no risk-taking in the banking business.

3.2 Rules of BBA and Murabahah

As BBA falls under the category of sale (*bay muajjal*), *Shari'ah* rules on sales differ very little from those on *murabahah* and are applicable as follows:

- The object that is the subject of the contract must exist, otherwise the contract is void.
- The object must be owned and possessed by the seller (the bank).
- The price must be fixed, otherwise the transaction would be tantamount to two sales in one, which is prohibited by the Prophet Muhammad (*SAW*).
- No conditions should be attached. (Usrah Discourse Module, n.d.)

3.3 *Legality of BBA and* Murabahah

Although, in reality BBA and *murabahah* have not fulfilled some of the above prerequisites, there is evidence to uphold the legality of them on the following grounds:

> O you who believe! When you contract a debt to a fixed term, record them in writing. (Qur'an 2:282)
>
> The Prophet Muhammad bought a camel from Jabil and the payment was made in Madinah after arrival: the *Mejelle* (Article 245) says that a sale for deferred payment by instalments is good.

Time value of money. *Shari'ah* recognizes the time value of money. There are certain contracts based on the prevalent rate, such as dowry (*mahr*), salary or wage (*ujarah*), compensation(*'iwad*). (Usrah Discourse Module, n.d.)

3.4 *Practical Scenario and Applications*

3.4.1 Bai' Bithaman Ajil (BBA) *Financing*
Bai' bithaman ajil (BBA) (a deferred payment sale) refers to the sale of goods on the basis of a deferred payment at a price that includes a profit margin agreed by both the buyer and seller.

See http://maybank.com.my.

Scope

- Financing purchase of residential properties;
- Financing completed properties under construction;
- Refinancing/redeeming a housing loan from another financial institution;
- Redraw facility (i.e. for existing housing loan customers with a good repayment track record);
- Re-mortgage.

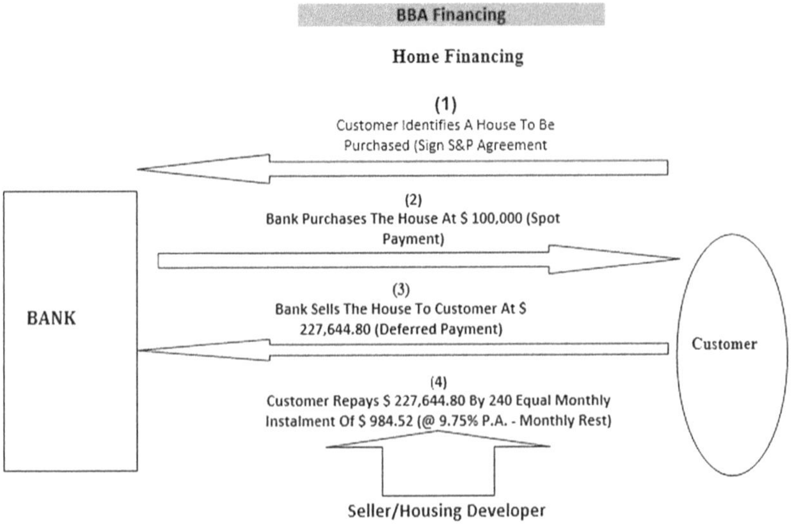

Fig. 1 *Bai' Bithaman Ajil* (BBA) financing

Features

- Fixed financing cost throughout the tenure of financing;
- No security deposit is required;
- 100% financing of mortgage reducing term assurance (MRTA)/ Long-term house owner *takaful* premium;
- Conversion of conventional housing loans to BBA house financing, subject to an applicant's execution of fresh legal documentation;
- Minimum property value of $75,000 and a minimum financing amount of $25,000 (Fig. 1).

4 *Murabahah* Overdraft

4.1 Concept

Murabahah is another type of sale and purchase contract with a deferred payment element. The contract of sale may take place when a buyer who wishes to purchase assets requests the bank to purchase assets at cost (purchase price) and, in return, the bank will charge the buyer an agreed profit margin that is incorporated into the selling price. The selling price is subsequently payable on a deferred single payment.

4.2 *Eligibility*

Murabahah is available to:

- Muslims and non-Muslims individuals, or to joint account holders;
- Companies incorporated under the Companies Act.

4.3 *Scope*

- For working capital requirements;
- For personal consumption;
- For purchase of assets/properties.

4.4 *Features*

- Fixed financing cost throughout the agreed tenure of financing;
- No commitment fee on unutilized amount;
- Maximum financing period (tenure) for a particular profit rate is 12 months; however, the availability period is unlimited, subject to periodical review;
- Also available for shorter financing periods of three, six and nine months;
- The profit rate will be reviewed and/or re-priced on a periodic basis;
- The profit rate is on a par with the consensual overdraft rate at the time of application;
- Third-party financing is allowed.

Further details are available by visiting http://maybank.com.my.

5 The Application of *Al-Murabahah* in Modern Islamic Banking

5.1 *Letter of Credit Under Contract of* **Al-Murabahah** *(Deferred Lump-Sum Sale or Cost Plus)*

At times, a customer engaged either in trading or manufacturing may need to purchase merchandise or raw materials in the course of his business. In this case, the customer requires a letter of credit together with the necessary financing over a certain period of time. The bank would offer him a letter of credit *al-murabahah* facility. The customer then informs the bank of his letter of credit requirement and requests the bank to purchase or import the goods, indicating thereby that he is willing to purchase the goods from the bank on the principle of *murabahah*. The bank establishes the letter of credit and pays the proceeds to the negotiating bank utilizing its funds. The bank sells the goods to the customer at a price comprising its cost and a profit margin under the principle of *al-murabahah* for settlement on the deferred terms (BIMB 1994).

6 Working Capital Financing Under the Principle of *Al-Murabahah*

The customer may approach the bank to provide finance for his working capital requirement to purchase stock and inventories, spares and replacements, or semi-finished goods and raw materials. In this case, the bank either purchases the required goods, or appoints the customer as its agent to purchase the required goods on its behalf, and settles the purchase price from its own funds. The bank subsequently sells the goods to the customer at an agreed price comprising the cost price and a profit margin, allowing the customer to settle this sale price on a deferred term of 30 days, 60 days, 90 days or any period that may be agreed between the parties. On the due date, the customer pays the bank the agreed sale price (BIMB 1994).

6.1 Issue on Islamic Debt Financing

The rate that is imposed on the BBA facility is fixed. This also means that the bank's profit from BBA products is fixed (Rosly 1999). The rate cannot be adjusted because changing the rate would mean that there would be an element of probability in the product offered; this is considered *riba* and thus makes the contract null and void. Since Islamic banks cannot change the contractual rate of the contract, this situation would cause an Islamic bank to be vulnerable to economic volatility. This means that Islamic banks have very little choice in defending their market share in financing products and the proportion of bank revenue they represent because Islamic banks cannot change the rate to suit their need to react to interest rate changes. Table 1 presents an example of such a situation.

Table 1 Debt Financing

Conventional banks	*Islamic banks*
Bank Profit = (contractual interest rate on loans × size of loans) – (interest rate on deposits × size of deposits)	Bank profit = [**contractual BBA profit rate (fixed)** × size of BBA] – (costs of deposits × size of deposits)
Example	
Bank profit = (10% × $100 million) – (6% × $100 million) = $4 million	Bank profit = (10% × $100 million) – (6% × $100 million) = $4 million
(1) If interest rate increases from 10 to 12%	**Interest rate has to remain constant**
Bank profit = (**12%** × $100 million) – (6% × $100 million) = $6 million	Bank profit = (**10%** × $100 million) – (6% × $100 million) = $4 million
(2) If interest rate decreases from 10 to 8%	**Interest rate has to remain constant**
Bank profit = (**8%** × $ 100 million) – (6% × $100 million) = $2 million	Bank profit = (**10%** × $100 million) – (6% × $100 million) = $4 million
(1) If interest rate increases from 10 to 12% and deposit interest increase to 8%	**Interest rate has to remain constant, but Islamic deposit interest increase to 8%**
Bank profit = (**12%** × $100 million) – (8% × $100 million) = $4 million	Bank profit = (10% × $100 million) – (6% × $100 million) = $2 million

Source Author's own

There are several situations whereby Islamic banks, conventional banks, Muslim customers, non-Muslim customers, Muslim depositors and non-Muslim depositors are affected.

Example 1 Assuming that deposit interest remains constant, suppose that conventional banks increase their interest on loans so as to follow the current market interest rate from 10 to 12%. Islamic banks, however, have to keep their interest on their BBA facility at 10%. This gives conventional banks an increase in profit of 2% (or $2 million), and Islamic banks an opportunity loss of $2 million. A consequence of this is the promotion of the BBA facility by Islamic banks, as it offers customers a lower premium rate. This will attract non-Muslim customers and also gives Muslim customers already enjoy the benefits of a BBA facility assurance that their BBA facility is at a lower cost than that of conventional loans.

Example 2 Assuming that deposit interest remains constant, conventional banks decrease their interest on loans so as to follow the current market interest rate from 10 to 8%. Islamic banks, however, have to keep their interest on their BBA facility at 10%. Due to the decrease, conventional banks experience a 2% (or $2 million) loss in their revenue, giving Islamic banks an opportunity gain of $2 million. A consequence of this is a decrease in the number of customers requiring the BBA facility because it now offers customers a higher interest rate. This will drive away non-Muslim customers and is confirmation to Muslim customers who already enjoy the benefits of a BBA facility that they are paying a higher interest rate compared with conventional loans.

Example 3 This is similar to Example 1, in which the interest rate increased from 10 to 12%, but the deposit interest rate is different. Here, the Islamic bank increases their deposit interest from 6 to 8% so as to capture more customers, but this gives rise to a decline in their profit margin. This situation shows that Islamic banks have very few options to increase their profit margin because the only controllable variable they have is the deposit interest.

The examples given above demonstrate that Islamic banks seem to be in a situation where their fate is predetermined by changes in the market interest rate (although these changes do not affect the fixed interest or premium rates): interest rate changes can work in favour of them or against the m. The situations described above can also work to the benefit of Muslim customers and non-Muslim customers using Islamic banks' BBA facility. These are the issues that Islamic banks have to face when offering BBA and *murabahah* facilities (both of which have fixed interest rates) to the public; demand for the products may increase or decrease.

7 Conclusion

Nowadays, the application of Islamic financing is expanding throughout Muslim countries, especially Malaysia. One of the common features of debt financing today is the fact that it is free from *riba*. This is probably the one clear feature of debt financing from the Islamic perspective that we can see today, even though there is more to Islamic debt financing than that. We can see how the application of BBA and *murabahah* contracts in Islamic debt financing act as an alternative to conventional debt financing.

However, Islamic finance is not only about interest-free financing. What is important is the human relationship itself, in which the elements of *amanah* and cooperation are the major features to focus on. This is proven by the problems entailed in principal and agent relationships that complicate financial transactions undertaken by society. The problem is not simply about the debt or equity instrument but, rather, how the contract is drawn up to fulfil man's desire for financial gain.

In fact, the implementation of interest-free banking is considered to be similar to the basic tenets of fasting, as reported by Saiful Azhar in his article 'Business and Islam' published by *The Sun*. Muslims may find it difficult to see the inner meaning behind the prohibition of *riba*, which calls for an equitable approach to wealth creation. Muslims are well aware that fasting is not only about refraining from eating or drinking, but also including the acquisition of steadfastness (*samadiya*). Unfortunately, most Muslims did not know how to perform fasting exactly as required by the *Shari'ah*. They only know how to abstain from eating and drinking, and no more than that.

It is therefore not wrong to conclude that Islamic financing today is similar to ordinary fasting. Legally, it is *halal* but, in spirit, it has yet to show how justice is put into practice in commercial life. The fact is that Islamic banking is not sufficiently eager to venture into new value-added investment activities to compete with conventional banks.

What is more, there are certain weaknesses in Islamic financing. The practice of an Islamic bank to use a BBA contract to finance a customer wishing to buy a house under construction should be reviewed in light of the fact that the object of the contract does not yet exist. Certain Islamic scholars have proposed that an Islamic bank should adopt *al istisna* contracts instead, because they fulfil *Shari'ah* requirements.

References

BIMB. (1994). 41, 102.

Rosly, S. A. (1999). BBA as an alternative to conventional loans, *The Sun*, Malaysia, 2 February.

Rosly, S. A. (n.d.). Business and Islam, *The Sun*, Malaysia.

Usrah Discourse Module. (n.d.). Muamalat, 3rd year, 2nd semester, IIUM.

CHAPTER 12

Islamic Trade Financing Instruments and Mechanisms

1 Introduction

This chapter examines and discusses Islamic trade financing products, which include *al-murabahah*, *al-kafalah*, *al-wakalah*, *salam*, *istisna'*, *al-musharakah*, *bai-al-dayn* and *al-bai-bithamin ajil* (BBA). It provides the modern application of those products in the current Islamic financial institutions, especially the banking sector, giving relevant examples. All of these examples are supported by *Shari'ah* rulings so that it can be seen that the applications are in line with *Shari'ah*. The main aim of the chapter is to highlight the applications in Malaysia and certain other Islamic countries. Therefore, we are going to take Bank Islam Malaysia Berhad (BIMB) as our example for current applications. It is the writer's hope that this chapter will make clear some of the applications of the products in the Islamic banking sector. The chapter first presents the central idea, followed by practical scenarios with *Shari'ah* rulings, recommendations and, finally, a conclusion.

2 Central Idea

There are many types of human need for financial facilities and services, such as financing needs that are used to carry out economic activity in a particular community, whether Muslim or non-Muslim. This activity may be in relation to production, distribution, or consumption (Bank Islam Malaysia Berhad 1994).

M. M. Billah, *Islamic Financial Products*,
https://doi.org/10.1007/978-3-030-17624-2_12

3 Debt Financing

Personal capital and equity-financing will not be considered in our discussion; for the purposes of this chapter, we are going to focus on debt financing, of which trade financing forms part. For debt financing, needs for this arise at various economic levels (Bank Islam Malaysia Berhad 1994):

- Consumer financing for residential buildings, furniture, fixtures and fittings, private vehicles, consumer durables and consumer goods;
- Domestic trade finance, domestic trade credit purchases and credit sales;
- International trade finance, import trade purchase and sales credits; export trade purchase and sales credits;
- Corporate finance, in the various forms of debt components of corporate finance;
- International finance, public sector foreign debt requirements, private sector foreign debt requirements;
- Governmental financial operations, Treasury bills, government bonds.

The above categories give the general idea of the current practice of Bank Islam Malaysia Berhad regarding debt financing. To clarify the position, we need to compare the same types of financing during the pre-Islamic period. During that time, the Arabs effected debt-financing through two main categories of contract: deferred contracts of exchange, and interest-based lending (Bank Islam Malaysia Berhad 1994).

3.1 Deferred Contracts of Exchange (Al-Bai, Al-Tijarahand Al-Dayn)

- *Al-bai bithman ajil* (deferred instalments sale)
- *Bai al-murabahah* (deferred lump sum sale)
- *Al-ijarah* (leasing)
- *Bai al-istisna'* (sale on order)
- Others.

3.2 *Interest-Based Lending* (Riba Al-Nasiah)

This type of lending is not *halal* in Islam and is therefore not relevant to our discussion.

4 Debt Financing in Pre-islamic Arab Society

- *Al-bai bithaman ajil* (deferred instalments sale)
- *Bai al-murabahah* (deferred lump sum sale)
- Interest-based lending
- *Al-ijarah* (leasing)
- *Bai al-salam* (salam sale)
- *Bai al-istisna'* (sale on order).

Classes of Islamic trade financing as practised today:

- *Al-murabahah* (deferred lump sum sale, or cost plus)
- *Al-kafalah* (guaranteed)
- *Al-wakalah* (agency)
- *Bai al-salam* (salam sale)
- *Bai al-istisna'* (sale on order)
- *Al-musharakah* (letter of credit)
- *Bai al-dayn* (debt-trading)
- *Al-bai bithaman ajil* (deferred instalment sale).

4.1 Al-Murabahah *(Deferred Lump Sum Sale or Cost Plus)*

Murabahah, a term in Islamic *fiqh*, refers to a particular kind of sale. In a *murabahah* transaction, a seller agrees with his buyer to provide a specific commodity with a certain amount of profit added to the initial cost (http://www.ambg.com.my/e/tf/alk_bankq.asp).

4.1.1 Shari'ah *Rulings*

From an Islamic perspective, *murabahah* is a contract for sale. Therefore, all Muslim scholars agree that *murabahah* is lawful according to the Qur'an, the Sunnah and *ijmah*.

4.1.2 Al-Qur'an

> That is because they say: 'Trade is like usury', but Allah hath permitted trade and has forbidden usury. (2:275)

4.1.3 Al-Sunnah

The Holy Prophet (*SAW*) said:

> if the two types are different, sell your products as you wish, if its hand by hand.

4.1.4 Real Practice by BIMB of Al-Murabahah *(Letter of Credit)*

At times, customers engaged either in trading or manufacturing may need to purchase merchandise or raw materials in the course of their business. In these cases, the customer requires a letter of credit together with financing over a certain period of time. The bank would offer him a letter of credit *al-murabahah* facility (Bank Islam Malaysia Berhad 1994).

- The customer informs the bank of his letter of credit requirements and requests the bank to purchase or import the goods, indicating thereby that he would be willing to purchase the goods from the bank on negotiation of a letter of credit on the principle of *al-murabahah*. The bank appoints the customer as its agent to purchase the required goods on its behalf.
- The bank establishes the letter of credit and pays the proceeds to the negotiating bank utilizing its own funds.
- The bank (BIMB) sells to the customer at a sale price comprising the cost of the goods and a profit margin under the principles of *al-murabahah* for settlement at a deferred time.

4.1.5 Working Capital Financing Under the Principle of Al-Murabahah

The customer may approach the bank (BIMB) to provide financing for his working capital requirements to purchase stock and inventories, spares and replacements, or semi-finished goods and raw materials (Bank Islam Malaysia Berhad 1994).

- The bank first purchases the required goods, or appoints the customer as its agent to purchase the required goods on its behalf, and settles the purchase price from its own funds.

- The bank subsequently sells the goods to the customer at an agreed price, which comprises its purchase price and a profit margin, and allows the customer to settle such sale price on a deferred term of 30 days, 60 days, 90 days, or any other period that may be agreed.
- On the due date, the customer pays the bank the agreed sale price.

4.2 Al-Kafalah *Bank Guarantee (KBG)*

An *al-kafalah* bank guarantee (KBG) is an irrevocable obligation in the form of a bank's written undertaking to pay an agreed sum in the event of default by a third party in fulfilling their obligations under the terms of the KBG (http://www.ambg.com.my/e/tf/alk_bankq.asp).

4.2.1 Shari'ah *Rulings*

Al-Qur'an

> They said: 'We miss the great beaker of the king; for him who produces it, is [the reward of] a camel-load; I will be bound by it.' (12:72)

> Ibn Abas said: bound by, means *kafil.*

Al-Sunnah

> *Kafil* is liable. (Sunan Abu Daud)

4.2.2 The Application of al-Kafalah *in BIMB*

Guarantees are issued for the following purposes:

- Tender guarantee
- Performance guarantee
- Guarantee for sub-contracts
- Guarantee in lieu of security deposits, or special guarantee
- Guarantee for exemption of customs duties
- Customs bond
- Guarantee for maintaining a ledger account.

The customer applies for a credit line. The bank processes the application and, if it is satisfied with the credit standing of the customer, it will extend the letter of credit facility to the customer by means of a written offer. On meeting the terms and conditions of the offer and the offer having been duly accepted by the customer, the bank will issue the relevant letter of credit on request (Bank Islam Malaysia Berhad 1994).

4.2.3 Al-Kafalah *Shipping Guarantee*

An *al-kafalah* shipping guarantee is an indemnity document issued by a bank, addressed to a shipping company on the instruction of an importer customer to take delivery of goods from the shipping company (or its agent) pending receipt of the bill of lading relating to the shipment (http://www.ambg.com.my/e/tf/alk_shipg.asp).

The customer approaches the bank for a guaranteed surety. The bank agrees to discharge the customer's liability in the case of default and gives the guarantee under the concept of Al-Kafalah. An *al-kafalah* shipping guarantee is not a financing instrument but merely an indemnity.

4.2.4 How Does It Work?

- The customer requests the issuance of a Kafalah shipping guarantee.
- The bank issues an *al-kafalah* shipping guarantee provided all requirements, including *Shari'ah* principles, are met.
- The bank must honour the guarantee and effect immediate payment in the event a claim is made by the beneficiary, provided the claims meet all the conditions of the guarantee.

4.3 **Al-Wakalah** ***(Letter of Credit)***

Under this concept, the bank acts as the agent of the customer.

4.3.1 Shari'ah *Ruling*

Al-Qur'an

> Now send ye then one of you with this money of yours to the town. (18:19)

> (Yusuf) said:

> Set me over the store-houses of the land: I will indeed guard them, as one that knows [their importance]. (12:55)

4.3.2 How Does It Work?

- The customer informs the bank of his letter of credit requirements and requests the bank to provide the facility.
- The bank may require the customer to place a deposit of the full amount of the price of the goods to be purchased or imported, which the bank accepts under the principle of *al-wakalah yad dhamanah*.
- The bank establishes the letter of credit and pays the proceeds to the negotiating bank utilizing the customer's deposit; the bank subsequently releases the documents to the customer.
- The bank charges the customer fees and commission for its services under the principle of *al-ujr* (fee).

4.4 Bai Al-Salam *(Sale by Deferred Delivery)*

Salam refers to a sale whereby the seller undertakes to supply specific goods to a buyer at a future date in exchange for an advanced price (http://www.islamiq.com/knowledgecenter/salam.php4#def).

4.4.1 Shari'ah *Ruling*

Al-Qur'an

> O ye who believe! When ye deal with each other, in transactions involving future obligations in a fixed period of time. (2:282)

Al-Sunnah

Salam during the time of the Holy Prophet (*SAW*) was permitted under specific conditions. Originally, the purpose of a *salam* sale was to meet the needs of small farmers who needed money to grow their crops and feed their family until the time of harvest (Bank Islam Malaysia Berhad 1994).

The most famous *hadith* in this context is the one in which the Holy Prophet (*SAW*) said:

> Whoever wishes to enter into a contract of Salam, he must affect the *salam* according to the specified measure and the specified weight and the specified date of delivery. (2:282)

Unfortunately, this type of trade financing is not practised in Malaysia; that may be because of the economic system, and also because *salam* is not mentioned in the Islamic Bank Act 1983.

4.4.2 How Does Salam *Work?*

Salam was initially allowed as a form of financing for small farmers and traders. In contemporary economics, banks and financial institutions may use *salam* as a financing method.

- As the price in *salam* can be fixed at a lower rate than the price of commodities delivered instantly, the difference between the two prices may be a valid profit for banks and financial institutions. In order to ensure that the seller will deliver the commodity on the agreed date, banks can also ask the buyer to furnish a security (either in the form of a guarantee, or in the form of a mortgage or hypothecation). In the event of default in delivery, the guarantor may be asked to deliver the same commodity and, if there is a mortgage, the buyer or the financier can sell the mortgaged property and use the sale proceeds either to realize the required commodity, or to recover the price advanced.
- *Salam* may, however, not be appreciated by banks and financial institutions as a means of settlement as goods are not so straightforward as money. As modern financing for houses is typically only dealt with in money, having to accept various commodities from a variety of clients and to resell them in the market presents banks with a complicated situation. In addition, in order to accord with *Shari'ah*, it is not permissible for a bank to sell such commodities before it has actually taken delivered of such goods.
- After purchasing a commodity by way of *salam*, financial institutions may sell it through a parallel contract of *salam* for the same date of delivery. The period of *salam* in the second (parallel) transaction being shorter, the price may be a little higher than the price of the first transaction; the difference between the two prices will be the profit earned by the institution. The shorter the period of *salam*, the higher the price and the greater the profit. In this way, institutions may manage their short-term financing portfolios.
- If a parallel contract of *salam* is not feasible, a promise to purchase can be obtained from a third party. This promise should be unilateral from the expected buyer. Being merely a promise, and not the

actual sale, their buyers will not have to pay the price in advance. Therefore, a higher price may be fixed. When the institution receives the commodity, it will be sold to the third party at a pre-agreed price, according to the terms of the promise.

4.5 Bai' al-Istisna' *(Manufacturing Contract)*

'Istisna is a form of sale where a commodity is transacted before it comes into existence. It related to placing an order with a manufacturer to make a specific commodity for the purchaser. If the manufacturer undertakes to make the goods with material the manufacturer's own materials, the transaction of *istisna* comes into existence. However, it is necessary for the validity of *istisna* that the price is fixed with the consent of the parties and that the necessary detailed specification for the commodity is fully settled between them (http://www.islamiq.com/knowledgecenter/istisna.php4#def).

4.5.1 Shari'ah *Ruling*

In fact, *istisna* is a form of sale. This topic has been discussed by all scholars and they have agreed it to be *halal* because society needs that type of transaction.

4.5.2 Al-Qur'an

> That is because they say: 'Trade is like usury', but Allah hath permitted trade and forbidden usury. (2:275)

4.5.3 Istisna *as a Method of Financing*

- One of the main uses for *istisna* as financing is the house purchase. If a client has their land and seeks financing for the construction of a house, the financier may undertake the 'contract' to construct the house on the basis of *istisna*. If the client has no land and wishes to buy both a plot land a house, the financier may undertake to provide him with a constructed house on a specified piece of land.
- Since it is not necessary for *istisna* that the cost is paid in advance or the time of delivery, the time of payment may be fixed in whatever manner the parties wish. The payment can also be made in instalments.

- It also is not necessary for the financier to construct the house. A parallel contract of *istisna* with a third party can be established, or the hire of a contractor (other than the client). In both cases, the cost should be calculated and added to the price of the *istisna* contract with the client. The payment of instalments by the client may begin from the day when the *istisna* contract is signed by the parties, and may continue during the construction of the house and after it has been handed over to the client. In order to secure the payment of instalments, the title deeds to the house or land, or any other property of the client, may be kept by the financier as a security until the client pays the last instalment.
- The financier will be responsible for the construction of the house in full conformity with the specifications detailed in the agreement. In the event of any discrepancy, the financier will undertake such alterations as are necessary at their own cost in order to bring the property within the terms of the contract.
- *Istisna* may also be used for project financing. For example, if a client wishes to instal an air-conditioning plant in their factory and the plant needs to be manufactured, the financier may undertake the preparation of the plant through a contract of *istisna*. Similarly, a contract of *istisna* can be used for building a bridge or a highway.
- The modern 'buy, operate and transfer' (BOT) agreements can also be formalized on the basis of *istisna*. If a government wants to construct a highway, it may enter into a contract of *istisna* with a builder. The price of *istisna*, in this case, may be the right of the builder to operate the highway and collect tolls for a specified period.

Unfortunately, this type of trade financing is not practised in Malaysia; this may be because of the economic and industrial systems that Malaysia has, and also due to *istisna* not being mentioned in the Islamic Bank Act 1983.

Each party has the option to rescind the contract before it is implemented, but is bound by it once it has been constituted. Once constituted, if the *al-masnoo* does not conform to specification, the *mustasni* has the right to revoke the contract.

4.6 Al-Musharakah *(Letter of Credit): Trustee Profit Sharing*

'*Musharakah*' in Arabic literally means 'to share'. In the context of business and trade, it refers to a joint enterprise in which all the partners share the profit or loss of a venture (http://www.islamiq.com/knowledgecenter/musharakah.php4).

4.6.1 Shari'ah *Ruling*

Al-Qur'an

> but if it be a transaction which ye carry out on the spot among yourselves there is no blame on you. (2:282)

4.6.2 Modern Application by BIMB

In an instance where a customer of the bank has won a contract for the supply of certain merchandise to a particular organization, he may propose a joint venture scheme whereby the bank grants him a credit facility in order that he may import and supply the merchandise. The joint venture proposal, known as *al-musharakah*, will be operated on the basis of profit-sharing (Bank Islam Malaysia Berhad 1994).

4.6.3 How Does It Work?

- The customer informs the bank of his letter of credit requirements and negotiates the terms of *al-musharakah* financing for his requirements.
- The customer places with the bank a deposit for his share of the cost of goods to be purchased or imported in accordance with the *al-musharakah* agreement, which the bank accepts under the principle of *al-wadiah yad dhamanah*.
- The bank establishes the letter of credit and pays the proceeds to the negotiating bank utilizing the customer's deposit together with its own share of the financing, and subsequently releases the documents to the customer.
- The customer takes possession of the goods and disposes of these in the manner agreed in the agreement.
- The bank and the customer share in the profit from the venture as provided for in the agreement.

4.7 Bay' Al-Dayn

This term can be defined as the sale of a payable right that normally arises from a transaction, service, loan or damage to the debtor himself or to any third party. Usually, this type of sale is made at a discount price and as a spot payment from the buyer. In other words, the seller will discount the price in order to have a payment from a buyer in cash. For example, Ahmad (the debtor) bought a good for $15,000 from Rashid for which the payment is due on a deferred payment basis. Ahmad confirmed that he would settle his debt on 31 December 2002. On 31 August 2002, Rashid (the seller) decided to sell this good either to Ahmad himself or to some other person at the discount price of $14,000. This new contract may take place between Rashid and Ahmad, or between Rashid (the seller) and some other person. This contract is known as *bai' al-dayn*. A new contract between Rashid and Ahmad would be known as *bay' al-dayn lil-ma'adin* (sale of debt to a debtor). However, if a new contract takes place between Rashid and some person other than Ahmad (the debtor), such contract would be known as *bai' al-dayn lil-ghair* (sale of debt to a non-debtor).

4.7.1 Bay' Al-Dayn *as Practised in BIMB*

The Bank finances exports and sales on the concept of *bai al dayn*. *Bai al dayn* (debt purchase) is a short-term financing facility whereby the Bank purchases the customer's rights to the debt; this is normally securitized in the form of a bill of exchange. An exporter wishing to avail himself of *bai al dayn* prepares export documents as required under the sales contract or letter of credit. He presents these documents to the Bank to be purchased. As the export documents have to be sent to the buyer overseas, the Bank requests the exporter to draw another bill of exchange drawn on the Bank, now known as IAB- Exports. IAB- Exports may subsequently be sold in the secondary market. (Securitization and Export Financing; Contract: Bai Al Daynor Debt Trading.)

The mechanics of Islamic *bai al-dayn* factoring are summarized in Fig. 1.

The *muqasah* (rebate) is determined in accordance with the following formula:

$$M = \text{NIV} - \text{PP}(1 + 0.12 \times n)/365$$

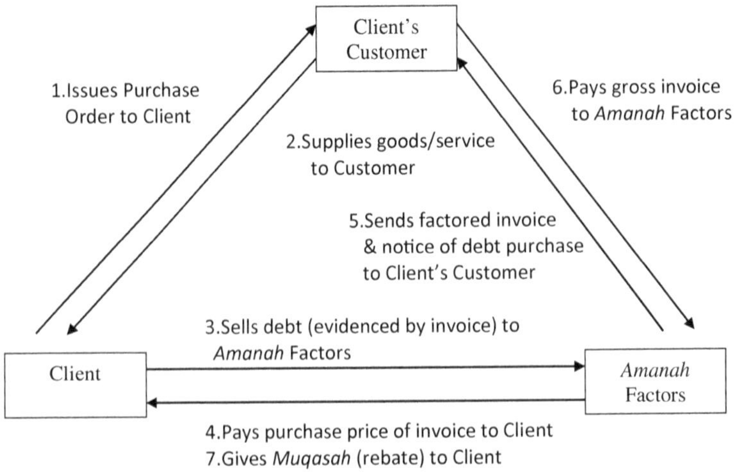

Fig. 1 *Bay' al-Dayn* as practiced in BIMB (*Source* Author's own)

where M = the total amount of *muqasah* (rebate) payable; NIV = the net invoice value (i.e. after deducting the factoring fee); PP = the purchase price; n = the number of days elapsed between the date of payment of the purchase price and the date of receipt by the *amanah* factors of the invoice value.

4.8 Al-Bai-Bithamin Ajil

Generally, BBA is a sale and purchase between a bank and its customer. The transaction of the sale has to be agreed by both parties when the payment by instalments is made over a period of time. Actually, the sale is made when the bank buys the property or good at the previous market price and then sells it to the customer at the current market price. The profit arising from the sale is lawful from a *Shari'ah* perspective as the transaction is based on a sale contract.

4.8.1 Shari'ah *Ruling*

As mentioned, BBA is a type of sale; therefore the *Shari'ah* rulings are as follows:

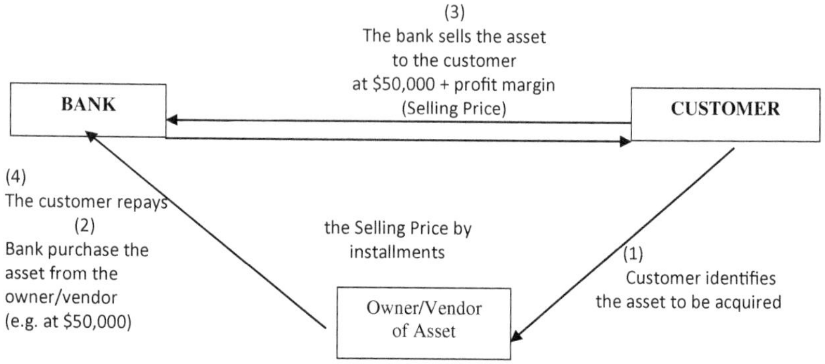

Fig. 2 *Al-Bai Bithamin Ajil* financing operation (*Source* Author's own)

Al-Quran

> That is because they say: 'Trade is like usury', but Allah hath permitted trade and forbidden usury. (2:275)

Regarding this topic, here is an example of this type of transaction. Suppose A wants to buy a house the current price of which is $250,000. He chooses a bank that practises interest-free financing. The bank buys the house and sells it to A at $500,000, payment being made in installments over 20 years. Each month, A has to pay the bank $2291. After two years, A decides to sell the house. A buyer is willing to purchase the house at $400,000.

A now has to find out the exact balance that must be paid to the bank before the house can be sold to the new buyer. Over the two years, A has paid the bank $54,000 and there is an outstanding balance of $446,000 due to the bank. The outstanding balance of $446,000 means that A has to find another buyer.

Figure 2 presents an example of a BBA financing operation.

5 Recommendations

Regarding today's practice by Islamic financial institutions, most Islamic countries either have no code to ensure that their practice is in line with *Shari'ah*, or have their own standards in place. We will now make some recommendations to enable further improvement.

There should be one code of practice and standards for all Islamic financial institutions to follow to ensure their work and practices stay in line with *Shari'ah*. Allah (*SWT*) said in the Holy Qur'an:

> Be not like those who are divided amongst themselves and fall into disputations after receiving Clear Signs: for them is a dreadful Penalty. And hold fast, all together, by the Rope which Allah [stretches out for you], and be not divided among yourselves. (3:105–106)

Nowadays, Islamic financial institutions are focusing on Islamic trade financing rather than equity financing; this is because equity financing is very risky for banks due to their being private enterprises. Hence, Islamic banks should be owned by government in order to help society even when a transaction is risky and the investment is long-term.

The Holy Prophet (*SAW*) said:

> all of you are responsible, and all of you are responsible of their servant.

All Muslim countries should apply *Shari'ah* in all their systems, rather than having dual banking systems. Dual banking systems prevent Islamic financing institutions from being truly Islamic.

> O ye who believe! Obey Allah and His Messenger, and turn not away from him when ye hear (him speak). (4:159)

> Let not the Believers take for friends or helpers Unbelievers rather than Believers: if any do that, in nothing will there be help from Allah: except by way of precaution, that ye may guard yourselves from them. But Allah cautions you [to remember] Himself; for the final goal is to Allah. (3:28)

6 Conclusion

We would conclude saying that Islamic banking and other financial institutions are gradually increasing. Islamic trade financing products nowadays are not only offered by Islamic financial institutions, but are also successfully practised by non-Islamic financial institutions by virtue of the *Shari'ah* Council. In addition, the Islamic full range of trade financing products is not available in some Islamic countries. For instance, *istisna* and *salam* are not practised in Malaysia, perhaps because of the type of banking system operating in Malaysia. However, all those Islamic products are taken up by Muslims and, in some cases, by non-Muslims. Islamic civilization is coming back to lead this corrupted world again, that is very clear in all life aspects, economic, social, political and so on, because Islam is a comprehensive way of life.

References

Bank Islam Malaysia Berhad. (1994). *Islamic Banking Practice, From the Practitioner's Perspective*, BIMB, Kuala Lumpur, 1st edn.

Rosly, S. A. (n.d.). *Islamic Banking and Finance*, Department of Economics, IIUM, Vol. II.

http://www.ambg.com.my/e/tf/alk_bankq.asp.

http://www.ambg.com.my/e/tf/alk_shipg.asp.

http://www.islamiq.com/knowledgecenter/istisna.php4#def.

http://www.islamiq.com/knowledgecenter/musharakah.php4.

http://www.islamiq.com/knowledgecenter/salam.php4#def.

CHAPTER 13

Islamic Trade Financing Frameworks

1 Introduction

The banking system comprises monetary institutions and non-monetary institutions. Monetary institutions are those institutions comprising Bank Negara Malaysia (BNM) (being the sole currency issuing authority in the country) and commercial banks (as the only institutions that are allowed to operate current accounts). A distinct form of commercial bank is the Islamic banks that operate commercially but apply Islamic principles in their transactions, with particular emphasis on the prohibition of *riba* (interest).

Non-monetary institutions include institutions that are closely linked to monetary institutions and whose liabilities are generally accepted as near money. Institutions that also come under the supervision of the BNM are finance companies, merchant banks and discount houses.

When Islam came into being, the Qur'an and Sunnah laid down various injunctions forming the basis of the Islamic banking and financial system; for example:

> When the prayer is ended, disperse through the earth and seek something of God's bounty. (62:10)

The above verse signifies the balance that Islam advocates between worldly affairs and religious affairs.

M. M. Billah, *Islamic Financial Products*,
https://doi.org/10.1007/978-3-030-17624-2_13

All the services offered by Islamic banks are bound by *Shari'ah* standards; therefore, all transactions should be disclosed properly according to such standards. The accounting standards to which they refer are MASBi-1 (Presentation of Financial Statement of Islamic Financial Institutions and Accounting and Auditing Standards for Islamic Financial Institutions).

2 Islamic Banking

Islamic banking business means a banking business the aims and operations of which do not involve any element that is not approved by the religion of Islam (Banking and Financial Institutions Act 1989) Islamic banking governs by the Banking and Financial Institutions Act 1989 (BAFIA). The introduction of the BAFIA was intended to provide for an integrated system of supervision of the Malaysian financial system and to modernize and streamline the laws relating to banking and financial institutions.

Islamic banks (BAFIA 1989) appeared on the world scene as active players at the end of the 1990s. However, many of the principles on which Islamic banking is based have been commonly accepted worldwide—for centuries, rather than decades. The basic principle of Islamic banking is the prohibition of *riba* (usury or interest). Some revelations of the Qur'an and the Sunnah relating to the prohibition of *riba* are:

> Devour not usury [*riba*], doubled and multiplied; but fear God; that you may [really] prosper. (3:130)

> God is with the debtor until he pays his debt, as long as it is not for something God disapproves. (Ibn Majah)

The above divine sources may conclude that the central pillar of the Islamic banking system is that financing can only be on an interest-free basis. In addition, the universal nature of these principles is immediately clear, even at a cursory glance of non-Muslim literature. Usury was prohibited in both the Old and New Testaments of the Bible, holding it to be a barbaric practice.

Islam not only prohibits dealing in interest but also in liquor, pork, gambling, pornography, and anything else that the *Shari'ah* (Islamic law) (MASBi, n.d.) deems *haram* (unlawful). Islamic banking is an instrument for the development of an Islamic economic order. Some of the most important features of this order may be summarized as follows:

- While permitting an individual the right to seek his economic well-being, Islam makes a clear distinction between what is *halal* (lawful) and what is *haram* (forbidden) in pursuit of such economic activity. In broad terms, Islam forbids all forms of economic activity that are morally or socially injurious.
- While acknowledging an individual's right to ownership of wealth legitimately acquired, Islam makes it obligatory on such individual to spend his wealth wisely and not to hoard it, keep it idle, or to waste it.
- While allowing an individual to retain any surplus wealth, Islam seeks to reduce the margin of the surplus for the well-being of the community as a whole—in particular, the poor and deprived sections of society—through participation in the process of *zakat*.
- While making allowances for the ways of human nature and yet not yielding to the consequences of its worst propensities, Islam seeks to prevent the accumulation of wealth in a few hands to the harm of society as a whole through its laws of inheritance.
- Viewed as a whole, the economic system envisaged by Islam aims at social justice without inhibiting individual enterprise beyond the point where it becomes not only collectively injurious, but also individually self-destructive.

The Islamic financial system employs the concept of participation in an enterprise, utilizing the funds at risk on a profit-and-loss sharing basis. This by no means implies that investments with financial institutions are necessarily speculative. This can be excluded by careful investment policy, diversification of risk and prudent management by Islamic financial institutions. (The term 'Islamic financial institution' refers to Islamic banks, commercial banks, finance companies, merchant banks and discount houses that carry out Islamic banking business or Islamic financial business.)

It is possible that investment in Islamic financial institutions can provide potential profit in proportion to the risk assumed to satisfy the differing demands of participants in the contemporary environment and within the guidelines of the *Shari'ah*. The concept of profit-and-loss sharing as a basis for financial transactions is progressive, as it

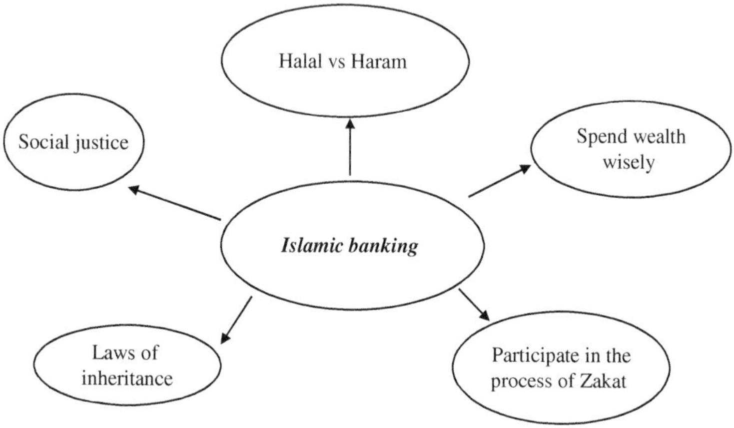

Fig. 1 Islamic banking (*Source* Author's own)

distinguishes good performance from the bad and the mediocre. This concept therefore encourages better resource management.

Islamic banks are structured to retain a clearly differentiated status between shareholders' capital and clients' deposits in order to ensure correct profit sharing according to Islamic law (Fig. 1).

3 Status of Islamic Banking

When the concept of Islamic banking with its ethical values was propagated, financial circles worldwide treated it as a utopian dream. Having lived for centuries under a valueless capitalist economic system, people asked what ethics had to do with finance? Attitudes are changing gradually and in recent years the value of neutral, conventional banking has begun to trouble the conscience of an increasing number of people. There is a reluctance to hand over funds to banks and financial institutions that invest in companies engaged in unethical and socially harmful activities. The emerging Islamic banking scene has succeeded in achieving general acceptance.

Today, Islamic banking is estimated to be managing funds to the tune of US$200 billion. Its clients are not confined to Muslim countries but are spread over Europe, the United States of America and the Far East. Islamic banking continues to grow at a rapid pace because of its value-orientated philosophy, which enables it to draw finances from both Muslims and non-Muslims alike. Keeping pace with sophisticated techniques and the latest developments, Islamic bankers have evolved investment instruments that are not only profitable, but are also ethically motivated. Today, more than 250 Islamic financial institutions are operating worldwide. Countries in which Islamic financial institutions operate include Algeria, Bahrain, Bangladesh, Canada, Djibouti, Egypt, France, Germany, India, Indonesia, Malaysia, Pakistan, Palestine, Switzerland, Turkey, United Kingdom, United States and Yemen.

4 Islamic Trade Finance

Islamic banking—which is based on the concept of sharing profits and risks, rather than charging and paying interest—is playing a growing role in financing trade and development projects. Banks operating on this principle have established a significant presence in Asia, Africa and Europe. According to some estimates, the total funds available to the Islamic banking system worldwide could be as much as US$80 billion (see *Trade and Project Finance in Emerging Markets*, Michael Rowe).

The Qur'anic prohibition of usury—taken to encompass all forms of interest—provides one of the basic religious cornerstones of this system. At the same time, this prohibition reflects a positive belief that the best economic and social results are obtained through a dynamic interaction of capital with human thought and effort.

5 E-banking

Islam does not prohibit the use of electronic devices for improving the efficiency of Islamic commercial banking transactions. Instead, the use of such systems (i.e. e-banking) is encouraged and commended by the religion, as it facilitates transactions and removes any difficulties parties may experience from having to meet physically, especially when they are located in different parts of the world.

Value-added services, such as the facility to pay alms (*zakat*) online, also prove that the e-banking Islamic banks provide is convenient for customers. A legal framework set up by the relevant regulatory bodies would ensure that Islamic e-banking could provide safe and efficient services and products to those who wish to manage their wealth in line with the requirements of the religion.

6 Recommendation

We think that two recommendations should be taken in hand to ensure the improvement of Islamic banking in Malaysia:

- *Institutional capacity*: Strategic steps should be taken to prepare Islamic banking industry players to become among the best-managed institutions, capable of capitalizing on the unique features of Islamic banking to achieve a significant competitive edge.
- *Financial infrastructure development*: The legal, regulatory and *Shari'ah* framework of Islamic banking should be further strengthened by means of a review of existing laws and guidelines governing the industry. A code of ethics should be one of the core determinants in disciplining the industry, with less emphasis placed on BNM's intervention.

7 Islamic Bank

7.1 Products and Services

There are many similarities in the range of Islamic financial products and services and that of conventional banks. Four concepts applicable to trade financing products are: *al-kafalah*, *al-wakalah*, *al-murabaha* and *bay' al-dyan*.

7.1.1 Al-Kafalah

Kafalah (a guarantee) is an undertaking by one party of another's obligations. The concept of this product is that the bank acts as a guarantor; in the event that the customer fails to perform his obligations, the bank will be responsible for honouring the beneficiary's claims. The types of *kafalah* are the *kafalah* bank guarantee and the *kafalah* shipping guarantee.

7.1.2 Al-Wakalah

Wakalah (agency) is services rendered by a bank on behalf of its customer. *Wakalah* products are the *wakalah* letter of credit and *wakalah* documentary collection.

7.1.3 Al-Murabaha

Murabaha (cost-plus sale) is where the bank appoints a customer as its purchasing agent, the customer purchases the merchandise on behalf of the bank at the invoice price and thn bank then resell the merchandise to the customer at a new selling price, which is the invoice price plus the bank's profit margin. *Murabaha* products are *murabaha* working capital financing and Islamic acceptance bills (purchase/import). *Murabaha* working capital financing is appropriate where the customer needs to ask the bank to provide financing for his working capital requirements to purchase stock and inventories, spares and replacements, or semi-finished goods and raw materials.

7.1.4 Bay Al-Dyan

Bay' al-dyan (debt trading, securitization of debt) is where the bank purchases the customer's debt at a discounted price, which is the invoice price minus the bank's profit margin and is normally securitized by a bill of exchange. On the maturity of this arrangement, the customer purchases their debt back from the bank at the full invoice price. There two *bay al-dyan* products: Islamic acceptance bills (sales/exports) and *bay al-dyan* financing (bill purchase).

Other products that offer by Islamic banking are: *bay' bithaman ajil*, *al-mudaraba*, *al-musharakah* and *al-ijara*.

7.1.5 Bay' Bithaman Ajil

Bay Bithaman Ajil (deferred payment sale) is a form of financing in which the customer wishes to acquire a given asset and agrees to repay the bank in instalments within an agreed period. The bank will purchase the asset required by the customer and then sell it to the customer at an agreed price that includes the bank's profit margin (MASBi, n.d.).

7.1.6 Al-Mudaraba

Mudaraba (profit sharing) is a form of partnership in which one party, the *rab-ul-maal* (principal), provides only capital to the business venture, with or without conditions, while another party, the *mudarib* (agent), contributes labour only. At the end of the *Mudaraba* period, profits from the venture are shared between the two parties according to a pre-agreed ratio. In the event of loss, such loss is borne solely by the capital provider.

7.1.7 Al-Musharakah

Musharakah means 'sharing', and is used to describe joint business enterprises in which the partners share the profit or loss of the venture.

Musharakah also can be translating as 'partnership'. In this situation, two or more financiers provide finance for a project. All partners to the arrangement are entitled to a share in the profits resulting from the project in a ratio that has been mutually agreed. However, any loss is to be shared in the same proportions as the capital put into the partnership. There is no guaranteed rate of return on the investment, as income is based on the profit earned by the joint venture; involvement may possibly result in loss. Partners also have a right to participate in the management of the project. However, they also have a right to transfer the right of participation to any specific partner or person. There are two types of *musharakah*: which are permanent *musharakah* and diminishing *musharakah*.

7.1.8 Al-Ijara

Ijara (leasing) is a contract where a bank or financier buys and leases equipment or other assets to a business owner for a fee. Under the terms of this arrangement, an investor or lessor is able purchase equipment from a manufacturer and lease it to the company or lessee for an agreed period of time. During the predetermined period, the title or the ownership remains in the hands of the lessor, whereas the actual possession and usage of the asset is for the benefit of the lessee. Over the life of the asset, the lessee pays an agreed rental to the lessor.

7.2 Other Services

Islamic banks also provide other services to customers under various Islamic concepts.

7.2.1 Money Transfer

A bank will transfer funds from A to B at the request of a customer. The bank acts as an agent, on behalf of their customer (on the basis of *wakalah*), the transfer taking place by means of demand drafts, mail transfer, or telegraphic transfer. The bank will then utilize the services of its branches or agent in B's locale. Normally, the bank would maintain an account with its agent. A demand draft or a mail transfer only takes place when the bank orders the agent to pay to the beneficiary by mail, authorizing the agent bank to debit its account once the transfer has been completed. The bank will sell foreign currency to the customer if the transfer is required to be made in foreign currency. The bank would then charge a small fee for its services.

7.2.2 Collection of Proceeds of Trade Transactions

A bank will act as a collecting agent for an exporter/seller on the basis of *wakalah* and will receive all necessary documentation. According to International Chamber of Commerce publication No. 322, the bank (the collecting bank) will send all necessary documents, together with its collection order, to its agent in the buyer's country.

7.2.3 Imports/Purchases

A bank will acts as a collecting agent on behalf of the exporter's banker. When the bank receives the document from an exporter's banker, the bank will collect payment from the importer, who may or may not be the bank's customer. After being satisfied with the documents, the importer makes payment and takes control of the documents.

7.2.4 Trade Information

A bank has agents worldwide. Sometimes, a customer may request the bank to provide certain information with regard to a particular commercial organization in a foreign country with which the customer has business dealings (Fig. 2).

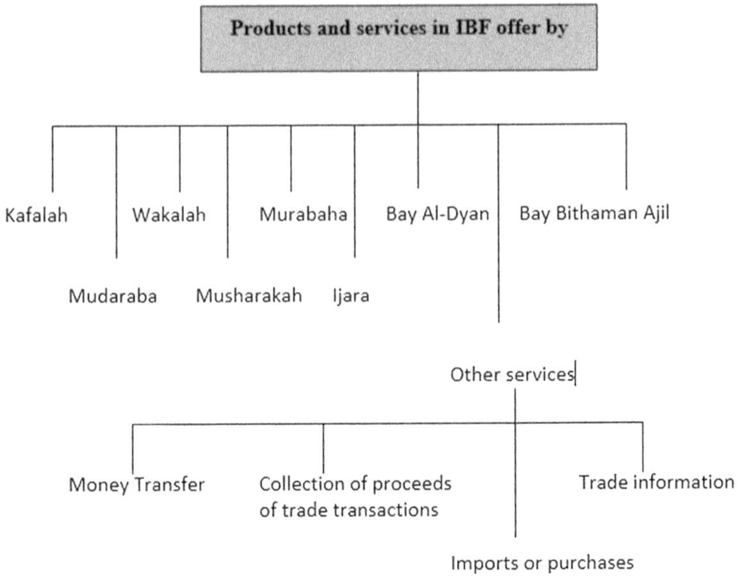

Fig. 2 Products and services (*Source* Author's own)

8 Conventional Bank

8.1 Products and Services

HSBC *amanah* finance also provides products that are quite similar to Islamic bank products. These products are:

- *Murabaha*: The *murabaha* transaction offered by HSBC *amanah* finance includes the trading of commodities, non-precious metals, goods made to order and so on.
- *Wakalah*: They also able to arrange letters of credit and letters of guarantee (*kafalah*).
- A range of Islamic products in which to invest excess liquidity.

These products offer short-term maturities comparable to those in the conventional treasury market and structured under Islamic principles; for example, a short-term *murabaha* programme based on the financing of commodity trades. Other liquidity management products offered include the Islamic commercial chapter programme and Islamic bonds. These products will offer investors a high return dependent on the underlying risk of the products.

9 *Shari'ah* Standard

9.1 Overview

Islamic economics is based on *Shari'ah* (Islamic) law, for which the main resources are the Qur'an and Sunnah. The basic objective of *Shari'ah* is to ensure general human well-being and socio-economic justice. It teaches that all wealth belongs to Allah and humans are only the trustees of this wealth; thus, they should spend some of the wealth for the sake of Allah (*SWT*) (Al-Qur'an, 57:7). Therefore, the purpose of using *Shari'ah* standards is to make sure the welfare of the *Ummah* is protected.

10 The Need for Islamic Accounting Standards

Islamic banking operations in Malaysia have been in existence since the end of the 1990s and have experienced rapid growth due to wider understanding and public acceptance, as well as to the introduction by the government of a structural framework and a set of facilitative measures to nurture the healthy development of the industry. Islamic banking financial reporting practices have been under the scope of the central bank of Malaysia (BNM), the Company Act (1965) and the MASB standards. Therefore, in the absence of a comprehensive set of accounting standards, Islamic banks and other Islamic financial institutions, together with the conventional banks that provide Islamic banking services, have relied on the guidelines issued by BNM and on *Shari'ah* ruling issued by *Shari'ah* advisors appointed by their respective banks. The existing MASB standards have not been able to address accounting issues within Islamic banking operations adequately. This is because the MASB standards and the current International Accounting Standards are inadequate for the accommodation of *Shari'ah* precepts, which form the basis of all Islamic transactions.

10.1 Objective

The objective of the suggested standard is to lay down the basis for the presentation and disclosure of the financial statements of Islamic financial institutions that conduct Islamic banking activities. The suggested standard would also provide guidelines for the structure and basis of the content of financial statements to ensure conformity with *Shari'ah* requirements.

10.2 Accounting Treatment: Al-Murabaha

10.2.1 Measurement of Asset Value at Acquisition by an Islamic Bank

Financial accounting statement No. 2 stipulates that historical cost should be the basis used in measuring and recording assets at the time of acquisition. As a result, assets possessed by an Islamic bank for the purpose of selling them on the basis of *murabaha* or *murabaha* to the person who placed the purchase order should be measured at the time of their acquisition on an historical cost basis (AAIOFI).

10.2.2 Measurement of Asset Valued After Acquisition by an Islamic Bank

In the case of *murabaha*, the cost to the person who placed the purchase order, who is obliged to fulfil his promise, should be measured at the historical cost. In cases where the asset value decreases to below cost—whether due to damage, destruction, or from other unfavourable circumstances—such decrease should be reflected in the valuation of the asset at the end of each financial period. However, in the case of *murabaha* or *murabaha* to the person who placed the purchase order, who is not obliged to fulfil his promise, the asset should be measured as the cash equivalent (i.e. its net realizable value). This should be achieved by creating a provision for a decrease in asset value to reflect the difference between its acquisition cost and the cash equivalent value.

10.2.3 Potential Discount to Be Obtained After Acquisition of an Asset

When an Islamic bank concludes a contract with a client and the discount is to be received subsequently, such discount shall not be treated as revenue for that Islamic bank; instead, the cost of goods shall be reduced by the amount of the discount. Consideration should be given to the effect on both the profit of the period and the deferred profits. However, the discount may be treated as revenue for an Islamic bank if the *Shari'ah* supervisory board of that Islamic bank decides this should be so. If so, then the revenue should be recognized in the income statement.

10.2.4 Al-Murabaha *Receivables*

There are five options to review for the measurement of *murabaha* receivables at the end of a financial period:

- that they should be measured at their cash equivalent value.
- that they should be measured at their book value (the amount required from the client at the end of the period), no provision being made for doubtful debts or loss arising from non-collection recognized at the time of its occurrence and after making sure collection is unlikely.
- that they should be measured at their book value and that doubtful debts should be treated within a general provision for investment risks.
- that they should be measured at their book value less provision for doubtful debts. An Islamic bank should also make a general provision for investment risks to cover *murabaha* receivables that are impaired but that will not be specifically identified as such until some point in the future.

- that they should be measured at their book value and the Islamic bank determines the valuation method, provided the Islamic bank discloses such method within its accounting policies.

10.3 *Accounting Treatment:* Al-Mudaraba

10.3.1 Recognition of Mudaraba *Capital*
Mudaraba financing capital (cash or kind) should be recognized when it is paid to the *mudarib* or placed at his disposition (AAIOFI). However, if it is agreed that the capital of a *mudaraba* is to be paid on an instalment basis, each instalment should be recognized at the time of its payment.

10.3.2 Measurement of Al-Mudaraba
Capital is the amount of money given by the provider of funds to the *mudarib* with the purpose of investing it in a *mudaraba* activity. There are some conditions to be satisfied: the amount of capital should be known the currency in which it will be paid; capital should be in cash. However, some jurists allowed *mudaraba* capital to be paid in trading assets; for example, inventory. At the time of contracting, the historical value of such assets should be considered as the *mudaraba* capital. The capital should be readily available in cash, rather than in the form of debt.

10.3.3 Disclosure Requirements
Disclosure should be made in the notes to the financial statements of any financial reporting period if the Islamic bank has made provision for a decrease in the value of *mudaraba* assets. Such disclosure should be observed, as required by Financial Accounting Standards No. 1 of General Presentation and Disclosure in the Financial Statements of Islamic Banks and Financial Institutions.

10.4 *Accounting Treatment:* Al-Musharakah

10.4.1 Recognition of Musharakah *Capital*
An Islamic bank's share in *musharakah* capital (cash or kind) should be recognized when it is paid to the partner, or made available to him

on account of the *musharakah*. This share should be presented in the Islamic bank's books under a *musharakah* financing account (indicating the client's name) and should be included in the financial statements (AAIOFI).

10.4.2 Measurement of Musharakah *Capital*

An Islamic bank's share in the *musharakah* capital provided in cash should be measured by the amount paid, or made available to the partner on account of the *musharakah*.

An Islamic bank's share of *musharakah* capital provided in either trading assets or non-monetary assets for use in venture should be measured at the fair value of the asset and, if there is a difference in the valuation between the fair value and book values, the differences should be recognized as profit or loss to the Islamic bank itself. The Islamic bank's share after contracting is measured at its historical cost because *Shari'ah* rules of *musharakah* require the determination of capital and its maintenance up to the point of final settlement in order to determine profit. The latter is defined as the amount earned in excess of the initial *musharakah* capital. This conforms to the accounting measurement provided for in the Statement of Concepts (para. 98).

11 Conclusion

In conclusion, it is enlightening that the Malaysian Islamic financial system has grown from a one unit bank into a large pool of players, thus signifying that Islamic banking services are now within the reach of every Malaysian—Muslims and non-Muslim alike. It is obvious from the foregoing discussions that Islamic banking and finance will continue to play an important role in the Malaysian economy. Further, efforts by the government to sustain and foster the industry bode well for the future of Islamic banking in the country. *Shari'ah* standards give guidelines to Islamic banks and Islamic institutions on how to present their income statements and disclose all the information required by current standards. This is so as to care responsibly for the benefits of users or their customers.

CHAPTER 14

Shari'ah Model of International Trade Financing

1 Introduction

Islamic financing has been in development over the past three decades, since the late 1980s, so several methods of financing have been developed to expand its market share in international finance, especially among Islamic countries. It was reported in 1995 that exports from Muslim countries totalled $340 million and imports $350 million (IDB Statistical Monograph 1997). From that report, it can be concluded that exports and imports between Islamic countries represent less than 10% of international trade financing. So, Islamic financial institutions are able to service all trade financing between Muslim countries. This chapter seeks to explore the problems of implementing international trade financing and the implementation of *Shari'ah* international trade financing.

First, the chapter discusses the capacity of Islamic financial institutions to respond to the needs of international trade financing. Thus, this issue is presented in three sections: the basic foundations of Islamic finance, the emergence of Islamic banks and the salient characteristics of Islamic finance.

Islamic methods of financing are discussed in Sect. 4, which examined whether Islamic financing is suitable for international trade. The chapter also discusses the main challenges faced by Islamic international institutions in international trade financing.

M. M. Billah, *Islamic Financial Products*,
https://doi.org/10.1007/978-3-030-17624-2_14

2 Basic Principles of Islamic Finance

The basic principles of Islamic finance are justice and harmony based on the reality of human nature. The principles of Islamic financial institutions are simple, pure and clear: they provide for the factors of production, goods and services on the basis of deferred payment. The justice of Islamic finance is made evident in profit and loss sharing. The financier and entrepreneur share the risk of the actual result. If the investment makes a profit, the profit is distributed equally; if the investment makes a loss, the financier loses their money and the entrepreneur loses the energy and time they have dedicated to that project.

In the Islamic system, the owner has the right to increase their property. Although such property is entrusted to another party through financing, the profit is still owned by the financier, but the entrepreneur's effort to raise profit should be considered. The profit should be divided equally between both of them. Debt, by its very nature, cannot grow or increase. Debt is the relationship between one person and another. A lender gives money to the borrower. So, lending money changes its nature from cash to commitment that remains entailed until the debt is settled.

Savings and real goods still can make use of this sharing basis. The owner still has ownership of the savings and the entrepreneur tries to make the goods grow. For example, if a farmer were to offer the use of his land for crops; the profit from the crops is distributed equally. In this case, both the farmer (as landlord) and the entrepreneur (as tenant) are creating profit. So, both parties have their individual rights to the profit gained. Under the Islamic financing concept, finance invested should not be guaranteed; if the finance were guaranteed, this would mean that, if the user failed in their efforts, the financier could take legal action to obtain the return of their money. Fairness requires that the financier and the user share the outcome of the arrangement, whether loss or profit.

When the financier is affected by the outcome of the user's efforts, it opens the route to direct investment. Corroboration between the bank and the user will minimize the risk of the finance invested by means of proper evaluation of the user's performance and the offering of solutions to unexpected problems. Whether resulting in a loss or a gain, the risk entailed in making a direct investment is equal; this makes direct investment appropriate not only for small and micro-enterprises, but also for high-risk projects. Direct investment is the principle of Islamic financial institutions—a method of financing that conventional banks rarely make available.

> In the absence of full information, banks tend to allocate credit to firms with reliable track records or available internal funds, even if other firms present better investment opportunities. Financial intermediaries … can acquire information that is superior to that of outsiders by developing and maintaining close long-term relationships with their customers. They can play an important role in screening projects, monitoring behavior and outcomes, and managing corporate distress. (However), in many countries, commercial banks favor lending for low-activities. They are generally less willing to finance high-risk project with long payback periods, even if these projects may yield higher overall returns. They are generally also reluctant to finance small firms that lack adequate collateral, even though such firms may be more innovative and promising than others. (Vittas and Cho 1996)

3 Emergence of Islamic Banks

Islamic history refers to banking practices emerging 1200 years ago in Baghdad, Damascus, Fez and Cordoba. At that time, banks offered current account and cheque facilities, and traders applied *mudharabah* as their mode of financing.

However, contemporary Islamic banking made its appearance in the 1960s when Malaysia established funds for people who wished to go on a pilgrimage. Egypt followed suit by establishing a small savings bank at Myt Ghamr, near Cairo. The IDB was established in 1974 with an authorized capital of Dinar 2 billion. By 1997, the worldwide number of registered Islamic banking institutions had increased to 177. If the present growth of Islamic banking rate were to continue, within 10 years Islamic banking would handle about 40–50% of the total savings of the Muslim *Ummah* (*Wall Street Journal* 1996). This figure does not include the branches of Islamic banking available in non-Muslim countries and in the conventional banks in Islamic countries.

The following quotation describes Islamic banking:

> As an international quasi-parallel financial system … from the US through Europe, Africa and the Middle East into the Indian subcontinent to the Far East.

Islamic banks are registered under the International Association of Islamic Banks. Based on the IDB report (1997), there were 177 registered Islamic banks: 51 in South Asia, 36 in Africa, 31 in Southeast Asia, 37 in the Middle East, and 112 in Europe, Central Asia, Australia and America.

4 Salient Characteristics of Islamic Finance

The main characteristic of Islamic banking is that the full range of financing services offered is based on Islamic law. Some authors have expressed a wish to see Islamic banking to be more than Islamic finance. Islamic banking cannot be anything other than Islamic finance; to argue otherwise is to argue for the separation of religion and economics. The concept of *Shari'ah* is that it is both law and religion.

The responsibility of Islamic banking is to ensure to that its main characteristic is the following of *Shari'ah* law. Islamic banking activities show how the relationship between financiers, suppliers and the users of funds operates to make ensure that the *Shari'ah* is followed.

Since the late 1980s, Islamic banking has provided three services:

- A relationship between banks and depositors;
- Integration of financial and real markets in financing;
- Incorporation of ethics and values in investment and financing decisions.

5 Relationship with Depositors

For many centuries, the relationship between banks and depositors was based on the banks' lending depositors' capital to those who needed capital for a project, in return for which the banks would pay interest to the depositors. Islamic banking is changing this method from lending to partnership; depositors entrust their capital to the banks to invest their money on their behalf. The profit and loss is shared equally. The sharing principle introduced by Islamic banking is different from conventional banking practices. In a conventional banking system, the banks demonstrate their good performance in the utilization of funds to attract the depositors, which enables the banks to attract depositors by offering a higher interest. In Islamic banking, profit is distributed equally to depositors; any covering up of information regarding liabilities will therefore have greater ongoing effects on shareholders and the board of directors, rather than on the depositors.

6 Closing the Financing Gap

The contribution of Islamic banking is to integrate financial and real markets. Islamic banks limit their functions to financing the creation or exchange of goods and services. Islamic banks also can finance economic activities such as:

- The purchase of consumer goods;
- The leasing of means of production, such as machinery and consumables;
- The establishing of new productive projects.

There are two categories of traditional financing that are not similar to Islamic banking methods:

- Financing is providing for government and corporate budgets But the banks ignore the purpose for which funds are used.
- A result of debt rescheduling is increased indebtedness.

7 Ethics and Banking

For a long time, people have accepted that banks deal with money, but not ethics. Islamic banking is therefore trying to adapt the ethical values in its practices. As mentioned earlier, Islamic banking is based on *Shari'ah*. The *Shari'ah* itself is founded on ethics. Since the establishment of Islamic banking, the banks have been financing the commodities and services that are recognized by *Shari'ah*. Examples of excluded goods and services are tobacco, gambling, casinos and alcohol.

One could claim that the moral values in banking are derived from the West; Islamic banks only adapt and extend their practices. This statement still can be argued still further: Islamic banks are derived from Islamic funds such as *baitul mal* and the Islamic Investment Company. So, the core statement is that Islamic banks are derived from the principles of mutual funds that were established at the time of the Prophet Muhammad.

The other contribution made by Islamic banking is the giving of opportunities to Muslims who do not wish to deposit their money in the bank purely for it to attract interest. When they deposit their money in the bank, it is safer than it would be if kept at their home and placing it in the custody of the banks ensures that their money will be used effectively. In other words, the emergence of Islamic banks will increase the number of newcomers to the financial market.

8 Modes of International Trade Financing

Islamic finance has a wide range of definitions, from the very narrow (interest-free banking) to the very broad (financial operations conducted by Muslims). Generally, it can be defined as Islamic financial institutions whose objectives and operations are based on Qur'anic principles. This means that the operation of the institutions is in line with the Qur'an, *hadith* and Sunnah, and also with *Shari'ah* regulations. This presents a different image of financing operations when compared with conventional institutions, in which interest (*riba'*) plays a major factor in their borrowing, financing and other transactions, where the effect of the transaction is injustice to the borrower (Fig. 1).

So, to help Muslims finance transactions—especially for exporters, importers and producers, since we are talking about international trade—there are three means of Islamic financing: sharing, sale and leasing (Fig. 2).

Here, sharing means the principle of sharing the outcome of the arrangement, whether a profit or a loss. It is the most authentic form of Islamic finance, as it replicates the transactions that were common in

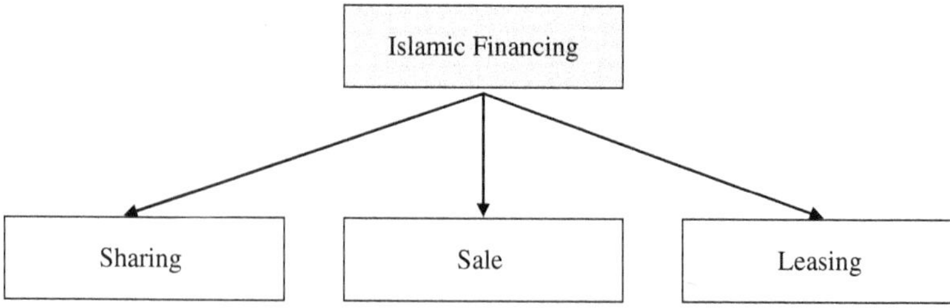

Fig. 1 Modes of international trade financing (*Source* Author's own)

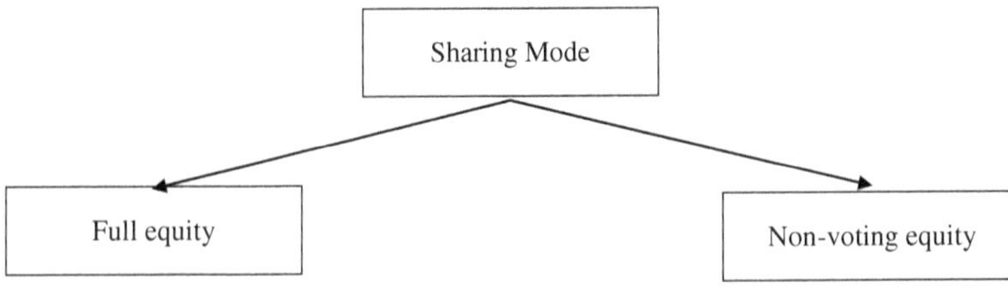

Fig. 2 Sharing (*Source* Author's own)

the early days of Islam. Generally, in this method, Islamic banks provide financing for projects in the expectation of a share in the returns; if the project makes a loss, all those that provided capital and finance lose proportionately. In conventional finance, the bank will lend the money at a fixed rate of interest.

Sharing can be divided into two methods: full equity sharing and non-voting equity financing.

In full equity sharing, a bank will partner its client in a joint venture in which both share the contribution of equity capital and also the management of the project or deal. This form of application is also known as *musharakah*. In *musharakah*, profits will be divided on a predetermined basis and any losses will be shared in proportion to the capital contribution. This method can be combined with *mudharabah*. For example, the initial capital of a project can be financed by *musharakah*, while later working capital may be provided according to *mudharabah*.

In non-voting equity financing, a bank will entrust the money to the fund user, who is to utilize it in an agreed manner. Here, the bank will receive the principal and a pre-agreed share of profit, while the fund user will keep the remaining profits. Should the project make a loss, both parties will share such losses. This method is also called *mudharabah*, the rules of which are that the division of profits between the two parties must necessarily be on a proportional basis and that settlement cannot be in a lump sum or a guaranteed return; the bank is not liable for losses beyond the capital it has contributed; and the fund user does not share in the losses except for the loss of his time and efforts. For example, during medieval Arabic times, when wealthy merchants financed the caravan trade, they would share in the profits if the operation was successful, or lose all or part of their investment if the merchandise was stolen, lost or sold for less than its cost.

These sharing methods or principles may also be applied in various other ways to finance either exporters or importers. Export financing may be undertaken on the basis of *musharakah* and *mudharabah* to finance a quantity of goods that have already been produced. In export financing, the bank will finance the principal amount; this is equal to the cost of the goods ordered from the exporter that are ready to be shipped. The active partner (the exporter) will manage the both the cash and the commodities. Any promissory notes and other guarantees—for example, bank acceptances and so on—that are obtained during the course of the business will be kept until maturity, at which point the profit will be distributed between the two parties.

In the financing of importers, they can either use the sharing principle, as in export financing, or they can use *musharakah*. With its promise to buy, *musharakah* means that the importer will promise the bank to buy out the financing partnership or the goods at a marked-up price once the imported goods are received. In this case, the active partner (the importer) will act as an agent for the bank in receiving the delivery of the imported goods (Fig. 3).

In import finance, the bank will purchase the goods and then sell them to producers or consumers, meaning that such payment will be received in the future. There are several forms of sale mechanism that can be applied. The typical method used is the sale contract, in which the bank purchases and sells the goods, equipment or machinery to producers or customers at an agreed on marked-up deferred price.

There are two other forms in sale method: construction or manufacturing contracts, and deferred delivery contracts.

Construction or manufacturing contracts are normally used to finance land development, infrastructure, and industrial and residential construction. Deferred delivery contracts are typically used to finance farmers

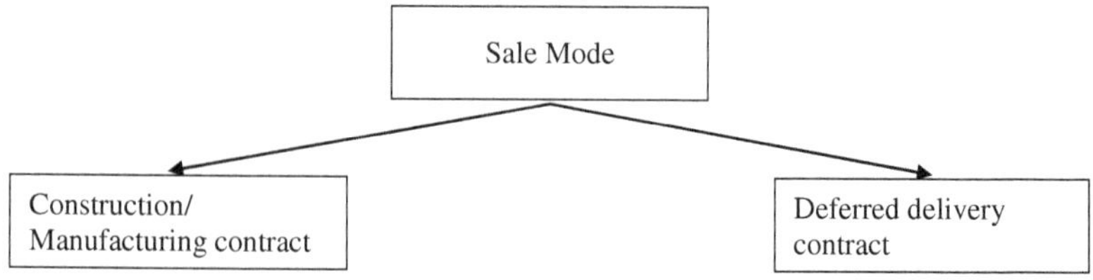

Fig. 3 Sales (*Source* Author's own)

who need funds for their operations against the production of grain at the end of the season. Under this type of contract, payment can either be made in a deferred lump-sum, or it can be settled by instalments spread over a period of time.

In international trade, the sale method helps finance importers by means of documentary credit which is undertaken on the principle of *murabahah* with its promise to buy. The importer will make a sale contract with the bank whereby the payment is deferred. The bank will act as the importer of the ordered goods and the delivery of the goods will be taken by the importer on the basis of being the bank's proxy or agent. A further form of sale method used by Islamic banks is *istisna'* financing. It consists of two *istisna'* sale contracts: the first, between importer and the bank; and the second, between the bank and the exporter.

In financing inventory replenishment for future delivery of goods to the international market, *salam* and a parallel *salam* contract is sometimes applied. It is utilized in standardized contracts for main commodities. Financing the exporter can also be done on the basis of two sale contracts: one on a cash basis and the other on the basis of a marked-up, deferred payment. Where settlement is on a cash basis, the sale contract will be between the exporter and the Islamic bank; on a marked-up, deferred payment basis, the sale contract will be concluded between the exporter as an agent of the Islamic bank and the importer.

8.1 Leasing Methods

Leasing (*ijarah*) is probably the fastest growing activity offered by Islamic financial institutions. Leasing methods come in a variety of forms—with fixed or variable rents, declining or fixed ownership, or of an operational or financial nature—together with various conditions regarding the status of leased assets at the end of the lease period, as practised by leasing companies and, recently, in many traditional banks. It is essentially used in financing the importation of equipment, machinery and other fixed assets.

It is virtually identical to conventional leasing, where a bank leases an asset to a third party in exchange for a specified rent. The amounts of payments are known in advance and the asset remains the property of the lessor. Only in a few respects do Islamic contracts differ. It can be seen in the principle of *ijarah wa iqtina* (a lease-purchase agreement), whereby, at the expiration of the lease, the lessee becomes the owner of the asset.

Ijarah, from the perspective of classical Islamic *fiqh*, constitutes a sale of benefit or usufruct (*manfa'a*), which means its rules are similar to the ordinary sale principle. In order to avoid the elements of *riba'* and *gharar*, there are a few minor differences between *ijarah* and conventional leasing. The law views some benefits and burdens of the property as belonging naturally and unchangeably to the lessee, others to the lessor. For example, the law provides that the duty to repair the goods always fall on the lessor, since the repair benefits him as the owner. Also, usufruct does not yet exist and is intangible; rather, it is a stream of use extending into the future, which is risky and unstable. Islamic law thus gives broad scope to the lessee to cancel the lease if the usufruct proves less valuable than expected. Finally, the price at which the asset may be sold to the lessee at the expiration of the contract cannot be predetermined.

Although, initially directed primarily at businesses, *ijarah* is increasingly used in retail finance, mainly for the mortgaging of homes, cars and household needs.

9 Conclusion

Islamic financing has become one of the fastest growing means of financing compared to that of conventional banks. It not only fulfils the needs of Muslim society in financial matters by being in line with Islamic teachings and the *Shari'ah* rulings, but is also free from prohibited elements—for example, *riba'* (interest). *Riba'*, as we know, only favours the rich and those who are already in business; also, it is only marginally concerned with the success of the ventures it finances. Islamic financing offers a variety of instruments or methods—for example, profit and loss sharing, which promotes risk sharing and avoids *riba'*. This method not only places emphasis on lending being on an interest-free basis, but also, more generally, demonstrates a pursuit of justice. Islamic financing allows a capital-poor but promising entrepreneur to obtain working capital. The bank, being an investor, as opposed to a lender, has a stake in the long-term success of the venture; the entrepreneur, rather than being concerned with debt-servicing, can concentrate on a long-term endeavour that, in turn, may provide economic and social benefits to the community. Disappointingly, despite its benefits, profit and loss sharing constitutes only a small part (about 5%) of the activities of Islamic banks.

Islamic banks need to make special efforts, especially in the areas of economies of scale and marketing, if they wish to increase their share in financing international trade. Islamic banks should increase their direct contact with businesses and become more comprehensive bankers, rather than straightforward lenders. They should also branch out, especially overseas and in trade centres that export to and import from their headquarters, and also try to incorporate domestic conventional banking that accepts the creation of branches and windows for Islamic financing transactions in an attempt to Islamize inter-Muslim country trade financing. Such banks usually have better capabilities and a larger international clientele, and enhance Islamic financing if they could transform inter-Islamic financing markets into Islamic bodies.

References

IDB. (1997). Statistical Monograph, October.

Vittas. D., and Cho, Y. J. (1996). Credit Policies: Lesson from Japan and Korea. *World Bank Research Observer*, vol. II, no. 2, August.

Wall Street Journal. (1996). Special Supplement on Islamic Banking, 9 April.

CHAPTER 15

Islamic Model of International Trade and Shipping

1 Introduction

Islamic banking has been involved in the financial industry since the late 1980s. Numerous products have been put into practice, particularly with regard to international trade and shipping between Islamic countries. There are several instruments and facilities provided by conventional banks to facilitate international trade and shipping; for example, bankers' acceptance bills, trust receipts, pre-shipment refinancing and post-shipment refinancing. However, all these products run contrary to the Islamic approach to trade and financing as all of these products are based on the element of *riba*.

As Allah (*SWT*) says in Al-Qur'an:

> Those who eat *Riba* [usury] will not stand [on the Day of Resurrection] except like the standing of a person beaten by *Syaitan* [Satan] leading him to insanity. That is because they say: 'Trading is only like *Riba*, whereas Allah has permitted trading and forbidden *Riba*. So whosoever receives an admonition from his *Rubb* and stops eating *Riba*, shall not be punished for the past; his case is for Allah [to judge]; but whoever returns [to *Riba*], such are the dwellers of the Fire – they will abide therein. Allah will destroy *Riba* and will give increase for *Sadaqat* [deeds of charity, alms]. And Allah likes not the disbelievers, sinners. Truly, those who believe, and do deeds of righteousness, and perform *As-Salat* [*Iqamat-As-Salat*], and

M. M. Billah, *Islamic Financial Products*,
https://doi.org/10.1007/978-3-030-17624-2_15

> give *Zakat*, they will have their reward with their *Rubb*. On them shall be no fear, nor shall they grieve. O you who believe! Be afraid of Allah and give up what remains [due to you] from *Riba* [from now onward].' (2: 275–279)

Abdullah bin Mas'ud (May Allah be pleased with him) reported:

> The Messenger of Allah (*PBUH*) cursed the one who accepts *Riba* [usury] and the one who pays it.

2 General Concern

There is rising concern in Islamic banking that international trade and financing facilities should not be based on *riba*. Islamic banking has introduced numerous of products and facilities for international trade and shipping that are not based on *riba*; for example, the Islamic accepted bill (IAB), *murabahah* financing, *musharakah* financing and Islamic export credit refinancing (IECR). Some conventional banks have also followed suit by introducing products not based on *riba*.

3 Islamic Accepted Bills: Import

IABs are orders to a bank by a bank customer to pay a sum of money at a future date. When the bank endorses an order for payment as accepted, it assumes responsibility for the ultimate payment to the holder of the acceptance. This bill can be used for import or purchase, and export for sales, and is conditional on the trade being for permissible and *halal* goods (http://www.bankislam.com.my). IABs offer a facility whereby a customer can approach the bank to provide financing for his working capital requirements; for instance, to purchase stock and inventory, spares and replacements, or semi-finished goods and raw materials (Fig. 1).

- The bank purchases or appoints the customer as its agent to purchase the required goods on its behalf and settles the purchase price from its own funds.
- The bank then sells the goods to the customer at an agreed price comprising its purchase price and a profit margin, and allows

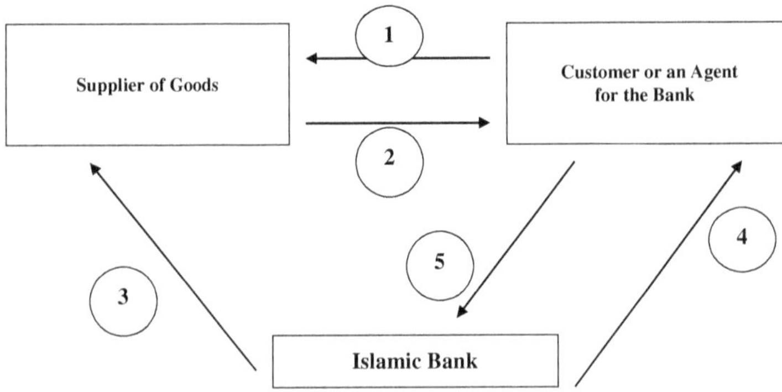

Fig. 1 Islamic accepted bill (IAB): Import (*Source* Author's own)

the customer to settle this sale price on a deferred term of 30 days, 60 days or 90 days or such other period as is appropriate.
- On the due date, the customer pays the bank the agreed sale price on the maturity date of the financing.

IABs can be traded in the secondary market to another party. Bank Negara Malaysia has allowed this trading, subject to certain guidelines. Being a negotiable instrument, it affords a very attractive price (Mahayudin 1997).

4 Islamic Accepted Bills: Export

IABs for exports or sales are a facility whereby the bank finances exports and sales under the principle of *bai al-dayn*. *Bai al-dayn* (debt purchasing) is a short-term financing facility whereby the bank purchases the customer's rights to the debt, which is typically securitized as a bill of exchange. An exporter wishing to benefit from this facility prepares export documents as required under the rules of a sale of contract or letter of credit. He presents these documents to the bank to be purchased. As the export documents have to be sent to the buyer overseas, the bank requests the exporter to draw another bill of exchange drawn on the bank. This bill is known as an IAB: Exports. IAB: Exports also can be traded in the secondary market.

The formula for calculating the purchase price is as follows:

$$\text{Market value} = \text{face value} \times (1 - \text{annual rate of return} \times \text{number of days to maturity})$$

5 Letter of Credit: *Murabahah*

Murabahah financing (deferred lump sum sale) was introduced into the market for those who wish to import commodities and goods for their operations. Banks will offer the financing for working capital requirement to purchase stock and inventory, spares and replacements, or raw materials and semi-finished goods. The bank either makes the purchase, or appoints the customer as its agent to purchase the required goods on its behalf, settling the purchase price from its own funds. The bank subsequently sells the goods to the customer at an agreed price comprising its purchase price and a profit margin. The bank provides this financing under a contract of *murabahah* (mark-up or cost-plus). Under this agreement, the customer will be appointed by the bank as an agent. The following is an illustration of the workings of the *murabahah* financing method:

- The customer, as himself or as an agent for the bank, places an order for the goods from the supplier (purchase order).
- The supplier will supply the goods to customer on an order basis.
- Once the supplier delivered the goods, the bank will make a settlement payment to the supplier for the purchase price on a cash basis.
- The bank sells goods to the customer on a deferred payment basis.
- The customer settles the bank's selling price on a mandatory basis.
- According to the agreement, the customer has to settle the sale price on a deferred term of 30 days, 60 days, 90 days, or such other period may be arranged.

6 Letter of Credit Financing: *Musharakah*

Islamic banks have introduced letter of credit facilities under a contract of *musharakah* financing. A *musharakah* is a partnership contract between two or more parties whereby each party will contribute the capital. The portion of capital will be determined between the parties at agreed ratio. The profit is shared among the parties based on the profit sharing ratio agreed in the contract, and any loss is shared between the parties based on the contribution ratio.

- Customers who use this facility have to submit a request for a letter of credit and negotiate the terms of the *musharakah* financing.
- The bank requires a deposit from the customer for his share of the cost of the goods to be purchased or imported in accordance with the *musharakah* agreement, which the Bank accepts under a *wadiah* contract.
- The bank establishes the letter of credit and pays the proceeds to the negotiating bank, utilizing the customer's deposit as well as its own share of the financing, and releases the documents to the customer.

7 Letter of Credit Financing: *Wakalah*

Another facility offered by Islamic banks is a letter of credit that is based on *wakalah*. *Wakalah* means 'agency'; this means that a bank will act as an agent on behalf of an importer or exporter. In other words, the banks will be an agent for the customer.

- Customers have to place a deposit for the full amount of the price of the goods to be purchased or imported, which the Bank accepts under a *wadiah* contract.
- The customer gives an instruction to the bank to make payment to the seller at a specific future date.
- The bank establishes the letter of credit and pays the proceeds to the negotiating bank, utilizing the customer's deposit, and releases the documents to the customer.

8 Islamic Export Credit Refinancing

The primary objective of the IECR scheme is to promote the export of products manufactured in Malaysia; these are agricultural products and primary commodities. The bank offers a competitive profit rate to Malaysian exporters through commercial banks participating in the scheme (http://www.exim.com.my).

Companies that can enjoy IECR financing are those involved in manufacturing activities, agricultural producers and trading companies.

There are two IECR facilities: pre-shipment and post-shipment. Pre-shipment IECR is either a sum advanced to manufacturers and agricultural producers to facilitate the production of eligible products, or a loan advanced to trading companies for the purchase of domestic intermediate or final products for export prior to shipment. The operational method for pre-shipment IECR is similar to that for the IAB.

Assume that the inception date is 1 January 2004 and the maturity date is 5 February 2004. The cost of the materials is equivalent to a refinancing amount from Bank Negara Malaysia of $100,950.50. This amount should not exceed the value of the export order. In this case, the value of the export order is US$1,000,000 @ 3.80 = $3,800,000.

An Islamic bank will finance its customer at 7% per annum by using the following formula (Mahayudin 1997):

$$\text{Selling Price} = C\,[R \times T + 1]$$
$$= 36{,}000$$

where C = the cost price of goods to be financed, R = the annual rate of return, and T = the tenor.

Post-shipment IECR is advanced to finance the period after shipment and pending receipt of the export proceeds, should the export be conditional on being of an acceptable standard following inspection by the buyer (Export Import Bank: Exim Bank). Exporters who sell goods and apply for finance using this facility may obtain the finance for the period of credit extended to the buyer. The period of financing may be extended to include the standard en route period (i.e. the expected number of days for the documents to reach the importer's banker).

9 Multilateral Trade Using the Islamic Gold Dinar

Another method that should be introduced for international trade and shipping between Islamic countries is a bilateral and multilateral payment agreement (MPA) between countries by using the Islamic gold dinar (Meera 2002).

To illustrate the efficiency of the MPA, let us assume that three countries are involved in a transaction: Malaysia, Saudi Arabia and Egypt.

- Assuming that the volume of trade between Malaysia and Saudi Arabia were the same as in the example with BPA, and we add the additional trade of those two countries with that of Egypt.
- In the earlier example, a total of 10.7 million gold dinars of trade takes place between the three countries, with a net payment of only 0.1 million gold dinars.
- In other words, the only payment required is for Egypt to pay Saudi 0.1 million gold dinars, but the total value of trade among the three countries is substantial, at 10.7 million gold dinars.
- It is also possible to refine the mechanism further, whereby the credit or debit outstanding at the end of each quarter can be forwarded to the subsequent quarters and final settlement is made at the end of the year.

The advantage of this refinement is that a net import position for a country during a particular quarter may be offset by a net export position in the subsequent quarter so that, for the year as a whole, the payment flows are further minimized.

10 Conclusion

Being in the Islamic financial market, we are eager that there be a new wave that is more committed to Islamic products. As we are hungry for more organized and modern methods of trading, we should not ignore the fact that the traditional ways of international trading, such as bartering or using gold dinar as the medium of exchange, are highly relevant to our objective to avoid *riba*.

Islamic banks also need to place greater emphasis on economies of scale, if they wish to be a major player in the provision of international trading and shipping financing. The potential for Islamic Banks in this area is considerable. However, there are several other tasks that could be put on the main agenda, such as increasing business contacts and being more comprehensive bankers, rather than simple lenders.

Islamic countries also need to be major league players to support Islamic banks in their business. Islamic banks also could be involved in incorporating with conventional banks overseas, so as to provide Islamic windows and thereby promote the Islamic method of financing for international trade.

References

Mahayudin, I. (1997). *International Trade Operations—A Guide*. BIMB Institute of Research and Training, Sdn Bhd.

Meera, A. K. (2002). *The Islamic Gold Dinar*. Subang Jaya: Pelanduk Publications.

http://www.bankislam.com.my.

http://www.exim.com.my.

CHAPTER 16

Islamic Accepted Bills

1 Introduction

Islamic accepted bills (IABs) are one of the Islamic financial instruments traded in the Islamic inter-bank money market (Yakob 1995). IABs are traded based on the concepts of *murabahah* and *bay' al dayn*, and are similar to other financial instruments such as green banker's acceptances, Islamic mortgage bonds and Islamic private debt securities. The Islamic inter-bank money market, in turn, is the place where various activities are carried out, including the purchase and sale of Islamic financial instruments among market participants, inter-bank investment activities, and cheque clearing and settlement facilities.

IABs arise from a situation when a customer, on behalf of a bank, buys goods that they want, the bank subsequently selling the goods to the customer on the basis of a deferred payment. The bank makes a lump sum payment to the seller for the goods purchased by its customer. These due payments represent profit for the holders of the IABs that are traded in the secondary market. IABs are mostly used to finance imports and exports, or local purchases and sales, provided that the traded goods are *halal*.

This chapter will analyse IABs in terms of structure and operation. First, we define IABs and discuss their operational procedures. Next, we present some of the guidelines imposed on the trade and issuance of IABs. The chapter goes on to explain how IABs are traded in the

M. M. Billah, *Islamic Financial Products*,
https://doi.org/10.1007/978-3-030-17624-2_16

secondary market, their users and traders, and the pricing basis used. Finally, we address the *Shari'ah* point of view on IABs in terms of their acceptability.

2 Understanding IABs

The IAB is one of the instruments traded on the Islamic inter-bank money market and is based on the concept of *al-murabahah/bai' al-dayn* (Bank Negara Malaysia 1993). An IAB is an order to a bank by its customer obliging it to pay a certain amount of money to the holder of the acceptance bill. The bank makes a lump sum payment for the goods purchased by its customer on its behalf and sells those goods to the customer on the basis of a deferred payment. These due payments represent profit for the holders of the IABs that are traded in the secondary market to another party. They attract a very attractive price because they are a negotiable instrument. The customer is, therefore, financed at a very attractive rate.

IABs are similar to banker's acceptance bills. A banker's acceptance bill is a bill with a specific face value issued by a bank to the customer at a discount (Rosely 2003). The discounted value of the bill is credited to the customer's account while the customer pays back the face value of the bill on the maturity date. For example, a banker's acceptance bill may have a face value of $2 million, while the amount of money credited to the customer's account is $1.9 million. The difference between the face value and the discounted value (the amount of money credited to the customer's account) represents an interest payment. Banker's acceptance bills are used for project financing and are traded on the secondary market. The IAB was introduced as an alternative to banker's acceptance bills in view of the need to provide customers an Islamic alternative.

The difference between banker's acceptance bills and IABs is the absence of interest payments in the case of IABs. Interest is not allowed in Islam and, therefore, the profit in IABs is said to be derived from trading, which is permissible. The profit by trading is derived through the contracts of *murabahah*. *Murabahah* refers to the sale of a good at a price based on cost-plus profit margin agreed by both parties to the contract. Here, the Islamic bank appoints a customer as agent to purchase the goods at cost. The bank guarantees the payment to the supplier. The bank then sells the goods to the customer, offering credit but to be settled in, say, 90 days. The selling price includes cost and profit, which is called a marked-up price. The bank then draws a bill on the customer who accepts the bill at the marked-up price. The holder of the bill (i.e. the bank) can sell the bill to a third party at a price not less than the cost (Bank Negara Malaysia 1993). Such sale is based on the *bay' al dayn* contract. *Bay' al dayn* refers to the sale of a debt arising from a trade transaction with a deferred payment.

IABs are widely used in financing imports and exports. It is an alternative to the banker's acceptance bills that are used to finance purchases and sales by conventional banks. IABs, however, are used only in transactions involving *halal* goods and services.

2.1 IAB: Imports (Al-Murabahah/Bai' Al-Dayn)

A customer can approach their bank to provide financing for their working capital requirements to import inventory or raw materials. The bank purchases the required goods and settles the purchase price from its own funds. The bank then sells the goods to the customer at an agreed price comprising the purchase price and a profit margin, and allows the customer to settle this sale price on a deferred term of 30 days, 60 days or 90 days. On the due date, the customer pays the bank the agreed sale price. The sale of goods by the bank on a deferred payment term constitutes the creation of debt. This debt is securitized in the form of a bill of exchange drawn by the bank on the customer for the full amount of the bank's selling price payable on maturity. IABs are traded in the secondary market based on the concept of *bay' al dayn*. This makes them an attractive, low-cost financing instrument.

2.2 IAB: Exports or Sales (Bai' Al-Dayn)

The bank finances exports and sales under the principle of *bai al-dayn*. Under the terms of this bill, an exporter prepares export documents as required under the sale of contract or letter of credit. He presents these documents to the bank to be purchased. As the export documents have to be sent to the buyer overseas, the exporter is requested by the bank to draw another bill of exchange drawn on the bank. This bill is known as an IAB: Exports. The IAB: Exports can be traded in secondary market.

3 Determining the Price of an IAB

The holder of an IAB may sell it on to any other person. The price of an IAB used for financing sales is determined using the following formula (Bank Negara Malaysia 1993):

$$P = \text{FV}\ (1 - rt/36{,}500)$$

where P = the market price or sale proceeds, FV = the face or maturity value, r = the annual rate of profit (in percentage) and t = the number of days remaining to maturity.

The price of an IAB used for financing purchases is determined using the following formula:

$$P = \text{IV}\ (1 + rt/36{,}500)$$

where P = the market price or sale proceeds, IV = the invoice value, r = the annual rate of profit (in percentage), t = the number of days remaining to maturity.

A certain commission may be charged for services related to IAB acceptance. In the case of IABs for sales, the drawer of an IAB may pay the bank the commission for the acceptance service. On the other hand, in case of IABs for purchases, the drawer may charge the acceptor a commission for the drawing services. Where such a commission is payable, the rate of commission is determined on the basis of the agreed proportion of the maturity face value of the IAB, expressed in percentage per annum.

4 Features of an IAB

As mentioned earlier, IABs are similar to banker's acceptance bills and but were introduced as an alternative for Islamic institutions so that they could benefit in the same way as customers using the banker's acceptance bill facility offered by conventional banks. There are a number of features that make IABs distinct from banker's acceptance bills.

- There are two types of financing available under the IAB facility: imports and local purchases financing; and exports and local sales financing.

- The financing is done under the *murabahah* concept whereby a customer purchases the required goods from the seller on behalf of the bank, which pays for the goods and resells them to the customer at a price inclusive profit margin and based on deferred payment. The maximum time allowed for a deferred payment is 200 days.
- The deferred payment constitutes a creation of debt. This debt is securitized in the form of a bill of exchange drawn by the bank and accepted by the customer for the full amount of the bank's selling price, including cost and profit margin, payable on the day of maturity. IABs can be sold in the secondary market at an agreed price using the concept of *bay' al-dayn*. Here, it is the bank that draws an IAB while the importer or purchaser becomes the acceptor.
- Similar to a letter of credit arrangement, an exporter who wants to use an IAB prepares and sends export documents to the importer's bank. The exporter draws a new bill of exchange on the domestic bank and this becomes an IAB. The bank purchases the IAB at a mutually agreed price using the concept of *bay' al-dayn*. The proceeds will be credited to the exporter's account. In this case, it is the exporter who draws the IAB and the bank is the accepting party.
- IABs can be purchased and sold using forward purchase and forward sales agreements. Forward purchase is a separate agreement whereby the purchasing party agrees to purchase IABs at an agreed price on a future specified date. On the other hand, forward sale is an agreement to sell IABs at an agreed price on a future specified date. There are two undertaking agreements in forward purchase and forward sale transactions.

5 Guidelines and Regulations on IABs

After its introduction in 1991, the IAB facility became very popular in the areas of trade and finance. With such significance development in the product, in 1992 the Bank Negara Malaysia saw a need to revise the guidelines on banker's acceptance bills and undertook, which had first been issued in 1989. These guidelines are presented below in brief (Bank Negara Malaysia 1993):

- An IAB can be drawn on and accepted by a bank or purchaser under the following circumstances only:

- The IAB is drawn to finance genuine trade transactions;
- The drawer, in the event of an IAB sale, makes a declaration that he has neither obtained nor will obtain another source of financing;
- The goods involved in the trade transaction are tangible and *halal* goods;
- Services will not be eligible unless specifically provided for in the guidelines;
- Adequate documentary evidence must be presented to the accepting or drawing bank.

- An IAB may be drawn to finance a trade transaction between two related companies, provided that:

  - The related companies are separate legal entities;
  - The transaction was undertaken resulting in a genuine transfer of title to the goods concerned, evidenced by the proper documents.

- An IAB shall not be drawn to finance any trade transaction between two business entities of sole proprietorships where the proprietor is the same person, or between two business entities of partnerships where the majority of partners are the same persons.
- An IAB shall not be drawn to finance a sales transaction on which the seller has provided a leasing, hire purchase or factoring facility to the buyer for the settlement of that transaction.

6 Application of IABs

As was mentioned earlier, there are two types of financing under the IAB facility: imports and local purchases financing, and export and local sales financing.

6.1 Imports and Local Purchases

The financing of this type of contract will be under the *murabahah* working capital mechanism. For this concept, the bank appoints the customer as the purchasing agent for the bank. The customer then purchases goods required from the seller on behalf of the bank, then the bank pays the seller and resells the goods to the customer at a price inclusive of a profit margin. The customer will be allowed a deferred

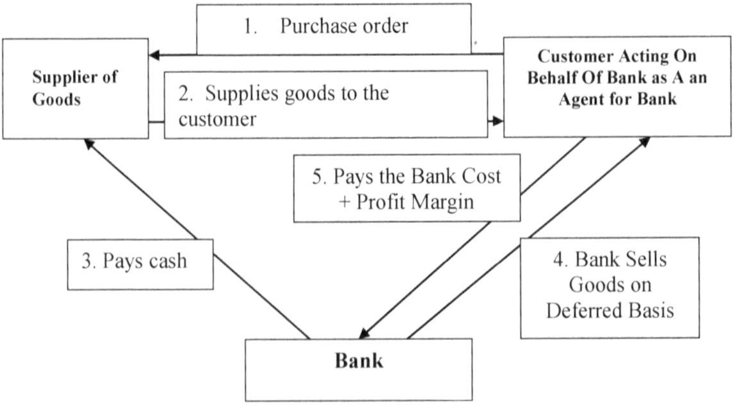

Fig. 1 Al-murabahah working capital financing (*Source* Author's own)

payment term of up to 200 days. After the maturity of the *murabahah* financing, the customer will pay the bank the original cost plus the profit margin (Bank Negara Malaysia 1993).

6.1.1 Al-Murabahah *Working Capital Financing*

Figure 1 presents an example of *al-murabahah* working capital financing.

6.2 Export and Local Sales

With this arrangement, the bank finances exports and sales according to the concept of *bay' al-dayn*. *Bay' al-dayn* (debt financing) is a short-term financing facility. It is where the bank purchases the customer's right to the debt, which is typically securitized as an IAB. The customer's account will be credited with the purchase price less the bank's charges. The price of *al-dayn* will be agreed between the customer and the bank. Following this, *al-dayn* may be sold to a third party.

The sale of goods on a deferred payment basis creates debt. This debt is in the form of a bill of exchange drawn by the bank on, and accepted by, the customer for the full amount of the bank's selling price and is payable on maturity. The bank may sell the IAB to a third party, then the concept of *bay' al-Dayn* will be used whereby the bank will sell the IAB at an agreed price (Bank Negara Malaysia 1993).

The purchase of debt by the bank takes place at the current financing rate of the market. However, Bank Negara Malaysia, in an attempt to encourage exports from Malaysia, has introduced a scheme known as the Export Credit Refinancing Scheme. Using this scheme, the bank may resell this debt (*al-dayn*) to Bank Negara Malaysia at a special price. Bank Negara Malaysia, however, limits the availability of this financing scheme to certain goods only.

7 *Shari'ah* Perspective on IABs

As has been shown, the application of an IAB creates debt (*al-dayn*). This section of the chapter discusses the *Shari'ah* perspective regarding the sale of *al-dayn*.

7.1 *The Nature of* Bay' Al-Dayn

The issue of *bay' al-dayn* arises when the IABs are traded in the secondary market. Let us now discuss *bay' al dayn* so as to show its nature according to an Islamic perspective.

According to *al-Majallah* (*Majallah al-Ahkam al-Adliyyah*, Art. 158), *dayn* defines what is due; that is, the amount of money owed by a certain debtor. Therefore, a sum of money that does not exist is also considered a debt, as also is a specific sum of money from things that exist or are present, or from a heap of wheat that is present before it is separated from the mass. *Al-dayn* can be either a sum of money or a commodity, such as food or metal. Based on the aforementioned definition of *al-dayn* and the literal meaning of *bay' al-dayn*, we can define it as the sale of a payable right either to the debtor himself, or to any third party. This type of sale is usually for immediate payment or for deferred payment (*al nasi'ah*).

7.1.1 Sale of Al-Dayn *to a Third Party*

According to most *Hanafi*, *Hanbali* and *Shafi* jurists (Al-Zuhili, *Bay' al dayn in the Shari'ah*), it is not permitted to sell *al-dayn* to a non-debtor or to any third party. Such opinions are based on the forbidden sale of *al kali bil al kali*, sale of a *gharar*, or the sale of something that the seller does not possess.

A prophetic tradition clearly states: 'Do not sell what you do not possess.'

Selling *al-dayn* to a third party is allowed under certain conditions.

As an exception, *Maliki*, *Hanafi* and some *Shafi* jurists allowed the selling of *al-dayn* to a third party. They stated that there is no authentic source that prohibits this kind of sale. Therefore, it should be allowed and permitted, since the *dayn* is *mustaqir* (confirmed debt). Since this pronouncement, the creditor has had the right to sell *al-dayn* to the debtor as well as to a third party, provided the following rules are observed:

- The *dayn* must be *mustaqir* (confirmed debt) and the contract must be performed on the spot. It may not be a deferred sale in order to avoid any relationship with the sale of a debt for a debt, which is prohibited by Islamic law.
- The debtor must be financially capable, and must accept and recognize the sale, in order that he will not deny that the sale took place. This condition aims to avoid any dispute between the parties, and the debtor must be easily accessible so that the creditor knows whether he has the capacity to pay his debt.
- The sale should not be based on selling gold with silver, or opposite, because, any exchanges between these items necessitates immediate possession and, if the debt is money, its price in another debt should be equal in terms of amount and quantity.

Furthermore, the selling of *al-dayn* must avoid the occurrence of *riba* between the two debts, and must also avoid any kind of *gharar*, which could come about should the buyer be unable to take possession of what he bought, as it is not permitted that the buyer sells before actual receipt of the purchased item.

It is important to note that Muslim scholars have unanimously prohibited the trading of debt (*bay' al-dayn*) at anything other than face value. Where the price paid for a debt is not the same as the face value of that debt, the transaction would be tantamount to *riba al-nasi'ah* and is therefore prohibited. Any profit created from the sale and purchase of a debt is *riba*.

> And whatever *riba* you give so that it may increase in the wealth of the people, it does not increase with Allah. (Ar-Rum 30:39)
>
> Prophet Muhammad (*SAW*) said: 'That every loan entailing benefit is usury'. (Al-Shirazi, n.d.)

The IAB would have been acceptable from an Islamic point of view if the application of the method of financing were based on the legal maxim of *al-ghunmu bil ghurmi* (*Majallah al-Ahkam*, Art. 87), meaning that no person is allowed to invest in a way that generates profit without exposing himself to the risk of loss. It would expose both parties to the outcome of their deal, be it a profit or a loss, and thus avoid usury as matter of Islamic principle.

8 Conclusion

IABs are a low-cost form of finance for businesses in the purchase and sale of inventory, raw materials and finished goods. The low cost is due to the exchange of IABs in the secondary market. After its introduction in 1991, the IAB facility in Malaysia became very popular in the areas of trade and finance. A set of guidelines have been issued by the Bank Negara Malaysia to regulate the transactions involving IABs. IABs are based on the concepts of *murabahah* and *bay' al dayn*. Consequently, the *Shari'ah* ruling for IABs is similar to that applied to *bay al inah*, which involves *bay' al dayn*. That is, the majority of*'ulama* in the Middle East do not agree with such transactions, although some of the*'ulama* have accepted them based on the valid external evidence of sale.

References

Al-Shirazi. (n.d.). *Al-Muhadhab*, vol. 1.

Al-Zuhili, *Bay' al Dayn in the Shari'ah.*

Bank Negara Malaysia. (1993). *Guidelines on Interest-Free Accepted Bills*, 4 March.

Majallah al-Ahkam al-Adliyyah.

Rosely, S. A. (2003). 'Islamic Project Financing in Malaysia'. A Collection of Articles on Islamic Banking and Finance.

Yakob, N. M. (1995). 'Money Market in Islamic Banking: The Problems of Thin Trading'. Paper Presented in the Conference on SPTF and Islamic Banking Products, December.

CHAPTER 17

Islamic Lease Financing (*Al-Ijarah*)

1 Introduction

Islamic financing is a widely used modern application nowadays. Most of the banking institutions in Malaysia have used Islamic financing products as an alternative to those of the conventional banking system. One of the modes of financing in Islamic banking is *ijarah*. *Ijarah* is a term of Islamic *fiqh*. Literally, it means the 'sale of the usufruct' (*bai' al manfa'ah*) (Islamic Financing: *Ijarah*). The terminological meaning of *ijarah* also reflects its literal meaning. The *Hanafis*, for example, define *ijarah* as 'a contract for the use of usufructs for a counter-value or price'. The *Shafi'is* give a more detailed definition in which they define *ijarah* as 'a contract for the use of a permissible, determined and known usufruct, capable of being spent, for a known counter-value or price'. The *Malikis* and *Hanbalis* define it as 'the transfer of the use of the usufruct of a permissible thing for a known counter-value' (al-Zuhaili, n.d.). From the definitions given, we can conclude that the basic meaning of *ijarah* is 'the contract to use the usufruct of a permissible thing for a known counter-value'. Hence, the main subject of *ijarah* is usufruct (*manfa'ah*), and not an object (*'ain*), taken in lieu of the payment of a counter-value ('iwadh). The term *ijarah* is used for two different situations: employment and usufruct.

- The employment of the services of a person for wages given to him as a consideration for his hired services. The employer is called the

M. M. Billah, *Islamic Financial Products*,
https://doi.org/10.1007/978-3-030-17624-2_17

musta'jir while the employee is called the *ajir*. For example, a person hiring the services of a porter to carry his baggage to the airport is a *musta'jir*, while the porter is an *ajir*. The wages paid to the *ajir* are called '*ujrah*'.

- The second type of *ijarah* relates to usufructs of properties, not to the services of people. *Ijarah*, in this sense, means to transfer the usufruct of a particular property to another person for a rent claimed from him. In this case, the term *ijarah* is analogous to the English term 'leasing'. Here, the lessor is called the *mu'jir*, the lessee is called the *mustajir* and the rent payable to the lessor is called *ujrah*.

The second type of *ijarah* is more relevant because it is generally used as a form of investment, and also as a method of financing. The rules of *ijarah* in the sense of leasing are very much analogous to the rules of sale as, in both cases, something is transferred to another person for a valuable consideration. The only difference between *ijarah* and sale is that in the case of a sale the property is transferred to the purchaser while, in the case of *ijarah*, the property remains in the ownership of the transferor—only its usufruct (i.e. the right to use it) is transferred to the lessee.

2 *Shari'ah* and Legal Basis of *Ijarah*

Jurists generally agree as to the legality of *ijarah*. The *jumhur* based their view as to the legality of *ijarah* on the *Qur'anicayat*, Sunnah of the Prophet (*SAW*) and *ijma'*.

Among the Quranic *ayat* relied on is the following:

> Lodge them [the divorced women] where you dwell, according to your means, and do not treat them in such a harmful way that they be obliged to leave. And if they are pregnant, then spend on them till they deliver. Then if they give suck to the children for you, give them their due payment, and let each of you accept the advice of the other in a just way. But if you make difficulties for one another, then some other woman may give suck for him [the father of the child]. (Al-Talaq: 6)

Another *ayat* is in *Surah* Al-Qasas: 26–27, which narrates the story of Prophet Shu'aib (*AW*) and the Prophet Musa (*AW*), whereby, the former offered the latter a contract of employment for the hand of his daughter in marriage:

> And said one of them [the two women]: 'O my father! Hire him! Verily, the best of men for you to hire is the strong, the trustworthy.' (Al-Qasas: 26)
>
> He said: 'I intend to wed one of these two daughters of mine to you, on condition that you serve me for eight years, but if you complete ten years, it will be [a favour[from you. But I intend not to place you under a difficulty. If Allah will, you will find me one of the righteous.' (Al-Qasas: 27)

From the Sunnah, it was narrated that the Prophet Muhammad (*SAW*) said:

> Give the hired man his wages before his sweat duties. (al-Zuhaili, n.d., in Ali, n.d.)
>
> When you employ a laborer, you must notify him of his *ujrah* (wages).

Both the Quranic *ayat* and the Sunnah seem to deal with *ijarah* for work. A narration relevant to the *ijarah* for usufruct is a narration from Sa'id bin Musayyib from Sa'ad, whereby he said:

> We used to lease out land for some portion of the agricultural products, and the Prophet (*SAW*) prohibited us from such [practice]. Instead, he asked us to lease it out for gold or money. (al-Zuhaili, n.d., in Ali, n.d.)

Fuqaha agree on the legality of contract of *ijarah*. Except for a very few of them, this minority group argued that the contract of *ijarah* is a contract on benefit that does not satisfy the element of *'aqd* (i.e. the existence of the subject matter [benefit] during the *majlis*). However all four schools of law (*Hanafis*, *Malikis*, *Shafi'is* and *Hambalis*) agreed with the contract of *ijarah*. The jurists also claimed an *ijma'* among the companions of the Prophet regarding the legality of *ijarah*. This is because there is real need for such a transaction (al-Zuhaili, n.d., in Ali, n.d.).

3 Elements of an *Al-Ijarah* Contract (Islamic Financing: *Ijarah*)

There are four elements required in order to make a valid *ijarah* contract:

- *Contracting parties*: Every contract must have an offeror and an acceptor. The contracting parties must fulfil the basic requirement of legal capacity.
- *Offer and Acceptance*: The contracting parties must have mutual free consent in order to make the contract. They must not make the contract under duress, or be influenced by each other.
- *Al-ujrah*: An *ijarah* contract must contain an element of *ujrah*, such as wages, a fee and consideration.
- *The benefit of the subject matter*: The subject matter must give benefit to the person who pays the consideration; for example, services or usufructs.

4 Conditions of *Al-Ijarah*

- It is necessary that the subject matter of the hiring must be lawful in Islam.
- The benefit derived for what is being hired (the benefit) must be determined and known to both contracting parties at the time of the contract. The duration of the contract should be limited to a specified period.
- It must be possible for the benefit to be enjoyed.
- Delivery of the benefit is required. The benefit must be delivered as soon as possible in order for the acceptor to have full enjoyment of the hire.
- The benefit must be free from any defect. For example, if there is any defect to the benefit that interrupts the enjoyment of the service and usufruct, the contract will void.
- It is necessary that the price to be paid for the hire is known and determined. The Prophet Muhammad (*SAW*) said: 'If a person hires another, let him inform him of the wages he is to receive.'
- It is required that both parties have the legal capacity to enter into the contract of hire. Mutual free consent between them is also required.

5 Determination of Rental

Rental must be determined at the time of contract for the whole period of the lease. It is permissible to fix different amounts of rent for different phases during the period of the lease. However, this is dependent on the rent for each phase being specifically agreed at the time the lease is effected. If the rent for a subsequent phase of the lease period has not been determined, or has been left at the option of the lessor, the lease is not valid.

Example 1 A leases his house to B for a total period of five years. The rent for the first year is fixed at $2000 per month and it is agreed that the rent for every subsequent year shall be 10% more than the previous year. The lease is valid.

Example 2 A now puts a condition in the agreement that the rent of $2000 per month is fixed for the first year only. The rent for subsequent years shall be fixed each year at the lessor's discretion. The lease is void, because the rent is uncertain.

As is normally the case with financial leases, the determination of rental on the basis of the aggregate cost incurred in the purchase of the asset by the lessor is permissible according to the rules of *Shari'ah*. This is only applicable if both parties agree and all other conditions of a valid lease prescribed by the *Shari'ah* are fully adhered to. The lessor cannot increase the rent unilaterally, and any agreement to this effect is void. The rent, or any part thereof, may be paid in advance before the commencement of the lease. However, the amount collected by the lessor shall remain an 'on account' payment and shall be adjusted to the appropriate rental sum after it is due. The lease period shall commence from the date on which the leased asset has been delivered to the lessee. If the leased asset is no longer functional for the purpose for which it was leased out, the lease shall be terminated on the day on which such loss has been caused. However, if the loss was caused by the misuse or the negligence of the lessee, then liability for compensation for the depreciated value of the asset falls to the lessee.

6 Types of *Al-Ijarah*

There are two types of *al-ijarah*: operating *ijarah* and financial leasing.

- *Operating ijarah*: This is an operating lease that does not include a promise that the legal title in the leased asset will pass to the lessee at the end of the lease.

- *Financial lease (ijarah wa iqtina)*: This is a lease that concludes with a promise that the legal title in the leased assets will be passed to the lessee. Such transfer of ownership may be effected under any of the following three methods:
  - By means of gift, which is the transfer of legal title to the lessee for no consideration;
  - Through the transfer of legal title to the lessee by way of sale at the end of the lease for a token consideration or other amount as specified in the lease;
  - Through the transfer of legal title by way of sale prior to the end of the lease term for a price that is equivalent to the remaining *ijarah* instalment (Bank Muamalat Malaysia Berhad 2000).

7 Application of *Al-Ijarah* Financing

Instead of giving a simple interest-bearing loan, some financial institutions have begun leasing equipment to their customers. While fixing the rent of this equipment, they calculate the total cost they have incurred in the purchase of an asset and add an agreed profit margin. The aggregate amount so calculated is divided by the total number of months in the lease period, and the monthly rent is fixed on that basis.

7.1 Procedure

The *al-ijarah* financing procedure is as follows:

- The bank first determines the requirement of the customer in relation to the use of the equipment and the lease period. The use of the equipment must be in conformity with *Shari'ah* principles.
- The bank purchases the equipment from vendor.
- The bank subsequently leases the equipment to the customer at an agreed rental sum over an agreed period of time. The total lease rentals of the bank comprises of:
  - the actual cost of the equipment;
  - the bank's margin of profit (Bank Muamalat Malaysia Berhad 2000).
- Even though the leased asset is in the customer's possession, the bank still retains ownership. However, if the customer fails to honour his payment obligation, the bank may repossess the leased equipment immediately.

- The flow of the transaction is as follows:
  - Customer identifies the asset to be acquired.
  - Bank purchases the asset from the vendor (e.g. at $500,000).
  - Bank leases the asset to the customer at $500,000 + profit.
  - Customer pays $500,000 + profit by periodic rental payments in accordance with the lease.

In the case of a sale and leaseback transaction, the procedure is as follows:

- The difference in the flow of transaction of a sale and leaseback compared with operating *al-ijarah* financing is that, in the former, the customer has already taken possession of the asset.
- The bank then purchases the asset from the customer and leases it back to him.
- the flow of a sale and leaseback transaction is as follows:
  - Customer takes possession of the asset.
  - Customer sells the asset to the bank (e.g. at $500,000).
  - Bank leases the asset back to the customer at $500,000 + profit.
  - Customer pays $500,000 + profit by periodic lease rental (Bank Muamalat Malaysia Berhad 2000).

8 *Al-Ijarah Thumma Al-Bai (Aitab)*: Car Financing

- The term *al-ijarah* means hire, lease or rent, whereas *al-bai* means purchase.
- Under *Shari'ah* principle, *aitab* refers to two contracts undertaken separately. These are:
  - *al-ijarah* contract (hiring); and
  - *al-bai* contract (purchase).
- *Aitab* car financing follows the *Shari'ah* principle as well as the spirit of the Hire Purchase Act (Bank Negara Malaysia 2001).

8.1 Procedure

- Hirer will select the car to be financed from the dealer and pay a deposit.
- Dealer or seller sells the goods to the finance company, which become the owner.

- Owner hires the goods to hirer for rental payment as stipulated in the *aitab* agreement.
- On settlement of the hire rentals, the purchase agreement will be executed automatically, thus transferring the ownership of the vehicle from the finance company to the hirer.
- An *aitab* transaction proceeds as follows:
  - Hirer pays deposit to dealer;
  - Dealer sells good to owner;
  - Owner pays dealer;
  - Dealer delivers good to hirer;
  - Hirer pays rental to owner;
  - At the end of the hire period, a purchase contract will be executed between the owner and the hirer.

9 *Al-Ijarah* Financing in the Modern Islamic Banking System

9.1 *Operating* Ijarah *Versus Financing* Ijarah

Financing *ijarah* is not allowed under *Shari'ah* law due to the fact that the transaction of giving financing to the hirer is similar to a contract of sale. Under *Shari'ah* principles, an *ijarah* contract must be for operating *ijarah* and the ownership of the property must be in the bank's name. However, most of the banks that introduced *ijarah* financing as one of their products use the concept of financing *ijarah*. This can be verified by examining the banks' financial statements, in which the amount in respect of financing outstanding appears in the financing section rather than the fixed assets section.

Despite leasing being adopted by many Islamic financial institutions, some institutions have heeded the fact that a 'financial lease' has a number of characteristics more similar to interest than to an actual leasing transaction. Furthermore, the usage of model leasing agreements, similar to those within conventional financial institutions, does not conform to *Shari'ah* principles.

Although leasing was not originally a means of financing, it may be used as an action for financing, subject to certain conditions. However, it is insufficient to substitute the word 'interest' with the word 'rent', and replace the word 'mortgage' with the words 'leased asset'. A substantial difference between leasing and an interest-bearing loan must clearly exist.

9.2 Accounting Treatment and Taxation Implication

Under *ijarah* financing, the ownership of the property must be in the bank's name. Therefore, the initial accounting treatment should be as follows:

DR: Fixed Assets (property)	XXXX
CR: Cash	XXXX

However, in the current banking environment most banks perform the accounting treatment as follows:

DR: Fixed Assets (property)	XXXX
CR: Cash	XXXX
DR: *Ijarah* Financing	XXXX
CR: Fixed Assets	XXXX

Source Bank Muamalat Malaysia Berhad (2000)

From the second accounting treatment, we can see that the ownership of the property is no longer in the bank's name, since the property purchase is not recorded under the fixed assets listing. Therefore, there may be issues regarding non-compliance with *Shari'ah* requirements since, under the *ijarah Shari'ah* requirement, the lessor must be the absolute owner the property rented. However, in this case, the issue of absolute ownership is questionable, if we base our opinion on the accounting treatment. As a result of not using the more appropriate accounting treatment, the bank is unable to obtain a taxation incentive from the capital allowance.

9.3 Valuation and Residual Value of the Leased Asset in Property Financing

An important feature of modern 'financial leases' is that, after expiry of the period of the lease, the leased asset is usually transferred to the lessee. As the lessor has already recovered any cost together with a profit thereon, the lessor has no further interest in the leased asset. Similarly, the lessee wishes to retain the asset after the expiry of the lease.

Therefore, the leased asset is generally transferred to the lessee at the end of the lease, either free of any charge, or at a nominal token price.

In order to ensure that the asset will be transferred to the lessee, the lease contract may include an express clause to that effect. Although such a condition may not be mentioned in the contract expressly, it is understood between the parties that the title of the asset will be passed to the lessee at the end of the lease term.

This condition, whether expressed or implied, is not in accordance with the principles of *Shari'ah*. It is a well-settled rule of Islamic jurisprudence that one transaction cannot be attached to another transaction so as to make one a pre-condition for the other.

According to the principles of *Shari'ah*, the asset shall be the sole property of the lessor. After the expiry of the lease period, the lessor shall be at liberty to take the asset back, or to renew the lease, or to lease it out to another party, or sell it to the lessee. However, in the current Islamic banking environment, almost all of the Islamic banks or conventional banks that offer Islamic banking products have no wish to own the property or retain it on their bank's balance sheet; hence the intention of offering *ijarah* as one of their products. With regards to the lessee, the intention of approaching an Islamic bank is to obtain financing for the equipment or property and, at the end of the hiring period, for a sum equal to their bank's cost plus a profit, the lessee expects that ownership will be transferred him or her.

9.4 Expenses of Maintenance Costs, Takaful *Premium*

It is the liability of the lessor, as the owner, to pay all the expenses incurred in the process of the purchase and import of an asset even though it was purchased from the supplier through an agent. All these expenses can be included in the cost and taken into consideration while fixing rental details. However, as a matter of principle, the liability to bear all expenses falls on the owner of the asset. Any agreement to the contrary is not in conformity with *Shari'ah*. However, in the current banking environment, all maintenance costs are borne by the lessee.

The lessee is responsible for any loss or damage to the asset caused by any misuse or negligence on his part. There can also be a liability for normal wear and tear. However, liability cannot be placed on the lessee for loss caused by factors beyond their control. The agreements of the traditional 'financial lease' generally do not differentiate between the two situations. In a lease based on Islamic principles, the two situations should be dealt with separately. However, in the current banking environment, if loss has been caused by factors beyond the lessee's control, the lessee still has to service the hiring instalments.

Insurance of the leased property, if insured under the Islamic concept of *takaful*, should be at the expense of the lessor and not at the expense of the lessee. However, in the current environment, all *takaful* premiums are borne by the lessee, rather than of by the lessor.

9.5 Termination of Lease

Under *Shari'ah* requirements, the lessor has the right to terminate the lease contract unilaterally if the lessee contravenes any term of the agreement. However, if there is no contravention on the part of the lessee, the lease cannot be terminated without mutual consent.

In current Islamic banking practice, in some 'financial lease' agreements the lessor has unrestricted power to terminate the lease unilaterally according to his sole judgement. This is contrary to the principles of *Shari'ah*. Similarly, in some agreements a condition has been found to the effect that, in the event of the lease being terminated, even if this is the lessor's decision, the lessee is responsible for paying the rent for the remaining period of the lease.

Such conditions are contrary to *Shari'ah* and to the principles of equity and justice. The logical consequence of the termination of a lease is that the asset should be returned to the lessor, and the lessee should pay the rent due up to the date of termination. If the termination has been brought about due to misuse or negligence on the part of the lessee, the lessee should compensate the lessor for the loss caused by such misuse or negligence.

10 Recommendations

10.1 Operating Ijarah *Versus Financing* Ijarah

Since the introduction of *ijarah* financing by Islamic banks and conventional banks participating in interest-free banking, the number of customer has continued to increase over the years. This shows that the response from customers, whether Muslim or non-Muslim, is very encouraging. However, a strong response does not mean that the participating banks can launch products without making any necessary study on *Shari'ah* requirements. In the case of Islamic banks and banks that take part in the Skim Perbankan Islam (SPI) initiative using financial *ijarah* as a means of providing *ijarah* finance, the method can be improved by switching to operating *ijarah*. This can be brought about by using a different accounting treatment by recording the assets finance as part of the fixed assets, but segregating the classification of the assets in terms of *ijarah* fixed assets as well as the bank's fixed assets.

10.2 *Accounting Treatment Together with Taxation and* Zakat *Implication*

Accounting treatment is the most important tool with which to identify whether the property leased is in the ownership of the bank. Under *Shari'ah* principles, the ownership of the property leased is vital to determining the non-contravention of *Shari'ah* requirements. Therefore, the existing accounting treatment may be changed to ensure it is more reflective of the ownership of the property leased. The proposed accounting treatments are as follows:

On the purchase of fixed assets or equipment	
DR: Fixed Assets/Equipment	XXXX
CR: Cash/Bankers Cheque	XXXX
On receipt of rental income	
DR: Cash	XXXX
CR: Rental Income	XXXX

10.3 *System Maintenance*

On the purchase of fixed assets/equipment	
DR: *Ijarah* Financing (Cost + Profit)	XXXX
DR: Unearned Income	XXXX
CR: Fixed Assets/Equipment	XXXX
On receipt of rental income	
DR: Cash	XXXX
CR: *Ijarah* Financing (Cost)	XXXX
CR: Unearned Income	XXXX

As a result of using the proper accounting treatment, which reflects the bank's ownership of the property, the bank would be able to claim a taxation benefit (i.e. capital allowance and annual allowance).

10.4 Valuation and Residual Value of the Leased Asset of the Property Financed

Under *ijarah* financing, the ownership of the property will remain with the lessor after the end of the period of the lease. Although the ultimate purpose of the leasing transaction is for the lessee to own the assets and for the lessor to dispose of the assets at the end of the lease period, the mechanism of a leasing contract could be improved by executing two separate contracts at the beginning of the period as follows:

- Contract of leasing between lessor and lessee for a specified period of time that equals the cost plus profit of the assets leased.
- Contract containing an option to purchase that the lessee should execute if they wish to own the assets. If, at the end of the period of the lease, the lessee does not pursue their option to purchase, the bank is unable to take any legal action against the lessee. The bank still has the advantage of owning the assets, for which the cost and the profit has already been recovered. In order to benefit further, the bank may sell the assets to a third party at a minimal value.

Under the *Shafi'i* school of law, the option to purchase contract is permissible, even though the intention is the same as in the examples in Sect. 10.2 regarding the current practice of Islamic banks and SPI. The reason for this is that, under the *Shafi'i* school of law, the form of a contract is more important than its substance. Therefore, the practice of executing two separate contracts is greatly preferred to executing two conditional contracts within one contract, as executing two separate contracts is *Shari'ah* compliant.

10.5 Expenses of Maintenance Costs: Takaful Premium

Under *Shari'ah* requirements, all expenses relating to purchasing and maintaining assets—such as servicing costs, for example—is the duty and responsibility of the owner/lessor. In the case of banks that offer *ijarah* financing as one of their products, all servicing costs and maintenance costs should be borne by the bank. *Shari'ah* principles allow that all such expenses can be included in the cost and be taken into consideration when fixing a rental value, provided that both the lessor and lessee agree the rental payment. In addition, the lessor can also set a new rental payment, provided that the lessee is made aware of the new terms in advance and that they are agreed by the lessee. Therefore, the bank can change the method of calculating a rental payment by, first, paying all maintenance costs and incorporating those costs, together with the *takaful* premium, into the rental payment. The bank will also have to generate a projected cash flow in order to determine the rental payment, so that the rental will not vary within a short period of time so as to maintain a good banker–customer relationship.

10.6 Termination of Lease

Under *Shari'ah* requirements, the lessor has a right to terminate a lease contract unilaterally if the lessee contravenes any term of the agreement. However, if there is no contravention on the part of the lessee, the lease cannot be terminated without mutual consent. In current Islamic banking practice, therefore, improvements should be made to ensure a product is *Shari'ah* compliant. Since the advantage of *ijarah* is that the ownership of the product remains with the banks, if the lessee terminates the contract, the bank has the right either to take back the assets and lease them another person, or to dispose of the assets. Regarding the lease contract, the bank should exclude clauses giving it unrestricted unilateral power to terminate the lease contract. This will give equal rights to the lessor and the lessee.

11 Conclusion

After examining the *ijarah* tool provided in Islamic banking in light of the *Shari'ah* texts, views of the jurists, and practitioner policies and guidelines, it is hoped that a better understanding of the operation of the *ijarah* tool according to *Shari'ah* can be achieved. It is clear that *ijarah* is generally accepted by the jurists and is practised by most of the banks in Malaysia because of the clear indication of their legality in the *Shari'ah* texts. Only with regard to the detailed rules and conditions of such tools do the jurists differ.

However, there are some practices that are controversial and questionable that need more attention to rectify the situation immediately. Nevertheless, it is the view that Islamic banks should try their best to stick to the accepted methods of banking according to the *Shari'ah* texts and Muslim jurists. They should avoid the wide use of less accepted methods, or methods that are the subject of much controversy, except when it becomes impossible to dispense with such methods.

References

Ali, E. R. (n.d.). *Islamic Banking Tools: The Shari'ah Principles.*

Bank Muamalat Malaysia Berhad. (2000). *Al-Ijarah Financing Procedures.* Kuala Lumpur.

Bank Negara Malaysia. (2001). *Frequently Asked Questions on the Aitab Financing Scheme.* News Strait Times Press.

CHAPTER 18

Islamic Leasing Leading to Ownership (*Al-Ijarah Tantahi Bi Al-Tamleek*)

1 Introduction

The focus of this chapter is the analysis of *al-ijara wa al-iqtina'* (leasing leading to ownership) and its relationship with *takaful*, and also the implications of the principles of *al-ijara wa al-iqtina'* with regard to socio-economic reality. The chapter will also discuss about different practices of different banks. *Al-ijarah wa iqtina'* is a long-term contract whereby the lessee asks their bank to purchase assets that they require. The bank will act as the lessor and lease out the assets to the lessee for a certain period of time for which the lessee will pay agreed monthly instalments. In addition, we found that there are several reasons why Islam recognizes the principles entailed in *al-ijara wa al-iqtina'* and why profit from this means of financing is *halal*.

2 *Al-Ijara wa Al-Iqtina'* (Leasing Leading to Ownership)

The establishment in Malaysia of banks that base their operations on Islamic principles is good news in terms of the acceptance of the Islamic financial system by other countries. The Islamic financial system has proved itself to be sound, free from *gharar*, free from *riba*, involved solely in trading transactions and also free from investments prohibited

M. M. Billah, *Islamic Financial Products*,
https://doi.org/10.1007/978-3-030-17624-2_18

under *Shar'iah* law. In Malaysia, there are many financial principles that are exercised by Islamic banks, such as *al-mudharabah*, *al-musharakah*, *al-wadiah yad amanah*, *al-murabahah* and *al-ijarah*.

Al-ijara or *al-ijara wa al-iqtina'* is one of the long-term methods of financing capital equipment or real property. Under such contracts, the customer selects the capital equipment or real property (assets) to be financed by the bank or the Islamic financial institution. The bank or Islamic financial institution then purchases these assets from the manufacturer or supplier and leases them to the customer for an agreed period.

This type of financing can also be used to refinance assets already owned by the client in a sale and leaseback arrangement, under certain circumstances allowed by the *Shari'ah*. The structure of *al-ijara wa-iqtina'* is thus very similar to that of a conventional lease-purchase arrangement or hire purchase financing. To conform to the *Shari'ah*, the owner of the assets (in this case, the bank or the Islamic financial institution) must be paid rent (fixed or variable) and must exercise all the rights and obligations that are incidental to ownership, such as maintaining, insuring and repairing the assets. The lessee, on the other hand, obtains the use of the asset for the period of the lease, subject to paying the rent. The lessee may assume obligations such as maintaining, insuring and repairing the asset in return for a reduced rent.

3 Implications of *Al-Ijarah wa Al-Iqtina'*

Al-ijara wa al-iqtina' has several implications for daily life. There are two major implications: implications for economics and social implications.

3.1 Implications for Economics

With regard to economics, *al-ijara wa al-iqtina'* has substantial implications. When other countries are interested in participating in or practising this principle, it indicates that they are demanding more assets in that country, therefore increasing sales and production. This will cause an increase in the country's gross domestic product (GDP), which indicates that the economy in that country is growing and doing well.

3.2 *Implications for Society*

From a social perspective, the major implication is in relation to the welfare of the society in a country interested in participating in or practising *al-ijara wa al-iqtina'*. As mentioned, under this principle, a customer's bank purchases the assets their customer requires and then leases them out to their customer for a specified period, for which the customer pays a certain amount of money in instalments. At the end of the leasing period, the customer has the option to purchase the assets from the bank.

This principle exists purposely to help people who are in need, meaning that people without a substantial amount of cash can also enjoy the benefits of assets by renting them, rather than having to buy them. *Al-ijara wa al-iqtina'* has adopted the *takaful* principle, which is based on mutual cooperation and helping each other. The lessor helps the lessee to enjoy the benefit (usufruct) of the assets, and the lessee pays for the benefits he receives from using the assets. In addition, *al-ijara wa al-iqtina'* helps to increase one's standard of living. For instance, should Mr A ask his bank to buy a photocopying machine and rent it out to him, then, by renting the photocopying machine from bank, he is in a position to offer photocopying services and generate an income. He can therefore pay the bank the instalments due and also create disposable income for his family. This will cause his standard of living to rise.

4 *Shari'ah* Recognition of *Al-Ijara wa Al-Iqtina'*

There are several important elements that cause this financing technique to be recognized in Islam: is must be free from *gharar* and *riba*, it must be based on trading and it should not be invested in prohibited activities.

4.1 *Free from* Gharar

Any transaction made must free from *gharar*. *Gharar* is any uncertainty, chance or risk that can occur in trading. Of course, there are systematic and unsystematic risks in the business world, but those risks must be clearly defined. If such risks are not clearly defined, people will not know what they may face in the future. In the case of *al-ijara wa al-iqtina'*, a lessee must be informed and be aware whether there is a possibility that the assets could contain some defect and could fail due to certain technical problems.

4.2 *Free from* Riba

In addition, the trading transaction must free from *riba*, meaning that it must free from unjustified profit and increment. Here, the profit that the bank makes must have *'iwad* or an equivalent counter-value that contains ownership risks (*ghurmi*), or effort (*kasb*), or liability (*damn*).

4.3 *Based on Trading*

Furthermore, the transaction must be based on trading, which involves buying and selling. Under this principle, the bank will acquire the assets and sell the usufruct (benefits) of the assets to the lessee. At the end of the leasing period, bank will give option to lessee to buy the assets.

4.4 *Avoid Prohibited Investments*

Finally, the trading transactions must avoid any prohibited investments. In this case, *al-ijara wa al-iqtina* financing must not involve any harmful investment. The transaction must free from prohibited assets, such as gambling machines and so on.

5 Why Profits from *Al-Ijara wa Al-Iqtina'* Are Acceptable Under *Shari'ah*

There must be strong reasons why Islam recognizes the profit earned in this type of financing method. As mentioned, the profit earned must contain an equivalent counter-value, which can be ownership risk (*ghurmi*), or effort (*kasb*), or liability (*damn*).

5.1 *Ownership Risk* (Ghurmi)

Ownership risk means the risk the bank faces from the time it acquires the assets from the supplier or manufacturer. The capital the bank puts up in order to buy the assets is at risk because there is a risk of default; the lessee may choose not to lease the asset due to moral hazard and so on. For that reason, it is permissible for bank to charge the lessee a certain amount of instalments with a certain percentage of profit margin.

5.2 *Effort* (Kasb)

Effort means the value added that a bank has contributed, such as in maintaining the assets during the leasing period. It covers the cost that the bank has spent in order to ensure that the assets are functioning efficiently. The lessee may be interested in buying the assets from the bank at the end of the leasing period, if the bank has ensured the assets have been maintained effectively.

5.3 *Liability* (Damn)

Damn means the liability that a bank may face during the leasing period. The concept is quite similar to *kasb* and refers to the cost of maintaining the assets throughout the rental period.

6 Leasing Leading to Ownership in Relation to *Takaful*

The relationship between leasing leading to ownership (hire purchase) and *takaful* (Islamic insurance) can be viewed from two perspectives. The first is related to the terms and conditions of the hire purchase agreement itself. The second perspective is related to the rational outlooks of the concepts of hire purchase and *takaful*.

7 Terms and Conditions of a Hire Purchase Agreement

Under the Hire Purchase Act (1967), a hire purchase agreement must:

- Specify the date on which the hiring shall be deemed to have commenced.
- Specify the number of instalments to be paid under the agreement by the hirer.
- Specify the amount of each instalment and the person to whom and the place at which the payments of these instalments is to be made.

- Specify the time for the payment of each of those instalments.
- Contain a description of the goods sufficient to identify them.
- Specify the address where the goods under the hire purchase agreement are held.
- Among others, the hire purchase agreement must also set out in tabular form:

  (i) Cash price: the price at which, at the time of signing the agreement the hirer may have purchased the goods for cash.
  (ii) Deposit: the amount paid by way of a deposit.
  (iii) Delivery charges, if any: the amount included in the total amount payable to cover the expense of delivering the goods to the hirer.
  (iv) Vehicle registration fees: any amount included in the total amount payable to cover vehicle registration fees in respect of the goods.
  (v) Insurance: any amount included in the total amount, payable for insurance in respect of the goods.
  (vi) The total of the amounts referred to in conditions (i), (iii), (iv) and (v), less (ii).
  (vii) Terms charges or interest: the amount of any other charges included in the total amount payable.

- The annual percentage rate for charges, which must be calculated in accordance with the formula set out in Schedule 7 of the Hire Purchase Agreement.
- The total of the amounts referred to in conditions (vi) and (vii), described as 'the balance originally payable under the agreement'.
- The total amount payable.

If a hire purchase agreement does not comply with the conditions given above, it will be void. The Hire Purchase Act (1967) clearly shows that insurance is one of the important elements in the hire purchase agreement. Insurance expenses are the responsibility of the hirer. This means that the insurance cost will be borne by the hirer regardless of who paid the insurance initially (i.e. either the finance company, or the hirer himself). In addition, the goods to be insured must be in the name of the hirer. In respect of a motor vehicle, the hirer shall inform the finance company that they have renewed the insurance policy not less than

14 days before the expiry date of the current insurance policy. In the event that the hirer has failed to renew the insurance policy, the finance company is liable to renew the policy, but the insurance cost incurred must be borne by the hirer. According to the Hire Purchase Act (1967), a finance company cannot request the hirer to insure any risks with any particular registered insurer.

It can be seen from the above discussion that a leasing agreement leading to ownership has a close relationship to insurance companies. *Takaful* is an Islamic insurance that operates in the insurance industry and provides insurance options to the market. Therefore, as Muslims, to show our support of the Islamic insurance practice, we have a responsibility to choose this type of insurance policy. So, we can conclude that there is a relationship between hire purchase agreements (their terms and conditions) and *takaful* (Islamic insurance).

8 Rational Outlook of the Concepts of Hire Purchase and *Takaful*

There is a relationship between hire purchase and *takaful*. This relationship is implicit. Therefore, for us to understand this relationship, we have to go back to the principles that govern both of these concepts. The concept or the nature of hire purchase has already been discussed. Let us now discuss in the concept of *takaful* further. The concept of *takaful* is quite complicated. In order to simplify matters, we will only discuss and relate hire purchase to *takaful* in terms of its meaning, as well as the logic behind the practice of *takaful*. *Takaful* is a contract for a financial transaction of mutual cooperation between two parties. These two parties are the *takaful* operator and the participant. The participant pays an amount of money known as a premium (contribution). In the event that the participant incurs a loss within the policy period, the *takaful* operator will provide financial protection for him. However, if no loss is incurred by the participant, the *takaful* operator has to pay back the total of the premiums (contributions) paid plus a share of the profit made by the operator by their having had access to the accumulated premiums paid based on principle of *al-mudharabah*.

This clearly shows that this type of transaction is mutually supportive in terms of financial protection. Such cooperation is recommended by *Shari'ah Islamiyyah*. Allah (*SWT*) says in His Holy *Qur'an*:

> And cooperate ye one another in righteousness and piety and do not cooperate in sin and rancour. (5:2)

There are several reasons to have Islamic insurance. First, the basic purpose of having Islamic insurance is to protect people who are unable to protect themselves from unexpected future material risk when such risk may lead those people to hardship. The Holy Prophet (*SAW*) said:

> Narrated by Abu Hurairah from Holy Prophet saying that: 'whosever removes a worldly hardship from a believer, Allah will remove from him one of the hardships of hereafter, whosever alleviates the needy person, Allah will deviate from him in this world and the next'. (Nawawi, Forty Hadith)

The above *hadith* clearly shows that Allah (*SWT*) really appreciates and rewards anyone who helps needy people. The reward may direct or indirect, in this world or the hereafter, or both.

Second, the basic purpose of having Islamic insurance is to reduce the poverty rates in society. As we know, anyone may become poor resulting from material loss or damage. Situations such as these can be overcome if the person has an insurance policy that protects them from any material loss or damage. Therefore, we can conclude that, by having insurance policy, a person is guaranteed to have a comfortable life in the event of misfortune. Islam encourages its believers to seek a better life in this world, as well as in hereafter. Allah (*SWT*) said in *Al-Qur'an*:

> Our Lord gives us comfortable life in both the world and hereafter.

Third, another important reason for having Islamic insurance is to ensure the development of mutual cooperation and the spirit of brotherhood in society. As stated previously, Islamic insurance is based on mutual cooperation and supporting each other against unexpected risk. By helping other people, we will be able to develop and strengthen the brotherhood among us.

Furthermore, Islamic insurance policies contribute to producing a self-reliant society as, should any damage occur, the insurance operator will cover the cost. This material protection will therefore make policy-holders independent. In other words, the insured person will not depend on the assistance of others should they be in difficulty.

In this respect, Allah always has the intention to make our life easy and comfortable. It is clearly stated in the Holy *Qur'an*:

> Allah intends easy life for you while he does not want you are to be in difficulties.

In addition, *al-mudharabah* is one of the principles of Islamic insurance. This principle is based on profit sharing according to prior mutually agreed portions. In other words, this type of insurance does not practice *riba*. As we already know, *riba* (interest) is prohibited in Islam: this is because the practice of *riba* manipulates others. It is because those who practice *riba* actually practise making interest on interest. This type of manipulation causes the rich to become richer and the poor to become poorer. If we avoid *riba*, we are avoiding hurting others, as well as ourselves. In addition, by avoiding *riba* we are ensuring economic well-being and also avoiding something prohibited by Allah (*SWT*). By doing so, Allah will reward us not only in this world, but also in the hereafter. Allah (*SWT*) says in the Holy *Qur'an*:

> and Allah permits trading and prohibits *riba* [interest]. (2:275)

Furthermore, Islamic life insurance is intended to compensate and provide material protection for the unfortunate offspring on the death of a policy-holder. In this case, the Prophet Muhammad (*SAW*) encourages and advises Muslims to provide material protection for their offspring. The *hadith* that relates to this matter is as follows:

> Narrated by Amir bin Saad bin Abi Waqaas, the Holy Prophet said: 'Verily it better for you to leave your offspring wealthy than to leave them poor asking others for help.' (Sahih al-Bukhari)

The Prophet (*SAW*) further said:

> Narrated by Sahal bin Saad, the Holy Prophet said: 'I and the person who looks after an orphan and provides for him security will be in paradise like this.' (Sahih al-Bukhari)

Both of these *hadiths* show that there will be a significant reward for those people who help orphans.

Furthermore, Islamic life insurance also ensures the future material security for the widow and other dependents of a policy-holder. The Prophet Muhammad (*SAW*) said:

> Narrated by Safwan bin Salim, the Holy Prophet said: 'the one who looks after and works for the widow and for a poor person is like a warrior fighting for the cause of Allah or like a person who fasts during the days and prays over the night.' (Sahih al-Bukhari)

According to the above *hadith*, those who help widows and poor people are similar to those people who fighting to defend Islam. So, helping widows and needy people is considered a valuable contribution to the *Ummah*.

From the above, we can conclude that Islamic insurance or *takaful* insurance promotes mutual cooperation between the *takaful* operator and the policy-holders, as well as among the policy-holders themselves. Additionally, the practice of *takaful* insurance contributes to social responsibility as well as the economic well-being of the *Ummah* as a whole. If we analyse the concept of hire purchase, it also applies the concept of helping each other. Therefore, up to this point, we can clearly see the implied relationship between the concepts of hire purchase and *takaful*.

9 Different Practices of Hire-Purchase

In Malaysia, the first bank to practise the Islamic banking system in 1983 was Bank Islam Malaysia Berhad (BIMB). Today, many conventional banks have adopted this financial system. We will now discuss several banks that use the Islamic hire purchase concept.

10 Ambank Group

The Ambank Group practices *al-ijarah thumma al-bai* (*aitab*) industrial hire purchase. It is a financing arrangement of leasing/hire purchase and subsequent purchase for industrial vehicles based on the *Shari'ah*. This hire purchase practice comprises two contracts that are undertaken separately and sequentially: an *al-ijarah* contract (leasing or renting) and an *al-bai'* (purchase contract).

- *Al-ijarah contract (leasing or renting)*: Under the first contract, the hirer leases the goods from the owner at an agreed rental over a specified period of time.
- *Al-bai' (purchase contract)*: On the expiry of the leasing period, the hirer enters into a second contract to purchase the goods from the owner at an agreed price. This concept is applicable for the financing of consumer and durable goods.

Malaysian companies and non-resident companies (subject to the approval of Bank Negara Malaysia and the customer's bank) are eligible to enter into *al-ijarah thumma al-bai* industrial hire purchase agreements. This bank practice establishes a flat agreed profit margin and its margin of financing is up to 100%.

The hire purchase concept that has been practised by the Arab Malaysian Bank is called *al-ijara wa al-iqtina'*, which means lease finance. This is a lease agreement that allows the client to purchase the leased goods at any time during the term of the lease, at an agreed price. Therefore, this type of hire purchase agreement has one major difference. Under an ordinary hire purchase agreement, the client cannot unilaterally terminate the contract, and must meet all the payments before ownership of the asset is passed from the financial institution to the client. However, an *al-ijara wa al-iqtina'* agreement allows the client to terminate the contract at any time he wishes, and to acquire the asset at a pre-determined purchase price.

This type of hire purchase agreement has its own special features, which include that:

- At the expiry date of the lease agreement, the title of the asset is transferred under a new contract to the lessee on the condition that the lessee has met all the terms and conditions of the original agreement.
- A lessee can also exercise the option to acquire the leased asset prior to the expiry of the lease agreement at a price to be mutually agreed between the lessee and the lessor at the time of the execution of the lease. The purchase option price is usually determined by two elements:

- An expert will determine the fair market value of the assets at the time the purchase option is exercised.
- An estimated residual value is agreed in advance, at the time the lease is signed.

After discussing various hire purchase agreements that have been adopted by a variety of banks, we can conclude that these banks use two different contracts. The first is a leasing contract, and the second one is a purchase contract. Both of these contracts are implemented regardless of the names by which different banks identify them.

11 Conclusion

Al-ijara wa al-iqtina' does have similarities with ordinary hire purchase agreements, the main difference being the way profit is made. In *al-ijara wa al-iqtina'*, the profit margin must contain an equivalent counter-value (*'iwad*) and includes *ghurmi*, or *kasb*, or *damn*. A further consideration is that there are major implications that affect economics and certain social aspects. This chapter has also further discussed the main reasons why *al-ijara wa al-iqtina'* has been recognized by Islam and how a *halal* profit can be generated.

It is further submitted that there is an indirect relationship between the concept of *al-ijara wa al-*iqtina' and the concept of *takaful*. They are related to each other, first, by virtue of the terms and conditions in *al-ijara wa al-iqtina'* itself and, second, in terms of the purposes for both concepts exist.

Today, several conventional banks are trying to practise the concept of *al-ijara wa al-iqtina'* concept, for which they have different names for the product. Even so, the governing principles in *al-ijara wa al-iqtina'* are the same (i.e. in relation to a leasing and purchasing contract) regardless of the names that have been given to them.

CHAPTER 19

Islamic Hire Purchase (*Al-Ijarah Thumma Al-Bay'*)

1 Introduction

Consumers seeking bank financing to purchase a car or any other good would normally do so under a hire purchase agreement. Here, the term charges (interest payable on the hire) are calculated as though the transaction is based on a facility or debt where the element of *riba* is implicated. The Holy *Qur'an* says:

> Allah has made trade or commerce lawful but made *riba* unlawful. (2: 275)

An alternative to conventional hire purchase in which there is no element of profit or *riba* is a commercial contract in Islam known as *al-ijarah* (leasing). However, a conventional hire purchase contract provides the lessee with an option to buy the leased property. This may imply that *al-ijarah* or leasing alone may not be a suitable contract as an alternative to conventional hire purchase. As an alternative, Islamic jurists have introduced an Islamic version of hire purchase known as *al-ijarah thumma al-bay'* (AITAB) (leasing ending with a sale). This means that AITAB is a leasing contract with an option for the lessee to buy the asset.

M. M. Billah, *Islamic Financial Products*,
https://doi.org/10.1007/978-3-030-17624-2_19

2 Central Idea

The name *Al-ijarah* has its origins in the Islamic *fiqh* and means allowing someone the use of something on the basis of a lease or rental agreement. Islamic principles permit the purchase of personal and real property for subsequent leasing at a mutually agreed periodic rent. Under the concept of *al-ijarah*, the assets are rented with full maintenance. Therefore, in addition to owning an inventory of leasable assets, the lessor may also own, repair and maintain facilities. So, *al-ijarah* is a contract whereby an asset is transferred from the owner (the lessor) to another party (the lessee) at an agreed price (rent) for an agreed period of time (the term of the lease). There are two types of usufruct in *al-ijarah* (Rosly, n.d.):

- Usufruct of property or capital assets (*manfa'at al-a'yn*).
- Usufruct of labour, employment and service (*manfa'at al-'amal*).

Al-ijarah relates to the leasing not only of property, but also of services (which we would normally term 'employment'). In *al-ijarah* of services, the employer is called the *musta'jir* and the employee the *'ajir*. The contract between the two parties involves the employment of the services of the *'ajir* based on an agreed wage or salary (*'ujrah*) given to him as reward for the services rendered in the transaction. Thus, irrespective of whether the employer is making a loss or a windfall profit, he must pay the predetermined wage or salary of his employee as specified in the *al-ijarah* contract. For example, in a corporation the management receives compensation under *al-ijarah*. Likewise, a similar contract is used in government services.

The lessor is called the *mu'jir*, the lessee or hirer is known as the *musta'jir* and the rent payable to the lessor is called *'ujrah*. *Al-ijarah* is not a sale because in a sale transfers the ownership of property to a purchaser. In *al-ijarah*, the lessee only has the right to use the property, but not have ownership of the property. Some of basic rules of *al-ijarah* are as follows:

- *Al-ijarah* is valid only if both parties consent to the contract. That is, to avoid *gharar*, the contracted usufruct or *manfa'at* has to be defined precisely.
- The usufruct must be lawful and must have a valuable use.

- All liabilities arising from ownership shall be borne by the lessor. That is, hired goods must be delivered or executed legally and practically at a specified time.
- The rent, and the period and the purpose of the lease must be clearly specified.

3 Corporate Understanding

There are two different contracts in *AITAB*:

- Leasing contract (*al-ijarah*);
- Contract of sale (*al-bay'*).

Al-ijarah and *al-bay'* are both categorized under the term 'contract of exchange' (*'uqud al-mubadalah*). The former relates to the exchange of usufruct for money, while the latter involves the exchange of goods for money. The AITAB contract is not found in the book of *fiqh*, which is probably due to the need for such a contract not arising in Muslim history. However, today, certain assets cost high prices that most people are unable to settle on a cash basis so, in order to obtain such assets as they require, they must resort to settling payment by instalments. The need to create a new contract that not only satisfies *Shari'ah* requirements, but also affords customers convenience has resulted in the introduction of the AITAB contract.

The *al-ijarah* contract exists separately from that of *al-bay'*. Since both contracts are executed in succession, AITAB can be used to describe the process of converting an *al-ijarah* contract into a sale contract. What is available now is a new leasing contract where the hirer is given an option to buy the goods they have leased, which is a similar concept to conventional hire purchase. Under the AITAB contract:

- The customer or hirer elects to buy the good when all the rentals specified in the agreement have been paid; or
- The customer or hirer can return the goods at any time before the option to buy is exercised and thus terminate the agreements. The customer is not obliged to pay all the rental instalments.

The AITAB contract should not be perceived as being a combination of the *al-ijarah* and *al-bay'* contracts. Instead, AITAB consists of two stages involving two separate contracts:

Stage 1: Executing the leasing contract (*al-ijarah*);
Stage 2: Executing the contract of sale (*al-bay'*) at a nominal value agreed by both parties.

Based on this information, it is evident that AITAB is a leasing contract with a condition that affords the customer the option to buy the asset at the end of the leasing period. For example, if the monthly rental is $500 and the period of rentals is 60 months, he will be offered the opportunity to buy the asset for $500, which is equivalent to the last rental payment. This also means that the total rental payment is $25,000. If a customer has reasons for not continuing with the *al-ijarah* contract, they will be offered the opportunity to buy the asset at a price equivalent to the difference between the total rental and the amount already paid as rent. For example, if the total rental charges are $30,000 and the customer terminates the lease after three years, or has paid rental instalments equivalent to $21,000 ($500 × 36), the AITAB contract permits the customer to buy the asset for $9000 or ($30,000 – $21,000) less rebate (*muqasa*). Three parties are involved in an AITAB:

- Dealer/seller/original owner;
- Customer/hirer;
- Bank/finance company.

The objective of AITAB is therefore to provide customers with the opportunity to own an asset they could not have bought on a cash basis but would be able to afford at a future date after regular instalment payments have been made on a lease basis. AITAB is not a conditional sale. To that effect, transactions in AITAB will involve the following steps:

- The bank will buy the asset from the dealer. At this point, the dealer/original owner drops out of the picture.
- The bank will lease the asset to the customer according to terms and conditions specifying market rental values and the leasing period.

- As the owner of the asset, the bank will receive the lease payments. In the case of, say, a house purchase, the bank is responsible for ensuring that the customer exercises the option to buy the house at a nominal value. Theoretically, the price of the house should be equivalent to the total lease payments received by the bank during the leasing period.
- The transfer of ownership from the bank to the customer takes place at the end of the leasing period when the customer exercises the option to buy the goods.

Since AITAB has to operate within the Hire Purchase Act (1967), it is necessary to understand some features of the Act. The Hire Purchase Act (1967) came into force on 11 April 1968. Prior to this date, there was no specific legislation to control and regulate hire purchase in Malaysia. Instead, hire purchase agreements came under the ambit of the ordinary law of contract and were covered by the Sale of Goods Ordinance (1957) as 'agreements to sell'.

4 Practical Scenario and Application

In practice, the basic procedure of this type of financing is as follows (Bank Islam, n.d.):

- First, the finance company or bank providing this scheme determines the requirement of the customer in relation to the use of the equipment or asset and the lease period. Here, the use of the equipment or asset must conform to the policy of the company or bank. In other words, it must be in accordance with *Shari'ah* principles (for *al-ijarah*).
- Next, the company or bank purchases the equipment or asset concerned.
- The company or bank subsequently leases the equipment or asset to the customer at an agreed rent over a fixed period of time. The total lease rentals comprise:
  - the actual cost of the equipment or asset to the company or bank;
  - the company or bank margin of profit.
- Even though the leased asset is in the customer's possession, the company or bank still retains ownership. However, if the customer fails to meet their payment obligations (as in the conditions

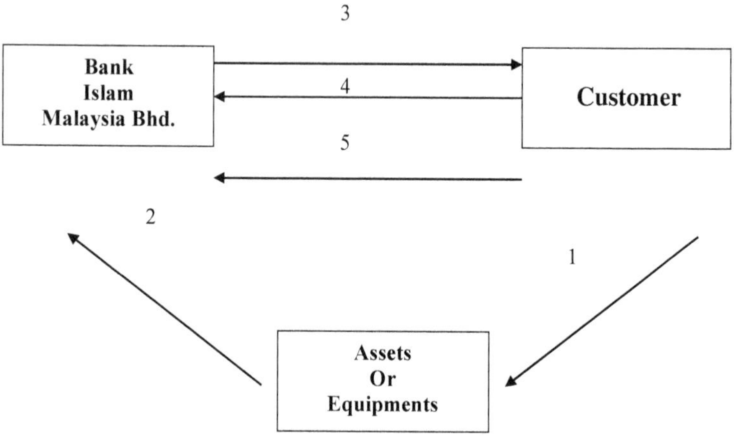

Fig. 1 Practical scenario/application (*Source* Author's own)

previously agreed), the company or bank may repossess the leased equipment or asset immediately.

- At the end of the leasing period, as in both parties' agreement, the customer purchases from the company or bank the equipment or asset concerned at an agreed price with the lease rentals previously paid constituting part of such price.

Various banks currently provide this of type financing lease, such as Bank Islam Malaysia Berhad and Bank Muamalat Malaysia Berhad. For example, Bank Islam Malaysia Berhad presently provides hire purchase (AITAB) for its customers under *Shari'ah* principles. The procedure practised by Bank Islam Malaysia Berhad is summarized in Fig. 1.

5 AITAB Procedure

- Customer identifies the asset(s) to be acquired.
- Bank purchases the asset(s).
- Bank leases the asset(s) to customer at an agreed amount.
- Customer pays the bank the lease rental over an agreed period.
- Customer purchases the asset(s) at the end of the period of the lease.

6 Recommendations

Financial institutions should not only provide leasing facilities to large companies; the eligibility of small and medium-sized companies should also be considered. Currently, for example, banks only provide the leasing facility to large companies that they believe will be able to service the debt.

Financial institutions should vary the period of payment and not adhere to common periods, such as five or seven years. The lessee should be given more options in terms of the duration of the payment period as this will help them to plan their financial budget.

7 *Shari'ah* Rulings

Al-Quran (Ali, n.d.):

> Said one of the [damsels]: 'O my [dear] father! Engage in him on wages: truly the best of men for thee to employ is the [man] who is strong and trusty'. (al-Qasas: 26)

This *Qur'anic* verse describes the rulings that allow Muslims to hire a third party as a *wakalah* in purchasing assets or equipment.

> Those who devour usury will not stand except as stands one whom the evil one by his touch had driven to madness. That is because they say: Trade is like usury, but Allah has made trade or commerce lawful but made *riba* unlawful. (2: 275)

Allah (*SWT*) prohibits *riba* (usury) in trade as practised in the conventional banking system. In Islamic trade financing, the existence of usury is not allowed; it is replaced by a *hibah* (service charge). It is because *riba* is a burden on the lessee or purchaser.

> if the debtor is in a difficulty, grant him time till it is easy for him to repay. But if you remit it by the way of charity, that is the best for you if you only knew. (2: 280)

The condition of hire purchase in Islam facilitates the lessee if they experience difficulty repaying the debt or an instalment by encouraging the bank or the lessor to extend the period of payment, or give it as charity:

> O you who believe. Eat not up your properties among yourselves in vanities; but let them be amongst you traffic and trade by mutual goodwill. (4: 29)

The transactions between two parties in trade financing should be undertaken by mutual consent. This means that both parties are satisfied with the conditions of the agreement.

8 Conclusion

The basic features of *al-ijarah* financing are the purpose for the financing, the total amount of the lease rental instalments, guarantees, security or collateral, and the early termination of *al-ijarah* (lease financing)

8.1 *Purpose of Financing*

The contract of *al-ijarah* financing can be used to provide customers with short- to medium-term financing to lease items that they are unable to purchase on a cash basis. Such items may include equipment, machinery, consumer goods, computers, motor vehicles, and other suitable and acceptable assets. The usage of the asset to be leased by the customer and to be financed by the bank must not be *haram* (forbidden); for example, the lease of a machine for the processing of intoxicants.

8.2 *Total Lease Rentals*

- The total lease rental comprises the amount of financing and profit that has been inserted in the contract (*aqad*).
- The total lease rental shall be derived on the method of a constant rate of return.
- The lease rentals must be maintained throughout the lease period.
- Additional profit in the form of a finance charge or penalty for late payment is not allowed; this is an exception to a lease transaction.

8.3 *Guarantee*

- The concept of guarantee in Islam is known as *al-kafalah*. Under *al-ijarah* financing, a guarantee is permissible. An *al-kafalah* guarantee also applies in a conventional leasing transaction.
- Guarantees may be personal, individual or corporate.

8.4 Security or Collateral

In Islam, the concept of security is known as *al-rahn*. Land and building or other property acceptable to a financier can be accepted as collateral for financing under *al-ijarah* and leasing.

8.5 Early Termination of Al-Ijarah *(Lease Financing)*

Since *al-ijarah* financing is a financial lease, it is a non-cancellable contract. However, in the event that early termination occurs due to voluntary surrender or repossession, the lessor will have to be compensated for any loss due to such premature termination.

References

Ali, A. Y. (n.d.). *The Holy Qu'ran*. Text and Translation.
Bank Islam. (n.d.). *Organisation and Operations Brochure* (4th ed.).
Rosly, S. A. (n.d.). *Islamic Financial System and Environment*. Malaysia.

CHAPTER 20

Islamic Manufacture Financing (*Al-Istisna'*)

1 Introduction

The increase in understanding of the suitability of Islamic concepts for the people has led to a huge demand for Islamic banking instruments. Most banks nowadays implement Islamic financing and contracts; for example, *al-murabahah*, *al-mudharabah* and many others. One of of the Islamic banking products is *al-istisna'*, which is related to sales. It is a contract to manufacture an item that does not yet exist. Several guidelines are in place regarding the use of *al-istisna'*; for example, there is no limitation to the time period and the price need not be paid in advance. Put simply, *al-istisna'* is the sale of an order. There is some confusion between *al-istisna'* and *bay al-salam*. *Al-istisna'* is different than *bay al-salam*. It is only similar in contract terms in that the item does not yet exist.

Islamic banks use *al-istisna'* widely as a method of financing. It can be used in the construction industry, such as for apartment buildings, hospitals, schools and universities. It also can be used in high technology industries, such as aircraft manufacture, and the locomotive and shipbuilding industries. One of the most important teachings of the *Qur'an* about conduct in business is to fulfil promises and the terms of the contract. The *Qur'an* demands that all contracts must be completed.

> God doth command you to render back your trusts to those whom they are due. (4:58)

M. M. Billah, *Islamic Financial Products*,
https://doi.org/10.1007/978-3-030-17624-2_20

The implementation of *al-istisna'* will inculcate in people a desire to be a trustworthy person and can create a moral obligation or sense of responsibility in manufacturers to fulfil their responsibilities. According to Al-Ghazali in his book *Ihya'Ulum al-Din* (*The Marvels of the Heart*), a good Muslim is one whose livelihood is moderate and who is responsible in their actions and promises. In this chapter, we will discuss the precise definition of *al-istisna'*, its implementation, characteristics and rules, present scholars' views on *al-istisna'*, and set out recommendations for further improvement of *al-istisna'* as a financing method.

2 Central Idea

Al-istisna' (progressive financing) is a contract of acquisition of goods by specification or order where the price is paid progressively in accordance with the progress of a job. In addition, it means sale by order; for example, the purchase of a house yet to be constructed. In this type of contract, payments are made to the developer or builder according to the stage of work completed. The flexibility of *Al-istisna'* contracts offers several possibilities in terms of business contracts, including some forms of future contract trading of processed commodities, as it permits the deferring of both ends of the contract—delivery as well as payment. Under this facility, the bank finances customers who wish to acquire assets in course of construction by means of delayed payment for an asset for a specific period, or payment by instalments (http://www.bankislaam.com.my/product_korpolistnaan.htm).

Al-istisna' is a contract of exchange with deferred delivery and is applied to specified made-to-order items. General agreement on the principles of practice is complex to define. However, it is often stated that the nature and quality of the item to be delivered must be specified in the contract. Therefore, the manufacturer must make a commitment to produce the item as described. The delivery date is also not fixed; the item is deliverable on completion by the manufacturer. Furthermore, the contract is irrevocable after the commencement of manufacture, except where delivered goods do not meet the contracted terms. In addition, payment can be made in a lump sum or on an instalment basis, and at any time up to or after the time of delivery. Finally, the manufacturer is responsible for the sourcing of inputs to the production process (http://www.alahli.com/bb/financing/Islamicfinanceproducts/alistisna).

Al-istisna' is defined as an alternative type of sale in which a commodity is transacted before it comes into existence. It means to place an order with a manufacturer to manufacture a specific commodity for the purchaser. If the manufacture undertakes to manufacture the goods, this creates the transaction of *al-istisna'*. For an *al-istisna'* contract to be deemed valid, the price must be fixed with the mutual agreement of both parties, and a detailed specification of the commodity to be manufactured agreed between them (http://www.albalagh.net/Islamic_economics/).

As in an article written by Ibn Abidin Radd-ul-Muhtar, the contract of *al-istisna'* creates a moral obligation on the manufacturer to manufacture the goods. However, provided notice is given before the manufacturer starts the work, either of the parties may cancel the contract. Moreover, according to *mufti* Taqi Usmani, after the manufacturer has started the work, the contract cannot be cancelled unilaterally (Ibn Abidin, Radd-ul-Muhtar, cited by Usmani 1988).

Al-istisna' differs from *al-ijara* in that the manufacturer must procure his own raw materials, otherwise the contract would amount to a hiring of the seller's waged labour in the same way as occurs under *al-ijara*. *Al-istisna'* also differs from *bay al-salam*, wherein the subject matter of the contract is always a made-to-order item. Additionally, the delivery date need not be fixed in advance. Further differences are that full payment in advance is not required and the *al-istisna'* contract can be cancelled, but only provided notice if cancellation is given before the seller commences manufacture of the agreed item(s) (Ibn Abidin, Radd-ul-Muhtar, cited by Usmani 1988).

3 Characteristics of *Al-Istisna'* (Manufacturing)

Al-istisna' is involved in many industries, such as the automobile, construction and heavy machine industries. *Al-istisna'* also can be used as a method of financing intangible assets, such as gas, electricity and others (http://www.oicexchange.com/docs.istisna.pdf.). Intangible assets are considered appropriate for a contract of *al-istisna'* since the assets are produced from raw materials that are unusable to a good that can benefit people. Today, *al-istisna'* is not only used as a means of manufacturing, it is also being used as a method of financing. People can use *al-istisna'* to finance certain transactions. For example, many banks offer this financial facility to customers to pay for a house or car, or some other major purchase. In the eyes of Islam, the transaction is considered as *al-istisna'*. An *al-istisna'* contract is based on the three parties entering into it: the bank, the customer and the manufacturer.

There are requirements for the implementation of *al-istisna'*. In an *al-istisna'* contract, the object or subject matter of the contract must be something that needs to be manufactured and the contract is only valid when the object can be produced. This type of contract is not valid for rice, corn, wheat, barley or fruit, or any other natural item. Natural items are only applicable in *bay al-salam*, not in *al-istisna'*. Moreover, assets or projects to be financed by the bank must be in line with *Shari'ah* principles. *Al-istisna'* financing may not be made available for a contract related to the production of liquor, or the construction of gambling houses as it is forbidden by *Shari'ah* and therefore means that any such contract would be invalid. Anything that contradicts with Islamic perspectives is considered as *haram* or unlawful. In addition, the item to be produced must also consider the sensitivities of the people that will be affected by its presence.

In an *al-istisna'* contract, there is no need for the price or cost to be paid in advance. The payment can be made in instalments during manufacture, or on the completion of the contract. The price must be fixed with the mutual consent of the customer and manufacturer in the early stages of the contract. Later, either the customer or the manufacturer may cancel the contract provided manufacture has not yet begun and provided that notice is given.

The time of delivery in *al-istisna'* differs from that of *bay al-salam*. In *al-istisna'*, the delivery time can be changed. However, the customer may fix a maximum time for delivery, which means that, if the manufacturer delays the delivery beyond the agreed time, the customer is not obliged to accept the goods and pay for the manufactured product: the customer has the right to reject the product. Moreover, the manufacturer is bound and obliged to deliver the goods within the agreed time. Any failure to meet the terms of the contract makes the manufacturer liable to pay the buyer liquidated damages in accordance with the contract (http://www.oicexchange.com/docs.istisna.pdf, p. 2).

It is the responsibility of the manufacturer to supply the materials. If the buyer supplies the materials, the contract is consider as *al-ijarah*. In certain circumstances, the customer may provide materials but, if the labour and skills are provided by the manufacturer, the contract will not be considered as *al-istisna'*.

4 Rules of *Al-Istisna'*

Al-istisna' is a sale involving a product and the services it performs where the terms of the contract are agreed before the product comes into existence. As mentioned previously, it means an order for a manufacturer to manufacture a specific commodity for the purchaser. If the manufacturer agrees to manufacture the goods for the purchaser, the transaction of *al-istisna'* comes into existence. It is necessary for the validity of *al-istisna'* that the price is fixed with the mutual agreement of both parties and that a detailed specification of the goods and services intended to be manufactured and provided is fully settled between them.

5 Conditions Relating to *Al-Istisna'*

An *al-istisna'* contract must state in the clearest of terms all the specifications required of the commodity being sold; this is a condition in all commutative contracts, the purpose being to avoid ignorance that may lead to dispute. The *Qur'an* instructs that the terms must be specified precisely (Mushtaq, n.d.). An *al-istisna'* contract is invalid for all natural products, such as corn, wheat, barley or fruit. The maker should supply the materials as, if they are supplied by the buyer, the contract is *al-ijara* and not *al-istisna'*. (http://albalagh.net/Islamic_economics/salam_istisna:shtml).

Al-istisna' is not limited to what the seller makes after the contract is made, but it is the maker's responsibility to produce an item conforming to all the specifications in the contract, whether he had already made the item before the contract was signed, or whether the item has been made by someone else. The contract is binding on both parties, and neither party has the right to retract; the only exception to this is if the commodity does not conform to the required specifications, in which case the buyer has the option to reject the good and cancel the contract (Mushtaq, n.d.). When the contract has been completed, the ownership of the asset passes to the buyer and due payment of the agreed price is made to the maker.

An *Al-istisna'* contract differs from a *bay al-salam* contract. In *bay al-salam*, the price of the manufactured item is paid in advance. In an *al-istisna'* sale, the price is not required be paid in advance, though it is permissible to pay in advance, or to defer payment, or to pay in instalments. Typically, part of the price is paid in advance and the remainder will be paid on receipt of the commodity.

It is a condition of an *al-istisna'* contract that the period of delivery is specified so as to avoid ignorance that may lead to conflict between the two parties.

Also, the place of delivery should be specified if the commodity requires loading facilities or if transportation expenses are involved. Lastly, the buyer may stipulate in the *al-istisna'* contract that the commodity is to be manufactured or produced by a specific manufacturer, or manufactured from specific materials. This is not permitted in the case of *bay al-salam*.

6 Application of *Al-Istisna'*

Generally, banks use *al-istisna'* to finance customers who are interested in purchasing property. There are two ways to settle the payment: deferred payment or payment by instalments. The manufacturer is responsible for providing the finished product at the agreed price as stated in the agreement. The price may be paid either prior to work commencing, at a specified time, or on delivery (http://www.altawfeek.com/glossaryofislamicfinancialterms.htm). As mentioned, *al-istisna'* is used widely in Islamic banking. Typically, it is applied in housing projects, the construction of industrial or commercial buildings, commercial projects and vehicle purchase.

Under *al-istisna'* financing, the bank purchases the ownership of the asset the customer requires to be made by putting the construction contract in place between the customer and the contractor. Subsequently, the bank immediately sells the ownership of the asset to be made to the customer at a sale price comprising the cost of the asset to the bank plus the bank's margin of profit (http://www.islamic-banking.com/ibanking.com/f_reports).

There are several ways in which a customer may make payment. The customer can settle the payment by instalments within an agreed period. The customer also can make payment through redemption. For instance, the bank's financing is usually released on a staged payment basis based on the presentation of a valid Architects' Certificate or such other acceptable documentary evidence (http://www.islamic-banking.com/ibanking.com/f_reports).

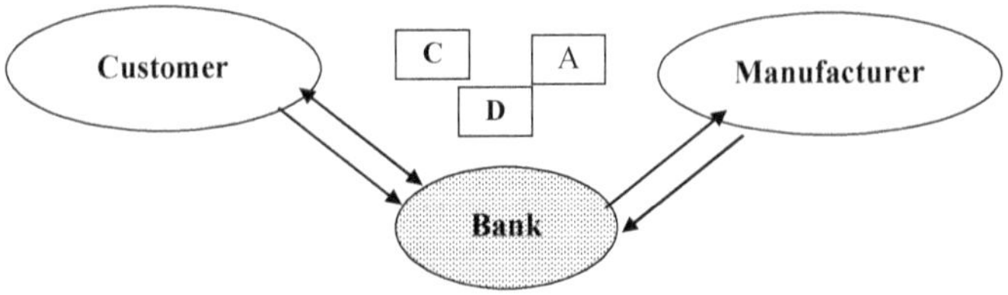

Fig. 1 Application of *al-istisna'* (*Sources* Authors' own)

7 Procedure of *Al-Istisna'*

Figure 1 shows the flow of *al-istisna'*: (A) shows the bank's purchase of the ownership of the asset being constructed for the customer. At the same time, the bank creates the construction contract between the customer and his contractor. (B) shows the transfer of ownership from the manufacturer to the bank. Simultaneously, the bank will sell the ownership of the asset to the customer at a marked-up price (C). Finally, the customer makes payment by instalments or deferred payment (D).

8 Application of the *Al-Istisna'* Financing Facility in Islamic Countries

There are various Islamic countries that apply the *al-istisna'* financing facility, for example, Malaysia, Negara Brunei Darussalam, Morocco, Qatar and Saudi Arabia.

In Malaysia, Bank Muamalat Malaysia Berhad applies *al-istisna'* for project financing. The *al-istisna'* facility improves a contractors' cash flow position and they are given total control over managing the performance of the contract. Under *al-istisna'* financing, a bank will purchase the contract at its cost price and resell it to the customer at the selling price, or for cost plus mark-up. However, the selling price may be paid in full or by instalments. There is a *Qur'anic* verse that deals with this type of financing:

> If the debtor is in difficulty, grant him till it is easy for him to repay. But if ye remit it by way of charity, then it is best for you if ye only know. (*Al-Qur'an*, 2: 280)

Other countries that use *al-istisna'* financing are Negara Brunei Darussalam, Morocco, Qatar and Saudi Arabia. Tables 1, 2, 3, and 4 present examples of projects supported by *al-istisna'* for each of these countries.

From the tables, it can be seen that *al-istisna'* financing has been used to achieve many major projects in Islamic countries (http://www.isdb.org/english_docs/idb_home/BussOpp.15.4.htm).

Other example of the application of *al-istisna'* is in the Kingdom of Saudi Arabia. At the beginning of 1993, the Al-Rajhi Banking and

Table 1 Brunei

Name of the project	*Paduka Seri Begawan Sultan Science College project*
Mode of financing	Istisna'
Project objectives	To construct, renovate, furnish and equip the science and classrooms, the library, the assembly area, the lecturer theater and home science buildings, girls and boy hostels, the admin block, the auditorium and dining hall
Project components	Demolition work, renovation, new construction, equipment and furniture
Project cost	US$20.704 million
Implementation period	2 years
Beneficiary	Ministry of Education/Government of Brunei
Executing agency	Ministry of Development

Source Author's own collection

Table 2 Morocco

Name of the project	*Water supply project for rural areas in Morocco*
Mode of financing	Istisna'
Project objectives	The project aims at constructing and providing the required infrastructure to secure potable water supplies to rural communities and other urban areas in Morocco
IDB components	100% of the cost, excluding taxes, of the components related to rural communities
Project cost	US$52.77 million
IDB financing	US$32.42 million
Beneficiary	The National Office for Potable Water
Executing agency	The National Office for Potable Water

Source Author's own collection

Table 3 Qatar

Name of the project	*West Bay complex office tower*
Mode of financing	Istisna' operation
Project objectives	The project aims the construction of a 29 story office tower to meet the ever-increasing demand for office space in Doha-Qatar
IDB components	Building construction works, substructure, and super structure
Project cost	US$45.25 million
IDB financing	US$16.50 million
Beneficiary	Advanced Real Estate Projects Company
Executing agency	Advanced Real Estate Projects Company

Source Author's own collection

Table 4 Saudi Arabia

Name of the project	*Dar Al Salam Waqf building project in Al Madinah Al Munawarah*
Mode of financing	Istisna' operation
Project objectives	Construction of a concrete building on a rented Waqf land in the North Central District of Al Madinah Al Munawarah, near the Prophet Mosque. The building will consist of three basements, 18 multi-stories, and helipad
IDB components	Building construction works, façade works, water and sanitary works, electrical works, air conditioning works, fire fighting works, infrastructure and utilities, consultancy services
Project cost	US$19.890 million
IDB financing	US$15.55 million
Beneficiary	Dar Al Salam Establishment for Pilgrimage and Umrah Services
Executing Agency	Dar Al Salam Establishment for Pilgrimage and Umrah Services

Source Author's own collection

Investment Corporation (a Saudi joint stock company) signed *al-istisna'* contracts with the Ministry of Education and General Presidency for Girls' Education. The project is guaranteed by the Ministry of Finance. This project involved the construction of 400 schools and was due to be completed within approximately 24 months. The value of the contract was payable in quarterly instalments over the course of 10 years. In accordance with the required standards, the Corporation classified its significant investments, such investments valued at an amortized cost, comprising of *al-mutajara*, *al-mutajara* by *wakala*, instalment sales, *al-istisna'* and *al-murabaha* (http://www.alrajhibank.com.sa/).

Furthermore, the Al-Rajhi Bank acknowledged its income as follows:

- Income from *al-mutajara*, *al-mutajara* by *wakala*, *al-murabaha*, *al-musharaka* after sale of shares, leasing, instalments sale and *al-istisna'* financing is recognized based on a constant rate of return using the outstanding balance method. No additional amounts are charged for delayed payments.
- Income from *al-istisna'* arises from the construction and financing of projects. Income from the construction part of an *al-istisna'* contract in progress is recognized based on the percentage of the contract that has been completed. However, if the cost to completion cannot be reasonably estimated, then the income is recognized on completion of the contract. Such income is included under *al-istisna'* income in the consolidated statement of income.
- Income from banking services is recognized at the time the related services are provided.

The practicality of *al-istisna'* financing can be seen from the above example, which shows that Islamic financing is applicable and suitable, and should be adopted not only by Islamic countries but also non-Islamic countries. Moreover, this financing method will help new contractors who have limited capital to use their skills and knowledge, and also provide easy payment methods for customers.

9 Scholars' Views on *Al-Istisna'*

Most jurists consider *al-istisna'* as one of the divisions of *bay al-salam* and therefore takes its definition. Various scholars hold differing opinions on *al-istisna'*. From the perspective of the *Hanafi* school of jurisprudence, *al-istisna'* is viewed as an independent and distinct contract. The jurists of the *Hanafi* school have given various definitions to *al-istisna'*; for example, 'A contract with a manufacturer to make something', and 'It is a contract for a commodity on the proviso of work' (http://www.albalagh.net/Islamic_Economics/salam_istisna:shtml). The purchaser is called the *mustasnia* contractor, the seller is called the *sania* maker or manufacturer, and the item to be manufactured, built or made is called the *masnooa*.

Hanafis allow *al-istisna'* based on *al-istihsan*. *Al-istihsan* is a contract that was devised so as to meet the needs of people and it has been in use for an extremely long time. Prophet Muhammad (*SAW*) made mention of it,

> What is good for a Muslim is good in the sight of Allah.

Shafi'is, *Hanbalis* and *Malikis* allow *al-istisna'* based on *bay al-salam* and *urf*. On one occasion, the Prophet himself ordered a manufacturer to manufacture a ring and a pulpit for him (Al-Amine, n.d.). Based on a resolution from the council of the Islamic Fiqh Academy, in its seventh session held in Jeddah, Kingdom of Saudi Arabia, from 7–12 Dhul Qi'dah 1412h (9–14 May 1992) regarding *al-istisna'* contracts, it was concluded that the *al-istisna'* contract, which has been mentioned with regard to work and goods on credit, is binding on both parties as long it meets the necessary requirements and conditions (http://www.oicexchange.com/docs/istisna.pdf). This discussion takes into consideration the purposes of *Shari'ah* regarding the interests of the people, the rules of *fiqh* regarding contracts and transactions, and considers that *al-istisna'* contracts play a vital role in stimulating industry, and increases the opportunities for the financing and promotion of the Islamic economy.

10 Recommendations

The range of applications of *al-istisna'* is quite broad; however, this form of financing is not currently fully implemented in business. This may be due to a general lack of information or knowledge among people, who are perhaps only aware of the conventional system of manufacturing, rather than the Islamic manufacturing system (*al-istisna'*). In order to improve the current application of *al-istisna'*, government and banking institutions should undertake the aggressive promotion of these instruments. This will impart awareness to people of the advantages of *al-istisna'* and how it can be implemented. The banks can introduce *al-istisna'* to their customers and show them how beneficial it can be as a financing method.

For instance, with regard to the house purchase sector, let us say a client has their own land. Their bank can provide the finance for the construction of a house on the basis of *al-istisna'*. If a customer has no land, a bank or financier can provide the finance for them to acquire it.

The bank is not responsible for the construction of the house but, rather, can hire another party to construct it. The cost should be calculated and added to the price of *al-istisna'* established with the client. The payment of instalments by the client may begin from the day on which the contract of *al-istisna'* is signed by the parties thereto, and may continue not only during the construction of the house, but also after it has been handed over to the client. In order to secure the payment of instalments, the title deeds to the house or land, or any other property owned by the client, may be retained by the financier or bank as security until the client has paid the final instalment.

The Islamic Development Bank is one example of the banks implementing *al-istisna'*. In addition, AmBank Group also offers this method of financing.

11 Conclusion

Al-istisna' should be implemented widely since it has many benefits for everyone. *Al-istisna'* means there is no burden to be borne by customers, despite which it can offer benefits in terms of payment and convenience to them. In addition, all parties benefit from *al-istisna'*. In order to make this method of business successful, everyone responsible for this type of business should spread the information *al-istisna'* as widely as they are able.

Lastly, from what has been discussed we can see that how beautiful Islam is. Islam relates to all aspects of life, from the smallest of matters to the most complicated and wide-ranging.

References

Al-Amine, M. A. M. (n.d.). *The Law and Practice of Istisna' in Islamic Banking.*

Ibn Abidin, Radd-ul-Muhtar, cited by Usmani, T. (1988). *Islamic Finance,* Saudi Arab.

Mushtaq, A. (n.d.). *Business Ethics in Islam*, International Institute of Islamic Thought, Islamabad.

http://albalagh.net/Islamic_economics/salam_istisna:shtml.

http://www.alahli.com/bb/financing/Islamicfinanceproducts/alistisna.

http://www.albalagh.net/Islamic_economics/.

http://www.albalagh.net/Islamic_Economics/salam_istisna:shtml.

http://www.alrajhibank.com.sa/.

http://www.altawfeek.com/glossaryofislamicfinancialterms.htm.
http://www.bankislaam.com.my/product_korpolistnaan.htm.
http://www.isdb.org/english_docs/idb_home/BussOpp.15.4.htm.
http://www.islamic-banking.com/ibanking.com/f_reports.
http://www.oicexchange.com/docs.istisna.pdf, p. 3.
http://www.oicexchange.com/docs.istisna.pdf, p. 2.
http://www.oicexchange.com/docs/istisna.pdf.

CHAPTER 21

Islamic Manufacture Financing Contract (*Aqd al-Istisna'*)

1 Introduction

The current conventional banking and finance system has taken long time to reach the point of developed at which it stands today. The system was not established for the purpose of social justice and welfare; rather, not only was it for self-interest, but also the whole system is based on creating interest (*riba*). Modern Islamic banking and finance began in Egypt in 1963, led by Dr. Alnajar. Other Muslim countries then followed suit, especially in the Gulf in the 1970s, in order to meet the growing demand for Islamic-based investment. The point we are trying to make is that Islamic banking and finance needs time to develop; therefore, what has been done so far has reached an acceptable level. Islamic banks offer financial instruments that are consistent with the teaching of *al-Qur'an* and *Sunnah*, such as *al-mudaraba*, *al-murabaha*, *bay' bithaman ajil* (BBA) and our topic of discussion: *al-istisna'*.

2 Central Idea

Al-istisna' is a debt-like contract that is based on mark-up. Some define an *al-istisna'* contract as a contract for the acquisition of goods by specification or order, where the price is paid in stages in accordance with the progress of a job towards completion (Hamwi and Aylward 1999). For the validity of an *al-istisna'* contract, it is necessary that the price is fixed with the mutual consent of the parties and that the necessary

M. M. Billah, *Islamic Financial Products*,
https://doi.org/10.1007/978-3-030-17624-2_21

specifications of the commodity to be manufactured are fully settled between them (http://www.albalagh.net/Islamic_economics/salam_istisna.shtml). An *al-istisna'* contract creates a moral obligation on the manufacturer to manufacture the goods but, before he starts the work, either of the parties may cancel the contract on giving a notice to the other. Once the manufacturer has started the work, the contract cannot be cancelled unilaterally (http://www.albalagh.net/Islamic_economics/salam_istisna.shtml).

3 Terms and Concepts

- *Mustasnia*: The purchaser or contractor (i.e. customer).
- *Sania*: The seller, maker, or manufacturer.
- *Masnooa*: The commodity manufactured (the object; i.e. house).
- *Al-istisna'* sale contract: The contract here is between two parties, a bank and its customer, or a customer and a manufacturer.
- Parallel *al-istisna'* contract: In this situation, the bank functions as an intermediary between the customer (who has asked the bank to finance the project) and the manufacturer. It is also called referred to as a back-to-back *al-istisna'* and is payable on a cash basis.

4 Terms and Conditions of the Islamic Development Bank

The following terms and conditions of the IDB, subject to change, may apply:

- The financing of capital goods shall be for a period not exceeding 12 years including a gestation period co-extensive with the period needed to manufacture and/or deliver the goods contracted, but not exceeding three years from the date of the contract.
- The mark-up currently applicable on IDB's project financing shall be either fixed at 5.5% per annum on Islamic Dinar, or floating at six months LABOR plus a 170 basis points spread. However, in case of export financing, the terms are: The rate of return will be valid for a period of six months from the date of approval of a

project by the Board of Executive Directors. The IDB reserves the right to apply a different rate if the Lease Agreement has not been signed within these six months.

- The manufacturer/contractor will provide a performance and refund bond guarantee issued by a commercial bank acceptable to the IDB, ensuring that the goods to be delivered conform to the specifications incorporated in the contract and to guarantee a refund of the progress payments made by the IDB should the manufacturer/contractor fail to deliver the goods, or if he delivers goods that do not conform to the specifications.
- The beneficiary (buyer) shall also furnish a guarantee to the IDB from the government, a first-class commercial bank or any other type of guarantee acceptable to the IDB to secure the repayment of the instalments on the due dates.
- The manufacturer will insure the assets under construction/manufacture and the IDB shall be named as the payee for the loss.
- The beneficiary (buyer), in consultation with and on behalf of the IDB, shall negotiate and conclude a contract and appoint a consultant to supervise the execution of the work of the manufacturer/contractor. The cost of such a consultant will be included in the IDB financing.
- Repayment instalments to be made on due dates by the beneficiary will be denominated in Islamic Dinar, and can be paid in a freely convertible currency acceptable to IDB. A 15% rebate will be applied to the applicable mark-up annually on the instalments repaid on or before the due date.
- It is permissible to include a penalty clause in an *al-istisna'* contract, if the parties so agree, save for cases of *force majeure* (http://www.isdb.org/english_docs/idb_home/MFIstMod_Home.htm).

In fact, the legality and acceptability of an *al-istisna'* contract show us that the Islamic state is an industrial state, too. So, *al-istisna'* is a very important contract in modern Islamic banking and finance, and it can help in the development of Islamic countries, which have been designated Third World countries! This is one of the reasons that encouraged us to write on the topic of *al-istisna'*, in order to develop and raise certain issues.

5 Legality of *Al-Istisna'*

Islamic *Shari'ah* is and always has been a suitable system of lifetime laws for all people at all time in. Moreover, the objective of *Shari'ah* is to make the life of Muslims and non-Muslims straightforward and easy. Therefore, in deciding the legality of any contract in Islam, we should take into consideration the needs of people within the teachings of *al-Qur'an* and *Sunnah*. Regarding the *al-istisna'* contract, there is no *Iya* from *al-Qur'an* or *hadith* from *Sunnah* that establishes the legality of *al-istisna'*; for that, the main basis for its legality is *istihsan*, according to some Muslim scholars.

On the other hand, the disagreement of Islamic scholars on the legality of *al-istisna'* arises from two points: first, the contract of *al-istisna'* is basically a future trading contract in which the subject matter is not in existence at the time of contract; second, we must consider the interpretation of the *hadith* 'Do not sell what is not with you'. Three scholars of law did not recognize the contract of *al-istisna'* as an independent contract and subsumed it under *salam* (Muhammad 2001). Moreover, some scholars do not allow the contract of *al-istisna'* and believe it is illegal, because it is the selling of what one does not have.

However, the *Hanafi* school considered *al-stisna'* an independent contract, and legal on the basis of *istihsan*, but they put in a condition that the contracting parties have the right to revoke the contract because it is a sale of what has not been seen (Muhammad 2001). If we could relate the above *Hanafi* opinion to modern times, it would be extremely difficult to apply. For instance, if a manufacturing company is working based on a just in time system, that company will only start manufacturing the product (i.e. a car) when they receive a customer's purchase order, which will include the specific style and options. So, is it possible for the customer or the manufacture to breach the agreement? Time is becoming money in our life today.

As has been mentioned, the first legal basis for the contract of *al-istisna'* is *istihsan*. *Al-Kasani*, in this regard, said: 'concerning the legality of *al-istisna'*, in principle it would not be allowed on the basis of *qiyas* because it is a state of what we do not have nor on the basis of Islam and the prophet had prohibited the sale of what we do not have, and it is allowed based on *istihsan* because people are unanimous about its need' (Muhammad 2001). *Al-istisna'*) has been used throughout the ages and the Prophet (*SAW*) said: 'My community shall never agree on an error' (Ibn Majah, Sunan Ibn Maja, *kitab al-fitan*, Hadith no. 3950).

In addition, some scholars claimed that *al-istisna'* is based on *ijma*—the unanimous agreement of the *Mujtahidin* of the Muslim community of any period following the demise our beloved Prophet Muhammad (*SAW*) on any matter: 'My community shall never agree on an error' (Ibn Majah, Sunan Ibn Maja, kitab al-fitan, Hadith no. 3950).

It is also legal based on public interest (*maslahah ama*). Al-Ashgar said: 'the use of this contract in building construction, shoes, furniture and other items without objection from the scholars is a demonstration of the general need. Therefore, it should be legal on the basis of public interest.' Moreover, Islamic jurisprudence admitted the validity of *al-istisna'* transactions on the grounds of custom (Billah 2003). Regarding the legality of *al-istisna'* contracts, we can say that nothing in the Holy *Qur'an* or *Sunnah* talks about the legality of this contract, it is an acceptable contract—according to some *fiqh* scholars, based on *istihsan*, *ijma* and public interest. However, the majority of the jurists consider *al-istisna'* to be one of the divisions of *salam*; therefore it is assumed under the definition of *salam* (http://www.barakaonline.com/products/Istisnaa.htm).

6 Current Scenario

6.1 Application

Al-istisna' contracts open broad fields of application for Islamic banks to finance public needs and the vital interests of the society in developing the Islamic economy. The *Al-istisna'* contract is applied in high technology industries, such as the aircraft industry, and the locomotive and shipbuilding industries, in addition to the different types of machines produced in large factories or workshops. The *al-istisna'* contract is also applied in the construction industry for apartment buildings, hospitals, schools and universities (http://www.alrajhibank.com.sa/instruments-istina.htm).

6.2 Al-Istisna' *Sale*

Al-istisna' sale contract:

- The buyer expresses his desire to buy a commodity and sends an *al-istisna'* request to the bank with a specific price. The timing of payment, whether in cash or deferred, is subject to agreement.
- The bank usually calculates what it will actually pay in the parallel *al-istisna'* contract plus the profit it deems reasonable.
- The bank puts itself under an obligation to ensure the manufacture of a certain commodity and to deliver it on a specific period subject to agreement (the bank takes into consideration that the due date either is the same as the due date, or after, for its receipt of the commodity in the parallel contract).

The parallel *al-istisna'* contract:

- The bank expresses its desire to order the manufacture of the commodity for which it has undertaken to ensure the manufacture in the first *al-istisna'* contract (with the same specifications as in the first contract) and agrees with the maker on the price and the date of delivery.
- The seller puts himself under an obligation to manufacture the specific commodity and to deliver the commodity on the due date agreed.

Delivery and receipt of the commodity:

- The seller delivers the manufactured commodity to the bank directly, or to any other party at the place decided by the bank on the contract.
- The bank delivers the manufactured commodity directly to the purchaser, or authorizes any other party to deliver the commodity to the purchaser, who has the right to make sure that the commodity satisfies the specifications he has demanded in the contract (http://www.alrajhibank.com.sa/instruments-istina.htm).

7 Payment Methods

The price of the goods in a contract of *al-istisna'* may be paid either in advance, or in arrears, and may be paid in one payment or by instalments during the manufacture of the goods or at a future date. The manufacturer is bound and obliged to deliver the goods within the agreed time. Failure to deliver within the agreed time will make the manufacturer liable to pay the buyer liquidated damages in accordance with the contract unless such delay is due to *force majeure* (http://www.oicexchange.com/docs/istisna.pdf) of instalments. The financier may retain the title deeds of the house or land, or any other property against which its financing has been secured until the client pays the final instalment.

8 Empirical Illustration

Islamic finance was successfully used in conjunction with conventional project finance for the landmark Hub River Power Project in Pakistan (total cost: US$1.6 billion). Importantly, financing included a US$92 million bridging finance facility in the form of an *al-istisna'* staged payment facility by the Al-Rajhi Bank to finance the purchase and installation of the power turbines for the facility (Hamwi and Aylward 1999).

9 Issues in *Al-Istisna'*

9.1 **Al-Istisna'** ***and Economic Development***

Economically, *al-istisna'* is more useful in industrial countries, so it can play a very important role in developing countries (Muslim countries). It allowed investment in the manufacturing and construction sector, such as cars, highways, airports and so on. The benefits of *al-istisna'* to those sectors come about due to the huge amount of capital that needs to be invested which, typically, is not immediately available. Therefore, through the use of *al-istisna'*, people can pay using BBA or *al-murabahah*. Infrastructure requires vast amounts of capital. The benefits of these huge investments are immense but many of them are indirect and all of them accrue gradually over a long period of time. In developing countries, especially, the private sector either lacks the means to undertake these projects, or the (low) returns and (long) time period involved are not suitable. So, the state is called on to undertake these projects in order to create an environment suitable for growth and development (http://www.soundvision.com/Info/money/financinginfrastructure.asp).

Infrastructure refers to roads, bridges, railways, waterways, airways, and other forms of transportation and communication, as well as water supplies, electricity and telephone lines (http://islamic-finance.net/islamic-economics/eco3.html).

9.2 *Foreign Exchange Risk*

Foreign exchange risk is a risk in which the value of the local currency will depreciate against the foreign currency (i.e. US$). As a result, investors (from other Muslim country, such as Al-Rajhi Bank) will lose some of their revenue. For instance, a report revealed that Al-Rajhi Bank funding known as *Al-istisna'*-I was initially for $92 million but was subsequently increased to $106 million under *Al-istisna'*-II (an Islamic means of financing). *Al-istisna'*-I comprised a sale and repurchase agreement whereby Hubco sold specified assets to Al-Rajhi Bank with an obligation to repurchase the same assets at a contracted price by a specified date. The repurchase price was predetermined to allow Al-Rajhi a margin.

This was, effectively, a financing cost to Hubco. Under *Al-istisna'*-II, Al-Rajhi Bank advanced $92 million to Hubco on 2 December 1992, in three amounts. Hubco was required to repay the three amounts grossed up to include the Al-Rajhi Bank's margin on 2 September 1993. Due to movements in the dollar exchange rates between the two dates, in addition to their financing cost up to the disbursement of *Al-istisna'*-II of some $7.4 million, Hubco had to bear a foreign exchange loss of around $6.5 million due to the fact that the foreign exchange risk had not been hedged (http://www.dawn.com/2001/09/13/top14.htm).

10 Findings and Recommendations

In today's world, an *al-istisna'* contract is a very important type of contract that should be widely practised by Islamic financial institutions to help in the development of our *Ummah*. *Al-istisna'* is an acceptable contract for the purpose of public interest, the price of the contract may be paid in advance or arrear, and it is even better if it can be paid in stages according the rate of progress of the contract. For instance, if 45% of the *masnoo* (the subject matter) is completed, 45% of the total cost should be paid by the customer. In addition, the customer (the beneficiary) should make a cash down payment (i.e. 15% of total cost) to ensure that a customer can be relied on, and to help the manufacturer start the work on time.

To protect a seller or manufacturer from foreign exchange risk, the price may not be fixed; we can use the floating rate, in the same way as *al-ijarah*. For example, the Islamic Development Bank use a fixed rate of 5.5% per annum Islamic Dinars, or floating rate at six months LABOR plus a 170 basis points spread.

In financing a major project, such as constructing highway or building a university, the government should guarantee publicly owned projects. In the event of default by the customer or a delay in delivery by the manufacturer, liquidated damages should be paid by the party who caused the damage, purely to ensure the project goes smoothly.

11 Conclusion

Al-istisna' is a debt-like contract for acquisition of goods by specification or order. Price can be paid in cash or by instalments, and it can be classified into two types namely *al-istisna'* sale contract and parallel *al-istisna'* contract. An *al-istisna'* contract is applied in high technology industries such as the aircraft industry, locomotive and ship building industries, and most importantly in house financing. In addition, under this mode of financing, it is possible to finance intangible assets like gas, electricity, etc. It is also possible, unlike under leasing and instalment sale, to finance working capital (http://www.isdb.org/english_docs/idb_home/MFIstMod_Home.htm). Regarding the legality of an *al-istisna'* contract, we can say that there is nothing in the holy *Qur'an* or *Sunnah* that speaks about the legality of this contract. It is therefore considered an acceptable contract—according to some *fiqh* scholars—based on *istihsan*, *ijma*, and public interest. However, the majority of the jurists consider *al-istisna'* as one of the divisions of *salam*; therefore it is assumed under the definition of *salam* (http://www.barakaonline.com/products/Istisnaa.htm). The application of *al-istisna'* could help in the economic development of the Islamic countries, however, *al-istisna'* is not widely used by Islamic countries such as Malaysia. The main problem which is facing the application of *al-istisna'* is the foreign exchange risk, especially for long-run *al-istisna'* financing Table 1.

11.1 Procedure for Al-Istisna' *Financing*

The procedure for *al-istina'* financing is presented in Table 2.

Table 1 Financing of customers

Group	*2001*	*2000*
	$'000	$'000
Al-Bai Bithaman Ajil	3,837,866	2,883,697
Al-Ijarah	231,871	279,389
Al-Musharakah	167,075	17,517
Al-Mudharabah	18,770	219,939
Al-Murabahah	1,455,955	1,156,849
Al-Qardhul Hassan	452,318	210,016
Al-Istisna	11,400	–
Staff financing	67,710	34,711
	6,242,965	4,802,118
Less: Provision for bad and doubtful financing	(442,250)	(302,790)
	5,800,715	4,499,328

Source http://www.bankislam.commy/ar/BIMB_Account%202(Engl).pdf

Table 2 Development projects

Scope of work: The project scope will comprise (i) substructyre (ii) permanent way which include doubling of the remaining track for length of 414 Km, including additional rails and Tunnouls (iii) extending the existing stations, from 450 to 950 m (iv) providing improved signing of telecommunication equipment and (v) project supervision

Sector transport & communications

Location: Tehran - Mashhad

Name of project: Doubling of Tehran - Mashhad railway line project

Project objectives: The primary objective of the project is to doubling of the existing single track at Tehran - Mashhad Railway line for the remaining distance of 414 Km out of 926 Km total length to meet the rapid transport demand growth of 8.3% per annum for freight and railway passengers respectively

Total cost US$ 106,94 million

Implementation period: 3 years

Co-financier: Government of Iran

IDB contribution: US$ 35, 0 Million

IDB financed components: Rails for the second track of 414 Km, additional rails for station (115 km) (28 stations) and tumouts of 229 units

Beneficiary: The government of Islamic Republic of Iran

Executing agency: Department of construction, and development of Railway (DCDR), under Ministry of Road and Transportation

Address no. 52 - Niloost - Brazil -ST- Vanak, Tehran, Iran

References

Billah, M. M. (2003). *Modern Financial Transactions Under Shari'ah*, Ilmiah, Malaysia.
Hamwi, B., and Aylward, A. (1999), Islamic Finance: A Growing International Market, Thunderbird International Business Review, Vol. 41, July–October.
Ibn Majah, Sunan Ibn Maja, *kitab al-fitan*, *Hadith* No. 3950.
Muhammad, M. A. (2001), *Istisna (Manufacturing Contract) in Islamic Banking and Finance (Law & Practice)*, A. S. Noordeen, KL.
http://islamic-finance.net/islamic-economics/eco3.html.
http://www.albalagh.net/Islamic_economics/salam_istisna.shtml.
http://www.alrajhibank.com.sa/instruments-istina.htm.
http://www.barakaonline.com/products/Istisnaa.htm.
http://www.dawn.com/2001/09/13/top14.htm.
http://www.isdb.org/english_docs/idb_home/MFIstMod_Home.htm.
http://www.oicexchange.com/docs/istisna.pdf.
http://www.soundvision.com/Info/money/financinginfrastructure.asp.

CHAPTER 22

Islamic Venture Capital

1 Introduction

In finance, there are two main ways available for a company or organization to raise fund and finance for its projects: equity financing and debt financing. Equity financing is where a company issues shares in a public offering; this is especially pertinent to listed companies. Debt financing takes place through the issue of bonds in the stock market or loans from a bank. As far as Islam is concerned, not all the elements of these means of financing are *Shari'ah* compliant or, at least, there are certain restrictions regarding the use of such methods of financing. This has specific regard to the case of debt financing, as it may involve *riba* or other *haram* elements such as *gharar* and gambling. Almost all Muslim scholars are of the opinion that buying, selling or holding shares is lawful provided that the company's main business is in line with Islamic law.

Islamic venture capital is a type of equity financing through the use of *al-musharakah*. In fact, venture capital as a concept is not new; it has a long history. Sami Al-Suwailem (2000) said: 'although the concept (venture capital) as such is not new, a formal market for venture capital in the U.S. started only after World War II. Venture capital institutions currently manage over $30 billion in the U.S. and another $30 billion in Western Europe'. People use venture capital to finance projects that may require a large amount of capital that may not be available to the project's owner. Nowadays, business uses venture capital in the full or partial financing of technology based projects. From this perspective, it is

M. M. Billah, *Islamic Financial Products*,
https://doi.org/10.1007/978-3-030-17624-2_22

strongly advisable for Muslim countries to have mutual contracts or win–win strategies to help each other in this era of globalization, in which strong will overpower the weak.

Most Muslim nations have sufficient resources but lack the skills and expert management found in the Gulf countries, although some Muslim countries seem to have highly skilled people, such as Malaysia. It would be a great advantage for Muslim countries to make mutual deals as, in order to thrive in this era of globalization, we Muslims need to stand hand-in-hand. In the next section, we explain the concept of *al-musharakah*, since it is the basis for the use of Islamic venture capital.

2 *Al-Musharakah*

Al-musharakah literally means 'sharing'. In the context of business and trade, *al-musharakah* refers to a joint enterprise in which all the partners share the profit or loss of a joint venture. It is a contract based on mutual consent and its strength is dependent on the most important aspects of *Shari'ah*. In *al-musharakah* all parties should be capable of entering into a contract, the mutual consent of all parties is required and the contract must be free from duress, fraud or misrepresentation.

2.1 *Rules of* Al-Musharakah

There are basic rules that need to be spelled out during the implementation of an *al-musharakah* contract. The distribution of profit and loss, the nature of the capital, the management of al-*musharakah* and the termination of *al-musharakah* must be clearly and precisely outlined.

2.2 *Distribution of Profit*

The proportion of profit to be distributed must be determined and agreed by all the contracting parties. If it is not determined, then the contract is invalid. The profit sharing ratio should be based on the actual profit accruing to the business and not on how much each party contributed. If the profit is distributed on a capital ratio basis and at a predetermined rate, then such contract is invalid; however, a question arises: Is it necessary that the ratio of profit of each partner conforms to the ratio of capital invested? There are differences of opinion among Muslim jurists about this question.

According to Imam Malik and Imam Shafi, a contract is valid if the distribution of profit is based on capital contribution. For instance, if A contributed 40% of the capital in the *al-musharakah* contract, he is entitled to 40% of the profit that arises from the business. If he receives more or less than the amount he contributed, then the contract is invalid. However, in the view of Imam Ahmad the contract is still valid even if the ratio of profit differs from the ratio of capital invested on condition that the partners agree to this. For example, A may invest 40% of the business capital, but they may receive, say, 60% of profit if the other partners agree. Imam Abu Hanifah agrees with views of Imam Ahmed, that ratio of profit to capital contributed may differ but on the condition that all partners are active on one is a sleeping partner. If there are any sleeping partners, then for such a contract to be valid their profit must be based on the proportion of capital that they contributed (Taqi Usman 2004).

2.3 *Sharing in Loss*

There is no disagreement among jurists regarding the sharing of a loss. All Muslim jurists unanimously agreed that, in the event of a loss, the partners must share it in proportion to the amount of capital they invested in the business. This argument is based on the principles of a maxim:

> Profit is based on the agreement of the parties, but loss is always subject to the ratio of investment.

2.4 *The Nature of Capital*

Most jurists are of the opinion that capital should be in monetary form, not commodities. However, there are different views in this respect. Imam Malik argued that partners can contribute capital in the form of money but that, as this is not a condition for the validity of *al-musharakah*, it is also permissible to invest in kind on condition that the partner's share is subject to the market price of that commodity.

Imam Abu Hanifah and Imam Ahmad disagreed, stating that no contribution in kind is acceptable in an *al-musharakah* agreement. Their argument was based on two reasons: first, commodities cannot be the same; even if they are the same type, they will differ in quality and value.

Hence, *al-musharakah* is invalid if the property can be distinguished from one another. Second, share capital redistribution is not possible, since commodities are subject to price fluctuations. However, there was agreement on commodity capital if the commodities are *dhawat-ul-amthal*. *Dhawat-ul-amthal* is applicable to commodities that, if destroyed, can be replaced with similar commodities; for example, rice. Imam Shafi was also of the opinion that, if the commodity is *dhawat-ul-amthal*, then it would be acceptable on the ground that it can be mixed with other commodities of the same type, but he disagreed regarding *dhawat-ul-qeemah* (commodities that cannot be replaced with similar commodities; for example, cattle (Taqi Usman 2004). Thus, share capital can be in the form of money or commodities, the market value of the commodities determining the share of the partner in the capital.

2.5 *Management of* Al-Musharakah

In the usual practice of partnerships, all partners have a right to take part in the management of a venture as well as to take part in the business activities. However, there are two possibilities here: first, management can be undertaken by one partner provided the remaining partners give their consent; in this situation, the sleeping partners will receive their profit based on capital they invested. Second, all the partners can work as a team and each partner will be considered an agent of the others in matters of business or with regard to any work, and all partners will have equal rights in the day-to-day dealings of the business.

2.6 *Termination*

Al-musharakah can be terminated in the following circumstances:

- *Right to termination*: Every partner has right to terminate the partnership any time. If the contract is terminated at will, and the assets are in the form of cash, then such cash will be distributed according to the share each partner contributed. If the assets are illiquid, then there are two options: distribution of the physical asset based on its value; in the event of dispute, the physical asset will be sold and the cash obtained distributed in an agreed ratio.
- *In the event a partner dies*: A partnership can be liquidated in the event of the death of one of the partners. However, if the heirs of

the dead partner are willing to continue with the *al-musharakah* arrangement, then this is also permissible.

- *In the event of insanity*: If one of the parties becomes mentally unwell, either the partnership can be terminated provided the remaining partners agree, or the remaining partners can continue with the business after buying out the share of the partner who has left the partnership.

These conditions of termination of an *al-musharakah* contract are allowed if all parties agreed to them at the commencement of the contract (Taqi Usman, 2004). As the Prophet (*SAW*) said in a famous *hadith*; 'All the conditions agreed upon by the Muslims are upheld, except a condition which allows what is prohibited or prohibits what is lawful.'

2.7 Modern Operation of Musharakah *Model*

When applying this *al-musharakah* model, a bank scrutinizes a prospective company to ensure it will be able to comply with due diligence. A company can issue *al-musharakah* preference shares to the bank at a discount if the bank wants to purchase them by means of *wadiah* or discount sale. In the event the bank does not intend to purchase preference shares, then the company can sell them to the investors directly by means of *al-musharakah* deposits. For example, a bank may require $70 million to finance four short- and medium-term investment projects. The bank will issue $70 million worth of *al-musharakah* shares to investors at $1 each. In this case, the bank acts as an agent for both the investors and the company, for which it will charges fees for services rendered. Let us say the value of the project increases to $90 million, the net asset value per unit will increase to $1.5. In this case, investors will enjoy capital gains. However, if the project fails to succeed, the investors will lose their capital.

2.8 The Practical Scenario

In reality, a venture capital project is a real business deal in which both parties, the venture capitalists (the venture capital company) and the financed company, work together and share the efforts and returns because, simply, there is no gain without pain; from this point on, we could start fighting the concept of *riba*. At the same time, we could also consider what the position would be if we minimized the use of banking services, especially loan services, and we establish investment companies that were based on *al-musharakah*.

Let us now identify some of the steps involved in the use of venture capital.

The company "The *Ummah*" deals in pharmaceuticals. It has the relevant skills to develop a new type of product but has insufficient capital to finance the project:

- The company founds a venture capital company that will finance about 90% of the total cost based on an *al-musharakah* contract; later, the profit or loss will be divided according to the principle of *al-musharakah*.
- After the establishment of the venture capital and the identification of the investment opportunities, the venture capitalist has the right to monitor the investment and analyse it step-by-step to make sure the project is successful and beneficial to both parties.
- The contribution of the venture capital company may be converted into common stock, but it is not Islamic to convert it to preference stock as a holder of preference stock typically receives a fixed dividend.
- The full amount of capital will not be provided in a lump sum but, rather, in instalments at each stage of the project as it progresses.
- The board of directors satisfies all parties, the recipient company and the venture capitalist.
- To minimize risk, the venture capital firm can build a portfolio investment by investing in other companies (diversification).
- After the project has materialized, the recipient company has the opportunity to go public.
- The profit earned from the project will be shared between the parties involved based on predetermined ratios (Al-Suwailem 2000).

3 Conclusion

To survive as a Muslim *Ummah* in the era of globalization, should the Islamic financial sector be considering innovation? Innovation and positive thinking on the part of Islamic scholars (*fiqh* scholars) are our motive force for becoming a civilized *Ummah* in order for us to lead the current corrupted world. Otherwise, we will only be dreaming of leading the world and we will be part of the problem.

What is harmful in using others' ideas if they can be maintained in line with Islamic law? We do not even need to use the term 'Islamic venture capital'; we use the venture capital as a mechanism to finance our project using equity financing. Muslims, especially businesspersons, should know what is wrong and what is right, what is *haram* and what is *halal*. He should invest using the appropriate mechanism for his investments; the names by which activities are known should not be our concern. Thus, to conclude: venture capital is a very important mechanism for the raising of funds through the use of the accepted Islamic concept of *al-musharakah*. Venture capital could help developing Muslim countries to exchange skills and resources, and go further in developing our *Ummah*.

CHAPTER 23

Sukuk Paradigm and Structure

1 Introduction

Sukuk are the *Shari'ah* alternative to the bonds used in the modern capital market. Interest in the product has expanded significantly since the mid-2000s, attracting both Muslim and non-Muslim participants with promising results. *Sukuk* now represents more than 70% of the total Islamic financial market across the contemporary world (Godlewski et al. 2014). Policies, strategies, instruments, mechanisms, structures, marketing, management and operations are strictly ruled as being totally non-compliant with the divine ethics and principles of *Shari'ah*, which are closely monitored by qualified *Shari'ah* scholars as to compliance with *Shari'ah* standards. Securities Commission Malaysia's guidelines provide that *sukuk* refer to certificates of equal value that function as evidence of undivided ownership or investment in assets using *Shari'ah* principles and concepts endorsed by the *Shari'ah* Advisory Council (Securities Commission Malaysia 2015). Thus, this chapter scrutinizes the *sukuk* model as an investment security by applying the *Shari'ah* spirit and standards as to universal value.

2 Phenomena

In modern practice, a bond is a debt security that vests in the holder a right of financial claim on the issuer. This claim protects the holder in circumstances in which the issuer is unable to pay the amount due.

M. M. Billah, *Islamic Financial Products*,
https://doi.org/10.1007/978-3-030-17624-2_23

Bonds bear certain similarities to savings accounts. When an investor deposits money in a savings account, that investor is, in effect, lending the bank money. The bank pays the investor interest on the deposit. Similarly, the investor who subscribes to bonds lends the issuer money in return for interest. When the bonds mature, the investor will receive the principle amount of the bonds back in the same way as if they had withdrawn the amount from the savings account (Al-Amine 2001). In this case, the bond functions as securitization. The major difference between savings accounts and bonds is that investors can dispose of their bonds in the secondary market before they have matured to end investors. Savings accounts, on the contrary, can neither be sold in the secondary market, nor be disposed of to other investors (Faerber 1993).

An enforceable bond must be supported by documentation that specifies the terms for both the interest and the principal payments. Interest can be paid monthly, bi-annually or annually. This makes a difference to the compounding of the interest and will affect the trading of a bond. The interest on most bonds is paid bi-annually with an agreed interest rate in North America. The interest on Eurobonds, which trade in Europe, is paid annually. The interest on mortgage-backed securities (MBS) and asset-backed securities (ABS) is paid monthly at an agreed rate, reflecting the payment terms of the underlying mortgages and loans. The currency of payments is important. Some bonds have the coupon paid in one currency and the principal in another. Bonds that pay part of their principal before maturity are said to 'amortize' their principal; this is the case with many mortgage bonds in use in North America in particular (Faerber 1993).

It should be noted that the bond market comprises two categories: the primary bond market and the secondary bond market. The primary bond market is where the bonds are initially issued, while the secondary market is where the bonds are resold to other investors. Islamic bonds also share conceptual similarities with modern practice by adapting the primary and secondary markets but, in practice, they contract with each other as to principles, technicalities, issuance and trading.

Sukuk is governed by the *Shari'ah* principles as an alternative to the bond practiced under modern economy. *Sukuk* is a financial instrument (document or certificate), which evidences the undivided pro-rata ownership of underlying assets. *Sukuk* is an Arabic term derived from *sak* (the singular of *sukuk*), which literally means 'freely tradable at par, premium or discount' (Faerber 1993).

The conceptual background of *sukuk* typically involves the structuring of pools of *Shari'ah* compliant assets or, without credit enhancement, into securities. It is structured based on a specific contract of exchange that can be made through the sales and purchase of an asset based on deferred payments, the leasing of a specific asset, or participation in a joint venture business. The issuance of Islamic bonds requires an exchange of a *Shari'ah* compliant underlying asset for a financial consideration through the application of various *Shari'ah* instruments; for example, *al-ijarah* (leasing), *al-mudharabah* (co-partnership), or *al-musharakah* (partnership). The structure of *sukuk* has to be approved by the *Shari'ah* advisors to ensure that they are in compliance. In addition, the structuring process may also involve the provision of additional protection for investors against late payments, prepayments, potential write-off and similar eventualities. Such protection is often provided in the form of a credit and/or liquidity enhancement scheme (Faerber 1993).

In the process of the issuance of *sukuk*, the doctrine of *al-tawarruq* (special purpose vehicle) is used to securitize the instrument in the primary market while, in the secondary market, *bay' al-dayn* is used in order to legalize the reselling of the bonds. Such process is mostly used in the Malaysian market, while most of the Middle-Eastern countries do not accept it. The proposed alternative is Islamic bonds based on *al-muqaradah* (profit sharing).

3 Modern Bond Market

A bond in the modern economy is treated as a debt security, similar to an IOU. When someone purchases a bond, they are lending money to a government, municipality, corporation, federal agency or other entity known as an issuer. In return for that money, the issuer provides you with a bond that promises to pay a specified rate of interest during the life of the bond, and to repay the face value of the bond (the principal) when it matures. Among the types of bonds available for investment are: US government securities, municipal bonds, corporate bonds, mortgage- and asset-backed securities, federal agency securities and foreign government bonds. The characteristics of several different types of US bonds are described in Sect. 5. Market practices described here apply to the US bond market, and may differ from those in other countries. Bonds can be also called bills, notes, debt securities, or debt obligations. To simplify matters, we will refer to all of these as 'bonds' (http://www.investinginbonds.com/learnmore.asp?catid=46&id=2).

The bond market—the primary market—is a financial market in which new issues of a security, such as a bond or a stock, are sold to initial buyers by the corporation or government agency borrowing the funds. The investment bank underwrites securities and then sells them to the public. The secondary market is a financial market in which securities that have been previously issued can be resold. It could be an organized market, such as KLSE in Malaysia, or an over-the-counter market in which dealers at different locations stand ready to buy or sell securities over the counter to whoever accepts their price (http://www.investinginbonds.com/learnmore.asp?catid=46&id=2).

Bonds may generally be traded anywhere in the world as long as a buyer and a dealer can strike a deal. Unlike publicly traded stocks, there is no central place or exchange for bond trading. The bond market is known as an over-the-counter market, rather than an exchange market. There are certain exceptions to this, however. For example, some corporate bonds in the United States are listed on the exchange, as are bond futures and some types of bond option. However, the majority of bonds do not trade on exchanges.

4 Market Participants

In a bond market, dealers, brokers and investors are among the lead participants.

4.1 Dealers

While investors can trade marketable funds among themselves whenever they wish, trading is usually done with bond dealers—more specifically, the bond trading desks of major investment dealers. The dealers occupy centre stage in the vast network of telephone and computer links that connect interested players. Bond dealers usually create the market for bonds. What this means is that dealers have traders whose responsibility it is to know all about a group of bonds and to be prepared to quote a price to buy and sell them. The role of the dealers is to provide liquidity for bond investors, thereby allowing investors to buy and sell bonds more easily and with a limited concession on the price. Dealers also buy amongst themselves, either directly or anonymously via bond brokers. The aim of trading is to take a spread between the price the bonds are bought at and the price at which they are sold. This is the main way that bond dealers make (or lose) money. Dealers often have bond traders located in the major financial centres and are able to trade bonds 24 hours per day (although not usually at weekends).

4.2 *Brokers*

Brokers are agents who match buyers with sellers of securities.

4.3 *Investors*

Bond investors include financial institutions, pension funds, mutual funds and governments from around the world. These bond investors, along with the dealers, comprise the 'institutional market', where large blocks of bonds are traded. A trade of $1 million in bonds would be considered a small ticket. There is no restriction to the amount of money that changes hands, and trades involving $500 million or $1 billion at a time can take place. Similarly, there is no restriction in the 'retail market', which essentially involves individual investors buying and selling bonds with the bond trading desks of investment dealers. However, the value of trades in the retail market is usually under $1 million.

5 Types of Bond

Among the bonds used in the modern economy are convertible bonds, extendable or retractable bonds, foreign currency bonds, government bonds, corporate bonds, high yield or junk bonds, inflation-linked bonds and zero coupon bonds.

5.1 *Convertible Bonds*

A convertible bond is a bond that gives the holder the right to convert or exchange the par value of the bond for common shares of the issuer at some fixed ratio during a particular period. As bonds, they share certain characteristics with fixed income securities. The fact they are convertible also gives them features of equity securities.

5.2 *Extendable or Retractable Bonds*

Extendable and retractable bonds have more than one maturity date. An extendable bond gives its holder the right to extend the initial maturity date to a longer-term maturity date. A retractable bond gives its holder the right to advance the return of principal to an earlier date than the original maturity date. Investors use extendable bonds and retractable bonds to modify the term of their portfolio to take advantage of movements in interest rates. The characteristic of these bonds is a combination of their underlying terms. According to whether interest rates rise or fall, as the dates on these bonds can be varied to suit the investor, the investor is able to maximize their gain or minimize their loss.

5.3 *Foreign Currency Bonds*

A foreign currency bond is a bond that is issued by an issuer in a currency other than its national currency. Issuers make bond issues in foreign currencies to make them more attractive to buyers and to take advantage of international interest rate differentials. Foreign currency bonds can be 'swapped' or converted in the swap market into the home currency of the issuer. Bonds issued by foreign issuers in the United States market in US dollars are known as 'Yankee' bonds; bonds issued in pounds sterling in the British bond market are known as 'Bulldogs' and bonds denominated in Yen by foreign issuers are known as 'Samurai' bonds.

5.4 *Government Bonds*

Governments have the power to print money to pay their debts, as they control the money supply and currency of their countries. This is why most investors consider the national governments of most modern industrial countries to be almost risk-free, from a default point of view.

5.5 *Corporate Bonds*

A corporate bond is a loan made by a corporation in return for a specified amount of interest and the repayment of the face value of the bond on a specified maturity date. The creditworthiness of corporate bonds is tied to the business prospects and financial capacity of the issuer.

The business prospects of companies are dependent on the economy and the competitive situation of industries. Industries with stable revenues and earnings are called 'non-cyclicals', whereas those whose revenues and earnings rise and fall with the economy and commodity prices are called 'cyclicals'. Companies that have financial risk because of high levels of debt, and variable revenues and earnings are called 'below investment grade' or 'junk' bonds because of their speculative nature. Higher quality bonds are considered 'investment grade'.

5.6 *High Yield or Junk Bonds*

A high yield, or junk, bond is a bond issued by a company that is considered to be a higher credit risk. The credit rating of a high yield bond is considered 'speculative' grade, or below investment grade. This means that the chance of default with high yield bonds is higher than for other bonds. Their higher credit risk means that junk bond yields are higher than bonds of a better credit quality. Studies have demonstrated that portfolios of high yield bonds have higher returns than other bond portfolios, suggesting that the higher yields more than compensate for their additional default risk.

5.7 *Inflation-Linked Bonds*

An inflation-linked bond is a bond that provides protection against inflation. Most inflation-linked bonds—such as the Canadian Real Return Bond, the British Inflation-linked Gilt and the new US Treasury Inflation-Protected Security are principal indexed. This means their principal is increased by the change in inflation over a period. In most countries, the consumer price index (CPI) or its equivalent is used as an inflation proxy. As the principal amount increases with inflation, the interest rate is applied to this increased amount. This causes the interest payment to increase over time. At maturity, the principal is repaid at the inflated amount. In this fashion, an investor has complete inflation protection, as long as the investor's inflation rate equals the CPI.

5.8 *Zero Coupon Bonds*

Zero coupon or strip bonds are fixed income securities that are created from the cash flows that make up a normal bond. Conceptually, a zero coupon security is similar to a Treasury Bill (T-Bill). The investor pays something up front in exchange for a promise to receive $100 on the maturity date.

6 Valuation of Bonds

The price of a bond, as with any other financial instrument, is equal to the present value of the expected cash flows of that instrument (http://www.investinginbonds.com/learnmore.asp?catid=46&id=2). The cash flows of a bond, in turn, depend on the value of its coupon payments, the length of time remaining until the bond matures and the current level of interest rates. In this section, we shall be looking at present value, yield to maturity, duration, coupon interest rate and market interest rate.

6.1 *Present Value*

Present value of a bond is the present value of its cash flows (coupons and principal) discounted at a suitable interest rate or rates. One convention used to simplify the calculation procedure is to assume a single rate for all cash flows. This is known as the yield-to-maturity.

6.2 *Yield to Maturity*

Yield to maturity (YTM) is the yield that equates the present value of all the cash flows from a bond to the price of a bond. It is an iterative (trial and error) calculation that accounts for the reinvestment of the coupons as well as any capital gain or loss on the price of the bond (which will be redeemed by the issuer at par, $100). Conversely, given the YTM, a price can be calculated. A rise in the YTM will cause the price calculated to decrease, while a fall in the YTM will cause the price to rise. Although it does simplify the calculations, this convention assumes that all the coupons from a bond can be reinvested at the same rate (which is unlikely). The actual return generated by a bond held until maturity depends on the future reinvestment rates at which the coupon payments received are invested.

6.3 *Duration*

Duration is a measure of the average (cash-weighted) term-to-maturity of a bond. The value of a bond will vary depending on the amount of the cash flows (coupon value), the timing of the cash flows (term to maturity), and the interest rate used for discounting.

6.4 Coupon Interest Rate

An interest rate is the cost of borrowing or the price paid for the rental of funds. Consequently, a coupon rate is the interest rate that the issuer of the bond promises to pay the bond holder. If, for example, the coupon rate is 5%, the issuer of the bonds promises to pay $50 in interest on each bond per annum (5% × $1000). Many bonds pay interest semi-annually, meaning that the bondholder would receive $25 per bond every six months (Fabozzi and Fabozzi 1989). There are different coupon interest rates on different types of bond depending on their risk level.

6.5 Market Interest Rate

A bond's price moves in the opposite direction to that of the change in market interest rates (Faerber 1993). As interest rates rise (fall), the price of a bond will fall (rise). For an investor who plans to hold a bond to maturity, the change in the bond price prior to maturity is of no concern; however, for an investor who may have to sell the bond before the maturity date, an increase in interest rates after the bond was purchased will mean the realization of a capital loss.

7 *Sukuk* (Islamic Bond) Market

Considering the fact that bond issuance and trading are important means of investment in the modern economic system, Muslim jurists and economists have been seeking *Shari'ah* alternatives. In order to meet the various demands of investors, Islamic bonds and certificates have been diversified. The results of these efforts are that *al-mudarabah* or *al-muqaradah* bonds, *al-musharakah* bonds, *al-ijarah* bonds, *al-istisna'* bonds, *salam* bonds and *al-murabahah* bonds have been developed and are thought well of in the global capital markets. However, it is noted that although some of these instruments have been generally accepted as being in compliance with Islamic principles so that they can be traded in the secondary market, the negotiability of some others is still a point of debate and controversy due to their legal acceptability or compliance with *Shari'ah*. Therefore, some of these bonds can be traded in the secondary market, while the trade of others is limited to the primary market because they can only be exchanged at face value.

In Malaysia, for instance, almost all the domestic Islamic debt chapters issued have been based on the principles of *al-murabahah*, *al-bay' bi al-thaman al-ajil*, *al-bay' al-'inah* and *al-bay' al-dayn*, despite the controversy surrounding the issuance of tradable bonds in the secondary market based on these four contracts. At the same time, there is a perceptible increase in the willingness amongst Malaysian issuers of bonds to explore other Islamic principles of financing; for example, the profit-oriented based *al-musharakah*, as well as the asset-backed method of *al-ijarah*. It had thus been anticipated in the late 1990s that the future issuance of Islamic bonds would focus on the widely accepted bonds, such as *al-musharakah* bonds, *al-mudarabah* bonds and *al-ijarah* bonds (Rosly and Sanusi 1999).

However, the problem with Malaysian Islamic bonds has been the application of *al-bay' al-'inah* and *al-bay' al-dayn*, which is not popular with Middle-Eastern investors. The contract of *al-bay' al-'inah* and *al-bay' al-dayn* is seen as something similar to *riba* based financing. This will certainly pose a great challenge to the Malaysian companies seeking Islamic funds in the Middle East via bond issues.

8 Three Main Steps of Bond Issuance

There are three main steps involved in bond issuance. These are:

- Securitization;
- Bond issuance;
- Trading of debt certificates (Rosly and Sanusi 1999).

8.1 The Creation of an al-Tawarruq *(Special Purpose Vehicle) Underlying Asset*

Assetsecuritization is the essence of Islamic bond issues, as a bond must assume the role of *al-mal* (property to qualify as an object of sale). An object of sale in the Islamic law of contract must be a property of value. When a bond certificate is supported by an asset as evidenced via the securitization process, it is transformed into an object of value and therefore qualifies to become an object of trade, whereby it can be purchased and sold in both the primary and secondary markets. Investors will then have to the right to sell (*haqq mali*) these bonds. In *al-tawarruq* asset securitization, the financier purchases an asset from the issuer and sells it back to the same party at a credit price through *al-tawarruq*. This buy-back through an *al-tawarruq* agreement will ensure that the issuer will receive the money in cash, while the financier will be paid a prefixed or contracted amount at a future date. Debt payments will be made by instalments through bond issues. The difference between cash and mark-up price will represent the profit due to the financier (Fig. 1).

The underlying asset is therefore crucial in determining whether these bonds are Islam. In Malaysia, these assets include factories, equipment, stock and inventory, and even intangible assets such as a list including buildings and properties.

8.2 Issuance of Islamic Debt Certificate (Shahdah al-Dayn)

This usually takes place in the primary market where, in settling its debt, the issuing company will sell debt certificates or bonds to investors. As mentioned, the issuance of debt certificates is valid only when it is supported by an asset. In other words, the bonds must be securitized. Here, the underlying security is the *al-buy bi than ajil* (sale by deferred long-term payment) or *al-murabahah* (sale by deferred short-term payment). The underlying asset need not be *al-buy bi than ajil* or *al-murabahah* alone. If the first stage involves a contract of *al-ijarah*, then the debt certificate is called a *sukuk al-ijarah*. If an *al-istisna'* (manufacturing) contract is used, we can called the debt certificate a *sukuk al-istisna'*. New issues of Islamic bonds can be put into two categories: bond issues with coupons (Islamic coupon bonds), and bond issues without coupons (Islamic zero coupon bonds).

8.3 Trading of Debt Certificates: Discounted Bay' al-Dayn

For liquidity purposes, bond trading in the secondary market is crucial. However, almost all Islamic bonds today were bought for long-term investments. The lack of a secondary market should not, however, imply that trading issues are no longer significant. This calls for a need to explain the Islamic view of bond trading in the secondary market. As mentioned, when a debt certificate is securitized it becomes property (*al-mal*), which is also an article of trade. As an article of trade, the bonds

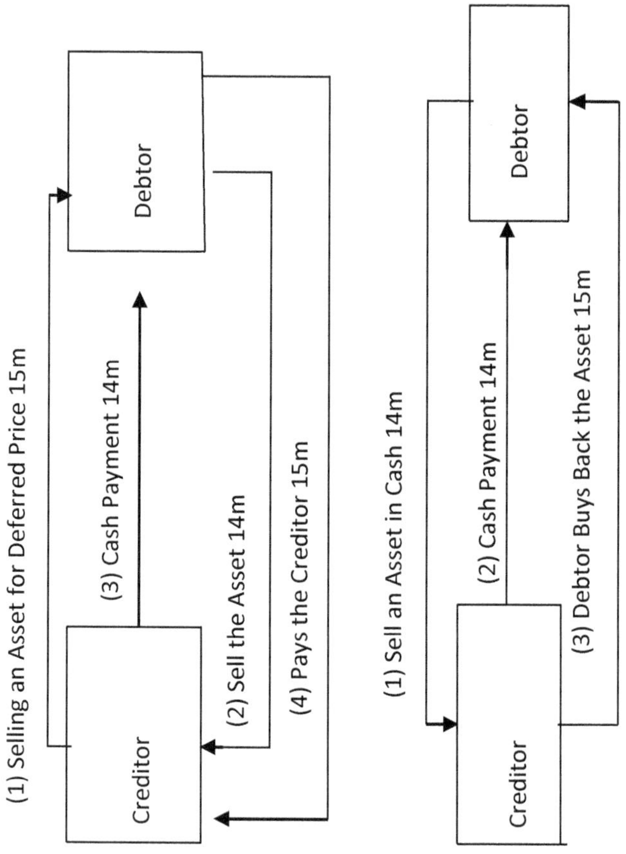

Fig. 1 The creation of a *Tawarruq* (*Source* Author's own)

can be sold by investors to the issuer or a third party if a secondary market for Islamic bonds exists. The trading (sale and purchase) of the debt certificates is called *al-bay' al-dayn*. In Malaysia, the contract of *al-bay' al-dayn* at a discount is acceptable, while the Middle-Eastern *Ulama'* consider it invalid, even though the debt is supported by underlying assets. Any profit created from the sale and purchase of a debt is *riba*.

> And whatever *riba* you give so that it may increase in the wealth of the people, it does not increase with Allah. (*al-Qur'an*, 30: 39)

Prophet Muhammad (*SAW*) ruled:

> That every loan entailing benefit is usury. (al-Shirazi, n.d.)

8.4 *The Nature of* Bay' al-Dayn

The issue of *al-bay' al-dayn* arises when the bonds are traded in the secondary market at a discount. We have to note that buyers in the secondary market are usually speculators and that they do not intend to keep the bond for long-term investment purposes. Their main objective is to make quick capital gains on the basis of market liquidity and interest rate movement. However, there is no indication that controversies exist in *al-bay' al-dayn*, where bonds are sold or redeemed at par. Let us now discuss *al-bay' al-dayn* to show its nature from an Islamic perspective.

According to *al-Majallah* (*Majallah al-Ahkam al-Adliyyah*), *dayn* is defined as the thing due (i.e. the amount of money owed by a certain debtor). So, a sum of money not yet existing is considered a debt, as also is a certain sum of money from things that exist or are present, or from a heap of wheat that is present before it is separated from the mass. *Al-dayn* can be either monetary, or a commodity, such as food or metal. Based on the definition of *al-dayn* given and the literal meaning of *al-bay' al-dayn*, we can define it as the sale of a payable right either to the debtor himself, or to any third party. This type of sale is usually for immediate payment or for deferred payment (*al-nasi'ah*).

8.5 *Sale of* Al-Dayn *(Debt) to a Third Party*

According to most *Hanafi*, *Hanbali* and *Shafi* jurists (Al-Zuhili, n.d.), it is never permissible to sell *al-dayn* to non-debtor or a third party. Such opinions are based on the forbidden sale of *bay' al-kali bil al kali*, the sale of a *gharar*, a sale of something that the seller does not possess. As an exception, *Maliki*, *Hanafi* and some *Shafi* jurists allowed the sale of *al-dayn* to a third party. Since the creditor has the right to sell it to the debtor, he also has the right to sell it to a third party, provided the following rules are observed:

- The *al-dayn* must be *mustaqir* (confirmed debt) and the contract must be performed on the spot, not deferred, in order to avoid any relationship with the sale of a debt for a debt, which is prohibited by Islamic law.
- The debtor must be financially capable of the sale, and must accept and recognize the sale in order that he will not deny the sale. This condition aims to avoid any dispute between the parties, and the debtor must be easily accessible so that the creditor knows whether he has the capacity to pay his debt or not.
- The sale should not be based on selling gold with silver or the opposite, because, any exchanges between these items necessitates immediate possession and, if the debt is money, its price in another debt should be equal in terms of quantity.

Furthermore, the selling of *al-dayn* must avoid the occurrence of *riba* between the two debts, and must also avoid any kind of *gharar* that may arise due to the inability of the buyer to take possession of what he has bought, as it is not permitted that the buyer sells before actual receipt of the purchased item.

It is important to note that Muslim scholars have unanimously prohibited the trading of debt (*al-bay' al-dayn*) at anything other than face value. Where the price paid for a debt is not the same as the face value of that debt, the transaction would be tantamount to *riba al-nasi'ah* and is therefore prohibited.

It is worthy of note that trading in bonds is a subject of dispute on two counts. First, bonds are normally sold at less than their nominal value. Second, the state or the issuer would use the *bay' al-'inah* and *bay' al-dayn* methods, and both of these sales transactions are regarded as *riba* by the majority of Muslim scholars. This is the very reason for the controversy about the legitimacy of Malaysian Islamic bonds, which are considered to be unacceptable by individual Islamic jurists and institutions outside Malaysia and the Middle-Eastern countries. Islam does not allow legal devices to be treated as a justification for transactions that Islam regards unjust and against Islamic belief. The bonds would have been acceptable from an Islamic point of view if the application of the method of financing were based on the legal maxim of *al-ghunmu bil ghurmi* (*Majallah al-Ahkam al-Adliyyah*), meaning that no person is allowed to invest in a way that generates profit without exposing himself to the risk of loss. It would expose both parties to the outcome of their deal, be it a profit or a loss, and thus avoid usury as matter of Islamic principle.

9 Types of Islamic Bonds (*Sukuk*)

In this section, we shall be looking at *sukuk al-ijarah* (lease bonds), *sukuk al-istisna'* (manufacturing bonds), *sukuk al-musharakah* (partnership bonds), the difference between an *al-musharakah* certificate and a conventional bond, and *sukuk al-muqarada* as an alternative to *sukuk al-dayn* (debt bonds/debenture certificates).

9.1 *Sukuk* Al-Ijarah *(Lease Bonds)*

Al-ijarah (leasing) is a contract according to which a party purchases and leases out equipment required by the client for a rental fee. The duration of the rental and the fee are agreed in advance and ownership of the asset remains with the lessor. Hence, the relationship between the parties differs from that of a debtor-creditor relationship, since it is based on there being a buyer-seller of an asset. *Al-ijarah* bonds, on the other hand, are securities of equal denomination of each issue, representing physical durable assets that are tied to an *al-ijarah* contract as defined by *Shari'ah* (Kahf 1997).

9.2 Sukuk Al-Istisna' *(Manufacturing Bonds)*

Al-istisna' (manufacturing) is a contract to sell a manufacturable good, with an undertaking by the seller to present the good manufactured from his own materials, according to a specified description and at a predetermined price. The suitability of *al-istisna'* for financial intermediation is based on the permissibility for the contractor in *al-istisna'* to enter into a parallel *al-istisna'* contract with a subcontractor. Thus, a financial institution may undertake the construction of a facility for a deferred price, and sub-contract the actual construction to a specialized firm (Al-Amine 2001).

9.2.1 Sukuk Al-Musharakah *(Partnership Bonds)*

Al-musharakah bonds based on the *al-musharakah* contract are relatively similar to *al-muqaradah* bonds. The only major difference is that the intermediary party will be a partner of the group of subscribers represented by a body of *al-musharakah* bondholders in a manner similar to a joint stock company. In *al-mudarabah*, the capital is provided by only one party. It should be noted that almost all the criteria applied to *al-mudarabah* bonds are also applicable to the circulation of *al-musharakah* bonds.

9.2.2 The Difference Between an Al-Musharakah *Certificate and a Conventional Bond*

An *al-musharakah* certificate represents the direct ownership of the holder of the assets of the project. If all the assets of a joint project are in liquid form, the certificate will represent a certain proportion of money owned by the project. A conventional bond, on the other hand, has nothing to do with the actual business undertaken with the borrowed money. The bond stands for a loan repayable to the holder in any eventuality, and mostly with interest.

9.3 **Sukuk al-Muqarada** ***Is an Alternative to*** **Sukuk al-Dayn** ***(Debt Bonds/Debenture Certificates)***

The Islamic financial system is a set of rules and regulations that govern the flows of funds from the surplus spending unit to the deficit spending unit. These rules and regulations are strictly governed by *Shari'ah* principles wherein there is neither possibility nor need to apply usurious financial instruments, such as debt related bonds. Hence, the solution to the dilemma for the Islamic financial system lies in the development of financial instruments in which the *Shari'ah* rulings are not violated. One such instrument is the *al-muqaradah* bond.

An *al-muqarada* bond is an Islamic bond on which no interest is earned, but whose market value varies with the anticipated or expected profits. It is the product of Muslim scholars and thinkers who developed and designed this financial instrument, which excludes interest or similar forms of return, which Islam has unequivocally prohibited. The Council of the Islamic Fiqh Academy of the Organization of Islamic Countries (OIC), during its fourth conference in Jeddah, Saudi Arabia, 18–23 Jamadul Akhir 1406H (6–11 February 1988), approved the *al-muqarada* method by issuing a *fatwa* after having reviewed various studies on *al-muqarada* bonds.

Al-muqarada bonds, as the term denotes, are based on the conclusion of lawful '*muqarada*' (*al-mudaraba*) with capital on the one hand and labour on the other, the shares of profit having been determined beforehand in definite proportions of the total. It is called a bond because it is terminal in nature, in that its maturity is determined by the tenure or project completion date.

10 Prospects for *Sukuk* in the Non-Muslim World

By virtue of the announcement on October 29, 2013 by the British Prime Minister that the United Kingdom ought to have been the first country outside the Islamic world to issue *sukuk* has reaffirmed the increasing interest in this Islamic mode of financing. Over the past decade, Islamic finance has shown a significant growth, with worldwide Islamic financial assets rising from US$150 billion in the mid-1990s to US$2.3 trillion by end of 2014. This result is not only in Islamic banking but also by the sustainable development of *sukuk*. By end of 2012, the value of outstanding *sukuk* was US$229.4 billion (with new issues amounting to US$131.2 billion), representing 14.6% of global Islamic equities. Malaysia accounts for the largest *sukuk* market with 74% of issues in 2012, but these securities are also usually issued in the GCC (Godlewski et al. 2014).

There are two observations: *sukuk* structures can be structured on either debt-based or equity-based principles. Debt-based instruments such as *al-ijara* (lease) and *al-murabaha* (sale by deferred payment) pay a predetermined rate of return to investors and are thus less eulogized under *Shari'ah* compared to equity-based investments. In contrast, equity-based investments by profit-and-loss sharing principles of *al-musharaka*, *al-mudaraba* and *al-qirad*, which are partnership contracts in which the financier and entrepreneur share profits based on pre-agreed ratios whereas losses are commensurate to their contribution (financial or physical) to the partnership. In light of their *Shari'ah* compliance questionability and since these instruments are likely to suffer from the adverse selection mechanism described by Godlewski et al., these *sukuk* may generate a negative stock market reaction in comparison to debt-based instruments (Godlewski et al. 2014).

Sukuk structures undergo a strict screening process by religious advisors to ensure their *Shari'ah* compliance. These instruments must notably be free from prohibitive elements such as *riba* (interest), *gharar* (uncertainty), *maysir* (gambling), but also from non-permissible activities (e.g. investments in pork, pornography, entertainment, drugs, and military activities) (Godlewski et al. 2014).

11 Process and Issuance of *Sukuk* (*Tawreeq*)

Tawreeq for the issuer and the investors is as follows.

The issuer shall effect:

- Liberty from the constraints of the balance sheet that provides financial and accounting rules to account for the principle of capital adequacy, and management of provision for doubtful debts that could hamper financial activities in general—more particularly, a slowdown of the capital cycle—and reducing the profitability of banks. Therefore, with regard to *tawreeq*, the substitution of an appropriately large part of the liberalization of bank funds required to meet the allotment of such debt is allowed.
- The development of the efficiency of the financial cycle, productivity and the rate of rotation through the conversion of non-liquid assets to liquid assets so as to re-employ them thus enabling the expansion of the scale of facilities without the need to increase the rights of ownership.
- The minimizing of credit risk through the distribution of financial risk in a wide range of different sectors.
- The opportunity for credit rating companies with a low capital base and low capital access to finance at the low rates obtained by the larger and more successful companies (Al-Maghlouth 2009).

The investors shall effect:

- Awareness of risk for financial investors and for the recovery of the capital market.
- Analysis of certain economic sectors of primary markets, such as real estate or cars. Moreover, revitalizion of the capital markets by providing new investment and financing tools, diversification of the

supply of financial products, and stimulation of the circulation of market instruments.

- Transparency, improving the structure of the information in the market and the entry of many institutions into the financing process, which will provide more information on the market.
- Impression of a variety of *tawreeq* investors, which will lead to the expansion of the scale of capital markets and their recovery.
- Facilitation of foreign exchange to banks and financial institutions' creditors in the event of cross-border *tawreeq*, since the buyer of an asset in this case is the bank or a foreign financial institution that will pay the local bank the value of the deal in foreign currency, which leads to an increase in domestic bank assets in foreign currency (Al-Maghlouth 2009).

12 Risk Factors in *Sukuk*

This section discussed the risks faced by the *sukuk* industry. They take several forms: market risk, credit risk and counter-party risk, the risk of *Shari'ah* non-compliance, operational risk and institutional rigidity. Also, one of the challenges facing the management of s*ukuk* financial risk is that of institutional reorganization. In addition, the section will talk about arguments that have been raised amid concern that most *sukuk* implementation does not follow *Shari'ah* rules. Undesirable risks affect the competitiveness of the pricing of assets. Therefore, the innovation of *sukuk* essentially involves a higher exposure to certain market and financial risks (Al-Maghlouth 2009).

12.1 Market Risk

Market risks can be either systematic or unsystematic. A systematic risk can arise due to public and economic policies; unsystematic risk arises because different firms' specific instruments are priced out due to comparison with other firms' instruments. Market risk is comprised of profit rate risks, foreign exchange risks, equity price risks and commodity risks. The profit rate risk is the rate of return risk on which *sukuk* is based; fixed rates that are exposed to this risk in the same manner as fixed rate bonds are exposed to the profit rate risk. Moreover, an increase in market profit rates leads to a decrease in the fixed-income *sukuk* values. However, all fixed return assets face this risk, whether from *al-ijarah*, *al-istisna'*, *salam*, *al-mudharabah*, *al-qiradh* or any other origin (Al-Maghlouth 2009). This also involves reinvestment risk and the opportunity cost of investing at the new rates, particularly if the asset is not liquid, as in case of the zero coupon non-tradable *sukuk*.

12.2 Credit Risk

It is likely that a bad-debt, or asset, or loan may become irrecoverable due to a default or delay in settlement, while the counter-party risk is the likelihood that the counter-party rescinds the contract, if there is a contractual arrangement. The consequences can be severe, causing a decrease in the value of a bank's assets. The credit and counter-party risks inbuilt in Islamic finance are unique owing to the nature of the Islamic financial instruments that become the foundation of the *sukuk* asset pools. Unlike conventional financial institutions, Islamic banks do not have access to derivative instruments and other credit risk management mechanisms due to *Shari'ah* considerations (Al-Maghlouth 2009).

12.3 Risk as to Shari'ah *Compliant*

The risk with regard to being *Shari'ah* compliant is the loss of asset value as a result of an issuer breaching its fiduciary responsibilities with respect to compliance with *Shari'ah*. For example, if the *sukuk* is based on a hybrid of *al-ijarah* and *al-istisna'* assets, *al-ijarah* must always have a stronger presence than *al-istisna'* in the pool, otherwise the *sukuk* deed will dissolve. Thus, broadly speaking, *Shari'ah* compliance risk must be defined as the rate of return foregone in comparison to the market rates as a result of complying with the *Shari'ah*. Moreover, fixed rate *sukuk* faces serious market risks. So, to match the market requirements for *sukuk* to be at a floating rate, and the *Shari'ah* requirements of rents to be fixed rate, the *al-ijarah sukuk* are based on a master *al-ijarah* agreement with several subordinate *al-ijarah* agreements. However, the investors could still face profit rate risk to a certain extent and, since the originator can only guarantee the fixed return on the underlying asset pools, the issue of floating rate returns still remains contentious, particularly in pooled or hybrid *sukuk* (Al-Maghlouth 2009). Therefore, the association of *Shari'ah* supervisors with *sukuk* issues will ensure investor confidence.

12.4 Management and Operational Risk

The management and operational risks are inherent in the structure of the issuances, rather than the underlying *Shari'ah* principles. The risks specifically related to the operation mirror those existent in conventional bond markets: default risk, coupon payment risk, asset redemption risk, investor specific risks and risks related to the asset. Default risk is when each party has provisions for the termination of a certificate in the event of default by the obligor. Coupon payment risk is when the obligor may fail to pay the required coupons on time. Asset redemption risk is when the originator has to buy back the underlying assets from the certificate holder. Investor specific risks arise when the certificate holder is exposed to several risks relevant to *sukuk* structures, such as liquidity management issues in Islamic finance. Risks related to the asset occur when the underlying assets of the *sukuk* certificates are subject to numerous risks to the extent that there is risk of the loss of the assets (Al-Maghlouth 2009).

12.5 Risk of Organizational Rigidity

The banking and financial infrastructure is weak in most emerging economies despite the significant moves that have been observed in some of these countries, such as Bahrain, Saudi Arabia, Malaysia, Brunei and Indonesia. However, *sukuk* requires unique *Shari'ah* compliant structures that create a state that can be considered one of institutional rigidity that cannot be removed in the short run and always increases the risks of *sukuk*. Furthermore, the features of this situation are the lack of hedging and financial engineering processes; non-existence of inter-bank money markets; lack of best practice uniform regulatory standards and regimes; weak support for litigation and legal frameworks, particularly in the handling of default; non-uniform accounting; auditing and systems for the acknowledgement of income and loss; insufficiently robust investment appraisal; promotion and monitoring infrastructure; ineffective external credit assessment systems; the rudimentary state of financial markets; and weak inter-segmental support and linkages (Al-Maghlouth 2009).

13 Managing *Sukuk* Risks

Sukuk serves to replicate the functions of conventional bonds and tradable securities in resources mobilization from markets, in injecting liquidity into an enterprise or government, and in providing stable resource of income for investors. Moreover, investing in *sukuk* issuances involves the funding of trade or the production of tangible assets. So, this section presents the challenges facing the management of the financial risks of *sukuk* that are created by institutional reorganization (Al-Maghlouth 2009).

13.1 Organizational Challenges

Government debt management, which affects the fixed income markets in developing countries, is dominated by government bonds. Therefore, the most important reorganization of the markets can come from the reorganization of public debt management. The introduction of derivative markets has further consequences on market and financing dynamics. Furthermore, markets role in the stabilization of futures and options markets depends on the speculator's information. Futures and options markets can also serve to stabilize the value of underlying assets by performing an insuring role, which can occur if these markets allow investors to pool risks more efficiently and share them. Therefore, in brief, the evolutionary changes of financial innovation, deregulation, globalization of financial services and introduction of novel financing instruments warrants the adoption of supporting risk management mechanisms, viable secondary markets and relevant regulatory bodies (Al-Maghlouth 2009).

The emergence of the market for asset-backed securities since the turn of the millennium has permitted banks around the world to free their capital by re-packaging and reselling portfolios of loans, assets and other receivables. This adjusts the criteria for lending by forcing financial institutions to meet the market's standards for loan quality and sufficient pricing for risk. It helps decrease funding risk by diversifying funding sources. Financial institutions also employ securitization to purge profit rate mismatches. Furthermore, it creates more complete markets by introducing formerly remote asset classes that better suit investor risk preferences and by increasing the potential for investors to achieve the benefits of diversification. Therefore, by meeting the needs of different market segments, securitization transactions can generate gains both for originators and for investors. The same benefits can be attributed to *sukuk* certificates. They allow the institution to manage balance sheet mismatches to securitize longer-term assets. Moreover, investors are also given the option to invest in asset grades that are suitable for their investment needs. Also, financial markets are more complete, as previously untapped assets are now available for public sector resource mobilization.

The liquidity and secondary markets portray varying risk preferences and a secondary market should be developed to reflect this. *Sukuk* certificates are unique, in that the investor becomes an asset holder and is directly tied to the nature and functioning of the underlying asset pools. *Sukuk* certificate holders therefore carry the burden of these unique risks. The primary concern of an Islamic secondary market is its marketability (Al-Maghlouth 2009). All things being equal, a certificate holder would rather participate in a well-structured and well-regulated secondary market rather than trade in a poorly run market. However, the challenges remain to provide increased risk management mechanisms, to increase market liquidity, to create a truer bond yield benchmark, and to expand the issuer and investor platform.

It is has been observed that the unfavourable risks facing the *sukuk* industry—such as market risk, credit and counter-party risk, *Shari'ah* compliance risk, operational risk and institutional rigidity that affect the competitiveness of the pricing of assets—lead to fact that the innovation of *sukuk* essentially involves a higher exposure to certain market and financial risks. However, I believe that we should pay most attention to unsystematic market risk and *Shari'ah* compliance risk. This is due to the fact that they are related to each other, in the sense that market risk will increase if *Shari'ah* compliance risks increase (Al-Maghlouth 2009). Furthermore, the current *sukuk* margin or profit is based on LIBOR, as an indictor only, but we still depend on it. This leads us to violate *Shari'ah* compliance, which will cause an increase in market risk, as most *sukuk* holders or investors are Muslims who search for *Shari'ah* compliant products in which to invest, choosing to avoid investing in non-compliant or questionable products. In our case, products will be questionable unless we try to avoid this risk.

The matter can be resolved with fixed percentages not related to any other matter, even if only as an indicator. It is true that *sukuk* issuers will, at some point, face problems with their projects due to economic crises or complexities, but they should be prepared to face this and make the sacrifice in order to avoid violating *Shari'ah* compliance (Al-Maghlouth 2009). Moreover, in order to develop the *sukuk* market and avoid the risks of *Shari'ah* compliance, the capital authorities of all Muslim countries should establish and create a *sukuk* an institutional body that reports to the Organization of Islamic Co-operation (OIC) and that, amongst other things, unifies the rules and regulations of *sukuk* issuance and the price of *sukuk*.

14 *Sukuk* and Its Rating Formula

14.1 Credit Rating

The Securities Commission Malaysia rules on matters regarding credit rating in *sukuk* that:

- All issues, offers or invitations to subscribe to or purchase *sukuk* must be rated by a credit rating agency.
- The final rating for the *sukuk* must be made available to the Securities Commission Malaysia at the time when the submission for approval to issue, offer or make an invitation to subscribe to or purchase *sukuk* is made to the Securities Commission Malaysia.
- Where the final rating is not available, an indicative rating must be submitted to the Securities Commission Malaysia.
- In the case of a *sukuk* programme where the rating is assigned not for the full amount but only for part of the amount (partial rating):
  - The first issue under the *sukuk* programme must be rated; and
  - The principal terms and conditions of the *sukuk* programme must include:
    a disclosure of all the preconditions, relevant risk factors and all material information relating to the partial rating; and
    a provision that states that all subsequent issues of the *sukuk* programme will be rated (Securities Commission Malaysia 2014).

14.2 Appointment of Credit Rating Agency

The guidelines further provide that:

- *Sukuk* rated on a local rating scale must be rated by a credit rating agency registered with the Securities Commission Malaysia.
- *Sukuk* rated on an international or regional rating scale must be rated by an international credit rating agency.
- An issuer incorporated in Malaysia may appoint an international credit rating agency to assign a rating for its *ringgit* denominated *sukuk*, provided that:
  - The issuer has previously issued a foreign currency denominated *sukuk* for which an international or regional rating has been assigned;

- The issuer is appointing the same international credit rating agency; and
- Any existing international or regional rating of the issuer's *sukuk* by that international credit rating agency is still valid on the date of submission to the Securities Commission Malaysia (Securities Commission Malaysia 2014).

14.3 Issuer's Obligations

The guidelines provide to the effect that:

- An issuer must provide relevant information on a continuous and timely basis to the credit rating agency. This is to ensure that the credit rating agency can continuously make available to investors the rating for the *sukuk*.
- An issuer must ensure that the rating report is published by the credit rating agency as soon as the rating has been finalised, or at least seven business days prior to the issuance of the *sukuk*.
- The issuer of the *sukuk* must not replace the appointed credit rating agency during the tenure of the *sukuk* unless the investors' consent has been obtained (Securities Commission Malaysia 2014).

14.4 Non-application of Requirements

Chapter 9 of the guidelines further rules to the effect that:

- Chapter 9 of the guidelines does not apply to an issue, offer or invitation to subscribe to or purchase the following types of *sukuk*:
  - Irredeemable convertible Islamic loan stocks;
  - Foreign currency denominated *sukuk*;
  - Convertible *sukuk* or Islamic loan stocks and exchangeable *sukuk* that fulfil the following requirements:

    Investors of the *sukuk* or Islamic loan stocks are given the right to convert or exchange the instruments into the underlying shares at any time or within a reasonable period or periods during the tenure of the *sukuk* issue; and
    The underlying shares are listed on a stock exchange;

  - *Sukuk*:

that are non-transferable and non-tradable; and
whose investors do not require a rating (Securities Commission Malaysia, 2014).

The principal adviser must ensure that both criteria are met prior to the issue, offer or invitation to subscribe to or purchase the *sukuk* and confirm this in writing to the Securities Commission Malaysia.

15 Conclusion

As has been noted, the conventional bond market comprises a primary market and a secondary market. The primary bond market is where the bonds are initially issued, while the secondary market is where the bonds are resold to other investors. Islamic bonds (*sukuk*) conceptually share similarities with the conventional model. However, the mechanism, technicalities, rules and standards of operation are different; thus, *sukuk* also requires primary and secondary markets. The main difference, however, is the way the bonds are issued and subsequently traded. In the process of Islamic bond issuance, *tawarruq* is used to securitize the instrument in the primary market, while in the secondary market *al-bay' al-dayn* is used in order to legalize the reselling of the bonds. This process is mostly used in the Malaysian market, while most of the Middle-Eastern countries do not accept it. The proposed alternative is Islamic bonds based on *al-muqaradah*.

Acknowledgement It is acknowledged that, the idea of this chapter has been shared with author's other research works for the common benefit of academia, regulators, researchers and industries as well.

References

Al-Amine, M. M. (2001), The Islamic Bonds Market: Possibilities and Challenges, *International Journal of Islamic Financial Services*, 3(1): 6.
Al-Maghlouth, A. K. (2009), *Sukuk: An Inside Study of Its Background, Structures, Challenges and Cases*, OUM.
Al-Shirazi, *al-Muhadhab*.
Al-Zuhili, *Bay' al Dayn in the Shari'ah*.
Fabozzi, F. J., and Fabozzi, T. D. (1989), *Bond Markets: Analysis and Strategies*, Prentice Hall.

Faerber, E. (1993), *All About Bonds and Bond Mutual Funds*, McGraw Hill.
Godlewski, C. J., Turk, R., and Weill, L. (2014), Do the Type of Sukuk and Choice of Shari'a Scholar Matter? IMF Working Paper WP/14/147.
Kahf, M. (1997), The Use of Assets: Ijarah Bonds for Bridging the Budget Gap, *Islamic Economic Studies*, 4(2), May.
Majallah al-Ahkam al-Adliyyah, Art. 158.
Rosly, S. A., and Sanusi, M. M. (1999), The Application of bay' al-'inah and bay' al-dain in Malaysian Islamic Bonds: An Islamic Analysis', *International Journal of Islamic Financial Services*, 1(2), July–September.
Securities Commission (Malaysia). (2014), Guidelines on Sukuk.
Securities Commission Malaysia. (2015), Guidelines on Issuance of Private Debt Securities and Sukuk to Retail Investors, SC-GL/5-2015.
http://www.aseam.com.my/dm/insight/islamdebtjan03.htm.
http://www.investinginbonds.com/learnmore.asp?catid=46&id=2.

CHAPTER 24

Islamic Loan (*Al-Qardh*)

1 Central Idea of *Al-Qard* (Loan)

The *fiqh* concepts of an *al-qardh* (loan) are:

Hanafi school, Ibn Abidin: 'What one party gives to the other to be returned in its own kind'.
Maliki school: 'Payment of valuables for repayment that is not different in kind'.
Hanbali school: 'Payment of money to someone who will benefit it by it and return its equivalent'.
Shafi'i school: 'Transferring the ownership of something to someone, provided he should repay its like'.

2 Divine Rulings on *Al-Qardh* (Loan)

2.1 Al-Qur'an

O you who believe! When you deal with each other in transactions involving future obligations in a fixed period of time, reduce them in writing, and let a scribe write down as faithfully as between the parties. Let not the scribe refuse to write as Allah has taught him, so let

M. M. Billah, *Islamic Financial Products*,
https://doi.org/10.1007/978-3-030-17624-2_24

> him write. Let him who incurs liability dictate, but let him fear his Lord Allah, and not diminish anything of what he owes. If the party liable is mentally deficient or weak, or unable himself to dictate, lets his guardian dictate faithfully. And get two witnesses, out of our own men, and if there are not two men, then a men and two women, such as you choose for witnesses, so that if one of them errs, the other can remind her. The witness shall not refuse when they are called on [for evidence]. Distain not to reduce to writing [your contract] for a future period, whether it be small or big; it is more just in the sight of Allah, more suitable as evidence, and more convenient to prevent doubts among yourselves. But if the transaction which you carry out on the spot among yourselves, there is no blame on you if you reduce it not to writing. But take witnesses whenever you make a commercial contract: and let neither scribe nor witness suffer harm. If you do [such harm], it would be wickedness in you. So fear Allah; for it is Allah that teaches you. And Allah is well-acquainted with all things. If you are on journey, and cannot find a scribe, a pledge with a possession [may serve the purpose]. And if one of you deposits a thing on trust with another, let the trustee [faithfully] discharge his trust with another, let the trustee [faithfully] discharge his trust and let him fear Allah his Lord. Conceal not evidence; for whoever conceals it – his heart is tainted with sin. And Allah knows all that which you do (2: 282–283).

2.2 *Al-Sunnah*

Abu Hurarira (*RA*) reported that the Messenger (*SAW*) said:

> Whoever relieves a Muslim in distress in this world will be relieved of distress on the Day of Judgement by Allah. Allah is in support of man so long as man is in support of his fellow man.

Anas (*RA*) reported that the Messenger (*SAW*) said:

> The night that I was taken on a nocturnal journey I saw inscribed on the Gate of Paradise that the act of alms is requited ten times, the loan eighteen. I asked Jibra'il, 'Why is the loan better than the alms?' His answer was, 'Because the one who asks for alms is not without means of subsistence, while the borrower does not borrow except when he is in need.'

3 Objectives

3.1 Linguistic Approach

Hadiyyah: To give to someone due to respect;
Hibah: To give to someone with no condition for repayment;
Sadaqah: To give to someone for the spiritual reward;
Loan: To give to someone who is in need.

4 Pillars of a Loan

- Debtors
- Creditors
- *'Aqad* (contract)
- Documentation:
  - Verbal
  - Witnesses
- Subject matter
- Payment period.

5 Loan Versus Sale Contract

- Transfer of ownership
- Mark-up price
- Exchange of subject matter.

6 Special Features in *al-Qardh* Contract

- Demise of one of the parties to the contract;
- Borrowers unable to pay a loan on time;
- Defects found in the subject matter;
- Demise of one or all of the parties to the contract;
- Based on *Shari'ah* principles, a person who holds an outstanding loan before they passed away, their heirs must be responsible for that debt;
- The Prophet Muhammad (*SAW*) said that all sins of a martyr will be forgiven by Allah (*SWT*) except his debts;

- From a practical perspective, borrowers are strongly advised to take up mortgage *takaful* or mortgage reducing term assurance (MRTA) on their loans. The reasons for this are given in the next section.

7 Practical Scenario

Example 1

- Ali and Aminah are taking out a *bai' bithaman ajil* (BBA) property loan but neither of them takes out *takaful* or MRTA.
- Should both of them pass away before the full settlement of the loan, the bank's attorney (normally a branch manager) may, at his own discretion, take possession of the property.
- The bank will sell the property and, if there is any balance after settling the whole outstanding balance, the remaining amount will be distributed to the deceased based on *farai'dh* principles. Normally, Amanah Raya Berhad (a Malaysian trustee company) is in charge for this type of transaction.

Example 2

- Ali and Aminah are taking out a BBA property loan amounting to $1 million and both of them share the mortgage *takaful* for the loan in equal proportions.
- Suddenly, Ali passes away and only $200,000 of the loan has been paid ($800,000 remains outstanding).
- Hence, 50% of the $800,000 ($400,000) will be recorded as fully settled.
- However, Aminah still has to continue paying off the remaining $400,000.

Example 3

- Ali and Aminah are taking out a BBA property loan amounting to $1 million and Ali is solely responsible for the full amount of the mortgage *takaful* instalments for the loan:
  - Suddenly, Ali passes away and only $200,000 of the loan has been repaid ($800,000 remains outstanding). Hence, 100% of the $800,000 will be recorded as fully settled.

- Should Aminah pass away, Ali has to settle the entire loan without any changes to his original commitment.

8 Borrowers Unable to Pay the Loan on Time

- Most of the prominent *Ulama'* have agreed that the following steps will be taken in case of a borrower's default. All the following steps involve the restructuring of the loan agreement:
  - More time will be given to the borrower to settle the arrears;
  - More time and part-payment;
  - The loan will be considered as fully settled (*al-Sunnah*).
- In practice in Malaysia, manual reminders as well as computer generated reminders will be forwarded to a defaulting borrower.
- The bank will telephone the borrower regularly in addition to sending reminders for up to three months after the date of the first default.
- Subsequently, the bank will start taking legal action against the borrower by sending a notice of demand to claim all the outstanding arrears within either 7 days or 14 days (depending on a bank's procedures).
- If the borrower still fails to settle the arrears within the stipulated time, the bank will send a notice of termination to the borrower to claim the full amount outstanding within 30 days (depending on a bank's procedures).
- In between issuing the notice of demand and the notice of termination, the bank will continue to telephone the borrower. The bank will still be willing to meet with the Borrower; that is, give the borrower advice based on Islamic principles (*Hadith*).

9 Defects Found in the Subject Matter

- A seller in a contract must disclose all the defects of the subject matter of a contract. (It is one of the *Ummah's* tasks in contemporary commercial activities under the principle of *Al-Itlau'* (which means 'disclosure'.)
- However, if a buyer is satisfied with the conditions of the subject matter, a contract can proceed even though there may be defects in the subject matter.

- A buyer can claim from a seller should a defect in the subject matter not be disclosed before the parties enter into a binding contract.

In practice in Malaysia, Section 45 provides that:

- If a person discovers defects in the subject matter within a reasonable time of the sale and purchase, they have the right to accept or reject it.

Furthermore, Section 46 provides that:

- In the event a consumer decides to reject the subject matter, then the dealer or the seller has to act:

  - To replace the goods in accordance with the terms and conditions of the contract; or
  - To pay compensation for the defective goods; or
  - To make a refund in respect of the goods sold.

Nevertheless, only a reasonable time is given for buyers to claim compensation or a replacement from the seller, which depends on the features and nature of the goods.

10 BBA Property Financing

- It is implied that, first, the bank will buy a property from the developer.
- Subsequently, the bank will sell the property to the borrower.
- Nevertheless, a current sales and purchase agreement is only signed between the developer and the borrower.
- Further, the 10% deposit is to be paid by the borrower, not the bank.
- Should the borrower fail to service the interest during the construction period, action will be taken against the borrower, not the bank.

11 Recommendations

- First, a sales and purchase agreement must be executed between the developer and the bank.
- Subsequently, the borrower will sign a sales and purchase agreement with the bank with a selling price determined by the bank.

- Before the execution of a sales and purchase agreement between the bank and the borrower, the bank has, first, to settle the 10% deposit based on the selling price between the developer and the bank.
- The bank must also settle the whole purchase price between the bank and the developer before having any contract with the borrower.
- Thus, the borrower will pay the deposit and construction interests to the bank and the bank can take action against the borrower should they fail to settle all the agreed payments.
- The developer will cease its involvement in the contract once the bank settles the selling price and when the contract between the bank and the borrower is executed.

Developing countries may grant a loan without interest (*qard al-hasan*) to less-developed countries. The borrowing countries may repay such loan by way of exporting their resources and products (e.g. foods, minerals, etc.) that are of equivalent or higher values in relation to the loan granted. The borrowing countries may repay the loan with a higher amount as an appreciation or gift to the lending countries, but this cannot be fixed by the lending countries.

CHAPTER 25

Islamic Financial Wealth Management

1 Introduction

Islamic financial planning is a new concept being developed and it has a relationship with the definition of Islamic financial marketing that was devised by Ibnu Abu Yusuf, Ibnu Taimiyyah and Ibnu Khaldun. They defined it as the creation, developing and delivery of unique competitive products and services to satisfy customers' needs at a profit to an organization in light of Islamic values and principles. In contrast, it is conventionally defined as the process whereby an individual's personal and financial goals are achieved through the development and implementation of a comprehensive financial plan.

Islam is a comprehensive, integrative and holistic religion that governs all aspects of life, major and minor, personal and social, spiritual and materialistic, and that relates this worldly life to the Hereafter. This means that we need to practise Islam while we perform our business and economic activities. Muslims are encouraged to plan for their life and put effort into achieving the goals they have set, then asking help from Allah (*SWT*). The final stage is *tawakal*, which is when the results materialize and we receive the destiny bestowed on us by Allah (*SWT*).

The prophet Muhammad (*SAW*) used to supplicate Allah (*SWT*):

> My Lord, help me and do not give help against me, grant me a victory, and do not grant victory over me, plan on my behalf and do not plan against me, guide me and make my right guidance easy for me, grant me

M. M. Billah, *Islamic Financial Products*,
https://doi.org/10.1007/978-3-030-17624-2_25

> victory over those who act wrongfully towards me. (Yusoff, n.d., narrated by Abu Daud)

In Islam, financial planning is not merely a process of acquisition and accumulating wealth; it has a broad definition that relates to the concept of vicegerent (*kalifah*).

According to the Holy *Qur'an*, God created man as his vicegerent (or ambassador) on Earth. Allah (*SWT*) says in *al-Qur'an*:

> Behold, thy Lord said to the angels: 'I will create a vicegerent on Earth.' They said: 'Wilt Thou place therein one who will make mischief therein and shed blood? – Whilst we do celebrate Thy praises and glorify Thy holy (name)?' He said: 'I know what ye know not.' (*Al-Qur'an*, 2: 30)

From the above verse, and others like it, we understand that, as the *khalifah* (vicegerent) of God on Earth, man is gifted with certain powers that other creatures of God do not possess. For example, he possesses (within limits, of course) intellectual faculties. We also read that God created all things on Earth for man.

> He it is who created for you all that is on Earth. Then He rose over [*Istawa*] towards the Heavens and made them seven Heavens and He is the All-Knower of everything. (2: 29)

The duty of man as God's *khalifah* is to make use of all the blessings of God on Earth to his own benefit. For this, man is given freedom; that is, freedom of choice and action (also within limits). It is because of man's special faculties and his freedom that he becomes the best of God's creatures.

Financial planning is basically a discipline of wealth management that applies to the unique needs and concerns of each individual. As a Muslim, even though a person does not possess any form of wealth, they still have to commit to a financial planning process because, in the event of their demise, either they would leave debts unpaid or the care of their children to a guardian. This chapter focuses on the comprehensive aspects of financial planning whereby an individual should take a balanced approached in order to achieve the golden goal. Financial planning quantifies and manages an individual's success on the basis of four financial pillars; wealth protection, wealth accumulation, wealth preservation and wealth distribution. Each of these different components is meant to play a different role in addressing unique issues and the objective must be in line with the principles of Islamic *Shari'ah*.

In Islam, we are confined within the concept of Allah's bounty or sustenance. This concept means that Allah is the sole giver of 'bounty' to every living creature in this world. Allah blesses His bounty on those who earn and spend it in compliance with His covenants. He does not bestow His blessing or mercy on those who earn it illegitimately and spend it irresponsibly. Allah (*SWT*) affirms:

> For Allah is He Who Gives [all] sustenance. (*Al-Qur'an*, 51: 58)

The concept of Allah's bounty is considered very important in Islam, as a good Muslim is required to have a proper balance between the fulfilment of his spiritual and worldly obligations (Yusoff, n.d.).

The Prophet (*SAW*) stated:

> A Muslim should prepare himself for the next world as if he is going to die tomorrow, but at the same time work hard to improve all his worldly comforts as if he is going to live forever. (Yusoff, n.d., narrated by Al-Dailami)

Islam covers the extremes of *zuhd* (abstinence) and *bulk* (avarice). A Muslim should not forego wealth. Neither should he be avaricious in the pursuit of wealth. *Zuhd* does not amounting to the rejection of pleasure but, rather, to leading a pious life through his ability to live moderately and within his means. This is why Islam encourages reasonable behaviour and moderation.

As Muslims, we are not discouraged from acquiring wealth; rather, we must know how to earn it and spend it in accordance with Islamic principles. Wealth should not be abused or misused, as Allah (*SWT*) has laid down very clear injunctions on how wealth is to be acquired and spent. All above, wealth is a form of trial by Allah (*SWT*) of His servants to see whether they follow His injunctions regarding the acquisition of wealth and disposal. As such, the owners of such wealth will be fully accountable on the Day of Judgement for what they have done with their wealth. In Islamic financial planning, an individual must understand the discipline of how to protect, to accumulate, to preserve and to distribute their wealth according to the Islamic *Shari'ah*. These are the components of

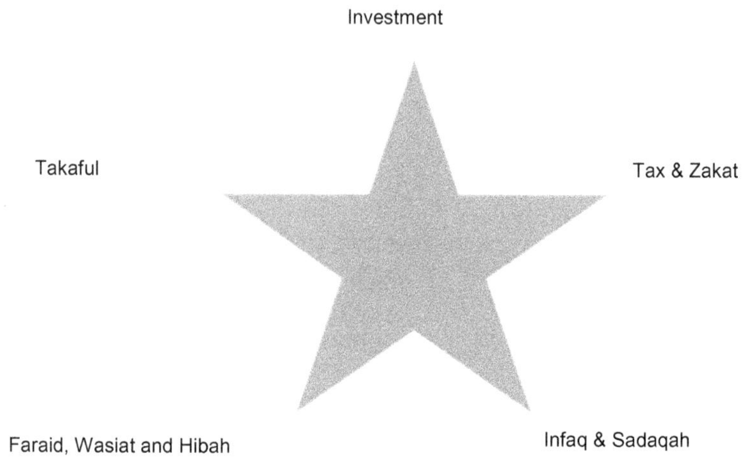

Fig. 1 Islamic financial planning (*Source* Author's own)

financial planning that need to be addressed in achieving financial goals (Fig. 1).

2 Protection in Islam

Wealth protection is the wealth management pillar that identifies and manages various sources of current and future income. This area of financial planning involves cash flow planning, tax planning, family security planning, disability income planning and critical illness income planning. In Islam, the concept of protection is slightly different than the conventional perception in performing the concept of mutual cooperation or *takaful* under the umbrella of *tabarru'* (donation). *Takaful* is an insurance concept that is grounded in Islamic *muamalat*, observing the rules and regulations of *Shari'ah*. In fact, this concept has been practised for over 1400 years (http://www.takafulnasional.com.my).

In principle, the *takaful* system is based on mutual cooperation, responsibility, assurance, protection and assistance between groups of participants. These fundamentals are based on the sayings of the Prophet Muhammad (*SAW*) that relate to *takaful*:

> Tie the camel first before putting it in the trust of Allah (*SWT*).

2.1 Basis of Cooperation

Help one another in *al-birr* and in *al-taqwa* [virtue, righteousness and piety]: but do not help one another in sin and transgression. (5: 2)

Allah will always help His servant for as long as he helps others. (narrated by Imam Ahmad bin Hanbal and Imam Abu Daud)

2.2 Basis of Responsibility

The place of relationships and feelings of people with faith, between each other, is just like the body; when one of its parts is afflicted with pain, then the rest of the body will be affected. (Narrated by Imam al-Bukhari and Imam Muslim)

2.3 Basis of Mutual Protection

By my life, which is in Allah's power, nobody will enter Paradise if he does not protect his neighbour who is in distress. (Narrated by Imam Ahmad bin Hanbal)

Thus, through these concepts, Muslims can plan ahead for any unwanted events that might involve illness, permanent disability or diseases. (Narrated by Imam Ahmad bin Hanbal)

2.4 Accumulation of Wealth in Islam

The wealth accumulation pillar of wealth management seeks to achieve reasonable capital growth with the primary objective of preserving accumulated wealth. This is the area that balances the risk of losing capital and the risk of losing purchasing power. Wealth accumulation involves asset allocation strategies, investment policy statement drafting, planning for financial freedom and planning for children's tertiary education. In Islam, before an individual decides on an investment, they must check whether the status of the investment fund they are considering is approved by the *Shari'ah* Board. Basically, the *Shari'ah* way of investing is that it must not be any of the following:

- Operations must not be based on *riba'* (interest); for example, activities of financial institutions such as commercial and merchant banks and finance companies that not comply with the Islamic principles. In Surah Al-Baqarah (275–281) Allah has prohibited *riba*:

> But Allah hath permitted trade and forbidden usury (*riba*) (*Al-Qur'an*, 2: 275–281)

- Operations involved with gambling. This is where one acquires something at the expense of another and that person suffers the loss of an asset and their dignity.
- Activities involving the manufacture and/or sale of *haram* (forbidden) products such as liquor, pork and meat not slaughtered according to Islamic rites and any other activities against the Islamic teachings, such as pornography.
- Operations containing elements of *gharar* (uncertainty), such as the conventional insurance business.

There are companies with activities comprising both permissible and unacceptable elements. The *Shari'ah* Council has applied several additional criteria for these companies:

- Core activities of the company must be activities that are not against the *Shari'ah* as outlined above and the *haram* element must be very small compared with the core activities.
- The public perception or image of the company must be good.
- Core activities of the company must have importance and give *maslahah* (benefit in general) to the Muslim *Ummah* (nation) and the country, and the *haram* element must be very small and involve matters such as *umum balwa* (common plight), *uruf* (custom) and the rights of the non-Muslim community that are accepted by Islam (Shari'ah Advisory Council, Securities Commission of Malaysia).

There are several channels of investment in which Muslims can participate in order to gain some profit, if any, such as *wadiah* savings accounts, *al-mudharabah* current accounts, *al-mudharabah* investment accounts, *tabung haji*, unit trusts, *takaful* (with saving elements) and Islamic bonds via Unit Trust Islamic equity (stock market) property, for example.

3 Wealth Preservation

The wealth preservation component aims to protect accumulated wealth against every conceivable financial risk and threat. For an individual who has accumulated a reasonable amount of wealth, a bad investment can cause major discomfort but a poor investment performance is not debilitating. As far as wealth is concerned, inadequate effort to preserve accumulated wealth creates an irrecoverable situation. The pillar of wealth preservation consists of wealth management, planning liability containment, planning business shareholding, planning business succession and debt management.

As Muslims, we must realize that, although we may have wealth, it is Allah's right to give it to anybody that He chooses. However, we are asked to work hard if we wish to succeed in acquiring wealth. Islam views wealth as a trial and man as responsible as trustee:

> And know you that your properties and your children are but a trial; and that it is Allah with whom lies your highest reward. (*Al-Qur'an*, 8: 28)

4 Wealth Distribution

Wealth distribution seeks to achieve proper planning so that your accumulated wealth can be managed and distributed according to your wishes with the minimum of inconvenience. This is important in the discipline of wealth management because of its inevitability and the spectre of Death, something that most of us tend to ignore. This area of wealth management definitely has a broader scope than a will is capable of addressing.

In addressing the issue of wealth, Muslims must not forget that the true owner of wealth is Allah and man is only a trustee. Allah (*SWT*) says:

> But seek, with that [wealth] which Allah has bestowed on you, the home of the Hereafter, and forget not your portion of lawful enjoyment in this world; and do good as Allah has been good to you and seek not mischief in the land. Verily Allah likes not the *Mufsidun* [those who commit great crimes and sins, oppressors, tyrants, mischief-makers, the corrupted]. (*Al-Qur'an*, Surah Al-Qasas: 77)

5 Financial Planning Process

Financial planning is a scientific methodology to manage wealth from a holistic viewpoint. It involves developing, coordinating and implementing a comprehensive range of strategies to address the challenges of wealth management. Financial planning is a process that encompasses the following six steps: establishing a financial goal, gathering relevant data, analysis the data, developing a plan for achieving the goal, implementing the plan and monitoring the plan (Hui 2003).

5.1 Establishing a Financial Goal

Setting a goal is critical to creating a successful wealth management plan. The whole financial planning process starts with establishing and prioritizing realistic financial goals and objectives. An appropriate time frame and risk tolerance level must also be clearly spelled out. It is important that the goals must be quantifiable, so that their attainment can be measured.

5.2 Gathering Relevant Data

After identifying your financial objectives, you need to gather as much relevant information as possible. This information must be accurate, up-to-date and relevant to the financial objectives. The more complex your situation and the more varied the number of your goals, the more challenging and risky the gathering of information becomes. This step requires a significant amount of time and patience.

5.3 Analysis of the Data

Analysis and evaluation of the data can begin when sufficient information has been gathered. The objective of this step is to establish where you are now in comparison to the financial goals that were established in Step 1. This is the point at which you determine the strengths and weaknesses of your present financial position.

5.4 Developing a Plan for Achieving the Goal

Typically, there will more than one way in which a financial objective may be achieved, and multiple alternatives should be explored and considered. The plan should be specific in nature, detailing who is to do what, when and with which resources. In order to increase commitment to the plan, the report describing the plan should be in writing.

5.5 *Implementing the Plan*

A financial plan is useful only if it is put into action. The success of a financial plan very much depends on someone's commitment to implementing the plan; for example, the implementation of plan is by writing or updating a will, restructuring current asset allocation and reducing debts and mortgages.

5.6 *Monitoring the Plan*

The financial planning process is dynamic and requires constant monitoring and reviewing. The plan should be reviewed at least once a year, or more frequently if changing circumstances warrant it. The review process should involve tracking the progress and performance of the implementation of the plan (Hui 2003).

6 Recommendations

There are several types of financial product introduced by financial institutions and professional bodies to facilitate our needs in managing and improving our financial planning; for example, Islamic Unit Trusts, family and general *takaful*, and Islamic bonds. However, we have chosen alternative products in this chapter, especially with regard to wealth distribution, that have been recognized worldwide for their powerful natures and effectiveness in application to our life, in this world and in the Hereafter. The three major instruments that are included in our analysis are *wasiyah*, *waqf* and *hibah*.

6.1 *Wasiyah*

Wasiyah is a legal document that outlines how you wish your assets to be distributed upon your demise. *Wasiyah* (a will) is one of the many acceptable modes of wealth disposal in Islam. It is similar to a gift, though with certain differences. It is executed following the demise of the benefactor and takes the form of gift of wealth, useful items (such as mosques, estates etc.), or even debt. The total of *Wasiyah* given cannot exceed more than one third of the total assets. The eligible heirs are not entitled to *Wasiyah* (Yaacob, n.d.).

Wasiyah should be in writing. It must be signed by the testator (will-maker) and witnessed by at least two persons. In Islam, it is not necessary for *wasiyah* to be in writing but it must be witnessed by two persons. It should comply with the requirement of *al-Qur'an* and the *hadith* of the Prophet (*SAW*).

The actual receipt of willed items is a precondition for the legal validity of *Wasiyah* such as gifts, according to Imam Malik. Others, such as Imam Shafie, opined that verbal acceptance alone may suffice.

The recommendation of *Wasiyah* has been prescribed by Allah (*SWT*) in *al-Qur'an* and whoever do *Wasiyah* will be rewarded.

> O you believe! When death approaches any of you, and you make a bequest [then take] the testimony of two just men of our own folk or two others from outside, while you are travelling through the land and death befalls you. (*Al-Qur'an*, 5: 106)

Although many scholars believe this verse has been abrogated by the more specific verses enjoining inheritance, it still enjoins *Wasiyah* to non-inheriting relations or according to *a-Tabari* for persons without heirs and for the *Ummah* in general.

Ibn Abbas relates a *hadith* of the Prophet (*SAW*):

> Prophet (*SAW*) says giving one third of your property by *wasiyah* is abundance.

Another *hadith* related by Saad that was written by Imam Shafie;

> The Prophet (*SAW*) forbids to *wasiyah* more than one third of property' (Ismail, n.d.)

The person who gives *wasiyah* has the opportunity to arrange the programme for alms or *sadaqah* and distribution of the remaining two thirds to the legal heirs. In Malaysia, anyone is allowed to make their own *wasiyah* but must comply with the rules and conditions of *al-Qur'an* and *hadith*, and also the Will Act (1949).

In the existing practices regarding financial services in Malaysia there is huge potential for financial planners and government itself to improve and to practise *wasiyah*. In current practice, it used mostly by financial institutions to nominate their customers' wealth for government agencies such as the Employee Provident Fund.

There are differences between *wasiyah* and nomination according to Islamic laws. A nominee may only act as a trustee. According to Section 167 of the Insurance Act (1996) Article 553, such nominee is entrusted to claim the policy money from an insurance policy for the payment of claims. Thereafter, the nominee must distribute the money to the rightful heirs or beneficiaries in accordance with Islamic laws or with their consent.

6.2 *Waqf*

Waqf means 'hold', 'confinement' or 'prohibition'. The word *Waqf* is used in Islam in the sense of holding certain property and preserving it for the restricted benefit of certain acts of philanthropy and prohibiting any use or disposition of it outside that specific objective. *Waqf* is a religious endowment, a property giving revenues, as regulated by Islamic law. The position of *waqf* is in the same category as *sadaqah* or *tabarru'*.

The legal definition *Waqf* includes two conditions. The first condition is to dedicate one's property rights to any public service and prevent of its re-ownership by others; the second condition is the perpetuity of this dedication.

The property must be real or have some sense of perpetuity. The property should be given on a permanent basis. Some jurists approve temporary *waqf* but only in the case of family *waqf*. An example of family *waqf* is the condition that the fruits and revenues of their *waqf* are first given to their own children and descendants and only the surplus, if any, should be given to the poor. If a person sets up a *waqf* for his children, they must treat males and females equally. Just as if they were to give something to their children, it should be shared equally among them so, too, if he sets up a *waqf* for them, they should have equal shares.

The *waqf* founder should be legally fit and able to meet the purpose of *waqf*. The purpose of the *waqf* must be, in the ultimate analysis, an act of charity. Hence, a *Waqf* on the rich alone is not permissible because it is not charity.

The revenues from the *waqf* finance mosques and other religious institutions. Hence, *waqf* is considered as a part of the mosque or the institution. According to Ibn Qudama, *waqf* means to bequeath the property and dedicate the fruit. As quoted from the Prophet's (*SAW*) words in His advice to Omar Ibn Khattab, when the latter consulted him about a plot of land of his:

> Bequest its stock and dedicate its progeny.

6.2.1 Advantages of Waqf

There are some points that should be highlighted on why we should include *Waqf* as part of our financial planning. Typically, when property holders indulge in gathering, developing, managing, protecting and diversifying the source of their wealth, their life, thinking and ambitions become slaves to its demand; hence, they become trapped in the process of protecting it. For this reason, they are more in need than others to be reminded to pay attention and to aspire to the Hereafter and to seek its merits. Especially through their money, complying with *al-Qur'an*, our endeavours should be with the Hereafter in mind.

> But seek the abode of the Hereafter in that which Allah has given thee. (*Al-Qur'an*, 2: 177) (Surah Al-Qasas: 77)

It can be considered as estate planning for the Hereafter. *Faraid* is the *rulr*, *wasiyah* is the bonus, *hibah* is the exception—but all are for preparing provisions for the legal heirs in this world. *Waqf* in all its categories, such *tabarru'* or *sadaqah*, is for all and truly for one's provision in the Hereafter. *Waqf* endowment saves the soul from worry, fear and a covetousness attitude to money; it also means that such endowment is used to be generous in spending.

Waqf also can be considered as a way of securing inheritance for the legal heirs. While the benefits from a *waqf* can be pious and good, the actual establishment of the *waqf* may have been anything but pious. In Muslim societies, regulations on inheritance have represented a problem for rich families; properties have been considered as belonging only to their owner, but not to his descendants. When the owner dies, the property would then be transferred to the ruler. But with *waqf*, rich families have established *waqf* and have nominated their children as trustees. In standard practice, a salary or allowances will be given out of about 10% of revenues. Through the *waqf*, the descendants have been secured a part of the fortune or wealth.

6.3 *Hibah*

The transfer of existing properties can be made voluntarily and without any consideration by the donor to the donee, and accepted by or on behalf of the donor during their lifetime.

> and gives his wealth in spite of love for it, to the kinsfolk, to the orphan and to *al-Masakin* [the poor], and to the wayfarer and to those who ask.

There will be some issues that arise from applications of *hibah* in our life. Therefore, the provisions for the implications of *hibah* transactions must be made. In Malaysia, Bumiputra-Commerce Trustee Berhad has introduced a new product named *hibah harta* to facilitate the needs of the whole Islamic community (Bumiputra-Commerce Trustee Berhad).

Property *hibah* is a private contractual arrangement between three parties whereby a person (the donor) allocates their property, during their lifetime, to their loved ones (the donees). In doing so, the property thus allocated will be held in trust and managed by Bumiputra-Commerce Trustee Berhad, which is then known as the trustee. This product has been approved by the Majlis Fatwa *Wilayah Persekutuan* (Yaacob, n.d.). On the donor's demise, the trustee will then transfer the gifted property to the donee. As *hibah harta* is a private contract undertaken during the lifetime of both the donor and the donee, the property will not form part of the donor's estate, and is therefore not subjected to the Probate and Administration Act and Will Act 1959 and *faraid*. Hence, this makes the transfer of the Donor's assets smoother and trouble-free.

Bumiputra-Commerce Trustee Berhad have introduced two types of *hibah harta*: *hibah umra* and *hibah ruqba*. *Hibah umra* is known as *hibah* without conditions, where the property will be transferred to the donee after the death of the donor. *Hibah ruqba* is a *hibah* with a condition that the property will be transferred depending on who died first. Should the donor die first, the property will be transferred to the donee. If the donee dies first, the property will not be transferred to the legal heirs but will be transferred to the donor.

Hibah ruqba is of crucial importance in today's *muamalat* (transactions). There were a few cases that involved *hibah* transactions that ended with unforeseen and unexpected circumstances. A similar transaction was *ruqba* (from *raqaba*: he waited), by which a man gives a house to another on condition that if the donor died first, the house became the property of the donee, and if the donee died first, the house reverted to the donor, as if each waited for the death of the other. Bukhari does not speak of *ruqba* which, according to the best opinion, is not allowed in Islam. With regard to *'umra*, it is agreed that when it is expressly stated that the property shall pass to the heirs of the assignee. In the event that no condition is laid down, it shall be a gift in all respects and shall not revert to the assignor. However, when an express condition is laid down that, on the death of the assignee, it shall revert to the donor or his heirs, there are two opinions: first, that the transaction shall take effect in accordance with the condition laid down, as if it were a loan; and, second, that it shall be looked on as a gift, the condition being dealt with as illegal and unenforceable.

Another example of *hibah* is where a couple gives away all their wealth and property to an adopted son as *hibah* without any conditions. The adopted son has no legal heirs and meets with an accident that causes his death. No one will inherit a single penny owned by the late adopted son except *baitul mal*. The parents who made *hibah* of all their wealth to the late adopted son have nothing in hand. *Hibah ruqba* is one of the tools that should be implemented to protect the situation and to hedge from any circumstances may arise in the future. *Hibah* is one of the best alternatives in our financial planning and should conclude well. However, the illustration given above is related to a *hadith* where Malik related that Umar Ibn al-Khattab said:

> What is wrong with men who give their sons gifts and then keep them and if the son dies, they say, 'My property is in my possession and I did not give it to anyone.' But if they themselves are dying, they say, 'It belongs to my son, I gave it to him.' Whosoever gives a gift and does not hand it over to the one to whom it was given, the gift is invalid, and if he dies it belongs to the heirs in general.
>
> The Prophet (*PBUH*) said: 'It is not lawful for a man to make a donation or give a gift and then take it back, except a father regarding what he gives his child. One who gives a gift and then takes it back is like a dog which eats and vomits when it is full, then returns to its vomit.' (Narrated from Abdullah Ibn Umar; Abdullah Ibn Abbas)

6.3.1 Advantages in Hibah

Hibah property will not be part of the original owner's estate because the contract concluded that the transfer of the property to the beneficiaries is legal. The person who gives their property as *hibah* will be protected against any legal action from creditors on that particular wealth.

In Malaysia, there are a few corporate and professional bodies that provide consultation on how to manage financial planning; one of these is Darul Hibah Consultant Sdn. Bhd. A person dealing with *hibah* will not experience any difficulty in completing a *hibah* transaction. It will not take much time in comparison with the documentation required to complete *faraid* matters.

Hibah can eliminate the problem of quarrelling among the beneficiaries in claiming ownership of the property. The owner of the property has the full right to transfer any amount of his wealth to anybody, whether his legal heir or not. *Hibah* has no limitation, unlike *faraid* and *wasiyah*. *Faraid* is strictly distributed to legal heirs only; *wasiyah* cannot be distributed to any family member and only a maximum of one third may be distributed in this way.

7 Conclusion

In Islam, the accumulation of wealth is allowed and, in some circumstances, mandatory. However, wealth should not be abused; it must be managed and planned properly, as Allah has laid down very clearly injunctions on how wealth should be acquired and spent. Above all, wealth is a form of trial by Allah to His servants, to see whether they follow His injunctions regarding the acquisition and disposal of wealth and, as such, the owners will be fully accountable on the day of the Hereafter.

References

Bumiputra-Commerce Trustee Berhad.

Hui, Y.M. (2003), Ensuring Fitness of Wealth Management, *BizWeek*, 16 August.

Ismail, A. (n.d.), *Islamic Estate Planning*, Darul Hibah Consultant.

Shari'ah Advisory Council, Securities Commission of Malaysia.

Takaful Nasional, http://www.takafulnasional.com.my.

Yaacob, O. (n.d.), *Amalandan Realiti Pengurusan Harta Orang Islam Di Malaysia*, Darul Hibah Consultant Sdn Bhd.

Yusoff, N. M. A. (n.d.), *Islam & Wealth: The Balanced Approach to Wealth Creation, Accumulation and Distribution.*

CHAPTER 26

Islamic Financial Planning

1 Introduction

Islamic financial planning is a guideline for people, especially Muslim society, as to how they can manage and use their wealth in a correct way that is in line with *Shari'ah* principles. The most important thing that is stressed in Islamic financial planning is the elimination of *riba* (interest) in all types of transaction. This is to ensure that exploitation among people can be eliminated, thereby establishing a just society.

There are several methods of financing in Islam, for example, through investment and insurance (*takaful*). Investment can be in the form of unit trusts, shares, bonds and other securities. As we have observed, people now use insurance as one of the ways to reduce the risk of loss due to misfortune. This concept is not against *Shari'ah* principles since it is in line with the principles of compensation and shared responsibility among the society. The concept of insurance already existed during the time of the Prophet and has been practised by the *Muhajirin* of Mecca and the *Ansar* of Madinah following the *hijra* of the Prophet over 1400 years ago.

As we can see nowadays, many financial institutions offer Islamic windows for their customers. This shows that the level of awareness and the demand for such services by the public have increased. That is why a further recent development has been that conventional banks have begun to offer Islamic financial services.

M. M. Billah, *Islamic Financial Products*,
https://doi.org/10.1007/978-3-030-17624-2_26

Such financial institutions have set up their own division, known as the *Shari'ah* board. The function of this division is to monitor the operation of the organization and to ensure that it does not operate against *Shari'ah* principles. *Shari'ah* boards also have to undertake thorough research and analysis before any actual investment is accommodated by the organization. In other words, any activities that are going to be executed must first be confirmed or approved by the *Shari'ah* board.

In this chapter, the focus is on the investment and insurance (*takaful*) in an Islamic economy. It includes the central idea, the *Shari'ah* rulings and a practical scenario for each type of financial instrument.

2 Central Idea

The Islamic financial system has certain guidelines and rules that organizations have to follow. This chapter discusses two types of financing: Islamic investment and insurance (*takaful*). Islamic investment can be in the form of unit trusts and securities, such as shares and Islamic bonds. As mentioned before, there are several principles that with which organizations have to comply. In Islamic investment, the transactions or activities must deal only with ethical sectors. For something to be ethical, when an organization makes an investment it has to invest in permissible activities. This is because the profit that the investment is going to earn should not come from unlawful activities such as gambling, the production of liquor, pornography and so on.

As we know, liquor is prohibited in Islam; Muslims are not allowed to drink it. Therefore, if someone makes a profit from the production or trading of liquor, then the return that they receive is a *haram* return. In addition, the profit from any investment made should not come from interest (*riba*). Such activities are unlawful and are prohibited in Islam. For instance, in Islam, if we owe a debt, we are not allowed to pay more than the amount that we owe, and we are also not allowed to buy something for a price that is lower than the regular price.

Another principle in Islamic investment is that the rewards should be earned from invested capital—meaning that profit only can be generated from the amount of capital that a person puts into their investment. In Islam, we are not allowed to make an investment that provides predetermined returns, such as bonds, bank deposits and the like. *Shari'ah* disagrees with bonds because the return does not come from invested capital but, rather, is calculated on a compound based.

For Islamic bonds, the return should come from the invested capital. For example, if someone buys a bond for $1000 with a coupon rate of 10% per annum, in the first year, a bondholder will receive $100 as a return. In the second year, he receives a further return of $100. This is unlike the performance of a conventional bond, under the terms of which, in the first year he will receive $100 but, in the second year, he will receive $110. This is because, in the second year, the return is calculated based on the principle plus the return of the preceding year, which was $1100. This type of bond is against *Shari'ah* principles since the return has not come from the invested capital; it includes an amount of return from the original investment.

Equity security, also known as 'shares', is another type of security acceptable to contemporary scholars: this is because the profits are tied to the returns of the underlying company and, hence, are risk related. It means that the shareholders will only receive returns if the company in which they invested is making a profit. If the company is not performing well and makes a loss from their business, then the shareholders are also responsible for that risk. That is what is meant by the term 'risk related'. In other words, wealth should be earned from a partnership between the investor and the user of the capital in which the returns and the risks are shared.

Another principle that must be complied with is that the money with which an investor is going to finance their investment should not come from money borrowed money at a rate of interest. Such money should not be invested or traded at margin. For example, let us say that someone takes a loan from a bank for $10,000 with an interest rate of 5% per annum. That money is then used to buy shares from an established company. Such transaction is prohibited in Islam since the investor used money that was borrowed at a rate of interest.

Furthermore, by making transactions in this way it seems as though we are taking advantage of such an amount of money—meaning that we make use of the borrowed money to purchase shares in the hope that we can obtain a high return on the money that we have invested. However, the same logic is permissible if, say, a unit trust company uses the fund that comes from a trustee to finance the investment. In conventional funds—such as hedge funds, arbitrage funds and similar types of fund—the funds used to finance their investments all come from borrowed money. Therefore, this kind of investment is prohibited in Islam.

In addition to investments, *takaful* (Islamic insurance) can be considered a good way to plan your saving. Today, *takaful* operators such as Takaful Malaysia, Takaful Nasional and others offer a variety of services or products. Islamic insurance transactions provide a policy of mutual cooperation, solidarity and brotherhood (Takaful Act 1984) against unpredicted risk. In Islam, this form of insurance is obliged to ensure both co-operation and mutual agreement between the participant and the *takaful* operator. In this way, Islamic insurance benefits both the participant and the selected operator. Hence, there should be a legitimate relationship between the parties in which the beneficiaries are not barred from claiming the benefits of the policy. This relationship is referred to as 'insurable interest'.

Therefore, the life insurance products for *takaful* practices, family *takaful* (Islamic life insurance) can only be determined based on the principles of *wasiyah* (bequest) and *mithrah* (inheritance). This is so as to ensure that one's loved ones will be safe in the future even if the assured is still alive on the maturity of the policy period. Moreover, *takaful* implements the concept of *al-mudharabah*. The money will be invested on a profit and loss sharing basis. This sharing of profit and loss is not contrary to *Shari'ah*, either in its operations or in the nature of its business. This is because all elements of the transactions follow Islamic and Malaysian rules and regulations. The *takaful* operator will be treated as *al-mudharib* that is in charge of the investment and the profit will be distributed according to the mutual agreement made earlier.

The profit gains for a transaction under *al-mudharabah* activity are paid, according to the agreed ratio, into a participant account and an operator account. In the event any loss occurs during the investment operation, only the *takaful* company shall bear such loss. There are many types of *takaful* offer in Malaysia:

- Family *Takaful* Plan
- *Takaful Siswa*
- *Takaful Ziarah*
- *Takaful Waqaf*
- *Takaful Rawat*
- *Takaful* Mortgage
- *Takaful Dana Pekerja*
- *Takaful Keyman*
- *Takaful Hawa*

- *Takaful Ma'asyi*
- *Takaful Sihat*
- Employees Provident Fund Annuity Scheme
- Family *Takaful* for Education
- *Takaful Wiladah.*

The above products are available to both Muslims and non-Muslims, except for *takaful wiladah.* However, for non-Muslims, the *takaful* operator will, first, investigate their income sources. If it is found that a potential investor commits any act related to prohibited activities—such as gambling, or selling pork or wine—their application will be rejected. Otherwise, they will be granted permission to participate in the scheme. Such investigation is important in order to investments are pure and receive the blessing of Allah (*SWT*).

The Takaful Act (1984) (the Islamic Financial Services Act, 2013) provides no further provision regarding the recipient of the benefits. So, in this situation, the Insurance Act (1996) is applied. Section 1672 of the Act provides that with regard to a life insurance policy held by a Muslim that nominates someone in the policy, the nominee shall be a mere trustee, agent, manager or executor. The nominee is the person that receives the benefits from the policy and their job is to distribute the benefits among the legal heirs in line with the principles of *faraid.*

3 Practical Scenario of Islamic Financial Planning

People are gradually accepting many types of Islamic financial planning. Many conventional banks are implementing and providing Islamic windows regardless of race or religion. Now, as we can observe, it is not only Muslims that seek Islamic services; non-Muslims are also using the Islamic practices of any kind of transaction. Individuals and corporate bodies, including multinational corporations, participate in the Islamic products provided by Islamic and conventional financial institutions. Here, we believe that the increase in the popularity of Islamic financial planning reflects not only its practicality, but also that its application is acceptable in our daily lives. As mentioned in detail in Section 2, Islamic financial planning can be divided into several categories. There are Islamic investments, Islamic *takaful* insurance, and more besides. Each type of Islamic financial planning affords a variety of choices.

People who have surplus money wish to make use of that money to invest in a business. For example, Mr. Kamarul has cash available of $100,000. He would like to invest that money so that it will give him a return from his investment in future years. So, it is recommended that he invest the money in businesses that operate in ethical sectors. In this case, Mr. Kamarul can use his money to buy shares from a company that deals with an Islamic operation.

For example, he could invest his money in a company, buying shares in that company and becoming one of the shareholders in it. The company will use the capital that has been injected by the investor to run their business. Then, at the end of each year or semi-annually, he will receive a dividend, declared by the company, in relation to the amount of money that he put into the business. However, he must first make sure that the company is not involved in any business that is not permissible by *Shari'ah*. Therefore, if the company declares a dividend to be a percentage of his investment, then the investor will receive $% as the return from his contributed capital. This return is a *halal* (permissible) since, the company is not involved in any prohibited activities.

> O ye who believe! Intoxicants and gambling, [dedication of] stones, and [divination by] arrows, are an abomination of Satan's handiwork; Eschew such [abomination], that ye may prosper. (5: 90)

According to this verse, Allah (*SWT*) has mentioned that gambling and alcohol is prohibited in Islam. Even though there may possibly have some benefit from it, the harm is greater than the benefit. Thus, it is prohibited in Islam. If any transaction or business deals with forbidden elements, it is prohibited and contradicts the *Shari'ah*. Therefore, if someone chooses to invest their money in such a company, then the return on the investment that they make can be regarded as unlawful.

> They ask you concerning the wine and gambling. Say: 'In them is great sin'. (2: 219)

According to this verse, it can be seen how strongly Allah prohibited wine and gambling. If people consume such things, it will create greater sin in the eyes of God. Allah (*SWT*) will punish those people in this world and in the Hereafter.

In addition to investing surplus money by purchasing shares in a company, people also can use their money to buy Islamic unit trusts. Nowadays, we can see that many organizations offer Islamic unit trusts. A unit trust is similar to the purchasing of shares. However, a unit trust is available to all groups of people. Unit trusts can be purchased in small units. For instance, X has $100. She would like to use that money and buy a unit trust so that, in future years, she will receive a return from the investment that she makes. X can use her $100 to buy a unit trust from an Islamic unit trust company. Let us say that the cost of one unit is $1. Therefore, X can buy 100 units of unit trust for the $100 that she has. Appendix 1 shows how X can get a return from her investment through the unit trust investment that she purchased.

As shown in Fig. 1, the profit that the company makes from *al-mudharabah* transactions will be distributed equally among the trustees. However, it should be based on the number of units held by the trustees. A trustee may sell or increase their unit trust holding at any time they choose.

4 Islamic Unit Trusts

Today, many financial institutions offer Islamic bonds with zero coupon rates as an alternative investment. In conventional bonds, the coupon payments can be regarded as *riba*; that is why Islamic bonds issued today have zero coupon rates—meaning that no additional payments are made on the par value of the bonds.

> Those who devour usury will not stand except as stands one whom the Evil One by his touch hath driven to madness. That is because they say: 'Trade is like usury, but Allah hath permitted trade and forbidden usury.' Those who after receiving direction from their lord, desist, shall be pardoned for the past; their case is for Allah [to judge]; but those who repeat [the offence] are companions of the fire; they will abide therein [forever]. (2: 275)

In this verse, Allah (*SWT*) mentioned *riba*, which we already know is prohibited in Islam. Allah also mentioned that trade is permissible but, if it involves *riba*, such trade will become unlawful. *Riba* has no benefit at all. This is because *riba* will oppress others, especially those who are poor: poor people become poorer under the burden of *riba*. This is

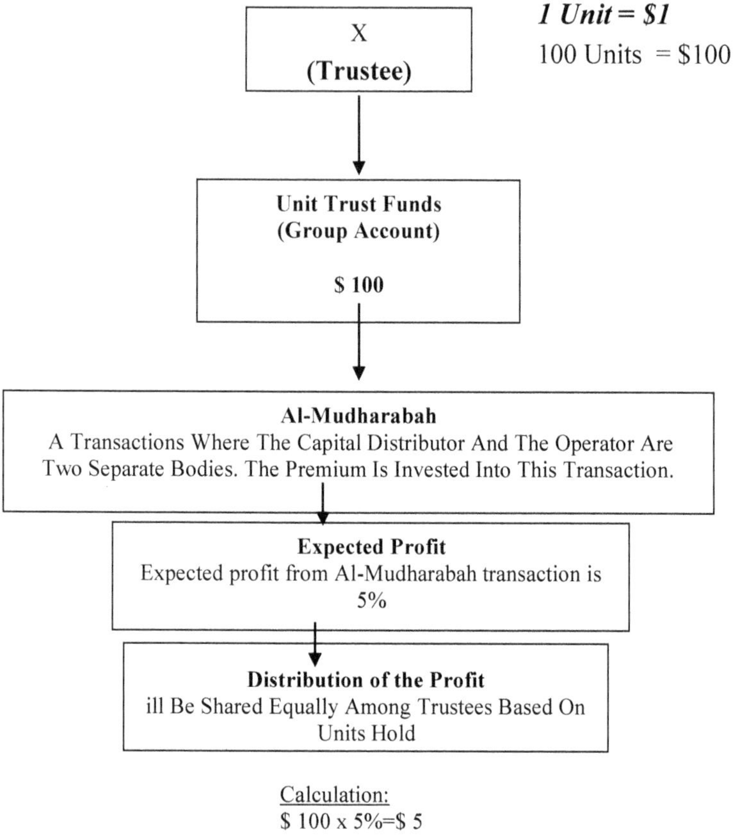

Fig. 1 Islamic unit trust fund (*Source* Author's own)

because they have to pay more than the amount that they owe. So, in Islam, it is unfair to let them pay more since the purpose of making a loan is because the recipient does not have enough money. Therefore, Muslims should not involve themselves in any transaction that involves the element of *riba* because Allah will punish them, either in this world or in the Hereafter.

There is one *hadith* that mentioned *riba*. It is reported by Abu Sa'id Al Kudri. The *hadith* says:

> The exchange of gold for gold, silver for silver, wheat for wheat, barley for barley, dates for dates, and salt for salt, must be on basis of equality and on the spot possession. Whoever adds or demands an addition commits *riba*. The giver and receiver of [additional quantity] are equally blameworthy.

This *hadith* tells how *riba* is incurred in a transaction. It shows that, in Islam, it is permissible to exchange of commodities of the same type provided they are equal in terms of quantity. Therefore, if someone accepts a loan from any party, he should pay the lender the same amount that he owes. If he pays more, or if the lender asks for a lesser amount than the actual amount borrowed, then *riba* will be involved:

> O ye believe! Do not involve with usury, double and multiple. (3: 130)

In this verse, Allah (*SWT*) prohibits Muslims from involving themselves in usury. This is because it encourages people to become more greedy and selfish. Such attitudes arise because, by committing usury, people will earn more money with little effort.

Let us say Mr. Zulkifli has the intention of buying Islamic bonds that will cost him $900. After a certain period of time (say, after one year), he may redeem the bonds at $1000, thus making a profit of $100. This type of contract is known as *bay' al-dayn* (the selling and buying of debt). Appendix 3 shows how Islamic debt securities work. There are three main steps:

- Debt securitization through *al-bai bithaman ajil* (BBA) purchases;
- Debt issuance through the contract of *shahadah al-dayn*;
- Debt trading through the contract of *bay' al-dayn*.

By referring to Appendix 3, we can see how *bay' al dayn* works. For example, Hijrah Sdn. Bhd. want to buy equipment for their office; however, they did not have sufficient money to finance the equipment. So, they will ask the bank to buy the equipment. The bank will then buy the equipment at the market price. Later, they will sell the equipment to Hijrah Sdn Bhd at a deferred price. The bank will sell the goods at the selling price plus a profit margin. This contract is called *al-bay bithaman ajil.*

Hijrah Sdn Bhd will settle the debt by paying through instalments. In order to settle the debts, Hijrah will issue Islamic Bonds to the public. Let say the purchase price for the goods are $2 million. So Hijrah will issue the bonds for the value of $2 million. The bondholders will be given a certificate. This contract is called a *shahadah al-dayn.*

Later, if the investors (bondholders) wish to sell their bonds to the issuer or a third party, the trading of such a debt certificate is known as *bay' al-dayn.* This type of bond is acceptable in Malaysia; the Middle-Eastern *Ulama'* consider it a null and void transaction.

5 Islamic Bonds (Sukuk)

A daily practical example of this would be if Mr. Imran wished to plan his money according to the Islamic *Shari'ah.* He wanted to buy insurance for his family. Islam allows Islamic insurance (*takaful*). So, it is appropriate for Mr. Imran to join the Family *Takaful* Plan, which comprises many types of product, such as those listed in Section 2. In this case, Mr. Imran is attracted to the Family *Takaful* Plan. He is therefore willing to pay the *takaful* scheme premium of $100 per month. He needs to obtain a clear picture of how the Family *Takaful* Plan works and how the operator (*takaful* agency) receives profit. In addition, how does the operator distribute the profit and what is the flow? The table in Appendix 4 provides the answers to Mr. Imran's questions (Fig. 2).

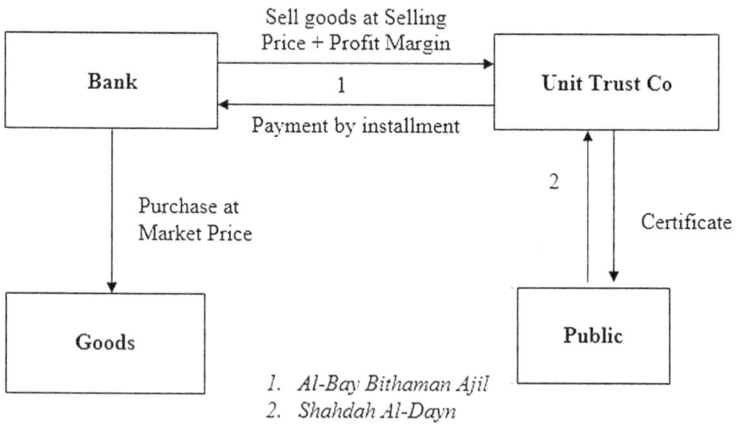

Fig. 2 Islamic bonds/Sukuk (*Source* Author's own collection)

As shown in Appendix 4, a participant's premium will be divided into two separate accounts: one is the participant's account, and the other one is a special participant account (SPA). The SPA is an account that is treated as charity with the mutual consent of the participant and the *takaful* operator. SPA practises the element of *al-tabaru'*, which is in line with the principle of a joint guarantee to help others.

> Muslim towards another Muslim is like a building that supports each other.
>
> Muslim among themselves live in '*mahabbah*', sympathy and cooperate between each other like a human body. If one of the limbs hurts, then the other will stay for the whole night to take care of each other.

These two *hadiths* of Prophet Muhammad (*SAW*) state that Muslims must support each other. Here, by implementing Islamic financial planning, Allah (*SWT*) will feel contented because we follow His commands. For those that disobey Him, they will be severely punished in Hell fire.

6 Family *Takaful* Plans

Let us consider another hypothetical example. Y has a daughter aged 5 years. Y plans to invest a portion of her monthly savings for her daughter, mainly for her child's education. As a Muslimah, Y needs the financing planning she implements to be Islamic based. Islamic financial institutions in Malaysia provide Islamic education plans for children. The most suitable Islamic financial plan is to buy *Takaful Siswa* for her daughter. The table in Appendix 5 shows how Y could save a fund for her daughter. Parents must comply with and accept certain regulations in order to participate in this kind of *takaful* (Fig. 3):

- The parents' age must not exceed 55 years old on the inception of the plan.
- Parents are treated as the trustee for that particular child.
- The maturity period for this scheme is 22 years.

Payment ceases when the child is 18 years old, when 20% of the accumulated fund will be placed into the *Takaful Siswa* Plan and will be paid every year towards its costs until the maturity period ends (when the child reaches the age of 22 years). The Prophet (*SAW*) said:

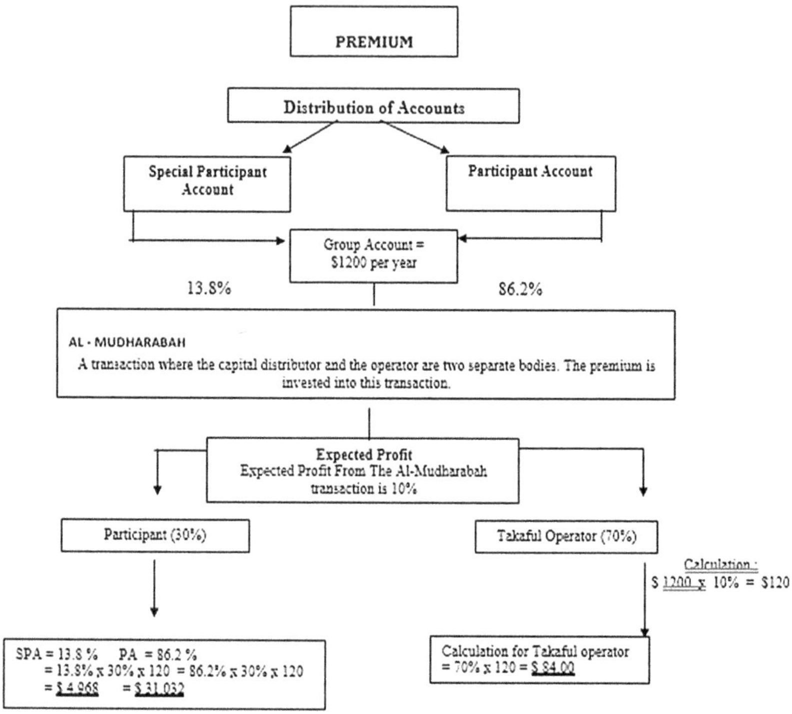

Fig. 3 Family *takaful* plan (*Source* Author's own collection)

> It is better to leave your offspring wealthy than to leave them poor, asking others for help. (Sahih al-Bukhari)

The above *hadith* from Prophet Muhammad (*PBUH*) narrated by Saad B. Abi Waqas insists that it is important to leave your belonging to your heirs. This can be applied to Islamic financial planning. *Takaful* is one of the best ways to plan your finance. The Family *Takaful* Plan is not a scheme that guarantees one's life, but it is financial protection for the needy in our society. Allah (*SWT*) says:

> Who [conducts] their affairs by mutual consultation, who spend out of what we bestow on them for sustenance. (42: 38)

The above verse explains the importance of mutual agreement. Muslims are encouraged to consult and interact with each other, which Allah (*SWT*) believes is the best way to obtain victory. In this *takaful* context, the mutual agreement made by the participant and *takaful* operator is expressed in terms of the agreed premium, ratio of profit and the period of maturity of the plan. Referring back to the case of Y, agreement has been made in advance. It is related to the above *ayat* of *al-Quran* that emphasizes the importance of mutual agreement. In many aspects of life, mutual understanding, mutual agreement and mutual support are examples of good ethical behaviour. Y had made an agreement with the *takaful* operator for her child's benefit in the future (Fig. 4).

Table 1 presents an example of proceeds payable under the *Takaful Siswa* Plan. It is divided into three packages depending on the *ringgit* contribution.

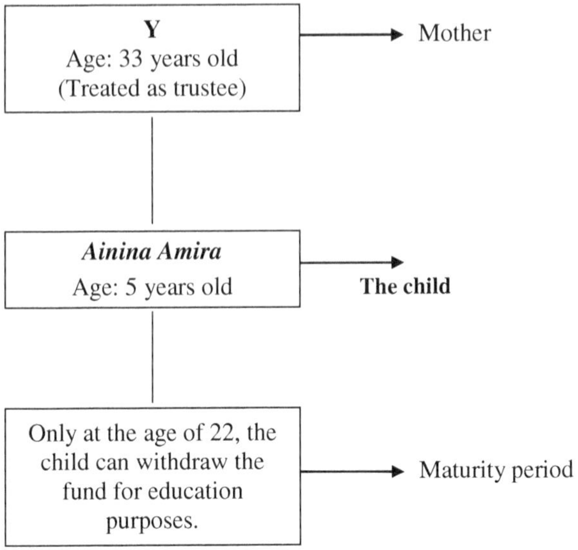

Fig. 4 Family *takaful* plan (*Source* Author's own)

Table 1 Family *takaful* plan

Example of the proceeds payable under the plan

	Package 1	*Package 2*	*Package 3*
Installment	$	$	$
1. Monthly contribution	10	20	50
2. SPA amount	1	2	5
***Takaful* benefits**	$	$	$
1. *Participant*			
Death	1000 + PA	1000 + PA	1000 + PA
Permanent disability	1000	1000	1000
Personal accident	5000	10,000	25,000
2. *Guardian*			
Death	1000 + 10× monthly Until the age of 18	1000 + 20× monthly Until the age of 18	1000 + 5× monthly
Permanent disability	1000 + 10× monthly Until the age of 18	1000 + 20× monthly Until the age of 18	1000 + 5× monthly

Source Author's own collection

7 Planning for Retirement

The next practical scenario concerns retirement. In Malaysia, private sector employees will enjoy their Employees Provident Fund when they reach the age of 55. Government employees will receive pension benefits, which is a portion of their last monthly salary. Yet, many people use their lump sum money improperly. If the money were to be spent in a matter of days without proper care and planning, this puts a person at risk. In our hypothetical case, Mr. Ali works in a private company as a manager and he is due to retire in seven years' time. Takaful Malaysia provides Islamic financial services planning. Depending on Mr. Ali's preference, he could participate in the *Takaful Ma'asyi* Plan.

The *Takaful Ma'asyi* Plan is a scheme where Mr. Ali receives his benefits in the form of a regular pension. Participants can pay the premium either in a lump sum or on an instalment basis. The contribution will be invested through *al-mudharabah* practice. It is in accordance with the principle of profit sharing in a ratio of 80% for the participant and the remaining 20% is for the operator. The plan equips the participant with unique benefits:

- Practising *al-mudharabah* principles, in which you have an entitlement to profit sharing and also an entitlement to profit on your investment income in the *Ma'asyi* account.
- A fixed income which will be monthly, quarterly, or at any other interval of your choice during your life-time until you reach the age of 100 years.
- A continuous act of good deeds, this plan is in line with *Shari'ah*.

Z can independently choose the *waqaf* period of participation. The *takaful* operator serves 10 years, 15 years and 20 years. Moreover, there are two type of *Takaful Ma'asyi* Plan. The first is the *Hasanah* Package. In this package, the participant may choose that the profit of the Participant Account be immediately paid out to him, instead of being re-invested. By this method, the participant would ensure a higher amount of *Ma'asyi* during the *waqaf* period. The operator, through the *al-mudharabah* principle, will not invest this Participant Account.

The second type of *Ma'asyi* Plan is the *Ahsan* Package. In this plan, instead of cashing in the profit of the Participant Account, the participant may choose that it be credited into the *Waqaf Ma'asyi* Account. Through this method, the participant would ensure a higher amount of *Ma'asyi* benefits for both periods of participation and after the *waqaf* period.

The following example shows the flow of the *Takaful Ma'asyi* Plan, which is very useful for Z to examine. By studying the flow chart, Z can contribute in instalments and in a lump sum.

8 *Shari'ah* Ruling

The *Shari'ah* ruling governing the *Takaful Ma'asyi*, as mentioned earlier, is that mutual consent and mutual agreement must in place before implementing this Islamic insurance. Allah adores Muslims that follow His commands. For the success of *Takaful Ma'asyi*, cooperation is needed the participant and the agent. The next verse emphasizes the importance of cooperation and doing good deeds.

> Cooperate with each other in righteousness and piety. And do not cooperate in sin and rancour. (5: 2)

Further to the verses above, Allah (*SWT*) stresses the importance of doing good deeds. Allah (*SWT*) condemns sin and rancour. So, it is important for Muslims to manage their money properly. Islamic financial planning can ensure that any investment in which you are considering placing your money is in line with the *Shari'ah*. This not only relates to *takaful*, but to any other form of Islamic financial planning available.

> But on Allah (*SWT*) put your trust [*tawakkal*] if you have faith. (5: 23)

The above verse mentions the concept of *tawakkal*. This is where we take out an insurance policy. We cannot put our trust in the insurer on certain events that we cannot foresee. In other words, we have to put our trust in Allah (*SWT*) with regard to all the unexpected events that could happen in our daily life.

9 Recommendations

Islamic investment, Islamic insurance and other forms of Islamic-based financial planning are wonderful for Muslims, especially for those who are concerned about good deeds and rewards from Allah (*SWT*). However, there is space for improvement: nothing is perfect, and there is no one best solution for anything. This section presents a few recommendations that we think may be useful and attractive for Islamic financial planning:

9.1 Exposure

The public should be widely exposed to the range of options offered by Islamic financial planning. There should be greater focus on college and university students, those who are about to graduate and begin searching for a job. They will need some element of support to be their guideline to plan their savings.

9.2 Attract More Non-Muslims

Participants in Islamic financial planning comprise Muslims and non-Muslims. Hence, the authorized parties who deal in the Islamic financial planning should devise plans to attract the attention of more non-Muslims.

9.3 Islamic Teachings

Islamic teaching is one of the fundamental elements to bring about a good daily life. The stronger one's belief in Islam, the greater will be the effort made to seek Allah's contentment. By emphasizing the commands of Allah to human beings, at least Muslims can differentiate between the good and bad. The problem of choosing the right method of Islamic financial planning should be easy and transparent.

9.4 Flexibility

It is vital to have flexibility in any transaction, but this has to be with the consent of both parties (participant and the operator/agent). This flexibility may lead participants to spread information about the benefits of the Islamic financial planning by word-of-mouth. They may spread the news to their family, relatives, peers and neighbours.

10 Conclusion

Islamic financial planning is established not only in Malaysia, but also worldwide. The public is aware of its existence and many people already participate and benefit from its application. Moreover, the number of participants is increasing daily. This shows that the Islamic financial planning products offered by financial institutions offer the best and most practical alternative for those who prefer to be in line with Islamic *Shari'ah.* By practising Islamic applications, people will come to believe in the rewards promised by Allah. This positive improvement is parallel to the increasing level of confidence the public has for using Islamic-based financial planning. Today, many people realize and understand how Islamic financial planning works and how practical it is. However, there is still a significant number of people who do not participate in it. Most probably Islamic financial planning does not promise a sufficiently high percentage of profit, or the absence of an interest rate proves unattractive.

Reference

Takaful Act. (1984), at S. 8(5)(b), repealed by the Islamic Financial Services Act (2013).

CHAPTER 27

Islamic Unit Trust (Micro-Saving)

1 Introduction

Currently, the development of the collective investment industry, particularly that of unit trusts, has become an important factor of growth for non-bank financial intermediaries within the Malaysian financial system. This reflects a significant contribution to the economy as a whole. As shown in Appendix 1, the percentage of asset holding in non-bank financial intermediaries increased from 5.8% in 1992 to 7.0% in 1998 (Malaysian Unit Trusts Industry 2000). Some of the factors that contributed to this growth are robust economic growth, low unemployment and low inflation rates, increased population growth and increases in per capita income. In addition, the introduction of unit trusts packages based on *Shari'ah* principles has also played a significant role in boosting the economy for the nation. So, in this chapter, the focus is on the Islamic model of unit trust, its development, its concept, its place within the local market, *Shari'ah* rulings to support unit trusts, the advantages and disadvantages of unit trusts, the regulatory body related to unit trusts, recommendations for further improvement in the practice of Islamic unit trusts and the future for the unit trust industry.

M. M. Billah, *Islamic Financial Products*,
https://doi.org/10.1007/978-3-030-17624-2_27

2 Overview of Unit Trust Industry

The unit trust industry in Malaysia started early in 1959 when the first unit trust—the Malaysian Unit Trust, managed by Malayan Unit Trust Limited—was introduced. In 1963, Malayan Unit Trust was transferred to the South East Asia Development Corporation Berhad. Later, Singapore Unit Trust Limited and Asia Unit Trust Berhad were formed as a result of separation from this company. In 1968, Amanah Saham MARA Unit Trust Management was established. The fund aimed to pool *bumiputra* savings, mainly from the rural areas. The introduction of the funds was very encouraging during that year. Amanah Saham MARA Unit Trust Management Berhad and Asia Unit Trust Berhad largely dominated the industry back in the 1970s.

The expansion continued on 20 April 1981 when Permodalan Nasional Berhad first introduced Sekim Amanah Saham Nasional. It was aimed at mobilizing savings and increasing the corporate wealth of the *bumiputra* in accordance with the new economic policy. The fund from the unit trusts was largely invested in the various companies run by the *bumiputra*. As a result of this, just one week after it was launched, Permodalan Nasional Berhad managed to attract about 170,000 *bumiputra* participants. One week after that, about 1 million *bumiputra* invested in Amanah Saham Nasional, which was worth $600 million. This is a record for the Malaysian unit trust industry. Later, the government believed unit trust could be a powerful tool with which to abolish economic differences among races. On the other hand, Malaysian Indians were also introducing their own unit trust to improve the standard of living among them. They introduced Amanah Saham MIC-TPG Berhad, with the main focus on promoting and mobilizing domestic savings among the Malaysian Indians.

The growth in economy in the 1990s as a result of growing per capita income, new international ventures, corporatization, rising consumer affluence and a booming stock market reflected greater heights of growth for the unit trust industry. The government became very concerned about the growth and development of the industry and so they introduced several regulatory frameworks and body to monitor the industry. Securities Commission Malaysia was established on 1 March 1993 as a regulatory agency to monitor all the unit trust transactions within the market. One of the Securities Commission Malaysia's roles is to rationalize and strengthen the fragmented regulatory framework of the industry (Malaysian Unit Trusts Industry 2000).

The unit trust industry has gone through optimistic performance in the past as well as the future. Appendix 2 clearly shows that the total net asset value for the industry was $15.72 billion in 1992. This value gradually increased to $43.3 billion as at 31 December 1999. This represents a 175% increment of the total amount. Underlying reasons for this are due to increase in new unit trust management companies, new funds launched and new accounts opened by the investors. This clearly demonstrates that the concepts of unit trusts and their products are feasible and are accepted by the people.

To support this argument, Appendix 3 clearly summarizes the development of the unit trust industry in Malaysia between 1992 and 1999. The number of government sponsored funds increased from 19 in 1992 to 30 in 1999. The net asset value for the funds also increased gradually from $15.334 billion in 1992 to $32.199 billion in 1999. Development in the private funds market was also attractive; 20 in 1992 to 77 in 1999. The net asset worth also increased, from $0.386 billion in 1992 to $11.058 billion in 1999. Overall, the market capitalization of the unit trust industry in Malaysia also improved year on year, from $6.39 billion in 1992 to $7.827 billion in 1999.

3 The Concept of Unit Trust

3.1 *Central Idea*

Unit trust can be defined as a collective investment scheme that obtained money by pooling the savings from various investors who share the same financial objectives, investment strategy and risk (Chong 2000). These funds are allocated in a diversified portfolio of authorized investments and managed by professional managers. The Security Commission Malaysia's Guidelines on Unit Trust set out the overall regulatory framework of the unit trust, such as a deed or an agreement that should be followed by the managers and unit holders. The authorized investments allowed by Security Commission Malaysia include, for example, approved stocks, bonds, commercial chapters, government securities, treasury bills, foreign securities, direct business ventures and unquoted securities.

3.2 *Mechanism of Unit Trusts*

The diagram in Appendix 4 presents the framework of how units trust work. First, a trust deed is created for the unit trust. It is an agreement between the trustee, the fund managers and the fund's investors (unit-holders). This agreement is made in order to identify the mutual interests of all the parties involved. The unit-holder is an individual, a group of individuals, or an institution that invests in the fund. Each of them will receive a certificate of entitlement, which is known as a unit trust certificate. They do not directly acquire the securities in the portfolio. Instead, the ownership of the fund is divided into separate units of entitlement or right. A decrease or increase in the portfolio will reflect the value of each unit. Typically, unit trust investors are small investors who do not have the time to look after a specific portfolio investment. Instead, they prefer to invest in a secure investment portfolio, thereby incurring minimal administration costs, marketing and research. The unit-holders can buy their units at a selling price. The calculation of price for each of the portfolio is recalculated daily and quoted in the newspapers. They can buy at any time before the fund reaches its maximum approved size. Alternatively, they can sell the units at a buying price at any time. This can be done through the fund management company with which they have invested.

The manager is the professional person appointed to manage the operation of the funds. He will invest the money in authorized investments as approved by the Securities Commission Act (1983): securities of companies listed on recognized stock exchanges, Malaysian Government Securities, Treasury Bills, Bank Negara Malaysia Certificates and Government Investment Certificates, Negotiable Certificates of Deposit, Banker's Acceptances and placements of money at call within discount houses, Cagamas Bonds, Unlisted Loan Stocks, Corporate Bonds and so forth. In certain exceptional cases, an external investment manager from a merchant bank or asset management company is appointed to manage the funds. As a return for services rendered by the managers, service fees are charged based on agreed charges. These charges may vary from company to company, as they able to set their own level of fees. Typically, the capital cost of a unit trust investment is reasonable and is based on the level of risk of the funds.

Unit trust provides a return on investment in the form of growth (capital appreciation) and dividend income. The dividend income is distributed to the unit-holders based on the number of units held. However, this is not a guaranteed sum as the investment is based on portfolio performance. To protect the funds, the fund management company is not allowed to retain the assets; for example, the share certificates and bank accounts. Instead, a trustee is appointed as custodian of the assets so as to ensure the interests of the unit-holders are protected.

3.3 The Difference Between Unit Trusts and Mutual Funds

The main difference between a unit trust and a mutual fund is the legal structure. Generally, a mutual fund issues redeemable shares. In contrast, a unit trust company issues units instead of shares. This difference has a significant impact on the performance of each type of investment. A mutual fund, being a closed ended fund, is normally traded in a secondary market. The performance of a share price is very much dependent on market demand and supply forces. Unit trusts, being open ended funds, can only be traded through the fund management company.

3.4 Types of Fund

Unit trust funds can be categorized based on their unique characteristics: equity, bond, income, growth, balanced, money market, Islamic funds and so forth. An equity fund is also known as a stock fund. The investments are mainly traded on the stock exchange. This fund comprises local shares, shares of unlisted companies and so on. A bond fund is focused on investments in bonds and other securities. It is less risky than an equity fund because, legally, it has first rights before the stockholders. Bond funds can be bank guaranteed, government guaranteed and so on. Income funds concentrate on securities, and derive their income from bonds, utility stocks, money market instruments and so forth. An Islamic fund concentrates on investing in businesses that follow Islamic principles. However, this type of fund does not limit the types of investor. It is open for all Malaysians, regardless of their race or religion.

3.5 *Shari'ah* Rulings

In Islam, investment in a unit trust is in line with *Shari'ah* rulings. The concept of risks and rewards shared by the unit-holders employing the expertise of professional managers conforms to Islamic principles and this type of investment is already being applied within the Islamic financial system. This can be related to specific financial contracts and products: *al-murabaha* and *al-musharakah*.

First, it complies with the concept of *al-mudaraba*. This concept is one of well-known investments permissible under Islamic *Shari'ah* and widely used by countries practising the Islamic system of banking, such as Iraq. Generally, *al-murabaha* is a concept of profit sharing where one party provides the capital and the other party provides the labour and will manage the money. The profit is shared by both parties according to an agreed ratio (Hasan, n.d.). This concept can be applied to a unit trust. In a unit trust, the capital for the venture is provided by the trust, and the business expertise and management will be the responsibility of a third party—in this case, unit-holders. The profit is divided between the unit-holders and the trust in accordance with the agreement. In addition to this, some unique elements of the concept of *al-mudaraha* are that it is limited to self-liquidating transactions; the assets must be easily recognizable, and must be realized and liquidated so that the profits are easily distributed; and its accounts must be recorded properly and be audited.

The concept of *al-musharaka* also can be applied to unit trusts. Following this concept, two or more financiers will engage in a new project or participate in an established project. All the partners have a right to share the total profits from a venture in accordance with the agreement made between them. The managers who manage a fund will be remunerated in the form of a service charge. This is in line with the unit trust concept, in which the mechanisms are the same. The main difference is mainly where the funds are being invested. In an Islamic unit trust fund, for example, the funds are placed in authorized investments approved by the Securities Commission Malaysia and the *Shari'ah* board. In addition to this, the profit is shared after deducting management fees and payment for *zakat*.

3.6 Examples of Islamic Unit Trusts

There are many types of unit trust in Malaysia. For the purposes of this chapter, we shall divide them into two categories: Islamic unit trusts and conventional unit trusts. The only clear difference between these two types is where the funds are invested. Some examples of unit trust companies are the Amanah Saham Bank Islam, Arab Malaysian Cumulative Growth Fund, BHLB Pacific Savings, Lifetime Trust Income and Amanah Saham Nasional. This section will discuss one example of an Islamic unit trust an example of a conventional unit trust.

First, Bank Islam Unit Trust Management Berhad introduced the Amanah Saham Bank Islam: Islamic Bond Fund on 27 December 2001. This fund has a size of about 400 million units. This fund aimed to invest in a portfolio of *halal* stock that would comply with the principles of *Shari'ah*. *Halal* stocks exclude all the companies involved in activities, products or services related to conventional banking, insurance and financial services, gambling, alcoholic beverages and non-*halal* food products. This fund also aimed to avoid the incidence of *riba* (interest from usury). One of the ways to achieve this is by direct deduction of *zakat* in each of the proceeds. The Bank Islam's *Shari'ah* board advises the fund. The funds can be categorized as being of the income type. Mainly, this type of fund aims to achieve a reasonable return by investing in a portfolio at a moderate level of risk. The minimum investment accepted for this fund is $1000 and the minimum additional deposit is $100. The service charge is between 0 and 5% of the net asset value.

Amanah Saham Nasional 3 was introduced on 16 October 2001. This fund was introduced by Amanah Saham Nasional Berhad, a wholly owned subsidiary of Permodalan Nasional Berhad. This fund's policy is to invest in a prudent portfolio of equities and other capital market instruments that are in line with the objective of achieving capital appreciation over the medium to long term. Amanah Saham Nasional 3 invested 70% of its assets in equities and the remaining 30% in other capital market instruments. The allocation may be reviewed based on market performance. This fund can be categorized as comprising equity and other capital market instruments. In other words, it is a balanced fund. The size of this fund is 1 billion units. In addition, this fund is suitable for investors who expect to achieve capital growth over the medium to long term. The service charge for this fund is between 5 and 10% of the net asset value (Prospectus of ASN 3 Imbang, 16 October 2001).

The difference between Amanah Saham Nasional 3 and Amanah Saham Bank Islam: Islamic Bond Fund is restriction by the *Shari'ah* board. Theoretically, Amanah Saham Bank Islam's fund must comply with the *Shari'ah* qualifications as listed below:

- Interest based transactions are prohibited.
- The outcome from the investments shall serve the interest for the benefit of the society.

- Capital (*maal*) should be managed through *halal* (religiously acceptable) channels. In other words, it cannot be invested in religiously prohibited activities, such as gambling.
- *Zakat* must be deducted from the proceeds and distributed to the needy through the proper channels.

3.7 *The Future of the Islamic Unit Trust Industry*

The prospects for Islamic financial products, particularly unit trusts, will be bright with further support and encouragement from the government. However, in order to become an international Islamic financial centre, several measures have to be implemented; for example, overcoming consensus among bankers and Islamic jurists, encouraging proactive participation in research and development, and educating the general public.

First, problems occur due to the different perspectives of conventional and Islamic practitioners. For example, in the case of unit trust, some companies may neglect to deduct *zakat* from their profit. In contrast, Islam suggests that *zakat* be paid to the needy and poor. In relation to this, the *Shari'ah* Advisory Council has to be more proactive in tackling this shortcoming. They should readdress the matters related to *Shari'ah* principles and conduct discussions to overcome the pertinent issues in a proper manner. As a result, better coordination and consistency of *Shari'ah* rulings will prevail in the future.

Second, research and development also play a significant role in reshaping the future of Islamic unit trusts. *Shari'ah* experts and professionals should sit, discuss and develop a versatile Islamic financial product that suits present and future needs. From discussions held by both parties, the knowledge gap can be diminished over time, which will directly reduce resistance and enhance cooperation in promoting any financial products.

Better education on the intricacies of the Islamic principles involved in Islamic financial product is very important, as it will provide a better understanding of the underlying concepts of Islamic finance. Lately, there have been comments from the public complaining about the calculation of profits, saying that there is little difference between Islamic products and conventional products. The government should therefore take a more proactive role to overcome this. Seminars and transmitting information through the mass media is a viable way to educate people about the concepts of Islamic finance.

To become a hub for Islamic finance countries, the government and the private sector have to make greater effort with regard to the Islamic financial sub-sector, particularly unit trusts. On the basis of this, our vision to see a fully Islamic based country could become reality (Izazee 2002).

References

Chong, D. (2000). *Unit Trust in Malaysia*. Sage Information Services, Kuala Lumpur.

Hasan, S. (n.d.). *Encyclopedia of Islamic Banking*. Institute of Islamic Banking & Insurance, London.

Izazee, M. I. (2002, April). *Islamic Private Debt Securities: Issues & Challenges*. RAMFoces.

Malaysia Unit Trust Directory. (2000). Permodalan Nasional Berhad, Kuala Lumpur.

Prospectus of ASN 3 Imbang, 16 October 2001.

CHAPTER 28

Islamic Financing for the Sustainable Development Goals

1 Introduction

This chapter focuses on financing that will improve the standard of living for low-income groups. According to World Bank data, a number of Muslim countries have been categorized as low-income countries. Malaysia, due to its stimulated economic development in recent decades, it is now categorized as an upper-middle country. Our discussion will be based on Malaysian data and statistics. It should be understood that, no matter how strong the economy is, there are still low-income groups that need to be catered for.

Since 1973, Malaysia has experienced a remarkable growth in its economy; this is shown by the increase in per capita income of 2.5 times from 1973 to 1995. Poverty had shrunk from half of the population to 78% (data sources: World Bank). The change in the poverty level has led to increased life expectancy, diminishing infant mortality, low public expenditure on health—only about 1.4% of gross domestic product (GDP) (World Bank 1994), as well as high government spending on public education, which led to secondary school enrolment for girls and boys increasing rapidly from 34% in 1970 to 58% in 1996. The impressive growth of the Malaysian economy has reduced poverty and income inequality. Table 1 shows Malaysia's reducing figure for income inequality distribution.

M. M. Billah, *Islamic Financial Products*,
https://doi.org/10.1007/978-3-030-17624-2_28

1.1 *Income Inequality Distribution*

The data in Table 1 use the Gini coefficient to calculate what caused the income inequality distribution among Malaysia's population to reduce by 4.2% between 1973 and 1989.

When talking about the low-income group, we always refer to the population in rural areas. However, in this new millennium, the low-income group can no longer be referred to as only comprising those who live in rural areas. Due to many pressure factors, those who live in urban areas can also be classified as a members of the low-income group, for example:

- Low income that is not enough to support their monthly expenditure.
- Prices of goods and services are much more expensive than in rural areas.
- High cost of living due to which housing rents, toll payments, parking charges and so on are high but the income received is low.
- Lack of education.
- A higher birth rate also forces some people who live in rural areas into the low-income group. Although the salary received is considered high, due to the large family size, purchasing power is still low.

In Malaysia, for instance, the low-income group is still a major concern for the government. To combat the effects of reduced earnings from lost employment or lower wages, the government is expanding income-earning opportunities for the poor by:

Table 1 Income inequality distribution

Economy	*Period*	*Measured variable*	*Gini coefficient (%)*	
			1973	*1989*
Malaysia	1973–1989	I/P	50.1	45.9

Source World Bank (1994)

- Giving low-interest loans to small farmers to increase food production;
- Expanding programmes run by a local NGO that provides small subsidized loans for income-generation in rural areas;
- Supporting a fund for loans to small- and medium-sized industries;
- Proposing an employer and employee exemption for contributions to the Employee Pension Fund for all new graduates hired;
- Establishing urban micro-credit programmes for hawkers, petty traders and small entrepreneurs; and,
- Building rural infrastructure to improve rural access to safe drinking water.

2 Low-Income Group

Low-income and middle-income economies are sometimes referred to as developing economies, according to World Bank classification. It is not intended to imply that all economies in the group are experiencing a similar level of development, or that other economies have reached a better or ultimate stage of development. Classification by income does not necessarily reflect development status. The World Bank divides economies according to the 2002 figures for gross national income per capita, calculated using the Atlas method:

- Low-income: $735 per month or less;
- Lower-middle income: $736–$2935 per month;
- Upper-middle income: $2936–$9075 per month; and
- High income: $9076 or more.

According to the Malaysian Economic Planning Unit, a monthly income of less than $1500 places that household in the low-income group; households earning $3500 and lower are classified as being in the middle-income group. The low-income group comprised 43.8% of the total population, and the middle-income group constituted 37%. These two groups represent 80.8% of society, which almost matches the types of houses planned to be built during the Plan period.

3 Determinants of the Low-Income Group

In determining the low-income group, the following factors are typically considered:

- Monetary income (this includes earnings, workers' compensation, social welfare, public assistance, pension or retirement income, interest, dividends, rents, royalties, income from estates, trusts, educational assistance, alimony, child support, assistance from outside the household, and other miscellaneous sources).
- Non-cash benefits (such as food stamps and housing subsidies).
- Income calculated before taxes.
- If a person lives with a family, the income of all family members is totalled. (Non-relatives, such as housemates, are not counted.)

Poverty thresholds are the dollar amounts used to determine poverty status. Each person or family is assigned one of 48 possible poverty thresholds. Thresholds vary according to:

- Size of the family;
- Ages of the members;
- Annual update for inflation using the Consumer Price Index.

Although the thresholds in some sense reflect families' needs, they are intended for use as a statistical yardstick, not as a complete description of what people and families need to live.

4 Poverty: An Islamic Perspective

Poverty has been a never-ending problem for the world, until today. One of the reasons behind the problem may be because of an unjust economic system practised in a country. History has proved that the system practised during the time of Jahiliyyah caused the poor to become poorer and the rich to become the richer, due to mankind's greed and selfishness through the practice of *riba'*. The same problems occur in the world today. *Riba'* or interest can be said to be among the major problems in economies. The world economic superpowers—for instance, the US government used its economic power to force the poor Islamic countries to be dependent on it through the *fiat* money system. The more the poor countries have to borrow from that country, the more that country gains and the more power it has over them.

Without a just economic system, poverty can never be solved. As Islam came with its full package for a perfect life, it provides guidelines for every aspect of life, including economic matters.

Islam seriously caters for the welfare of low-income earners (the poor and needy). This can be proved by the provision on *al-zakah* in an article of faith that obliged rich people to pay *al-zakah* from their surplus income to those who earn less. This responsibility cannot be taken for granted since, besides helping our poor Muslim brothers, *al-zakah* is a medium through which to purify our wealth. Allah (*SWT*) says:

> Take Sadaqah [alms] from their wealth in order to purify them and sanctify them with it, and invoke Allâh for them. Verily! Your invocations are a source of security for them, and Allâh is All-Hearer, All-Knower. (*Al-Qur'an*, *Al-Taubah*: 103)

In other verses, Allah (*SWT*) says:

> And strive hard in Allâh's Cause as you ought to strive [with sincerity and with all your efforts that His Name should be superior]. He has chosen you [to convey His Message of Islâmic Monotheism to mankind by inviting them to His religion, Islâm], and has not laid upon you in religion any hardship, it is the religion of your father Ibrahim [Abraham] [Islâmic Monotheism]. It is He [Allâh] who has named you Muslims both before and in this [*al-Qur'ân*, that the Messenger [Muhammad (*SAW*)] may be a witness over you and you be witnesses over mankind! So perform *As-Salât* [*Iqamat-as-Salât*], give *Zakât* and hold fast to Allâh [i.e. have confidence in Allâh, and depend upon Him in all your affairs]. He is your *Maula* (Patron, Lord, etc.), what an Excellent *Maula* (Patron, Lord, etc.) and what an Excellent Helper! (*Al-Qur'an*, *Al-Hajj*: 78)

> Verily, your *Walî* (Protector or Helper) is Allâh, His Messenger, and the believers,—those who perform *As-Salât* [*Iqâmat-as-Salât*], and give *Zakât*, and they bow down [submit themselves with obedience to Allâh in prayer]. (*Al-Qur'an*, *Al-Maidah*: 55)

> And in their properties there was the right of the beggar, and the *Mahrûm* [the poor person who does not ask of the others]. (*Al-Qur'an*, *Al-Zariyat*: 19)

As far as inequality among human beings in this world is concerned, *al-Qur'an* regards that it as the result of Divine will (Al-Maududi 1984). However, it is always Islam's objective to eliminate inequality in this world through the Divine teachings, which order everyone should receive equal distribution of wealth. That is why Islam condemns materialism and greed in mankind. *Al-Qur'an* says:

> The mutual rivalry for piling up of worldly things diverts you. Until you visit the graves [i.e. till you die]. Nay! You shall come to know! (*Al-Qur'an*: *Al-Takathur*: 1–3)

Al-Maududi (1984) stated in his book that one of the basic objectives of the Islamic system is to provide social justice and equitable distribution between the poor and rich. Muslims are not allowed to be greed and selfish. They have to realize that man is not an absolute owner of what we possess today. Allah (*SWT*) says in *al-Qur'an*:

> His is the kingdom of the heavens and the earth. It is He Who gives life and causes death; and He is Able to do all things. (*Al-Qur'an*, *Al-Hadid*: 2)

On the other hand, al-Qur'an also condemns a man who spends his wealth to secure luxury (Al-Maududi 1984). The Islamic way of living encouraged by Islam is to spend in a moderate way without wasting for the sake of extravagant spending and neglecting the fulfilling the rights of other Muslims who are suffering from poverty. Allah (*SWT*) says:

> And those, who, when they spend, are neither extravagant nor niggardly, but hold a medium [way] between those [extremes]. (*Al-Qur'an*, *Al-Furqan*: 67)

> But seek, with that [wealth] that Allâh has bestowed on you, the home of the Hereafter, and forget not your portion of legal enjoyment in this world, and do good as Allâh has been good to you, and seek not mischief in the land. Verily, Allâh likes not the *Mufsidûn* [those who commit great crimes and sins, oppressors, tyrants, mischief-makers, corrupters]. (*Al-Qur'an*, *Al-Qasas*: 77)

5 Islamic Financial System

The perfect Islamic economic system can be realized at a point when there need be no problem of poverty in a country. This perfect system was attained in the time of the caliphate of 'Umar ibn Abd Aziz (Al-Hasan 1999). In Islamic history, 'Umar was known to be a very humble and moderate caliph who succeeded in eliminating poverty until there were no more poor and needy that qualified to receive *al-zakah* except him. History proved that by implementing Islamic teaching and eliminating greed and selfishness, poverty can be abolished. Taxes imposed by governments are not the only way towards the equitable distribution of wealth. During the time of 'Umar (*RA*), it was proved that, without imposing any tax, he was able to return the rights of poor and needy and, at the same time, develop the country with just governance. In 'Umar's opinion, the abolishment of tax collections was based on the following verse:

> And O my people! Give full measure and weight in justice and reduce not the things that are due to the people, and do not commit mischief in the land, causing corruption. (*Al-Qur'an*, *Hud*: 85)

It may be concluded that poverty is not only a problem for the poor and needy. It could arise from spiritual greed and selfishness that ignore the rights of others. Inequality is a Divine will, the solution for which requires the spirit of brotherhood, cooperation, responsibility and respect between the rich and the poor so as to abolish it. If Muslims realize their responsibilities towards to others around them, there is bound to be a time when poverty will cease to exist.

6 How Does Islamic Finance Help to Grow the Low-Income Group Towards Sustainable Development Goals?

6.1 Al-Musharakah *(Venture Capital)*

Al-musharakah (or *shirkah*) is a valid contract in Islam to which the jurists of all schools (*mazhab*) of thought (*Shafie*, *Hanafi*, *Hambali* and *Maliki*) had agreed (Al-Harran, n.d.). Prophet Rasullullah (*SAW*) himself was also involved in business on the basis of *al-musharakah* and this

Structure of Musharakah:

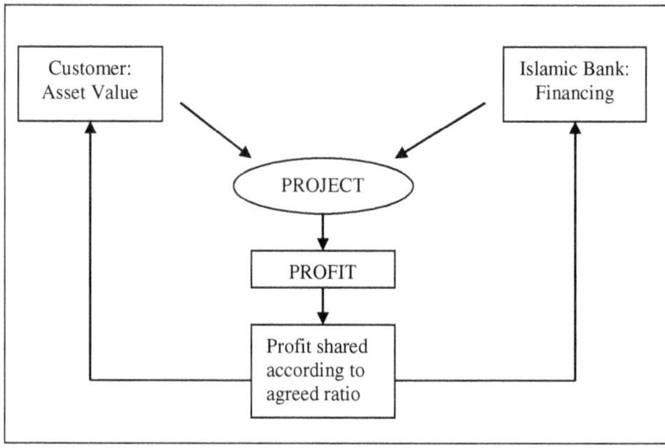

Fig. 1 *Al-musharakah* (venture capital) (*Source* Author's own)

practice already existed in Arab society, especially in commercial activities in Arabia. *Al-musharakah* (*shirkah*) can be simply defined as a form of partnership or joint venture where two or more persons agree to combine either their capital or their labour for the purpose of sharing the profits and business risk or liabilities (Fig. 1).

A bank and customer agree to cooperate in a project suggested by the customer to which both parties agree to contribute capital. The bank will offer the customer finance based on profit sharing, and will appoint the customer to manage the project. The bank, as a partner, is allowed to be involved in the project management. As a partner, the bank also has the right to advise his partner on how to manage the project properly, based on the bank's professional experience. The bank also needs to monitor the business project continually and follow up on the project from time to time to make sure the project will succeed and achieve the partners' objectives on time. If the project is profitable, then both parties will share the profit based on the proportions of capital that they contributed. Should any loss occur from the project, the loss will be shared based on the capital contributions of the partners.

6.2 Al-Mudharabah *(Profit and Loss Sharing)*

Al-mudharabah is similar in principle *to al-musharakah* (partnership) principle. The different between the two is that, under the principle of *mudharabah*, the capital is to be supplied by one party and the other contributes skills, labour and work. The capital provider is called the *rabb-al-mal* or *sahib ul mal* and the worker, who provides the entrepreneurship, is called the *mudharib*. Under the principle of *mudharabah*, a bank or financier provides finance and the client (a poor person) provides the labour, management and expertise. In terms of profit and loss sharing, the ratio will be predetermined so that if there is a profit, both parties will share it in pre-arranged proportions, let us say 70:30, 60:40. In this situation, the *rabb-al-mal* would receive either 30% or 40% from the profit and the *muhdarib* would receive 70% or 60% from the profit. Should a project incur a loss, the *rabb-al-mal* (financier) will bear the loss, and the *mudharib* will lose the effort and time that he put into the project. This system provides an entrepreneur more confidence and incentive to undertake a project that they think is profitable (Fig. 2).

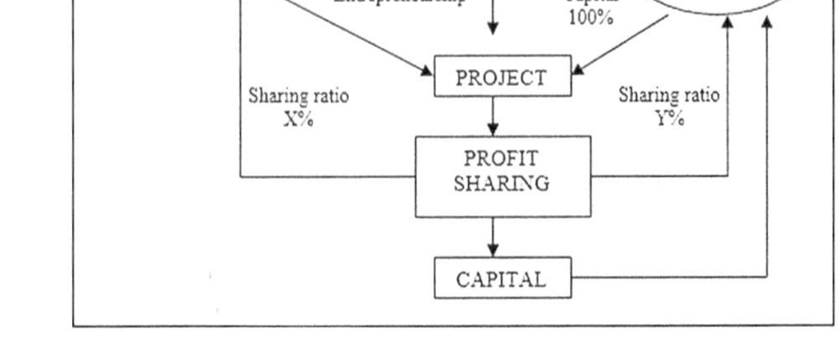

Fig. 2 *Al-mudharabah* (profit and loss sharing) (*Source* Author's own)

The financier, as *rabb-al-mal*, will provide the *mudharib* (entrepreneur) with capital for a particular project, let us say $100,000. The profit and loss ratio is 70:30. After three years, the project is worth $250,000 and net profit for this project is $150,000. The profit will be shared between the *rabb-al-mal* and the *mudharib*; the *rabb-al-mal* will receive $45,000 as a return and, at the same time, compensate the opportunity cost that the financier gave up. The *mudharib* will receive $105,000. In the event that the project has incurred a loss after the third year, the loss will be borne by the *rabb-al-mal* and the *mudharib* will have lost his time and effort.

We believe this system will trigger entrepreneurs to undertake any project that they think is profitable due to the incentive provided by this system, thereby growing the low-income group economy. We would like to support this statement with a comment quoted from *The Economist*:

> some people in the West have begun to find the idea attractive. It gives the provider of money a strong incentive to be sure he is doing something sensible with it. What a pity the West's banks did not have that incentive in so many of their lending decisions in the 1970s and 1980s. It also emphasizes the sharing of responsibility, by all the users of money. That helps to make the free market system more open; you might say more democratic. (A.L.M. A. G. 2003)

6.3 Al-Murabahah *(Cost Plus Financing)*

Al-murabaha can be defined as the sale of goods or commodities for the price at which a vendor has purchased them, with additional profit where the vendor must to disclose the marked-up price to the purchaser. *Al-murabaha* is a kind of business participation and it is permitted in Shari'ah. 'The legality of *Murabaha* is not questioned by any of the schools of law' (Al-Harran, n.d.) where *Shari'ah* assumes that the financier will buy the goods or commodity on behalf of his client and then sell it back to the client based on a marked-up price (A.L.M. A. G. 2003) (Fig. 3).

The customer or client will inform the bank of the details of goods that he intends to buy or import based on the terms and conditions agreed by both parties. The bank (financier) agrees to buy the goods on behalf of its customer and will use its own money to purchase the goods, subsequently selling the goods back to the customer at a marked-up price based on the principle of sales. After the supplier has received

Structure of Murabahah:

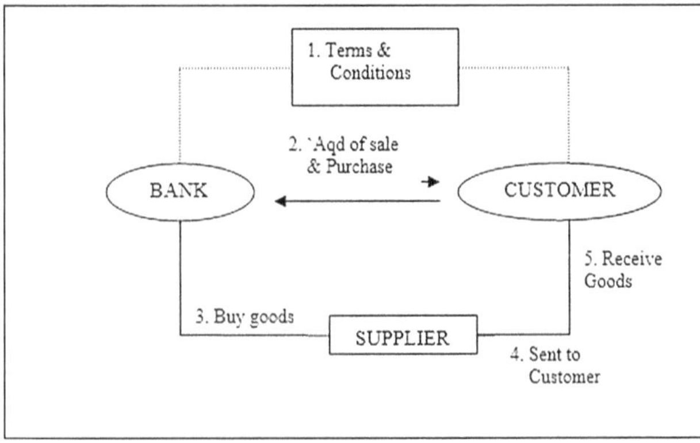

Fig. 3 *Al-murabahaha* (cost plus financing) (*Source* Author's own)

payment from the financier, the supplier will send the goods to the customer. In accordance with the terms of their agreement, the customer will pay off the loan from the bank either in a lump sum or on a deferred basis in instalments.

6.4 Al-Ijarah (Lease)

Al-ijarah is the agreement between two parties: the lessor and the lessee. The lessee agrees to pay a certain amount of rent to the lessor in return for which he will have the use of property. There are two categories of this type of arrangement: *ijarah wa iqtina* and *ijarah al-muntahia bittamlik*.

Ijarah wa iqtina is where the lessee agrees contract to buy the property that was leased out to him. *Ijarah al-muntahia bittamlik* is where the lessee does not intend to buy the property he leased. This means that the lessee will only pay a monthly or yearly rental to the lessor (Fig. 4).

Table 1 can best describe how Islamic banking can adopt this concept to help the low-income group. This principle can be applied to the banking system: the Islamic bank buys a product (e.g. a photocopy machine) from the supplier and then rents it to the customer. Following this principle, the ownership is in the Islamic bank's hand and the transfer of ownership from the bank to the customer will only take place at the end

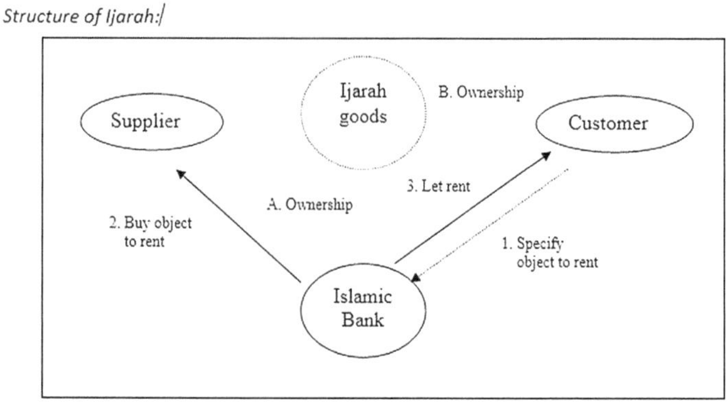

Fig. 4 *Al-ijarah* (lease) (*Source* Author's own)

of the *ijarah* contract (if it is an *ijarah wa iqtina* contract). Through the Islamic banks adopting the principle of *al-ijarah*, members of the low-income group can increase their productivity by being allowed to pay a monthly rent for a product that would cost them too much to buy. An increase in productivity would mean an increase in household income, too.

6.5 Al-Qard (Loan)

Al-qardhul hassan is an agreement between two parties; one party is the borrower and the other party is the lender. There is no collateral for the loan; if there were, it would be *al-rahn*, rather than *al-qard*. The principle behind *al-qardhul hassan* lending is it is a welfare loan made by someone who has no expectation of it being paid back to him in the future (unless the borrower gives the lender *hibbah*) and who wishes only to help the poor. This is consistent with the concept of brotherhood in the Islamic world (Fig. 5).

Under this principle, Islamic banks can help the low-income group by lending them money that they can invest in any project that, in return, gives them profit. The profit, however, does not belong to the bank; under *al-qardhul hassan*, the profit is for the borrower alone. However, the borrower may give the bank a portion of money as a *hibbah* (gift) in gratitude for the fact that the bank had initially enabled him to establish a project from which he would attain profit.

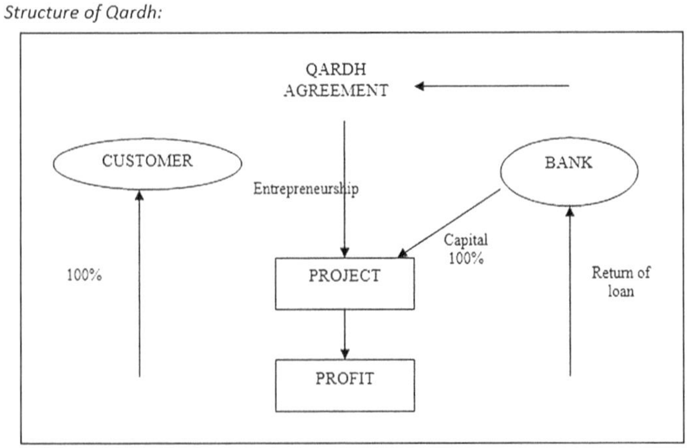

Fig. 5 *Al-qard* (loan) (*Source* Author's own)

6.6 *Method of Financing Through* Baitul Mal

Baitul mal has existed for a long time, since the days of the Prophet Rasullullah (*SAW*), with the objective of helping the poor (*fakir*) and needy groups such as orphans, *mualaf*, *al-riqab*, *al-gharimin*, *fi-sabilillah* and *ibnu sabil.* People who collect *zakah* for *baitul mal* called *amil.* They are two types of *zakah*: *zakah fitrah* and *Zakah* on properties. *Zakah* can be defined as a portion of property (*mal*) that one compulsorily spends on others. *Zakah* also can be defined as the process of purification and expansion (Radiah 2001). The *zakah* contribution is compulsory for every Muslim and it is one of the Islamic pillars. Command on *Zakah* contribution in *al-Qur'an* is as follows:

> And those in whose wealth there is a known right. For the beggar who asks, and for the unlucky who has lost his property and wealth, [and his means of living has been straitened]. (*Al-Qur'an*, *Al-Ma'ãrij*: 24–25)

> Take *Sadaqah* [alms] from their wealth in order to purify them and sanctify them with it, and invoke Allâh for them. Verily! Your invocations are a source of security for them, and Allâh is All-Hearer, All-Knower. (*Al-Qur'an*, *Al-Taubah*: 103)

These two verses explained that the role of *zakah* from the *Shari'ah* point of view is for purification purposes. There are two aspects that we have to purify:

- To purify the individual property where Allah had already determined the portion for everyone;
- To purify individual minds from negative characteristics such as selfishness, over-concern about *Ukhrawi* (worldly life) and with positive characteristics such as generosity and to tighten the relationship (*silaraturahmi*) among the *Ummah*.

6.7 *Distribution of Income*

Zakah can play a very important role and it seems to be an effective tool with which to ensure the equality of income distribution among the poor and the richest. *Zakah* can be used as a tool to close the income gap to a minimum level in society, where the richest will contribute a certain percentage of their income as *zakah* to help the poor. *Zakah* can be paid in the form of money or goods. Even though the individual *zakah* contributions are small, together they make a great difference to the poor. With the *zakah*, the poor can fulfil their daily needs and wants to ensure they can survive and live as comfortably as the others.

Zakah will always ensure the society wealth will channel or transfer to the society where the wealth is not own by a particular party or person only. Through the *zakah* system, properties owned by the richest will not only be used for their benefit, but also can be used as a channel to transfer the wealth the poor.

> What Allâh gave as booty [Fai'] to His Messenger [Muhammad *SAW*] from the people of the townships, it is for Allâh, His Messenger [Muhammad *SAW*], the kindred [of Messenger Muhammad *SAW*], the orphans, *Al-Masâkin* [the poor], and the wayfarer, in order that it may not become a fortune used by the rich among you. And whatsoever the Messenger [Muhammad *SAW*] gives you, take it, and whatsoever he forbids you, abstain [from it], and fear Allâh. Verily, Allâh is Severe in punishment. (*Al-Qur'an*, *Al-Hashr*: 7)

The continual *zakah* contribution from society will stimulate the country's economy due to the purchasing power of the low-income group increasing from time to time. When their purchasing power increases, this will cause the demand for goods to increase and, eventually, its will enhance or stimulate the country's economy. As a *zakah* contributor, the people will receive their rewards in the Hereafter and Allah will reward them in *dunia* with the increment in their income and profits due to the increment in productivity and national income. This process will ensure the *zakah* contribution from the society will increase from time to time. In addition to paying *zakah* to help the poor, the contributors hope that with the support of their small contribution today the poor, as receivers, will become contributors in the future.

7 Conclusion

Since the incident of 11 September 2001, there have been many negative perceptions of Muslim countries through which western countries have labelled Muslims as terrorists. The war between America, Britain and Iraq that followed this incident has generated even greater problems of poverty in Muslim countries. It is now the right time for Muslim governments to restructure their economic system so that Muslim countries do not have to depend on Western countries for funds. Restructuring the economic system is essential so that the government can find a sound solution to help the poor through Islamic methods of financing. Even though, from time to time, there are certain criticisms of Islamic methods of financing, we believe this system can be improved and become sound and stable in the future, and will accepted as a favourable method of financing not only among Muslim countries, but also in the western countries.

References

A.L.M. A. G. (2003). *Interest Free Commercial Banking: Islamic Banking*. Rev. ed. A. S. Noordeen.

Al-Harran, S. (n.d.). Musharakah Financing Model. *Journal of Islamic Banking and Finance Net.*

Al-Hasan, N. A. (1999). *10 Tokoh yang Mengubah Dunia, Pustaka Ilmi.* Selangor, Malaysia.

Al-Maududi, Abul A'la. (1984). *Economic System of Islam*. Islamic Publications Ltd. Lahore, Pakistan, p. 45.

Radiah, A. K. (2001). *Ekonomi Islam: Agihan Semula Pendapatan.* Zakah Univision Press Sdn. Bhd.

World Bank. (1994). Data Sources.

CHAPTER 29

Islamic Fin-Tech: Digital Financial Products

1 Introduction

Digital financial products are the financial services that are offered and delivered using the Internet. The Internet is a widely growing sector where new services and users are introduced every day and which allows immense savings in telecommunication costs for businesses. It also enables companies and customers to communicate with each other with greater efficiency and improved accuracy than paper-based systems allow. The Internet is typically available 24 hours each day, which makes it an attractive place for businesses as they can operate for long hours with relatively low running costs.

However, there are a number of security issues in providing online services; for example, authorized access, user and system identification, data integrity and confidentiality, and e-mail viruses, hacking, and denial of service attacks. To address these problems, several security solutions were developed such as authentication, digital signatures, encryption, protocol usage, gateways and firewalls.

Over time, the Internet has gone through drastic developments. It has expanded massively and the transactions it now handles include data and information that are crucial and could be sensitive for certain parties. Demands were made for cyberspace legislation when the era of e-commerce took off in the early 1990s. At this stage, any modification of the details of a transaction could lead to severe loss and damage for individuals and for organizations. This need for the provision of legal

M. M. Billah, *Islamic Financial Products*,
https://doi.org/10.1007/978-3-030-17624-2_29

jurisdiction and a system of enforcement applies to the many countries that are involved with the Internet in the globalization process. Without the appropriate bodies and systems in place to control Internet activity, countries and their companies are vulnerable to misconduct and unethical behaviour.

This technology also has an impact on Muslims and their chosen activities. This refers is to the *muamalah* (worldly activities) of Muslims, especially with regard to financial and business matters. Allah (*SWT*) has laid down certain rules and limitations on business transactions, such as buying and selling. As long as the parties involved in a transaction adhere to these rules and limitations, Islam can allow buying and selling online and other online financial activities. To resolve the issue of online transactions, we must refer to the primary sources (*Al-Qur'an* and *As-Sunnah*) and the secondary sources (*al-ijma'*, *al-qiyas* and *al-istehsan*).

2 Types of Digital Financial Product

The Internet has the potential to become a highly efficient electronic marketplace for goods and services. When payments are effected electronically, there is always a risk that organizations may resort to gathering information relating to individuals; for example, regarding the amounts that they have spent, the locations involved and the types of good purchased. Misuse of such information can give rise to serious breaches of personal privacy. If a payment system for the Internet is to receive widespread support, it must offer its users some form of protection against the gathering of such information. It should not be possible for an attacker to bypass a protection system, or falsely to obtain any data from the details of transactions. In this section, we discuss some of the online financial services—particularly, electronic payment systems.

3 Smart Authorization

Credit card fraud is a large and growing problem. Smart authorization was developed to solve this problem. It combines powerful fraud screening technology and credit card processing into a single easy to use service. Smart authorization is a solution to help combat credit card fraud and process a greater number of valid orders automatically without requiring recourse to a sophisticated fraud department, or the implementation or management of additional technical resources.

Many merchants rely on the card associations' address verification systems to detect credit card fraud. Unfortunately, these services are limited in their ability to identify fraudulent activity because they only analyse a very small amount of information. Smart authorization goes significantly further to identify more incidents of fraud with greater accuracy.

Smart authorization performs the following tests:

- *Address validation*: This verifies that both the card holder billing address and the shipping address are legitimate and deliverable.
- *Phone number validation*: This verifies that the customer's area code is legitimate and correctly matches the cardholder's address.
- *Data analysis*: This analyses customer data to determine whether there are any 'red flags', such as obscenities or nonsensical data that indicate potential fraud.
- *Negative file check*: This reviews each transaction against a file of historically 'bad' addresses and credit card numbers.

Smart authorization is a real-time credit card authorization service with effective built-in fraud screening technology.

3.1 Key Features

- Technology works with all major credit cards;
- Verification of both cardholder billing and shipping addresses;
- Verification of legitimate customer area code and address location match;
- Analysis of customer data for 'red flags', such as obscenities and nonsensical data;
- Review of each transaction against a file of historically 'bad' address and credit card numbers.

3.2 Key Benefits

- Authorizes credit cards rapidly, reliably, and securely;
- Effectively detects fraudulent orders in real time;
- Maximizes automatic acceptance of valid orders;
- Requires simple set-up and operation.

4 Credit Card Processing

This solution enables secure, reliable, real-time card processing in multiple currencies. Major cards and card types are supported across multiple processors, worldwide.

4.1 Key Features

- Exceptional real-time processing speed;
- Multiple card types, including bank cards, private label cards, cheque cards with Visa or MasterCard logo, American Express, non-PIN based debit cards, corporate cards and procurement cards;
- Multiple currencies, 120 worldwide;
- Multiple bank and processor connections, worldwide;
- Unparalleled processing scalability and security.

The following points illustrate how real-time, electronic credit card processing works using the CyberSource credit card processing service.

- Purchaser places order.
- Merchant securely transfers order information to CyberSource over the Internet using a secure, encrypted messaging protocol (SCMP).
- CyberSource receives order information and performs requested services.
- CyberSource formats the transaction details appropriately and securely routes the transaction authorization request through its payment gateway to the processor.
- The transaction is then routed to the issuing bank (purchaser's bank) to request transaction authorization.
- The transaction is authorized or declined by the issuing bank or card (e.g. American Express).
- CyberSource returns the message to the merchant.
- Issuing bank approves transfer of money to acquiring bank. The acquiring bank, in turn, credits the merchant's account.

4.2 Key Benefits

- Processes transactions at any time, regardless of the volume of traffic.
- Enables new sales channels quickly.

- Changes processor gateway connections as business needs evolve.
- Integrates easily with major commerce platforms, CRM, ERP and other business systems.
- Adds credit card fraud management. Uses smart authorization for basic protection, or investigates more robust fraud management strategies.
- Receives 24-hour support seven days a week from a skilled team of support engineers and operations professionals, and via access to an award-winning support centre.

5 Electronic Cheque Processing

Electronic cheque processing allows universities, government agencies, utilities, retailers and other businesses offer customers the option of using their chequing account to make payments online. Organizations can accept personal or business cheques online in real time. For example, using the Check-free option, the payer enters their user name and password in a Check-Free hosted window. The payer has an account with Check-Free (or registers at the time of their first purchase). Check-Free authenticates the payer and guarantees payment to the merchant. Real-time, electronic cheque processing using the CyberSource Payment Service works as follows:

- Payer (customer or bill payer) is prompted to authorize an electronic debit, enter a bank routing number (ABA#) and the account number.
- Merchant's sales system securely transfers order information to CyberSource over the Internet.
- CyberSource forwards bank routing number and account number to processor.
- The routing number and account number are validated, and the integrity of the account's chequing history is verified. Processor forwards status results (approved/declined) to CyberSource.
- CyberSource returns status message to merchant.
- If approved, CyberSource routes cheque for settlement through a processer to the automated clearinghouse system. Funds are deposited within approximately between one and three business days.

6 E-Dinars

E-dinars are for the electronic circulation of real gold dinars. They are backed at all times by the gold dinars physically held securely in the internationally renowned repository. E-dinars are integrated into a payment system that empowers people to use gold as money. The physical gold bullion backing e-dinar units is always equivalent to, or greater than, the value of all e-dinars in circulation. Transactions are executed globally using e-dinar units via the Internet. Account holders always have the option either to exchange their e-dinars into any major currency, or to redeem them and take physical possession of an equivalent amount in gold dinars. E-dinars have an unprecedented level of transparency. Total e-dinars in circulation in relation to the total gold bullion reserves held are provided in real time via the e-dinar examiner utility accessible from the e-dinar website, as well as statistics relating to the use and growth of the e-dinar system.

The physical bullion that comprises the value backing e-dinars must be insulated from physical, legal and political risks. The e-dinar Bullion Reserve Trust exists for the express purpose of holding bullion for the exclusive benefit of all e-dinar account holders, who collectively hold title. Gold is held free of any lien or encumbrance whatsoever and explicitly may not be attached to any entity.

An e-dinar unit is equivalent to 4.3 grams of pure gold, and is not allied to any other national currency unit. However, the e-dinar payment system allows spending to be expressed in terms of other national currencies. This means, for example, that a Singaporean can pay a Malaysian or an Indonesian the equivalent gold dinars (e-dinars) for a good or service as easily as if the price had been quoted in his own national currency. E-dinar payments clear instantaneously (with no chargeback risk), regardless of how large the payment and regardless of the geographic distance between the purchaser and merchant.

E-dinars are simply evidence of people using money. How do you presently use money? It is likely that any of the following activities would benefit from the increased soundness, security and efficiency afforded by e-dinars:

- E-commerce
- Business-to-business payments
- Point of service sales

- Person-to-person payments
- Payroll
- Bill payments
- Charitable donations
- Payment of *zakat*
- Monetary base of the economy.

The e-dinar system is absolutely free of any financial risk. There can be no debt or contingent liabilities associated with e-dinars. For this reason, e-gold Ltd. does not possess the national currency of any nation and has no bank accounts. The independent exchange services around the world support exchange between national currencies and e-dinars, accepting various remittance methods, including bank telegraphs, cheques, and money orders.

7 Financial Risk Versus Exchange Risk

E-dinars are entirely backed by a physical commodity, rather than by debt or other financial instruments; therefore, e-dinars are the only currency in the world free of financial risk. However, the absence of financial risk does not mean an absence of exchange rate risk. As with any currency, the value of other currencies will continually fluctuate relative to that of e-dinars.

However, precious metals—gold, in particular—enjoy a long history of monetary use worldwide. Thus, e-gold is ideally suited for international transactions.

8 Benefits in Digital Financial Products

8.1 Availability

The power of the Internet to reach millions of users around the world at any time has made the Internet the most powerful communications tool available. Marketers, consumers and business partners use the Web to collect information regarding products, services or companies with which they intend to do business. With just a click, people from around the world can buy or sell products within seconds. People are no longer required to queue up at a cashier's counter to purchase the products they have selected. They only have to choose the product they desire, key in their credit card number and the product is theirs. No more traffic jams, no more irritating inconvenience—one click will do it all.

8.2 Convenience

Business services online cover all aspects of buying, selling and exchanging information using the Internet as their medium. Business can be transacted anywhere at any time, 24 hours a day and seven days a week. One example of the online companies is Amazon.com, which has achieved tremendous success.

8.3 Efficiency

The Internet enables businesses to communicate with each other with greater efficiency and improved accuracy than that traditionally allowed by paper-based systems. Today, however, such activity is largely restricted to organizations that already know and trust each other. To exploit the potential market fully, there is a need in multi-third party trust, trust that can facilitate communication between parties that have never previously met or traded. This is the traditional business of the major banks, who offer to check business identities, credit ratings and to arrange various financial services. Once there is strong trust in the identity of an individual or legal entity, transactions can take place that are of higher value and greater risk.

9 Issues of Security in Digital Services

9.1 Confidentiality

Online financial management offers customers the benefit of convenience; however, wary customers cite the fear that their personal and financial information will be stolen as the primary reason for not conducting banking and other financial transactions online. For this reason, security concerns are a major obstacle to the rapid expansion of Internet-based banking and finance markets. For online business-to-business and business-to-customer financial services to be truly successful, customers must trust that the service has the necessary security systems in place to protect their data.

9.2 Authenticity

The first step to ensuring data security for any online financial transaction is to authenticate and verify the user's identity. This is done most effectively using two-factor authentication technologies; these require that a user proves their identity in two different ways. In the past, online identity authentication has typically been accomplished through some combination of things customers know: a user name, pin, account number and/or social security number. This system, however, has several inherent weaknesses, such as its lack of two-factor authentication technology.

9.3 Non-repudiation

Once a contract has been concluded online, there must be a sound system to ensure that the terms and conditions, and any other data are not altered. This is, again, a matter of securing the data from being spoofed (viewed by third party masquerading as an authentic body). To overcome security problems in online services, tools such as firewalls, anti-virus software, data encryption and authentication certification can be used.

10 Symmetric Key Encryption

The implementation of symmetric key encryption can be highly efficient, meaning that users do not experience any significant time delay as a result of the encryption and decryption. Symmetric key encryption also provides a degree of authentication, since information encrypted with one symmetric key cannot be decrypted with any other symmetric key.

Thus, as long as the symmetric key is kept secret by the two parties using it to encrypt communications, each party can be sure that it is communicating with the other as long as the decrypted messages continue to make sense. If anyone else discovers the key, it affects both confidentiality and authentication. A person with an unauthorized symmetric key not only can decrypt messages sent with that key, but can encrypt new messages and send them as though they came from one of the two parties who were originally using the key. Symmetric key encryption plays an important role in the secure sockets layer (SSL) protocol, which is widely used for authentication, tamper detection and encryption over transmission control protocol/internet protocol (TCP/IP) networks.

11 Public Key Encryption

The scheme shown above allows you freely to distribute a public key, and only you will be able to read data encrypted using this key. In general, to send encrypted data to someone, you encrypt the data with that person's public key, and the person receiving the encrypted data decrypts it with the corresponding private key. Compared with symmetric key encryption, public key encryption requires more computation and is therefore not always appropriate for large amounts of data. However, it is possible to use public key encryption to send a symmetric key, which can then be used to encrypt additional data. This is the approach used by the SSL protocol. It is also possible to reverse the procedure: data encrypted with your private key can be decrypted only with your public key. This would not be a desirable way to encrypt sensitive data, however, because it means that anyone with your public key, which is by definition published, could decrypt the data. Nevertheless, private key encryption is useful, because it means you can use your private key to sign data with your digital signature—an important requirement for e-commerce and other commercial applications of cryptography.

12 Using a Digital Signature to Validate Data Integrity

There are two items transferred to the recipient of signed data: the original data and the digital signature, which is basically a one-way hash (of the original data) that has been encrypted with the signatory's private key. To validate the integrity of the data, the receiving software first uses the signatory's public key to decrypt the hash. It then uses the same hashing algorithm that generated the original hash to generate a new one-way hash of the same data. Information about the hashing algorithm used is sent with the digital signature.

Finally, the receiving software compares the new hash against the original hash. If the two hashes match, the data has not changed since it was signed. If they do not match, the data may have been tampered with since it was signed, or the signature may have been created with a private key that does not correspond to the public key presented by the signatory. If the two hashes match, the recipient can be certain that the public key used to decrypt the digital signature corresponds to the private key used to create the digital signature. Confirming the identity of the signatory, however, also requires some way of confirming that the public key really belongs to a particular person or organization. The significance of a digital signature is comparable to the significance of a handwritten signature: once you have signed data, it is subsequently difficult to deny having done so—assuming that the private key has not been compromised or not within the owner's control. This quality of digital signatures provides a high degree of nonrepudiation; that is, digital signatures make it difficult for the signatory to deny having signed the data. In some situations, a digital signature may be as legally binding as a handwritten signature.

13 Digital Timestamping

A digital signature merely confirms that a particular private key was used to encrypt a document or, more probably, that document's message digest. A person could dishonestly try to repudiate a document by claiming that, at the time the signature was made, the key had been compromised. Alternatively, a person could sign a document even though the relevant key had already been revoked. Given the ease with which any time whatever can be associated with a file, there needs to be some other mechanism to tie such a signature to a particular moment in time. If the precise time that the signature was applied is known, then accurate judgement can be made as to its validity. Someone with a timestamped digital signature sends the message digest to a timestamping service, which then returns a timestamp certificate. Anyone who wants to verify the signing time then uses the certificate (along with an algorithm appropriate to and specified by the particular certificate) to verify that the time claimed is correct.

14 Certificate

A certificate is an electronic document used to identify an individual, a server, a company, or some other entity and to associate that identity with a public key. As with a driver's licence, a passport, or other commonly used personal IDs, a certificate provides generally recognized proof of a person's identity. Public key cryptography uses certificates to address the problem of impersonation.

15 Certification Authorities

Certification authorities are bodies that validate identities and issue certificates. They can be independent third parties or organizations running their own certificate-issuing server software (such as Netscape Certificate Server). The methods used to validate an identity vary depending on the policies of a given certification authority—just as the methods to validate other forms of identification vary depending on who is issuing the ID and the purpose for which it will be used. In general, before issuing a certificate, the certification authority must use its published verification procedures for that type of certificate to ensure that an entity requesting a certificate is, in fact, who it claims to be. The certificate issued by the certification authority binds a particular public key to the name of the entity the certificate identifies (such as the name of an employee or a server). Certificates help prevent the use of fake public keys for impersonation. Only the public key certified by the certificate will work with the corresponding private key possessed by the entity identified by the certificate. In addition to a public key, a certificate always includes the name of the entity it identifies, an expiration date, the name of the certification authority that issued the certificate, a serial number, and other information. Most importantly, a certificate always includes the digital signature of the issuing certification authority. The certification authority's digital signature allows the certificate to function as a letter of introduction for users who know and trust the certification authority but do not know the entity identified by the certificate.

16 The Secure Sockets Layer Protocol

The SSL protocol, which was originally developed by Netscape, is a set of rules governing server authentication, client authentication, and encrypted communication between servers and clients. SSL is widely used on the Internet, especially for interactions that involve exchanging confidential information such as credit card numbers. At the very least, SSL requires a server SSL certificate. As part of the initial 'handshake' process, the server presents its certificate to the client to authenticate the server's identity. The authentication process uses public key encryption and digital signatures to confirm that the server is, in fact, the server it claims to be. Once the server has been authenticated, the client and server use techniques of symmetric key encryption, which is very fast, to encrypt all the information they exchange for the remainder of the session and to detect any tampering that may have occurred. Servers may optionally be configured to require client authentication as well as server authentication. In this case, after server authentication is successfully completed, the client must also present its certificate to the server to authenticate the client's identity before the encrypted SSL session can be established.

The following simplified model shows how these different elements can work together to protect a message from casual scrutiny and ensure it is received with confidence that it has come from me, the authorized sender:

- I apply to my plain text message an appropriate process to generate a hash value to be used as a message digest.
- I encrypt this digest, but not the message itself, with my private key, confirming to anyone who can decrypt it with my public key that it came from me.
- I generate a one-time use secret key that I use to encrypt the text of the message.
- I encrypt this secret key using my recipient's public key and send the whole bundle to him.
- My addressee uses his private key to obtain the secret key, uses that in turn to decrypt the message, applies to it the same message digest algorithm and compares it with the message digest that he has decrypted using my public key.

Provided they match, he can be sure that the message came from me and is unchanged.

Although practical use may be more complex, this is fundamentally how the very widely used program Pretty Good Privacy (PGP), and certain other applications work, elegantly incorporating complementary elements that work together in an efficiently and rapidly.

Symmetric key methods are considerably faster than asymmetric methods and so are the preferred mechanisms for encrypting large chunks of text. A cipher such as DES (QV) will be at least 100 times faster than the asymmetric cipher RSA in software, and may be up to 10,000 times faster when implemented on specialist hardware. Secret key ciphers are most suitable for protecting data in a single-user or small group environment, typically through the use of passwords or passphrases. In practice, the most satisfactory methods for dispersed or large-scale practical use tend to combine both symmetric and asymmetric systems.

17 Secure Electronic Transmission

A secure electronic transmission (SET) protocol has been developed by the VISA and MasterCard banking consortia as a method for secure bank card transactions over open networks. It supports DES and triple DES for bulk data encryption and RSA for the public key encryption of the secret keys and the bank card numbers. Although SET is considered extremely secure, this very security leads to its being relatively slow. Further, users need properly issued digital certificates, meaning that it cannot be used in a simple ad hoc way, unlike the case with SSL or TLS. For these reasons, and for the added reason that many banks shift the risk and consequences of bank card security breaches onto their merchant customers, the take-up of SET has been much lower than was originally thought may be the case. However, there are indications that this is changing.

18 Secure HTTP

Secure HTTP (S-HTTP) is a security extension to HTTP, operating at the application layer. It is intended to provide privacy and authentication while supporting non-repudiation and allowing for a range of cryptographic algorithms and key management mechanisms to be used. RSA is typically used for the initial key negotiation, although keys may also be obtained from a Kerberos server that has been agreed on in advance of a session or generated in one session for use in the next.

19 *Shari'ah* Issues with Digital Financial Products and Services

Although the Internet and online transactions are new developments, there is some general guidance in Islam in dealing with online financial services. In fact, Islam is a complete source of guidance for mankind regardless of time when it is needed.

20 Reference to *Al-Qur'an* and *Al-Sunnah*

Under *Shari'ah*, legal enforcement is solely based on *al-Qur'an* and *al-Sunnah*. In the time of Rasulullah (*SAW*), whenever there was a problem or a situation arose, all the followers would consult Rasulullah (*SAW*) in order to find the exact solution to the problem. Rasulullah (*SAW*) would first refer to *al-Qur'an* to see whether there were any specific revelations pertaining to that matter. If there was no specific revelation, Rasulullah (*SAW*) would try to solve the problem through his remarkable knowledge and wisdom. This is what is known as the tacit approval of Rasulullah (*SAW*), otherwise famously known as *al-Sunnah*.

21 *Al-Ijma'*, *Al-Qiyas*, *Al-Istehsan* and *Masaleh al-Mursalah*

When Rasulullah (*SAW*) passed away and left the Muslim *Ummah*, the duty of solving any problems that may arise lay in the hands of all the companions of Rasulullah (*SAW*), since they has been the closest to Rasulullah (*SAW*) and the most trustworthy source available at that time. *Al-Quran* and *as-Sunnah* still remain the main sources for reference to find the right solution. After the era of the companions ended, the duty passed to the *Tabi'* and *Tabi'in*. However, at that time, as the result of rapid human development, many new problems arose that required very deep and specific reference, as *al-Qur'an* and *as-Sunnah* only provide general guidance in most cases. Due to this need, sources that are sufficiently trustworthy have been developed by the *ulama'*, but are still based on *al-Qur'an* and *as-Sunnah* as the main references. These new sources for solutions comprise *al-ijma'* (consciences of the *ulama'*), *al-qiyas* (legal reasoning), *al-istehsan* and *masaleh al-mursalah* (concern of public interest). Today, these sources are still used in order to apply *Shari'ah* ruling in civil applications.

The need for a *Shari'ah* response to online transactions has triggered the *ulama'* to come up with several ideas that could be supportive in dealing with Internet crimes. Among the ideas are:

- *Al-huquq* (rights)
- *Al-izzat, al-ikram wa al-hurmat* (dignity)
- *Al-amanat* (trust)
- *Al-salamat* (protection)

- *Al-hurriyah* (freedom)
- *Al-darar* (damage)
- *Al-gasab* (misappropriation)
- *Al-itlaf* (destruction)
- *Al-jinayat* (offence)
- *Al-mufawwadh* (authorization)
- *Al-aqd* (contract)
- *Al-sirr* (secrecy)
- *Al itlau'* (disclosure)

Also, the *ulama'* have defined the following limitations and procedures regarding online activities:

- Privacy
- Freedom
- Copyright
- Data protection
- Digital signature
- Computer crimes
- Liabilities and penalties.

Even though the sources are rather general, they are sufficient for the *ulama'* to proffer more specific and deep judicial reference. The financial service online can be seen, from an Islamic perspective, to depend on truthfulness, legitimate behaviour versus illegitimate behaviour, and publication ethics.

22 Al-Qur'an

22.1 The Choice of Infrastructure

> Ramadhan is the [month] in which was sent down in *al-Qur'an*, as a guide to mankind, also clear [Signs] for guidance and judgement [Between right and wrong]. So every one of you who is present [at his home] during that month should spend it in fasting, but if any one is ill, or on a journey, the prescribed period [should be made up] by days later. Allah intends every facility for you; He does not want to put you to difficulties. [He wants you] to complete the prescribed period, and to glorify Him in that He has guided you; and perchance ye shall be grateful. (Al-Baqarah 2: 185)

22.2 Freedom of Contract

O ye who believe! Fulfil [all] obligations. Lawful unto you [for food] are all four-footed animals, with the exceptions named: But animals of the chase are forbidden while ye are in the sacred precincts or in pilgrim garb: for Allah doth command according to His will and plan. (Al-Maidah 5: 1)

22.3 Protection of IP, Data Protection, Digital Signature and Certification

O ye who believe! Eat not up your property among yourselves in vanities: But let there be amongst you Traffic and trade by mutual good-will: Nor kill (or destroy) yourselves: for verily Allah hath been to you Most Merciful! (An-Nisa 4: 29)

23 Al-Sunnah

23.1 Prevention from Violation, Computer Crimes and Privacy

Muslim is brother of Muslim. He does not betray him, he does not lie to him and he does not insult him.

23.2 Fraud in Business Dealings

It is not permissible to sell an article without making everything clear nor is it permissible for anyone who knows (about its defects) to refrain from mentioning them. (Baihaqi)

24 Conclusion

It is essential to emphasize that whatever is good for mankind, whatever brings more benefits, is encouraged and permissible in Islam. Any regulation regarding the *halal* and *haram* in Islam is for the well-being of mankind. Therefore, any deal or transaction is permissible in Islam as long as it does not contradict the rules and limitations imposed by *al-Qur'an* and *al-Sunnah*. With regard to online financial services, it is permissible provided that there is a sound system that will prevent any theft and eliminate *gharar*.

CHAPTER 30

Islamic Cryptocurrency

1 Introduction

Even though a cryptocurrency management company is a digital financial platform operated in the borderless cyberspace, it should be required to be a registered company with a separate legal entity. Among the prerequisites of a *Shari'ah* (Islamic law) alternative cryptocurrency model is to be formalized under the company's rules, either onshore or offshore, as a separate legal entity. It should be managed based on an acceptable system, operational mechanism, standard planning and strategies, legitimate objectives and manifesto, documentation and manuals, policies and guidelines, all of which should comply to the *Shari'ah*, law and policies within *al-Maqasid al-Shari'ah* (Divine objectives) (Vejzagic and Smolo 2011). In this chapter, however, an attempt is made to analyse the operational mechanisms of cryptocurrency as they relate to *al-Maqasid al-Shari'ah*.

This concept for a strategic business model for a *Shari'ah* cryptocurrency management company was originated and initiated through intellectual discussions, writings and designations brought about by my humble initiative (Billah, n.d.) in early 2017. The idea has been shared among interested parties, presented in forums and written in periodicals, and promoted in the social media. Subsequently, some came forward to establish a *Shari'ah* compliant cryptocurrency model (Oziev and Yandiev 2017) capable of operating globally. A *Shari'ah* compliant cryptocurrency is a cryptocurrency platform initiated by cryptography

M. M. Billah, *Islamic Financial Products*,
https://doi.org/10.1007/978-3-030-17624-2_30

and operated based on block-chain technology. Its objectives and operational mechanisms shall be in conformity with the *Shari'ah* principles and be approved by the *Shari'ah* board before the operation takes place. It should be treated as a commercial entity, offering cryptocurrency globally based on *Shari'ah* standards (*Shari'ah* compliant) within *al-Maqasid al-Shari'ah*. For a *Shari'ah* cryptocurrency, it is a prerequisite to ensure that the entity and its total operations are backed by valued assets. In other word, a *Shari'ah* cryptocurrency should be an asset-backed operation within the ambit of *Shari'ah*.

Cryptocurrency generally means virtual, digital or cyber complementary form of money with an intrinsic commercial value that takes the form of tokens or coins. Some digital currencies have ventured into the physical world with debit or credit cards or other such instruments; the large majority remains entirely intangible or has a virtual existence in cyberspace. The term 'crypto' with regard to digital currencies refers to sophisticated cryptography, which allows for a particular e-coin or e-token to be generated, stored, and typically transacted anonymously, securely and smartly by digital encryption. The essence of the 'crypto' feature of these digital currencies is a common undertaking to decentralize; all digital currencies are typically designed and developed as a specific hash code by teams who build in mechanisms for issuance through a process called 'mining', in most cases, and other virtual devices. In contemporary practice, digital currencies are commonly designed so as to be free from government manipulation, control and influence, and such digital currencies have grown rapidly, with global market appreciation. Digital currencies, which are modelled after the bitcoin, are collectively known as altcoins and have tried to establish a presence in the cyber market as hybrid versions of bitcoin. Some of those digital currencies are easier to be managed than bitcoin, which is inclined to complexity. Today, there are more than 1600 digital currencies in existence, offered in cyberspace through block-chain technology (*Fintechnews*, Singapore, 1 November 2017), and many of those tokens or coins are popular in their micro-capacities or for their attributes among the virtual communities of investors and traders in cyber space (https://www.investopedia.com/tech/most-important-DigitalCurrencies-other-than-bitcoin).

A *Shari'ah* alternative cryptocurrency is a *Shari'ah* compliant cryptocurrency activated by the application of cryptography through block-chain technology within the ambit of *al-Maqasid al-Shari'ah* (Divine objectives). The fundamental dichotomy between conventional practices and the *Shari'ah* alternative model is the core objectives and the mechanisms adapted. In a *Shari'ah* cryptocurrency, its block-chain system, technology, model, objective, operational mechanisms, technicalities, culture, functions and all activities must be in total compliance with *Shari'ah* principles (*Shari'ah* standards), which should regularly be advised by the board of advisors, screened through and duly approved by the *Shari'ah* advisory board of the company before any implementation takes place.

Cryptocurrency using block-chain technology is a cyberspace economic revolution in the twenty-first century. Numerous players are in the market globally to offer different categories of digital currency but there are many shortcomings, such as the lack of regulatory support, poor strategic planning, uncertainty. Also most of such offerings have no backing assets but rely on virtual assumption. A *Shari'ah* model of cryptocurrency is a *Shari'ah* compliant cryptocurrency model is timely in filling the gap caused by the ongoing shortcomings in the cryptocurrency market. A *Shari'ah* cryptocurrency model (Oziev and Yandiev 2017) is thus backed by valued assets and operated based on valued assets (coins or tokens). Transactions are based on *Shari'ah* instruments such as *al-bay wa al-shira'* (trading), *al-musharakah* (partnership), *al-mudharabah* (co-partnership), *al-shuftaja* (exchange), *bai' al-sarf* (money exchange), *al-wakalah* (agency), *al-ujrah* (service charge), *al-ju'alah* (reward), *al-wadiyah* (deposit), *al-amanah* (trust), *al-tabarru'at* (charity) and *zakat* (alms). The *Shari'ah* cryptocurrency model is concerned for humanitarian well-being, regulated by the standard *Shari'ah* principles, opposed to uncertainty (*gharar*) in any component and in favour of the liberty to enjoy legitimate (*Shari'ah*) investment returns. Thus, the *Shari'ah* cryptocurrency model has greater opportunity to attract the global cryptocurrency market by offering a sustainable existence in the emergence of block-chain technology.

The prime objective of a *Shari'ah* cryptocurrency model is to create an enterprising entrepreneur-based community worldwide through a *Shari'ah* cryptocurrency management company and global participation therein. This may ultimately fight poverty, joblessness, domestic economic crisis and world eco-catastrophe. A *Shari'ah* cryptocurrency management company will be universally welcoming and encouraging, and will benefit all mankind regardless of religion, race, status, gender, colour or even nationality. Its operation is not only concerned with money making; 2.5% of each transaction will be deducted for humanitarian or charitable causes based on the holistic principles of *zakat*. Additionally, it is also recommended that all gross income in every transaction, account, management fee, activities, income and services will be subject to a reasonable deduction as *al-tabarru'at* (charity) for the noble causes of charity and solidarity.

The basic features of the *Shari'ah* cryptocurrency model is that it will be operated based on the *Shari'ah* standards (compliant with the *Shari'ah* principles), closely supervised and duly screened by a qualified *Shari'ah* advisory board, and advised by a team of scholars as a board of advisors. The management of the *Shari'ah* cryptocurrency operation will be strictly obliged to abide by the standard *Shari'ah* guidelines and ethical standards in all its activities, policies and functions within the rules of *al-Maqasid al-Shari'ah* (Divine objectives). All investors (coin or token holders) will be protected by transparent transactions and are formalized based on the *Shari'ah* justified doctrines and mechanisms.

A *Shari'ah* cryptocurrency model will be based on the following parameters and philosophy:

- The model will be operated based on the principles of *Shari'ah* (*Shari'ah* standards).
- The total operation of the model will be facilitated by a *Shari'ah* compliant hybrid structure.
- The model will evolve as both an asset-backed and an asset-based operation within the *Shari'ah* frameworks.
- The company will be backed by valued assets equivalent, at least, to the value of the initial coin offering (ICO), and its products and services (business operations) will be based on assets (valued coins or tokens).
- The total operation shall be facilitated by *Shari'ah* justified instruments and Divine principles such as *al-mudarabah* (co-partnership), *al-musharakah* (partnership or joint-venture), *al-shuftaja* (exchange), *bai' al-sarf* (money exchange), *al-wakalah* (agency with commission), *al-wadiyah* (deposit), *al-ju'alah* (reward or service charge), *al-amanah* (trust), *al-ujarah* (service charge), *al-tabarru'at* (donation) and *al-zakat* (alms or compulsory tax).

The structure of a *Shari'ah* model is thus a *Shari'ah* compliant hybrid platform of cryptocurrency backed by valued assets.

The operation of a *Shari'ah* cryptocurrency model will be facilitated and duly operated mainly based on *Shari'ah* principles with the concept of 'issuer coin or token' or of an 'exchange platform'. An operation based on 'issuer coin or token' shall primarily be executed by trading platform and decentralized direct (one-to-one) buying and selling (*bai' wa al-shira'*) mechanisms. However, exceptionally, it can be operated on an exchange platform based on a *Shari'ah* hybrid mechanism, facilitated by the doctrines of *al-shuftaza* (exchange), *bai' al-sarf* (money exchange), *al-hewalah* (transfer), *al-kafalah* (custodianship), *al-amanah* (trust), *al-wakalah* (agency by commission), *al-ju'alah* (reward for services) and *al-ujrah* (service charge) within the *Shari'ah* frameworks.

2 Objectives

Among the objectives of a *Shari'ah* cryptocurrency are:

- Offering and managing *Shari'ah* cryptocurrency with the rules of *Shari'ah* compliance.
- To create a legitimate income opportunity for all mankind (regardless of religion, race, status, gender, colour or nationality) within *al-Maqasid al-Shari'ah*.
- To create a micro-investment platform for all mankind with a universal holistic approach (regardless of religion, race, status, gender, colour or nationality) through a *Shari'ah* cryptocurrency management company.
- To create economic well-being for all mankind through a *Shari'ah* cryptocurrency platform based on the holistic principles of mutual cooperation and solidarity.
- To care about the poor and helpless by segregating part of the income of the *Shari'ah* cryptocurrency operation within the Divine principles of humanity (Bangash 2018).

3 Governing Principles

The governing principles of a *Shari'ah* cryptocurrency are as follows:

- All levels of products and services of a *Shari'ah* cryptocurrency management company will be designed, regulated and operated in accordance with the principles of *Shari'ah*.
- All activities, policies, technicalities and mechanisms of a *Shari'ah* cryptocurrency management company shall conform to *Shari'ah* standards and be within *al-Maqasid al-Shari'ah*.

- All activities, policies, technicalities, mechanisms, products and services of a *Shari'ah* cryptocurrency will be closely monitored, screened and approved by the *Shari'ah* advisory board of a *Shari'ah* cryptocurrency management company to ensure that complete *Shari'ah* compliance (Noordin 2018) is strictly observed.
- The *Shari'ah* cryptocurrency management company's board of advisors shall also play a vital role in advising the company to ensure that its policies, products and services conform to the *Shari'ah* principles within *al-Maqasid al-Shari'ah*.
- A *Shari'ah* cryptocurrency management company shall also strictly observe and duly comply with other applicable national or international laws and policies (Ahmat and Bashir 2017).

4 Ethical Principles

The ethical principles of a *Shari'ah* cryptocurrency management company are that:

- All levels of decision-makers, advisors, operators and facilitators of a *Shari'ah* cryptocurrency management company should observe the principles of *Shari'ah* (*Shari'ah* standards) in their activities with relation to a *Shari'ah* cryptocurrency management company that seeks to pursue the doctrines of *al-Maqasid al-Shari'ah*.
- Anyone involved in a *Shari'ah* cryptocurrency management company, whether directly or indirectly, should observe the Divine principles of honesty, transparency, rights and obligations while strictly opposing and avoiding an unlawful culture or unethical gain at the expense of others.
- None of the parties involved in a *Shari'ah* cryptocurrency management company, whether directly or indirectly, should be allowed to practice undue influence, misrepresentation, duress, malpractice, falsehood, manipulation, selfishness, deceit or any other unethical action.

5 Model and Structure

A *Shari'ah* cryptocurrency management company should be based on the following model and structure:

- A *Shari'ah* cryptocurrency management company is a cryptocurrency model based on the principles of *Shari'ah* (*Shari'ah* standards).
- The entire operation of a *Shari'ah* cryptocurrency management company is a *Shari'ah* compliant hybrid model.
- A *Shari'ah* cryptocurrency management company should evolve as both an asset-backed and an asset-based operation within the *Shari'ah* frameworks.
- The *Shari'ah* cryptocurrency management company should be backed by valued assets, while its products and services (business operations) are based on assets (valued coins/tokens).
- A *Shari'ah* cryptocurrency management company's total operation should be facilitated by *Shari'ah* justified instruments and Divine principles, such as *al-mudarabah* (co-partnership), *al-musharakah* (partnership or joint-venture), *al-shuftaja* (exchange), *bai' al-sarf* (money exchange), *al-wakalah* (agency with commission), *al-wadiyah* (deposit), *al-ju'alah* (reward or service charge), *al-amanah* (trust), *al-ijarah* (charge), *al-tabarru'at* (donation) and *al-zakat* (alms).
- The structure of a *Shari'ah* cryptocurrency management company is, thus, a *Shari'ah* hybrid platform for cryptocurrency backed by valued assets, and facilitated and duly operated mainly based on the *Shari'ah* principles of *al-musharakah* and others (shared profit) and *al-wakalah* (agency with service charge).
- A *Shari'ah* cryptocurrency operation should be based on an 'issuer coin or token' by trading platform by decentralized direct (one-to-one) buying and selling (*bai' wa al-shira'*).
- A *Shari'ah* cryptocurrency management company can also be operated through an exchange platform based on a *Shari'ah* hybrid mechanism, facilitated by the doctrines of *al-shuftaja* (exchange), *bai' al-sarf* (money exchange), *al-hewalah* (transfer), *al-kafalah* (custodianship), *al-amanah* (trust), *al-wakalah* (agency by commission), *al-ju'alah* (reward for services) and *al-ujrah* (service charge) within the *Shari'ah* frameworks.

6 Operational Mechanism

The operational mechanisms of a *Shari'ah* cryptocurrency management company are as follows:

- The operation adapts its prime operational tool based on a valued coin or token offering through the issuance of the ICO justified and duly screened in accordance with the general principles of *Shari'ah* and Divine ethical standards.
- The offered coins or tokens through the ICO may also be effectively transacted (buying/selling) further in the secondary market within the *Shari'ah* ambit.
- A *Shari'ah* cryptocurrency management company may also provide a platform for international *Waqf* cooperation and contribution through cryptocurrency.

7 Technological Model

- The products and services under a *Shari'ah* cryptocurrency management company (*Shari'ah* cryptocurrency in coins or tokens) shall be operated based on *Shari'ah* screened block-chain technology.
- Block-chain technology is a cyberspace platform provider with a reliable block-chain solution with which to systemize, manage, operate and perform all the activities of a *Shari'ah* cryptocurrency management company that seeks to pursue the doctrines of *al-Maqasid al-Shari'ah*.
- The block-chain technology for a *Shari'ah* cryptocurrency management company should be closely monitored by *Shari'ah* experts to ensure all technological support for a *Shari'ah* cryptocurrency platform are *Shari'ah* compliant (to *Shari'ah* standarda) (Alexandre 2018).

8 Scope and Limitations

The scope and limitations of a *Shari'ah* cryptocurrency management company are that:

- A *Shari'ah* cryptocurrency management company should be operated within the principles of *al-Maqasid al-Shari'ah*.
- All of a *Shari'ah* cryptocurrency management company's policies, activities, structures, systems, products and services should conform to *Shari'ah* principles.
- The general culture should be in compliance with the Divine ethical standards and *Shari'ah* principles.

9 Products and Services

The products and services of a *Shari'ah* cryptocurrency management company are:

- *Halal* cryptocurrency with valued coins or tokens commercialized by means of a trading platform using block-chain technology, or an exchange platform, or through halving excise or mark-up through the global payment innovation.
- In order to create a cashless society, a cashless payment through a cryptocurrency model may be introduced to ease society's day-to-day payment activities. A *Shari'ah* cryptocurrency management company offers a hybrid cashless or card-less digital debit account backed by cryptocurrency to be maintained on a block-chain platform and be operated by a mobile phone, iPad or laptop application such as is currently available in China. This system may have dual benefits:
  - Having an investment return through currency inflation;
  - Creating a cashless purchasing power by simply maintaining an image (barcode) with a digital credit capacity appearing on the mobile, iPad or laptop screen that enables the creditor or seller to appreciate the payment by digital swap.
- *Waqf* management through cryptocurrency.
- Investment through *Shari'ah* cryptocurrency.
- Trading platform through *Shari'ah* cryptocurrency.
- Humanitarian concern expressed through a *Shari'ah* cryptocurrency management company.
- A global *tabarru'at* (charity) foundation through a *Shari'ah* cryptocurrency management company.

10 Backing Assets

The company, its products and services shall be backed by valued assets. Thus, a certified proof of product shall be a prerequisite to ensure that the total operation of a *Shari'ah* cryptocurrency management company is backed by commercially valued assets. Backing assets for a *Shari'ah* cryptocurrency management company and its operation refers to a certified proof of product carrying the commercial value of a legitimate asset, product, property, intellectual property, IT, solution, program or such other matters as are recognized by *Shari'ah* principles. The proof of product shall carry the value of, at least, the equivalent of the ICO. For the valid operation of a *Shari'ah* cryptocurrency, the backing assets are a prerequisite to ensure that the total products and services or business activities of the entity are an asset-backed operation. The backing assets should only be treated as the backing assets of the company, its activities, products and services. The backing assets are simply for the purpose of supporting and facilitating the company's capacity.

11 Decision-Makers

The decision-making in a *Shari'ah* cryptocurrency management company shall be vested in the following authorities:

- Management team (general decision).
- *Shari'ah* advisory board (*Shari'ah* compliance, screening and approval).
- In-house advisor or consultant (technical advice).
- Board of advisors (overall advice).

12 *Shari'ah* Advisory Board

The *Shari'ah* advisory board of a *Shari'ah* cryptocurrency management company shall comprise qualified *Shari'ah* scholars, including a *Mufti*, *Shari'ah* judge, *Shari'ah* lawyer, Islamic finance expert, Islamic finance researcher, *Shari'ah* scholars in cryptocurrency and such other advisors as are necessary.

Among the functions of the *Shari'ah* advisory board are:

- To advise, supervise, monitor and approve a *Shari'ah* cryptocurrency management company and all its policies, systems, activities, operations and mechanisms to ensure the company and its operation are generally compliant with *Shari'ah* principles.
- The *Shari'ah* advisory board shall also screen and approve all activities of the *Shari'ah* cryptocurrency management company to ensure all are compliant with the *Shari'ah* principles (*Shari'ah* standards).
- The *Shari'ah* advisory board shall also contribute to the *Shari'ah* cryptocurrency management company by training its employees and also the public in accordance with the required *Shari'ah* compliant cryptocurrency model (Wardhani 2012).

13 Board of Advisors

The board of advisors of a *Shari'ah* cryptocurrency management company may comprise renowned scholars including academics, financial experts, business operators and other key people in the Islamic financial industry.

Among the functions of the board of advisors are:

- To advise the *Shari'ah* cryptocurrency management company to ensure that the company is moving forward dynamically within the doctrines of *al-Maqasid al-Shari'ah.*
- To contribute to a *Shari'ah* cryptocurrency management company by training its employees and also the public in accordance with the required *Shari'ah* compliant cryptocurrency model.

14 The Management Company

A *Shari'ah* cryptocurrency management company should be managed by a qualified management team that applies business dynamism, quality management and smart strategies within the holistic spirit of *Shari'ah* ethical principles. The management team shall be headed by a well-qualified managing director or chief executive director with a corporate attitude who is also an Islamic finance expert.

15 The Road Map of a *Shari'ah* Cryptocurrency Operation

For the establishment and operation of a *halal* cryptocurrency model capable of achieving effective results, the road map present in Table 1 may be adapted, provided that the full range of activities on the road map comply with the spirit of *al-Maqasid al-Shari'ah* (Divine objectives).

16 The Public Statement

In every operation of a *Shari'ah* compliant cryptocurrency, it is recommended that a public statement be made through social media, soft-launching or organizing a summit prior to the actual operation taking place with an ICO, or initial product offering, or initial token offering. A model of such a public statement could take the following form:

Table 1 The road map of a *Shari'ah* cryptocurrency operation

Tasks (Concurrent)	*Details*	*Timeframe (Concurrent)*	*Action (Concurrent)*
Brain-child idea	Background, paradigm, objectives, structure, strategies, mission and vision	15 days	Initiator
Model sharing	Model in reality	7 days	
Team building	Brain-sto$ing key persons	5 days	
Ownership/decision makers	Identification and confirmation of the owners (Management team)	3 days	
Corporate agreement	Formalization by agreement among the proposed Management team (owners) and duly notarization	3 days	Management team (BoD)
Team selection	Management team, Shari'ah Advisory Board (SAB), Board of Advisers (BoA), Technical Board, Consultant and Marketing team	3 days	
Ad-hock management team	A team of management to be assigned with primary tasks to be carried out till the official appointment is out	3 days	
Corporate formality	Licensing/registration of a company with separate legal entity based either in offshore or onshore	30 days	Management
Corporate office	Setting up, documentations and readiness	30 days	
Corporate bank accounts	A company account plus an additional account for each BoD shall be opened and duly maintained with any established bank	3 days	
Corporate profile	The profile shall include details about the company, its system, principles, objectives, planning, management and operation	21 days	
Mission and vision	Objectives within ***Maqasid al-Shari'ah***	2 days	
Planning	5 years action plan within ***Maqasid al-Shari'ah***	15 days	
Strategies	Corporate strategies complying with the *Shari'ah* principles	15 days	
Official website	Website with details of components and activities besides objectives and mechanisms to be established and duly maintained through own registered domain	30 days	
Policies and guidelines	Detail policies and guidelines to be established within the spirit of ***Maqasid*** *al-Shari'ah*	30 days	
Appointments	Formalization of all levels of appointments	5 days	BoD and management
Backing asset	Confirmation of the valued backing asset (with certified Proof of Property (POP) in creating the corporate capital capacity to support the total operation with real asset (POP) with intrinsic value, in opposing to the conceptual support by virtual asset (extrinsic value)	7 days	POP provider

Tasks (Concurrent)	*Details*	*Timeframe (Concurrent)*	*Action (Concurrent)*
Technology provider	Identification and confirmation of a block-chain technology provider	7 days	Block-chain
Forming technical specification	Instrumental and technological preparation for the block-chain platform	10 days	
Design draft	Block-chain mind-mapping	7 days	
Block-chain/technology platform	Designing and establishment of the model and the operational platform in the block-chain technology	45 days	
Technology platform/halal screening	Establishment of the block-chain platform and duly screened through with *Halal* compliance	5 days	Block-chain and SAB
System	Designation of the system of operation	30 days	Block-chain
System/halal screening	Establishment of the system of operation and duly screened through with Halal compliance	5 days	Block-chain and SAB
Testing	Block-chain technology	5 days	Technology team
	Block-chain platform	5 days	
	System of operation	5 days	
	Management structure	5 days	Management
	Operation in action	5 days	
	Marketing mechanisms	5 days	Marketing team
	Market	5 days	
White chapter	Preparation of the standard 'White Chapter'	3 days	Management
SAB approval page	Approval of the system and model by the *Shari'ah* Advisor Board (SAB) in writing and duly signed by the SAB chai$an on behalf of the board in confirming it with the *Shari'ah* compliance	2 days	SAB
BOA approval page	Approval of the system and model by the Board of Advisors (BoA) in writing and duly signed by the BoA chai$an on behalf of the Board in confirming it within the spirit of ***Maqasid al-Shari'ah***	2 days	BoA
Pre-ICO-Demo	Prior to the actual initial offering of coin (IOC) takes place, a pre-ICO-demo is recommended so to ensure the actual ICO will go through smoothly without any undesirable obstacle	5 days	Block-chain and operating team
ICO-full scale development	Preparation for the full scale of ICO	10 days	

(continued)

Table 1 (continued)

Tasks (Concurrent)	*Details*	*Timeframe (Concurrent)*	*Action (Concurrent)*
Soft launching	For the pre-ICO public awareness of the product, a soft-launching is recommended to be organized by inviting selected key individuals, entrepreneurs, corporate entities, regulators, professionals and media	2 days	Operating and marketing teams
Traditional summit	An effective gathering shall be organized prior to the ICO is required, which shall comprise of potential purchasing (Coin) groups. The summit shall focus on various aspects of the ready coin, benefits and opportunities besides satisfactory Q and A sessions	2 days	
Public statement	A public statement shall be prepared and duly published in the social media in particular, providing the summary of the product (coin), securities, mechanisms, benefits and opportunities	1 day	Management
Media summit	A media summit is more effective as compared to what a traditional one is? At least seven days prior to the actual ICO takes place a media summit is strongly recommended to be organized. The summit shall comprise of at least five to ten media groups (traditional or social) from each country of the targeted market zones. The summit shall provide fundamental ideas of the coin, benefits, opportunities, securities and other related aspects. The media group shall publish the summit message in the respective media at least three days prior to the ICO takes place. This may spread the news of the ICO across the world and thus, may create a sound market to participate in the ICO effectively	3 days	Marketing team
ICO (Phase I)	30% as the initial kick-off by creating furtherance market demand	30 days	Operating team
ICO (Phase II)	35% (only after selling out of Phase I)	30 days	
ICO (Phase III)	45% (only after selling out of Phase II)	30 days	
Real-time transaction in Seconds (trading in the block-chain platform)	Real transactions by trading activities among the coin owners shall be continued in the block-chain platform	30 days	Market and investors

Source Author's own

A *Shari'ah* cryptocurrency management company offers a *Shari'ah* compliant cryptocurrency. It is backed by valued assets with legal authentic proof of property. Its establishment, policies, management, operation, activities and general culture are compliant with the spirit of *Shari'ah* standards and within the doctrines of *al-Maqasid al-Shari'ah*.

Its block-chain technology, ledger system and operational mechanisms are designed as a *Shari'ah* hybrid model based on the *Shari'ah* doctrines of *silsalat al-katl*, *al-ta'awun*, *al-musharakah*, *al-bai' wa al-shira'*, *al-wakalah*, *al-fudhuli*, *al-ju'alah* and *al-tabarru'at*.

All activities of a *Shari'ah* cryptocurrency management company are generally screened by experts in Islamic finance and a *Shari'ah* cryptocurrency expert, supervised by a *Shari'ah* advisory board comprising a team of renowned *Shari'ah* scholars and further advised by a board of advisers comprising a group of academics, economists and industrialists to ensure the activities and operation of a *Shari'ah* cryptocurrency management company are compliant with the spirit of *Shari'ah* standards.

Among the prime objectives of a *Shari'ah* cryptocurrency management company are to create economic and entrepreneurial opportunities for all mankind (particularly for those who are less fortunate), universally embracing all (regardless of religion, colour, status, gender or nationality) within the holistic spirit of *al-Maqasid al-Shari'ah*.

It is also the strict policy of a *Shari'ah* cryptocurrency management company that there be special provision to segregate part of all levels of its income for humanitarian causes within the broad principles of *zakat* and *al-tabarru'at*.

17 The White Paper

A white paper for a *halal* cryptocurrency operation may include the following information:

17.1 Introduction to Shari'ah *Coin*

17.1.1 The Shari'ah *Coin*

This is a *Shari'ah* compliant (*Shari'ah*) cryptocurrency management company platform with global prospects. Its block-chain system, technology, model, objective, operational mechanisms, technicalities, culture and all its activities shall be in total compliance with *Shari'ah* principles (*Shari'ah* standards), which shall regularly be advised by the company's board of advisors, screened by the Company's in-house advisor prior to the approval of the *Shari'ah* advisory board of the company and thereafter shall be operated or executed globally.

17.1.2 Emerging of Block-Chain

Cryptocurrency achieved through block-chain technology (Bank Negara Malaysia) is a cyberspace economic revolution of the twenty-first century. Numerous players are in the market globally to offer cryptocurrency platforms but these have many shortcomings, such as lack of regulatory support, poor strategic planning, uncertainty and, typically, with no backing assets, relying only on virtual assumption. A *Shari'ah* model of cryptocurrency is a timely means to fill the gap left by the ongoing shortcomings of the cryptocurrency market. The *Shari'ah* cryptocurrency model is, thus, backed by valued assets (proof of product), operated based on valued assets (coins), transactions are based on *Shari'ah* instruments of *al-musharakah*, *al-shuftaja* (exchange), *bai' al-sarf* (money exchange), *al-wakalah*, *al-ju'alah*, *al-tabarru'at* and such. It is concerned for humanitarian well-being, regulated by the standard *Shari'ah* principles, opposed to uncertainty in any form and offers liberty to enjoy legitimate (*Shari'ah*) investment returns. Thus, a *Shari'ah* cryptocurrency model has greater opportunity to attract the global cryptocurrency market by offering a sustainable existence in the emergence of block-chain technology.

17.1.3 Background of Shari'ah Coin

The idea of a *Shari'ah* cryptocurrency model was initiated in early 2007 by considering how a *Shari'ah* cryptocurrency model with a unique model could be developed and duly operated globally to meet contemporary demand as to cryptocurrency operation with *Shari'ah* standards in keeping with *al-Maqasid al-Shari'ah*. It was initiated with grassroots ideas, strategies, mechanisms and structures. It has been continued by sharing in different events in countries around the world, both in Muslim and non-Muslim environments, reaching out through social media, in particular. To strengthen the idea further, this book project on a *Shari'ah* cryptocurrency management company has been undertaken by focusing on numerous specialized issues as among the pioneering and leading works on *Shari'ah* cryptocurrency models in the contemporary world of cryptocurrency.

17.1.4 How Shari'ah Coin Could Help to Solve Some Problems

The prime objective of a *Shari'ah* cryptocurrency model is to create an enterprising and entrepreneur- based community across the world through a *Shari'ah* cryptocurrency management company and global participation. This may ultimately fight poverty, joblessness, the domestic economic crisis and world eco-catastrophe. A *Shari'ah* cryptocurrency management company is universal, welcoming and encouraging, and of benefit to all mankind regardless of religion, race, status, gender, colour or nationality. The operation is not only concerned with money making; part of its income (2.5%) is mandatorily deductible as *zakat* for charitable causes. Furthermore, all gross income in every transaction, account, management, activity, income and service may be encouraged to be subjected a reasonable deduction as *al-tabarru'at* (charity) for the humanitarian causes within *al-Maqasid al-Shari'ah.*

17.1.5 The Meaning of Shari'ah Coin

A *Shari'ah* coin refers to a *Shari'ah* cryptocurrency model to be operated based on *Shari'ah* principles. It is a coin- or token-based offering and is activated by transactions based on *Shari'ah* trading mechanisms through *Shari'ah* screened block-chain technology.

17.2 Shari'ah Coin Branding and Definition

The basic features of a *Shari'ah* cryptocurrency model are that, it should be operated based on *Shari'ah* standards (compliant with *Shari'ah* principles), closely supervised by a world-class *Shari'ah* advisory board, advised by team of scholars as a board of advisors, and further monitored and screened through in-house *Shari'ah* experts. The management of a *Shari'ah* cryptocurrency management company is to abide by the standard *Shari'ah* guidelines and ethical standards. All investors (token holders) are protected by transparent transactions and are formalized based on the *Shari'ah* doctrine of *al-musharakah* (partnership), *al-shuftaja* (exchange), *bai' al-sarf* (money exchange), *al-jualah* (service charge) and *al-wakalah* (agency).

17.2.1 Shari'ah Coin Structural Analysis

A *Shari'ah* cryptocurrency management company should be based on the following model and structure:

- The model shall be based on the principles of *Shari'ah* (*Shari'ah* standards).
- The total operation shall be based on a *Shari'ah* compliant hybrid model.
- A *Shari'ah* cryptocurrency management company evolves as both an asset-backed and an asset-based operation within the *Shari'ah* frameworks.
- The company is backed by valued assets, while its products and services (business operations) are based on assets (valued coins or tokens).
- The total operation is facilitated by *Shari'ah* justified instruments and Divine principles. Among those doctrines are: *al-mudarabah* (co-partnership), *al-musharakah* (partnership or joint-venture), *al-shuftaja* (exchange), *bai' al-sarf* (money exchange), *al-wakalah* (agency with commission), *al-wadiyah* (deposit), *al-ju'alah* (reward or service charge), *al-amanah* (trust), *al-ijarah* (charge), *al-tabarru'at* (donation) and *al-zakat* (alms or compulsory tax).
- The structure of the model is, thus, a *Shari'ah* hybrid platform of cryptocurrency backed by valued assets and, facilitated and duly operated based mainly on the *Shari'ah* principles within *al-Maqasid al-Shari'ah*.
- The operation should be based on 'issuer coin or token' but, exceptionally, it can be based on an exchange platform subject to strict *Shari'ah* ethical guidelines.
- A *Shari'ah* cryptocurrency operation should primarily be based on 'issuer coin or token' by trading platform, decentralized direct (one-to-one) buying and selling (*bai' wa al-shira'*). However, exceptionally, it can be operated on an exchange platform based on a *Shari'ah* hybrid mechanism, facilitated by the doctrines of *al-shuftaja* (exchange), *bai' al-sarf* (money exchange), *al-hewalah* (transfer), *al-kafalah* (custodianship), *al-amanah* (trust), *al-wakalah* (agency by commission), *al-ju'alah* (reward for services) and *al-ujrah* (service charge) within the *Shari'ah* frameworks.

17.3 Application of a *Shari'ah* Cryptocurrency

17.3.1 Financial Assets Exchange (Backing Assets)

The company, its products and services are strictly backed by valued assets. Backing assets for a *Shari'ah* cryptocurrency management company and its operation refers to certified proof of product with, at least, an approved value equivalent to the value of the ICO.

17.4 *Pass-Up Plan*

17.4.1 Total Volume

The total volume of the ICO could be recommended not to exceed 1,000,000,000 coins or tokens, the value of which may not exceed US$ 1.00 each. Thus, the total value of all phases of the ICO may not exceed US$ 1,000,000,000.

17.4.2 Launch Time and Its Checklist

The launch should be at any convenient time, but only after the following checklist has been confirmed:

- Registration of the company
- Documentation (manual, policies, guidelines, standards, planning and strategies)
- Complete tested model through block-chain technology
- System of operation
- Management team
- Equipped office
- *Shari'ah* advisory board
- Board of advisors
- Technical advisor
- Website
- White paper and public statement
- Bank accounts
- Summit
- Soft-launch
- Initial coin offering

17.4.3 Digital Asset Ratio

This is represented by the total value of the coins or tokens offered.

17.4.4 Shari'ah Cryptocurrency Appreciation Logic

No competitive model of *Shari'ah* cryptocurrency has yet been launched. There is a huge demand globally but, as yet, no supply owing to the absence of an available model. It is therefore timely for a *Shari'ah* cryptocurrency management company to open its arms to the global market with utmost appreciation.

17.5 *Project Progress and Team*

The project of a *Shari'ah* cryptocurrency model should be in hand with all modelling, strategic and structural solutions, required documentations, backing asset, decision-makers, advisory panel, supervisory panel, marketing teams, audit (compliance), procedure, mechanisms, technological supports, logistic supports and management team in place before the ICO (Rahajeng 2013).

17.6 *Operation*

A *Shari'ah* cryptocurrency management company may maintain its operating office in any offshore or other suitable location. It may maintain its corporate offices or branches in such different locations or jurisdictions as may, from time to time, be decided by the management team.

17.7 *Market*

A *Shari'ah* cryptocurrency management company should be at liberty to create its marketplace across the cyber world within legitimate frameworks, but it must be within the spirit of *al-Maqasid al-Shari'ah*. There are no restrictions on who may be customers and investors.

17.8 *Accounts*

A *Shari'ah* cryptocurrency management company may maintain the following accounts:

- Customer's or Investor's Account (coin holders)
- Management team Accounts
- Company's Management Account
- *Waqf* Cooperation Account
- Humanitarian Account
- *Tabarru'at* (charity) Account.

17.9 Significant Results

Among the significant results of a *Shari'ah* cryptocurrency operation would be:

- The creation of an atmosphere for all mankind to participate in investment opportunities through *Shari'ah* cryptocurrency within the doctrines of *al-Maqasid al-Shari'ah*.
- To help everyone generally, particularly those who are poor and the low-income group, to create an economic opportunity by participating in the activities of the *Shari'ah* cryptocurrency management company.
- The creation of a global awareness among all with the encouragement to enjoy supporting entrepreneurs and enterprising opportunities through a *Shari'ah* cryptocurrency management company.
- The creation of an economic empowerment with basic rights for all mankind through a *Shari'ah* cryptocurrency management company.

17.10 Humanitarian Concern Through Tabarru'at

A *Shari'ah* cryptocurrency management company would aim to create a *tabarru'at* (charity) fund through the contribution of part of its income to care and show concern for those who are poor, helpless and destitute, and for orphans and the otherwise underprivileged in any society, to meet their basic needs and natural rights of well-being within the holistic spirit of *al-Maqasid al-Shari'ah*.

18 Conclusion

In the contemporary digital space, there are numerous types of cryptocurrency in operation. However, there is no standardized system and no operational mechanisms for non-compliance with the legal requirements. This may be a negative phenomenon for participants in the cryptocurrency and also for the system in general. For a cryptocurrency to be sustainable, it should observe and maintain all legal requirements from its inception until its effective operation. A *Shari'ah* cryptocurrency model (Asif 2018) is in no exception; it should be recognizable only by its legal and *Shari'ah* compliance in its establishment, system, operation and code of ethics within the ambit of *al-Maqasid al-Shari'ah*.

References

Ahmat, N., and Bashir, S. (2017), Central Bank Cryptocurrency: A Monetary Policy Perspective, Bank Negara Malaysia, September.

Alexandre, A. (2018), Stellar Becomes 'First' Shari'ah-Certified Blockchain for Payments and Asset Tokenization, in *The Cointelegraph, The Future of Money*, 18 July 2018.

Anti-Money Laundering and Counter Financing of Terrorism (AML/CFT)—Digital Currencies (Sector 6), Bank Negara Malaysia.

Asif, S. (2018), The Halal and Haram Aspects of Digital Currencies in Islam, https://www.researchgate.net/publication/326398987_The_Halal_and_Haram_Aspects_of_DigitalCurrencies_in_Islam.

Bangash, A. (2018), Bitcoin, Digital Currencies, Blockchain Shari'ah Analysis and their Applications in Islamic Finance, February, https://www.linkedin.com/pulse/bitcoin-DigitalCurrencies-blockchain-Shari'ah-analysis-islamic-bangash/.

Malaysia Central Bank Publishes Study about Digital Currencies, *Fintechnews*, Singapore, 1 November 2017.

Noordin, K. A. (2018), Islamic Finance: Is Cryptocurrency halal? *The Edge*, Malaysia, 6 September.

Oziev, G., and Yandiev, M. (2017), Cryptocurrency from Shari'ah perspective, https://papers.ssrn.com/sol3/papers.cfm?abstract_id=3101981.

Rahajeng, D. (2013), Shari'ah Governance: Shari'ah Supervisory Board Model of Islamic Banking and Finance in Indonesia, in *SSRN*, 11 December.

Vejzagic, M., and Smolo, E. (2011), Maqasid Al-Shari'ah in Islamic Finance: An Overview, Paper presented at the conference on *Post-Crisis Economic Challenges for the Contemporary Muslim Ummah*, held in October 2011 at Universiti Sains Islam Malaysia (USIM), Nilai, Malaysia.

Wardhani, N. (2012), The Role of Shari'ah Board in Islamic Banks: A Case Study of Malaysia, Indonesia and Brunei Darussalam, Paper presented at the ISRA Colloquium on November 2012.

https://www.investopedia.com/tech/most-important-DigitalCurrencies-other-than-bitcoin.

Index

M. M. Billah, *Islamic Financial Products*,
https://doi.org/10.1007/978-3-030-17624-2

CPSIA information can be obtained
at www.ICGtesting.com
Printed in the USA
LVHW021243110819
627237LV00002B/5/P

9 783030 176235